BEYOND THE CONSTITUTION

BEYOND THE CONSTITUTION

Hadley Arkes

PRINCETON UNIVERSITY PRESS

PRINCETON, NEW JERSEY

LIBRARY OF CONGRESS CATALOGING-IN-PUBLICATION DATA

ARKES, HADLEY.

BEYOND THE CONSTITUTION / HADLEY ARKES.

P.   CM.

INCLUDES BIBLIOGRAPHICAL REFERENCES.

ISBN 0-691-07850-5 (ALK. PAPER)

1. UNITED STATES—CONSTITUTIONAL LAW—MORAL AND ETHICAL ASPECTS.

2. UNITED STATES—CONSTITUTIONAL HISTORY. I. TITLE.

KF4552.A75   1990   342.73′029—dc20   [347.30229]   90-30788   CIP

THIS BOOK HAS BEEN COMPOSED IN LINOTRON SABON

PRINCETON UNIVERSITY PRESS BOOKS ARE PRINTED

ON ACID-FREE PAPER, AND MEET THE GUIDELINES FOR

PERMANENCE AND DURABILITY OF THE COMMITTEE ON

PRODUCTION GUIDELINES FOR BOOK LONGEVITY

OF THE COUNCIL ON LIBRARY RESOURCES

PRINTED IN THE UNITED STATES OF AMERICA BY

PRINCETON UNIVERSITY PRESS PRINCETON, NEW JERSEY

1   3   5   7   9   10   8   6   4   2

For Judith Rena

[I]t is certain that there is [a law of nature], and that too as
intelligible and plain to a rational creature, and a studier of that
law, as the positive laws of commonwealths: nay, possibly
plainer; as much as reason is easier to be understood, than the
fancies and intricate contrivances of men, following contrary and
hidden interests put into words; for so truly are a great part of the
municipal laws of countries, which are only so far right, as they
are founded on the law of nature, by which they are to be
regulated and interpreted.

—John Locke, *Second Treatise on Civil Government*, par. 12.

I was summoned by Durieu [who had instituted a commission of
arts and religious buildings] to pass judgment on the process of
Haro, of which we are to get a demonstration at Saint Eustache.
I learned there what no one in the world will believe: that the
Cathedral of Beauvais lacks a wing which was never finished; the
cathedral is a mixture of Gothic and of the sixteenth century.
They are discussing seriously whether the part which remains to
be done shall be rebuilt in the style of the rest or in that of the
thirteenth century, which is the favorite style of the antiquaries
at this moment. In this way, we should give a lesson in living to
those ignoramuses of the sixteenth century who had the
misfortune not to be born three centuries earlier.

—From *The Journal of Eugène Delacroix*, February 26, 1850

CONTENTS

ACKNOWLEDGMENTS

T HIS BOOK was written during a period of academic leave that was supported by a bequest left by my late colleague Karl Loewenstein. For this timely and ample support, I would like to record my thanks to President Peter Pouncey and Dean Richard Fink, of Amherst College; to the colleagues who backed this project; and to Mr. William Dwyer, the Trustee of the Loewenstein Bequest. I am pleased that this is the first book to be published as a result of the work sustained by a Loewenstein Fellowship; I hope it will be the first of many.

During the season of celebration over the Bicentennial of the Constitution, I had the chance to offer lectures and papers at a variety of conferences, and to try out, on different audiences, the arguments that would make their way into this manuscript. Some sections of this book appeared, then, in earlier incarnations, in publications springing from these conferences. I would like to acknowledge my gratitude for the permission that was readily granted to me to draw from my writings in these earlier publications: " 'The Reasoning Spirit of It': the President, the Separation of Powers, and the Laws of Reason," in Robert L. Utley, Jr., ed., *Principles of the Constitutional Order* (Lanham, Md.: University Press of America, 1989); "On the Dangers of a Bill of Rights: A Restatement of the Federalist Argument," in Sarah B. Thurow, *Constitutionalism in America, Vol. I: To Secure the Blessings of Liberty* (Lanham, Md.: University Press of America, 1988); "A Word Unfitly Spoken: The Rejection of 'Contract' in the Argument over the Bill of Rights," in *The Jewish Quarterly* (1989), special supplement arising from the Conference on "The Judeo-Christian Tradition and the U.S. Constitution," at the Annenberg Research Institute. I would also like to thank Dean Jude Dougherty, of the Catholic University, for the occasion to develop, further, the argument I offer in the second chapter of this book. That occasion was provided by his kind invitation to speak in the series of lectures, in the fall of 1987, on "Philosophy and the Constitution." In all of these meetings, I had the benefit of receiving, from the audience at hand, searching questions, leading to further invitations, and the discovery, in certain cases, of new, lasting friends.

BEYOND THE CONSTITUTION

ONE

INTRODUCTION

H E SEEMED to me, even at the time, a curious figure. He had, planted on his desk, a bust of John F. Kennedy; his children had placed a McGovern sticker on the bumper of his car; and yet here he was, a civil servant of high rank, nestled in the Nixon administration. But more than merely nestled: He was the head of the office on civil rights in the Department of Housing and Urban Development. His responsibility was to enforce the federal laws against discrimination in housing, which meant that he was in a position to shape the litigation of the government in this field. He could pick and choose his targets, he could determine the conditions on which the government would sue, and that authority gave him a certain leverage in making things come out his way even without litigation. His deepest pleasures seemed to come with the settlements he could arrange on his own, with private developers and real estate companies; and there, he could move beyond the inventiveness of the courts. He could mold the terms of settlement to his own, demanding sense of what the spirit of the law required. For all of this, of course, he needed the cooperation of the attorney general, and by his own account, he was gratified by the support he had received, steadily, at the hand of Mr. John Mitchell.

Or so, at least, it might have been prudent to say for someone in his position, talking with an outsider. He was a liberal Democrat, litigating the liberal agenda, within a conservative administration. And he was talking with me, a professor, in his office, in the summer of 1972. I was working on a book on urban politics and law, and conducting interviews within the government. On the day I saw this seasoned lawyer, he was particularly pleased with a settlement he had worked out with a private real estate developer. The developer had agreed to advertise in newspapers and radio stations in black communities as a manifest of his commitment not to screen blacks from his new development of single-family homes. The developer had further agreed to encourage interest in his housing by advertising to a broader public, so that blacks and other minorities might be drawn to the project and take up as much as 25 percent of the homes he was selling. Under the Fair Housing Act of 1968 the laws forbade discrimination on the basis of "religion" as well as race. And so the lawyer for the government was working out settlements, with formulas that would include Jews as well as blacks, with the sword of the law held in obvious and ready reserve.

As he was recounting his successes here, I broke the line of his narrative—

and the chain of his thought—when I expressed a certain curiosity about the constitutional ground of the litigation he was threatening. If he were contemplating suits directed at *private* developers, the cases would not lend themselves to the formulas of the Fourteenth Amendment ("No State shall make or enforce any law . . ."). He could get around the need to show "state action" if he made use of the Thirteenth Amendment. In recent years the Supreme Court had restored an expansive understanding of that amendment: The Thirteenth Amendment had ended "involuntary servitude"; it invested the federal government with an authority to act directly on private persons in coping with the lingering "badges and incidents of slavery." With the authority of that amendment, the federal government could deal directly with those acts of intimidation and discrimination that were directed, in America, at a racial group that was still affected by the stigma of the experience in slavery.

And yet, it seemed to be understood that this authority under the Thirteenth Amendment was confined to the special problem raised by blacks in America. It was not apparently available, at the time, to deal with discrimination against Jews, even though Jews, too, had been delivered from slavery. Religion had been mentioned in the First Amendment, but it would have been hard to argue that discrimination in housing interfered with the rights of Jews to the "free exercise" of their religion. It was even more implausible to contend that this tenuous connection to the First Amendment invested the federal government with an authority to reach those discriminations practiced against Jews in the private exchange of real estate. Clearly, the Fair Housing Act of 1968 forbade discrimination based on religion—it was meant to cover Jews. But the question still had to be raised: Under what clause of the Constitution would the federal government claim the authority to reach these private acts of discrimination that did not involve blacks?

My interlocutor reflected on the question for a while—a short while, as I recall—and he conceded that the question did indeed pose an interesting "academic" problem. But he went on courteously to remind me that he was, after all, in the business of litigating cases. As with many other lawyers, he would fill his brief with references to any part of the Constitution that could offer even a slender connection: He would mention the Fourteenth Amendment and the Commerce Clause, and perhaps even the passage on letters of "marque and reprisal" if he thought that could help. It was not his business to divine just which one of these clauses or slogans would touch the credulity of the judges and produce the result he was seeking from the court. The rationales could be left to the judges to explain, or to the professors of law to work out, in their leisure, in the law reviews. But the concern to establish, with some precision and persuasiveness, the constitutional ground for the authority he was exercising on behalf of the government—that kind of exercise did not seem to mark, for him, an interest worth indulging at the expense of braking, even for a moment, the motor of litigation.

I was quietly put off, of course, by what I took to be his philistinism in these matters. I was struck by the contrast he offered within himself: On the one hand, he was the officer of the law, investing himself with the moral preten- sions of the Constitution, and vindicating the interests of justice. On the other hand, he was willing to affect a cavalier want of concern for the most elementary moral discipline that attaches to constitutional law, namely the discipline of establishing the constitutional "justification" for the use of the law.

And yet, after years of reflecting on these questions, I've come to the judg- ment that my interlocutor was, in a curious way, half right. His reflexes were the right reflexes, even though he could not begin to give a proper account of them. He was *not* right in his serene indifference to the grounds of justifica- tion for the law. But he was sound, I now think—unaccountably sound, sound beyond his reason to explain—in the assumption that apparently animated his efforts. He evidently presumed that if there was a wrong or injustice that came within the reach of the law, then the national government was as fully competent to the ends of justice—as fully competent to vindicate this interest of the law—as any other government within the territory of the United States. If the government of a state could reach acts of private discrimination in housing, then the federal government was no less a government than the government of a state, and it should require no strained pleading to establish the authority of the national government to deal with incidents involving the same kinds of wrongs. Precisely what clause of the Constitution would estab- lish that authority to act in any case was less important or less decisive. What was more critical was the conviction, rooted in the decisions of 1787, that the national government created by the Founders was a real government, that its powers were adequate to the ends of any legitimate government.

When this point is stated directly, it induces a certain surprise and skepticism among lawyers and judges. And yet, it is quite clear by now that many of the same lawyers and judges act upon this understanding in forming their judg- ments, even though they are far from recognizing the grounds of doctrine that would explain what they are doing. Instead, they have been content to use the familiar phrases, and the tenuous fictions, of the Constitution—to invoke the Equal Protection of the Law or the Commerce Clause, even when those phrases explain nothing and compel no conclusion. But by using them, even inaptly, our jurists may persuade themselves that they are somehow working under the restraints of the Constitution. And so we find the case of the Lake Nixon Club, a "recreational facility" in Arkansas that refused to accept blacks

as members. Since there was no action of the state, no policy of racial separation enforced by law, the Fourteenth Amendment appeared to be inapt. In
cases of this kind the government had usually switched to the Commerce
Clause. But as Justice Black would point out, the Lake Nixon Club was accessible only through country roads, it was distant from the main highways,
and there was no evidence that the proprietors had ever sought to have "commerce" with people traveling among the states.[1] Still, when there is a resolve
to use the law, the arts of argument will be strained to the implausible. The
food served at the Lake Nixon Club was purchased mainly from local sources,
and the soft drinks were bottled within the state. But a mind sharpened by
the study of the Constitution could notice here, as the district court did, that
"the bread used by defendants was baked and packaged locally, [however] . . .
the principal ingredients going into the bread were produced and processed in
other States. The soft drinks were bottled locally, but certain ingredients were
probably obtained . . . from out-of-State sources."[2] There was also a jukebox
on the premises. Had the records in the jukebox been pressed in Arkansas, or
had they come rather from New York? Had they, in other words, *traveled* in
interstate commerce?

On considerations of this kind the case appeared to turn. Quite apart from
the question of whether this exercise was worthy of grown-ups, there is a
serious concern that a jurisprudence that leads its practitioners along these
paths will divert their understanding from the things that are truly "juristic."
Instead of leading our jurists to focus on the substantive moral ground that
defines the wrong in any case, or instead of directing them to the principles
that truly bear on the jurisdiction of the national government, our jurisprudence has induced our lawyers to expend their genius in producing the most
contrived fictions. Those fictions may be taken as formulas that somehow
settle the case, even while they illuminate nothing about the grounds of judgment that are necessary for the law. And for the sake of fitting their decisions
to these formulas, the jurists have had to absorb canons of reasoning that must
ever be embarrassing to scholars who have any mildly rigorous training in
philosophy.[3]

But this much credit we must give to our men and women of the law:
Whether it is right or wrong for a restaurant to discriminate on the basis of
race is an issue that does not really turn for them on the question of whether
some of the ingredients in the Coca-cola came from outside the state. Nor
can we suppose that their passion for regarding this matter as a *federal* case
was really ignited by their discovery that there were, in the juke box, records
that came from New York. Plainly, these items were grasped as so many rationalizations, useful in a court, but they could hardly explain why the case
described, for attorneys in the government, a wrong that the federal government ought to vindicate.

The attorneys for the government played according to the script. They spoke these fictions with straight faces, pretended that the lines they spoke made sense, and the courts agreed that the federal law would indeed reach to the Lake Nixon Club. Justice Black observed, in dissent, that this construction would "give the Federal Government complete control over every little remote country place of recreation in every nook and cranny of every precinct and county in every one of the 50 States."[4] So it would; and so it has. Justice Black had as much to do, as any judge in the country, with the expansion of the federal government under the Commerce Clause; but he could still recoil, in surprise, when he himself described, plainly, the reach of that government.

The paradox is that the lawyers for the government would probably share that surprise. In their rendering of the Constitution, they would probably deny, as insistently as Black, that the authority of the national government would extend to "every little remote country place of recreation in every nook and cranny of every precinct." But they describe, in the course of their own conduct, in their reflexes on litigation, a wholly different understanding of the Constitution. Their theory and their practice do not come together, and I would submit that nothing else accounts for the behavior of the lawyers here: Regardless of what they say when they come to pronounce on the "constitutional bases" for their arguments, they act as though the federal government they are administering is fully competent to reach acts of racial discrimination even in the most trivial of private establishments that are open for business with the public. What remains is to explain—and explain without false rationalizations—the grounds on which they may be justified in their conviction.

Until we settle these questions on their proper ground, the current charade of legal fictions does not offer us a benign way of muddling through. At best, it offers a license for sophistry, and at worst, the terms of a crude political fix. It allows one set of political activists to use these formulas of the law with a knowing wink when they would extend the powers of the federal government and reach their favorite objects. At the same time, the lawyers schooled in this game would remain free to affect surprise and treat these formulas of the law with a feigned seriousness when their adversaries try to make use of the same powers of the government for notably different ends. Hence the spectacle played out not too long ago at the Yale Law School, in the form of a debate. On one side was Professor Burke Marshall, who directed the Office of Civil Rights in the Justice Department under Presidents Kennedy and Johnson, on the other side was Mr. Charles Cooper, representing the Justice Department of President Reagan. Professor Marshall had helped to expand the powers of the federal government with the Civil Rights Act of 1964, and now he found himself opposing the use of the same, expansive powers, when it came to the protection of newborn infants with Down's syndrome.

The issue arose with the celebrated Baby Doe cases in 1983. The Reagan administration sought to use one section of the Civil Rights Act against hospitals that withheld corrective surgery from newborns solely because they were retarded. The administration invoked Section 504 of the Rehabilitation Act of 1973, which dealt with discriminations against the handicapped. As the administration sought to press its concerns in the courts, it had every reason to expect support from a body of precedents that extended to hospitals the interest of the federal government in vindicating civil rights. But the administration met a steady resistance from the courts, which culminated in a rebuff from the Supreme Court itself in a narrow decision.[5] And the main opposition to the administration came from those lawyers and judges of liberal persuasion who had made it their project in the past to extend the powers of the federal government under the Civil Rights Act.

Professor Marshall represented the perspective of this party when he expressed his disbelief: How could the power of the federal government reach, in this way, to the decisions made by families and their physicians about the treatment of their children? And why should the administration wish to vindicate the civil rights of newborn children when it had not been anxious to enforce civil rights in the form of "affirmative action"? For the liberal mind in the law, the power of the federal government could rightly penetrate spheres of privacy—private hotels, private schools, perhaps even private clubs and families—when it came to protecting people against racial discrimination. For that cause, the federal government could reach Ollie's Barbecue in Birmingham, Alabama, or the Lake Nixon Club, in—if one could conceive the notion—the "hinterland" of Little Rock, Arkansas. But when it came to the "private right" of parents to withdraw medical care from their own children, the barriers of "privacy" were too grave—too bound up with civil freedom—to be pierced by the federal government.

Perhaps the administration might have rendered its position more plausible to the modern judicial mind if it contrived to show that this withholding of medical care from infants would have a depressing effect on interstate commerce, or that the failure to save a life deprived the child of its "freedom to travel" in its later years. But of course, the critics would have dismissed these "arguments" as the fabrications they have always been. All one can say, then, in summing up the score, is this: The federal government may be regarded as a real government, with the power to reach directly to individuals and private settings, when it comes to any vestige of discrimination on the basis of race, no matter how trivial the injury or the setting. But when it comes to protecting children of all races from the unjustified taking of their lives, the federal government must be constrained by the barriers of federalism and privacy. Clearly, the difference cannot be explained by the real nature and powers of the federal government. Rather, it is the federal government that is reconceived when there is a political interest in extending or contracting its reach.

Despite the recent setback to the administration, the Congress has provided another means of extending protection to retarded, newborn children. The Child Abuse and Protection Act was passed in 1984 with bipartisan support. That act should make it clear now that the Congress did indeed mean to engage the influence of the federal government in support of these vulnerable children, even in private hospitals, even against the designs of their own parents. And yet, even when the authority of the federal government is engaged, with the firmest resolve of the legislators, on a matter of moral consequence, that authority is bent into indirection. It is shaped in the most curious ways, to fit the fictions of federalism that have not really limited the power of the federal government, but which *have* compelled that authority to move in the most awkward paths. In the case of Baby Doe, the Congress would offer moral instruction to the community of pediatricians: It would mark off as a "wrong" the withholding of medical treatment from retarded infants, and it would refuse to that act of indirect killing the deference accorded to "medical judgment." The Congress would begin, in other words, where legislation has traditionally begun, with the awareness of a *wrong* that justifies the restraint or punishment of the law. But the analytic connection between moral judgment and legislation is then broken: Congress does not punish or restrain the people who commit these wrongs. Instead, it merely withholds federal funds from the private hospitals in which these wrongs are permitted. The task of proscribing and punishing these wrongs is left to the responsibility of state and local governments.

The response is, of course, logically inapt. If we come to the recognition, say, that it is "wrong" for parents to torture children, we do not give parents tax incentives to stop. Nor do we threaten to withdraw contracts or federal grants. The recognition of a wrong finds its expression in the logic of a *law*, which forbids and punishes what is wrong.[6] If the federal government holds back from marking, as wrongdoers, the people who withhold medical treatment from retarded infants, that judgment may betray a certain want of surety in condemning these acts as "wrongs." Or, it may mark a telling strand of doubt that the federal government really has the authority to reach wrongs of this kind. In either event, this backhanded approach of the national government must render the position of the government quizzical. It must raise the question of whether the national government is justified, or competent, in offering up censures, and threatening to intervene in the medical treatment of infants.

As we shall see later, there may be a case, drawn from the canons of prudence and statesmanship, for encouraging local governments to take the first responsibility in addressing the wrongs that are nearest to them. But as we shall also see, it is a curious, untenable position for the federal government:

The local governments are encouraged to take themselves seriously as governments by addressing directly, or in the first instance, the wrongs that come within the reach of the law. But the federal government is seen as a government of second instance, or second resort, which is not apparently competent to the ends of any other legitimate government, in acting directly to vindicate the wrongs it means to reach. It is a mistake to assume that this understanding flows, inescapably, from the nature of American federalism. The best of our jurists in the past did not assume that the federal government was constrained in such an artificial way, even while they were convinced that the federal government was seriously "limited" in its powers by the restraints of constitutionalism. They understood that the federal government had the authority to reach every legitimate object of its concern—to reach, if need be, past the states, and to act directly on individuals. This authority required no arcane renderings, no ingenious reading of passages hidden in the Constitution. As our jurists understood, that authority was contained in the simplest truths established about the national government that was created in 1787.

In recovering this understanding, there is no need, then, to invent anything new. The argument I will put forth here would have been understood without strain by the lawyers in our founding generation, and it would have been grasped quite as well by those jurists in the nineteenth century who had learned most precisely the lessons that the Founders taught. But our current lawyers and professors of law find it hard to speak seriously in this vein. They may speak the words with a sense of filial piety, but they could not be sure that any meaning attached to those words if they said, with John Marshall, that our judgments in law may be drawn from the "general principles of our political institutions," as well as from the "words of the Constitution."[7]

Without the words of the Constitution, our current lawyers would not feel confident that there is a body of principles, substantive, moral, juristic, to which they could appeal. In *Calder v. Bull*,[8] Justice Chase referred to those fundamental principles that flow "from the very nature of our free Republican governments." Those principles had the advantage, also, of being "the true principles of Government."[9] But to speak in this way of the principles of republican government, or of lawful government, is no longer to speak simply of the logic of a "national" government. To that sense of an integrated, national government it is necessary to add something about the moral principles that define the nature of a "just" and lawful government. In other words, if we would try to understand the principles of the *American* law, it would be necessary to move outside the Constitution. It would be necessary to speak, first, of the principles that define what is just and unjust, the principles that help us to tell the difference between good regimes and bad ones. We would be drawn back, then, as the Founders were, to those principles of "natural justice" that existed before the formation of any government. After all, the

Founders were able to speak about "the principles of law" before we had a Constitution; and by the principles of law, they understood what Blackstone described as "the law of nature and reason." For the Founders, these principles of right and wrong helped to explain, in the first place, just why they were morally enjoined to found a constitutional government rather than a despotism. And they were the principles that the Founders were able to draw upon as they set about to arrange the framework and the character of a new government.

But in our own day that appeal to natural justice has become suspect. Within our law schools, the claims of natural rights have been resisted, as a matter of high political interest, by conservatives as well as liberals.[10] The liberal commentators on the law have been quite willing to advance a "living Constitution," an arrangement in which judges are freer to adapt the law to the "sensibilities of our time," without being overly constrained by the text of the Constitution. In this temper, liberal writers have been inspired to find an "unwritten Constitution,"[11] or at least to discover again that the Founders were alert to principles of natural justice outside the text of the Constitution. But for liberal commentators, this argument suffices to move them outside the text. Once they are outside the text, however, the notion of "natural rights" does not provide, for them, the same guide, or the same constraint, that it provided for the Founders. During the First Congress, James Madison remarked that the natural right of human beings to be governed only with their consent was an "absolute truth." Lincoln would later insist, in the same vein, that this doctrine of self-government was "absolutely and eternally right." For the Founders, for Lincoln, the case for natural rights claimed its force and its coherence only with the recognition that it was grounded in certain necessary, moral truths. But in our own time, nothing is more likely to stir discomfort among liberals, in dining rooms or courts, than the willingness to speak seriously about moral "truths" that are "absolute" and "eternal."

And so, in a recent work, Professor Sanford Levinson has made an earnest appeal for a "constitutional faith" that runs quite beyond the text of the Constitution. He would not recruit the faith of any citizen to the constitutional text that incorporated a commitment to the return of fugitive slaves, or the text that originally omitted a Bill of Rights, or the text that failed to provide for the suffrage of women. His commitment to the Constitution, as the bond of our national life, depends on an understanding of the Constitution that moves quite beyond the text. But at the same time, Levinson is convinced that there are no moral "truths" that make one meaning of the Constitution more authoritative or compelling than another. Or at least, Levinson is inclined to say, in a paraphrase of Richard Rorty, that "nothing interesting can be said about truth. It is almost literally not worth talking about." In other words, no argument should be taken seriously if it makes a claim to its own truth. With that premise, Levinson was obliged to agree that a committed Marxist-Leninist may have a legitimate claim to profess in a school of law: In point of principle, it could not be said that there was anything in the premises of totalitarian Communism that finally made it incompatible with the premises of a regime of law, or with the character of the American Constitution. Levinson would summon our "faith" in the Constitution, and yet he could not say whether that Constitution contained any true principles that ruled out a Leninist dictatorship.[12]

In an earlier passage, Levinson had quite rightly pointed up the amorality of Justice Holmes when Holmes, in his characteristic thuggery, blithely embraced the possibility that the Constitution could accommodate "tyrannical" laws. As Levinson remarked, "It is at this point . . . that we are required to ask if the legal process . . . deserves our respect. Why should faith in the Constitution be affirmed rather than questioned?"[13] That is, why would a Constitution merit our faith if it were not committed, in principle, to justice rather than tyranny? But in the same way, it must be asked: Why *should* we summon our "faith" in the Constitution, if there is no moral ground of conviction to support that faith? Why would the Constitution deserve our respect if we finally could not say, with any claim to truth, that the Constitution supports a regime of freedom rather than a despotism?[14]

Levinson has aptly observed that " 'Truth' may continue to be a word within modernist culture, but only as a synonym for culturally shared conventions. At the very least there are, from this perspective, no self-evident, immutable, or eternal truths." But that is to acknowledge, with an unsettling candor, that modern liberals begin from premises that are radically at odds with the premises of the Founders and Lincoln. As artfully as they may write, and as subtle as the evasions may be, it will be necessary in the end for "modernist" liberals to detach the notion of "rights" from the claims to moral truth.

Professor Thomas Grey has been even more explicit in acknowledging this shift in the moral ground of jurisprudence for modern liberals, and he has been willing to put, more directly, the uncomfortable question:

> The intellectual framework [for the recent articulation of new "rights"] is different from the natural-rights tradition of the founding fathers—its rhetorical reference points are the Anglo-American tradition and basic American ideals, rather than human nature, the social contract, or the rights of man. . . . Conceding the natural rights origins of our Constitution, does not the erosion and abandonment of the 18th-century ethics and epistemology on which the natural-rights theory was founded require the abandonment of the mode of judicial review flowing from that theory? Is a "fundamental law" judicially enforced in a climate of historical and cultural relativism the legitimate offspring of a fundamental law which its exponents felt expressed rationally demonstrable, universal, and immutable human rights?[15]

Grey could be remarkably beamish in assuming that the moral ground of our constitutional rights would still be largely unaffected by this shift from the "epistemology" of the founders, from their understanding of "natural rights," to a jurisprudence that was pervaded by the premises of "historical and cultural relativism." That new jurisprudence would have to find its ground, as Grey said, in "the Anglo-American tradition." And that shift to "tradition" is no trivial alteration. It is a movement, as Grey concedes, from an independent ground of right and wrong—from a moral understanding that does not depend on the vagaries of local cultures—to a ground of jurisprudence that reduces to the "habits of the tribe," or to the opinions that are dominant in a particular country. In that respect, this "new" jurisprudence would be indistinguishable from the jurisprudence, in the nineteenth century, that found its ground in cultural relativism, or in the new social science of anthropology. That style of jurisprudence found its less attractive expression in the legal arguments cast up by Roger Taney and Stephen Douglas, in their defense of American slavery. In our own time, the words may be dressed in artier forms, with shades of modern literary theory, but the decisive marks are readily familiar: There will be an appeal, at a critical point, to "shared understandings" or "political traditions," in place of moral truths, as the ultimate ground of our jurisprudence.[16]

The project of liberation in the law has been thought to depend on the rejection of moral truths, as claims that are, in philosophy, spurious; in politics, reactionary. Governments swollen with the conceit of knowing moral truths may try to legislate against abortion. They may claim a license to restrain obscenity in literature and the arts. They may claim a moral ground of conviction in refusing to regard, on the same plane of legitimacy, all varieties of "sexual orientation." They may refuse to regard all species of political ends, or all brands of political speech, as equally legitimate. And so they may suffer fewer inhibitions in outlawing totalitarian parties, or restraining the speech of Nazis and Communists. Against these tendencies, liberals have set themselves firmly, even when they have had to set themselves against the sentiments dominant in the public. They have made it their mission to deny that the government, or anyone else, may claim to "know" what is morally right for anyone else, and on that basis, to "legislate morality."

Of course, when it comes to legislating against discriminations based on race, gender, or "sexual orientation," the liberals may profess that they are not legislating on "moral" questions. They invoke the language of right and wrong; they react to "injustice" with moral outrage; they show a willingness to impose a uniform policy through the law, and displace private choice. They look, in short, to be very much in the business of "legislating morality," even if they do not use the same words. This performance has merely confirmed the suspicions of the conservatives that the language of morality is simply manipulated in our politics to suit the ends of the liberal agenda. For that reason, conservatives have become ever more skeptical about the use of moral language in politics. But this concern for the uses of moral language has been fashioned by many conservatives into an extravagant skepticism toward the very notions of moral truth and natural rights. Writers such as Raoul Berger and Robert Bork have regarded any appeal to "natural rights"—any appeal beyond the text of the Constitution—as a pretext for evading the discipline of the Constitution. They have noticed that in recent years, the writers and judges who have claimed the license to make that kind of appeal, have not exactly been the kind of people who take seriously the notion of "moral truths." In the hands of these judges, the appeal to principles outside the Constitution may be nothing more than an appeal to the "values" of the judges themselves. As Robert Bork once put it, "If a judge should claim . . . to possess a volume of the annotated natural law, we would, quite justifiably, suspect that the source of the revelation was really no more exalted than the judge's viscera."[17]

But by casting their opposition to "natural justice," Berger and Bork have joined the modern heresy. Apparently, they and their liberal counterparts would join Bentham in regarding "natural rights" as "nonsense on stilts." They reject the possibility of knowing moral truths in the literal sense—i.e., truths that hold their standing as truths in all places and cultures. And so, Robert Bork has written:

> There may be a natural law, but we are not agreed upon what it is, and there is no such law that gives definite answers to a judge trying to decide a case.
>
> There may be a conventional morality in our society, but on most issues there are likely to be several moralities. They are often regionally defined, which is one reason for federalism.[18]

The translation has become familiar: The mere presence of disagreement on matters of moral consequence is taken as proof for the claim that there are no moral truths (or "natural law"). But I would be obliged to record my own, emphatic "disagreement" with *this* proposition, and by its own terms, by its own logic, that disagreement would be quite sufficient to establish the falsity of the proposition. No argument has become more familar in "explaining" the futility of natural law, and yet it seems to have slipped past the common understanding that this proposition stands in the class of what philosophers describe as "self-refuting" propositions.[19] That this "argument" has hung on so long, and engaged the credulity of so many estimable people, is a testament of sorts to the way that even the most patent fallacies may seem more plausible, with time, as they are more commonly repeated. For lawyers who have become tutored on this fallacy, there is no "morality" in the strictest sense— no understanding of right and wrong that is universal in its reach. As Mr. Bork remarked, there are only separate "moralities," for persons and countries. In place of moral truths that hold their truth in all places, we merely have "conventional" truths that are "posited" or set down or accepted, in different places, as a reflection of the opinions that are dominant in any country. By "right" and "wrong," then, we mean: that which has been accepted, or rejected, by a majority. In this manner, the cause of conservatism in politics has been attached to "positivism" in the law, and that kind of marriage will be the undoing of political conservativism. For it will insure that, in jurisprudence, conservativism will be brittle and unworkable, and that on matters of moral consequence conservative jurisprudence will have nothing to say.

But this problem for conservative jurisprudence is merely another phase of the same problem that afflicts the current liberal temper when it is turned to matters of law. To borrow a phrase from Henry James, the problems of liberalism and conservatism here are "simply different chapters of the same general subject." That subject is the displacement of natural rights, in our public philosophy, with one variety or another of "positivism" or moral relativism. Regardless of whether lawyers are liberals or conservatives, they are products of our law schools, and since the inception of law schools, their students have been tutored in the reigning orthodoxy of "legal positivism." Over a hundred years after the debate between Abraham Lincoln and Stephen Douglas, the teaching in our schools of law is cast almost entirely in the character of Douglas's positivism. So thorough, in fact, has been the triumph of this positivism, that there seems to be little awareness among lawyers that there was ever an argument on this matter, or that a choice had once been posed. Justice Holmes thought it would be a decided gain "if every word of moral significance could be banished from the law altogether."[20] And when we see jurists in our own time regarding "moral judgment" in the same way, as something alien to the logic and mission of law, we must understand that we are seeing the jurists who have absorbed the premises that Holmes sought to impart. Whether they regard themselves as liberals or conservatives, they have made themselves part of that modern project in the law that Holmes helped to launch.

We could hardly cite a figure more learned in the law of our own day, or more "established" in the profession, than Chief Justice Rehnquist. In his reflexes, the chief justice may be described as a "conservative," but his conservatism could not be the conservatism of Lincoln or the Founders, since his understanding has evidently been recruited, deeply, thoroughly, by the doctrines of legal positivism. The curious result is that this good man could hardly be more radical in his moral skepticism. In an address given at the University of Texas Law School in 1976, Mr. Rehnquist denied the existence of moral propositions in the strictest sense: What we regard as moral judgments are simply the products of personal belief, emanations from the "individual conscience." That is to say, these understandings of right and wrong are matters of subjective belief or private feeling. They cannot claim a content that is accessible to anyone but the person who holds these beliefs or experiences these feelings. Therefore, "there is no conceivable way in which I can logically demonstrate to you that the judgments of my conscience are superior to the judgments of your conscience, and vice versa."[21] In other words, there is no ground on which it can be shown that any of these beliefs is true or false for anyone apart from the one who holds them. Or to put it even more briefly, there are no moral truths in the literal sense.[22]

But if there are no moral truths, how do we know that the "wrongs" condemned by the law are really wrong? How can we be sure that they *deserve* the censure of the community and the proscription of the law? In Rehnquist's understanding, we cannot *know* those things, for there is no measure of right and wrong, finally, until a judgment has been consecrated in the law. As the chief justice has put it, the "value judgments" of individuals

> take on a form of moral goodness *because* they have been enacted into positive law. *It is the fact of their enactment that gives them whatever moral claim they have upon us as a society.* . . . Many of us necessarily feel strongly and deeply about our own moral judgments, but they remain only personal moral judgments until in some way given the sanction of law.[23]

In short, it is the classic recipe of legal "positivism": Whether anything is morally right or wrong in a particular place depends on the strength of the opinion that supports or condemns it. In Mr. Rehnquist, these strands were explicitly connected: "When adherents to the belief [of any individual] become sufficiently numerous, he will have the necessary armaments required in a democratic society to press his views upon the elected representatives of the people, and to have them embodied into positive law."[24]

These passages have the ring of familiarity, of course, because they reflect the terms in which "logical positivism" and "ethical emotivism" have been diffused in our public discourse. But what seems to have escaped the notice of the judges is that these doctrines have come under a serious challenge in the schools of philosophy, and even a modern relativist would be a bit sheepish about making his case in the terms put forth by Chief Justice Rehnquist. Still, the views of the chief justice do not seem threatening because they do not seem novel. And even liberals who profess to be threatened by his views can feel threatened only by the prospect of what the majority of voters, licensed by Rehnquist, will choose in their name as the sovereign majority. But even Mr. Rehnquist's critics cannot profess to be threatened by the philosophic apparatus that produces these results; for *his philosophic premises are theirs.* Mr. Rehnquist sharpens the differences only because he makes those premises more explicit.

We should be aware, then, that there is a radical separation between the jurisprudence of the Founders, and the jurisprudence offered by conservatives and liberals in our own day. The jurisprudence of the Founders was built on the connection that was traditionally understood between morals and law. The Constitution they finally produced, as our second Constitution, could be understood and *justified*, only in moral terms, only by an appeal to those standards of natural right that existed *antecedent* to the Constitution. My argument in this book is that the Constitution produced by the Founders cannot be understood or defended if it is detached from those moral premises. When we earnestly pledge to "preserve" the Constitution, we cannot pretend to undertake that project unless we can establish the essential character or the "meaning" of the thing we would seek to preserve. And that meaning of the Constitution cannot be established unless we can grasp again the moral understanding held by the Founders, antecedent to the Constitution—the understanding that governed the judgments of the Founders as they sought to convey, in a legal structure, the principles of lawful government. My burden in this book is to show that we cannot apply the Constitution, in the practical cases that arise every day, unless we can move, so to speak, "beyond the Constitution." We will persistently find a need to appeal to those moral understandings lying behind the text; the understandings that were never written down in the Constitution, but which must be grasped again if we are to preserve—and perfect—the character of a constitutional government.

To restore those understandings is not to engage in a quaint project in "historical" reconstruction. It is to begin unlocking a set of puzzles that confound lawyers every day in this country. The questions may come to us in prosaic forms, in cases of this kind: Would it violate the Constitution if the drivers of automobiles are compelled to stop and report on accidents in which they are involved? If their reports expose their own wrongdoing, would they be compelled, in effect, to be witnesses against themselves? Would that procedure violate the Fifth Amendment, or offend a principle bound up with the Constitution? Or to take another case we shall encounter later: A football player at a state university misses a punt. As a consequence, the player is benched, he loses his scholarship for athletics, and he drops out of school. He later sues the coach of the team for a violation of his civil rights, and our judges are compelled to consider whether the federal government may reach a case of this kind under the Civil Rights Acts. The lawyer I interviewed, years ago, at the Department of Housing and Urban Development, was not entirely clear about the constitutional ground on which the federal government might reach discriminations against Jews in the sale of private housing. And jurists have been quite as unclear today about the grounds on which the federal government might intervene in hospitals and protect retarded, newborn infants from the withdrawal of medical care. In another phase of that problem, might the federal government compel Catholic universities to perform abortions in their hospitals if any of their students received loans from the government? Under the banner of enforcing civil rights, could the government compel private corporations to cover abortions in their medical plans, even if those corporations received no grants from the federal government? These issues were raised, as we shall see, in the arguments over the Civil Rights Restoration Act of 1988. The answers, in this string of cases, cannot well up from the cases themselves. And it is plain that they cannot be found in the text of the Constitution. The grounds of judgment can be found, as the first generation of our jurists knew they could be found, in the principles that marked this new government, and in those principles of law that existed well before the Constitution.

I will take it as my purpose, in the next two chapters, to recall the arguments of the Founders themselves in order to restore a meaning that has been curiously filtered, in recent years, from the "original understanding" of the Founders: namely, that the Founders did think it was necessary to move, in this way, beyond the text of the Constitution to the principles of right and wrong that stood antecedent to the Constitution. The Founders did not think that they were entering the domain of arbitrary or "subjective" judgment when they were compelled to move outside the text of the Constitution. They did not understand that they were emancipated, at that moment, from a discipline of reasoning that could guide their judgments and properly claim to limit their discretion.

On this point, there is ample evidence in the original arguments over the Constitution, and in the early, signal opinions offered in the Supreme Court. That evidence also happens to be distinguished by the prose and reflections that were left to us by judges such as James Wilson and John Marshall. These men understood that they were establishing nothing less than the groundwork for a jurisprudence that had, as yet, almost nothing in the way of distinctly American precedents, formed under this new frame of government. The advent of the new Constitution was marked, almost immediately, by a debate on the meaning and necessity of a Bill of Rights. The objection was offered by some of our most notable juridical minds that the Bill of Rights would seriously misinstruct the American people about the ground of their rights: It would obscure the foundation of the Constitution in "natural rights," and it would blind people to the principal mission of the government in the securing of natural rights. For that reason, it would have the effect of contracting or narrowing our understanding of the range of rights that were protected under the Constitution. But beyond that, the Bill of Rights would become a source of civic miseducation: Instead of instructing the American people in the principles of free government, it would merely fix attention on an inventory of "rights" detached from their moral grounds. In this manner, the Bill of Rights would become the source of a crude civic teaching; it would beget generations of lawyers who had absorbed slogans rather than principles. Those lawyers might have, at their command, the convenient formulas produced by lawyers, but they would no longer know how to deliberate about constitutional rights by tracing their judgments back to the first principles of law.

Those urbane men, among the Founders, who were skeptical about a Bill of Rights did not fear that this collection of amendments would produce an immediate and palpable harm. Nor did they think that this parchment of rights would provide the sureties that its partisans were promising. Men like James Wilson seemed to be offended by what they saw as the incoherence of the Bill of Rights, and their deeper concern, I think, was with the way in which the misunderstandings fostered by the Bill of Rights would shape the sensibilities of lawyers and citizens in the coming generations. And on that point, we could show that their apprehensions have been richly borne out. I will return, then, to that original debate, to state anew, and perhaps state more fully, the issues that were raised by the skeptics among the Founders. For the serious questions that were passed by, in such a facile way, in that original debate, have persisted to our own time, and they have been at the center of the deepest confusions today in our constitutional law.

I recalled earlier that, in the classic debate between Lincoln and Douglas, Lincoln made a compelling case in the tradition of natural rights, a tradition that most lawyers no longer take seriously. The lawyers may remember being told that the argument for natural rights had been refuted, but exactly who refuted it, or the grounds on which it was refuted, slips from memory. Lincoln has had the benefit, in our own day, of the most talented writers and teachers of political theory, who have sought to preserve the substance of his thought on politics and law.[25] I had the occasion to offer a small chapter here myself, as I sought to incorporate the teaching of Lincoln in an effort to restore the teaching of "first principles."[26] There is no need to repeat here what has been done elsewhere. But I would revisit Lincoln briefly for the sake of recalling his clarity on a point that has been obscured in the law of our own day: Many commentators have written, with a hazy conviction, about the moral foundations of law; but Lincoln showed a more precise recognition that there was, behind the law, a logic and structure of moral understandings. Those moral understandings supplied the true justification for the law, and without them— as he demonstrated, with brilliance and wit—the law fell into a collection of shallow pretexts, without coherence.

As I move on, in the succeeding chapters, I will try to show, in that vein, that the various clauses of the Constitution and the Bill of Rights can be established, in their meaning, only by attaching them to the properties of a moral argument. And when we do that, we find ourselves tracing these clauses back to the structure of moral understanding that must lie behind the text of the Constitution. To understand the current import of Due Process, Equal Protection of the Laws, Privileges and Immunities, Self-Incrimination, Double Jeopardy—and indeed, almost any other part of the Constitution—it is necessary to understand again how lawyers such as Marshall and Lincoln were able to deliberate about the "rights" that were encompassed in the Constitution. There is a need to know again what was known by these men. There is a need to restore the sense of what Justice Johnson understood when he drew upon a line familiar to his generation and remarked that "the security of a people . . . must lie in a frequent recurrence to first principles."

TWO

THE "REASONING SPIRIT" OF THE CONSTITUTION

I T IS ONE of the ironies of the original debate over the Constitution that
some of the most illuminating commentaries on the character of the new
government were provided by the opponents of the Constitution. The
Anti-Federalist writers were moved to draw out, explicitly, the significance of
provisions that the supporters of the Constitution were willing to muffle for a
while with a prudent reticence. Some of the most thoughtful and penetrating
commentaries in this vein were supplied by the man who wrote, in New York,
under the pen name of "Brutus." In the simple passages, in the Constitution,
that established the judiciary, Brutus managed to unlock some rather precise
meanings about the nature of the national government and the understanding
of the framers on the sources of law. The framers had defined the authority of
the courts in Article III of the Constitution, and they had stipulated, in Section 2, that "the judicial power shall extend to all Cases, in Law and Equity,
arising under this Constitution." That passage is easily passed by, in any reading of the Constitution. But to someone with tutored sensitivities, that passage drew on a tradition of jurisprudence, and it marked the sweeping power
of the courts under the new government. As Brutus recognized, it was no
small gesture, no draftsmanship without purpose, in assigning to the Supreme
Court a jurisdiction in *Equity*. To explain what was meant by Equity, he
looked to the writings of Grotius and Blackstone, and he drew this understanding: When the courts are authorized to decide upon the meaning of the
Constitution in law *and equity*, "they are empowered to explain the constitution according to the reasoning spirit of it, without being confined to the
words or letter."[1] From Grotius he learned that "equity" involved the "correction of that, wherein the law, by reason of its universality, is deficient." Brutus
went on to explain that "since in law all cases cannot be foreseen, or expressed, it is necessary, that when the decrees of the law cannot be applied to
particular cases, there should some where be a power vested of defining those
circumstances, which had they been foreseen the legislator would have expressed."[2] Grotius had observed that "equity, thus depending essentially upon
each individual case, there can be no established rules and fixed principles of
equity laid down, without destroying its very essence, and reducing it to a
positive law."[3]

To put the matter a bit more carefully, Grotius was not saying that the
judges would be left on their own, without the guidance of principles of judgment, whenever they encountered a case that strained the terms of a statute—

or a case that could hardly have been anticipated by the men who had framed the legislation. As the jurists understood, those kinds of cases would commonly arise. When they did, the judges were not free to shape the law according to their own enthusiasms. They were obliged, rather, to move from the stipulations of the *positive* law to the guidance of the natural law, or what Blackstone called at different times "common reason,"[4] or "the law of nature and reason."[5] In the hands of Blackstone, this appeal to the natural law furnished an artful way of reconciling the supremacy of the Parliament, in the constitution of Britain, with the authority and integrity of the courts. The paradox took this form: The Parliament stood, in Britain, as the most sovereign agency of the positive law; the courts were also established through the positive law; and yet, the courts were also expected to be detached. They were expected to be the custodians for a law that did not always depend on the commands of the sovereign legislature. Blackstone sought to settle the problem in this way: He suggested that the jurists could acknowledge the supremacy of the legislature by respecting the words of a statute, even when those words command what is unreasonable. But at the same time, the statutes may be read precisely and narrowly, to cover no cases or objects beyond what they have explicitly mentioned. Blackstone remarked then that "where some collateral matter arises out of the general words, and happens to be unreasonable; there the judges are in decency to conclude that this consequence was not foreseen by the parliament, and therefore they are at liberty to expound the statute by equity."[6] In other words, they would be liberated by their tutored judgment to reconcile the statute with the commands of natural reason and justice. Blackstone offered this example:

> [I]f any act of parliament gives a man power to try all causes, that arise within his manor of Dale; yet, if a cause should arise in which he himself is a party, the act is construed not to extend to that; because it is unreasonable that any man should determine his own quarrel.[7]

Part of Blackstone's delicacy came in the suggestion that this office of the judges, in completing or perfecting the law, in appealing to "the law of nature and reason," would arise only rarely, as the judges were called on to fill in the interstices of the law. What was decorously held back, however, was the possibility that, for many statutes, this exercise formed the routine and dominant work of the judges. After all, cases were brought before the judges when there were arguable disputes about the meaning of statutes. And even when statutes were clear beyond caviling, it was the persisting experience of the law to encounter cases quite remote from anything the legislators could have imagined when they had drafted their statutes.

To draw a case from our own recent experience, the Congress has provided liberally for the protection of witnesses whose lives could be imperiled by their testimony. The witnesses would be provided with the support they would need in establishing new "identities" and concealing the tracks of their past. Yet, it seemed to slip past the imaginations of the legislators that some of these witnesses might be people divorced from their spouses, and that some of them would preserve the custody of their children. That arrangement created a sudden problem for the parent without custody, who nevertheless had rights, under the laws of a state, to visit his children. A case of this kind arose in the late 1970s, when Mr. William Franz pressed his proper claims to see his three children. His former wife had remarried a man who was a "contract killer" in what is usually called "organized crime." Her new husband agreed to testify in a federal trial if he and his new family were taken under the program for protecting witnesses. The government agreed to his request. The family was moved and hidden, and perforce, the children were hidden at the same time from Mr. Franz.[8] The courts were faced then with the question of whether the interest in protecting a witness, by concealing her identity and location, took precedence over the interest of the former husband in preserving the tie to his children. There was also a serious question of federalism: Did the ends of the federal program override the rights that were allocated under the laws of the states, in assigning the rights of custody and visitation? Patently, there were many tiers of judgment here, and it was necessary to appeal to some underlying canons of jural reasoning for the sake of resolving these conflicts.

The recognition, contained in Blackstone, was that most of the work of judges would come closer to this description, rather than to a notion of judges working with mechanical standards, routinely stamping out decisions to confirm the commands of the legislators. The nearly unmentionable secret was that those commands of the statute were not always clear or defensible. The work of the judges, in making the statutes both plausible and defensible, would indeed be steady work, and the men who performed it would not be trifling clerks. It was assumed by Blackstone, as it was assumed by our own Founders, that when the judges were forced to leave the text of a statute, they had access to principles of judgment quite apart from the things that were set down in the positive law. Brutus read this understanding of the Founders in the text of the Constitution itself, in the provision that settled on the federal courts a jurisdiction in "Equity." The written Constitution has been celebrated as a salutary novelty, but Brutus understood, at the very beginning, that the judges under the new government could not be confined to the written text of the Constitution. The judges would exercise a franchise to appeal beyond the text of the Constitution, to those canons of moral reasoning that guided the Founders themselves when they had set about to frame a new government. Brutus recognized, as he said, that the judges were authorized to "explain" the new Constitution—to draw out its implications, to fill out its meaning—through the "reasoning spirit" of the new instrument, "without being confined to the words or letter."

Five years later, in the case of *Chisholm v. Georgia*, the first set of opinions would be brought forth by the new, Supreme Court. James Wilson would explain, in an elegant opinion, that there were no cases built up as precedents under this new Constitution. It became ever more necessary then for the Court to speak about "the principles of general jurisprudence" before it would speak about the principles that marked the peculiar character of the American Constitution.[9] The Founders had referred to "the principles of law," or these "principles of general jurisprudence," even before they had drafted a Constitution. But now, Wilson took care to remind the audience of the Court that the principles of legal judgment were merely a *part of the laws of reason* and the principles of moral judgment. Before Wilson would invoke the authority of any case at law or any writer on matters legal, he would invoke the authority of "an original and profound writer . . . in the philosophy of mind." He would appeal to "Dr. [Thomas] Reid, in his excellent inquiry into the human mind, on the principles of *common sense*, speaking of the sceptical and illiberal philosophy, which under bold, but false pretentions to liberality, prevailed in many parts of Europe before he wrote."[10]

In other words, the Court would ascend to the task of judging only after it insisted, in the first instance, that it was indeed possible to judge: the Court would reject that "skepticism" in philosophy that denied the possibility of "knowing" moral truths, just as it denied the possibility of "knowing" almost anything else. Wilson would move from "the principles of general jurisprudence" to the principles that defined the distinct character of the American Constitution. As he moved through this train of reasoning to produce his conclusions, he advanced through the force of what he described as "fair and conclusive deduction."[11] Seventeen years later, Chief Justice John Marshall would offer a striking example of how a mind tutored in philosophy and law would derive certain constitutional rights through *deduction*. The case was *Fletcher v. Peck* (1810), and Marshall offered a remarkable echo of "Brutus" in his observation that the Court would be guided by the "reasoning spirit of the Constitution," rather than "the words or letter." Marshall could have rested his judgment in the case on a specific provision in the Constitution (the Contract Clause). But instead, he sought to establish the ground of his judgment in "the general principles of our political institutions," as well as in "the words of the constitution."[12]

The case involved a statute in Georgia that rescinded a grant of lands made by an earlier legislature. The law was a response to the famous "Yazoo scandals," in which legislators had been bribed by speculators as an inducement to make a grant of public lands. But the problem had become complicated by the fact that the land had since been sold, in many parcels, to third parties, who were innocent of the original wrongdoing.[13] *Fletcher v. Peck* would become notable as an early test of the provision in Article I, Section 10 of the Constitution, which barred the states from passing any law "impairing the Obligations of Contracts." Marshall summoned his arts of argument to show that a grant of land bore certain critical similarities to a "contract." It was not like the more familiar form of a contract "executory," in which a promise was made to deliver goods in exchange for a consideration or payment. The obligation of the contract would be focused then on the promise to "execute" the transfer, or convey the goods that were promised. In this case, there was no offer of a consideration, no tendering of a promise. The goods (i.e., the lands) were conveyed at once, and the granting constituted a "contract executed."

As one may readily see, the comparison was not without its strains. But Marshall's plausible point was that both arrangements entailed obligations, and the revoking of those obligations, in the case of a grant, would work an injustice quite as manifest as any failure to carry out a promise in conveying goods to a new owner. Let us suppose, for example, that a donor grants a large gift to a college. At a certain point the gift must be thought to "vest," to become part of the property of the college, and the college would be free to commit the funds to its own uses. The college might use the money for new construction; it might let out contracts with builders and workmen, and commit itself to the payment for this work. But then what if the original donor suddenly discovers that the recipients were unworthy, by his own exacting judgment, and decides to revoke the grants? The college might have made commitments or promises to these contractors because it reasonably expected that the gift had become its own property. The administrators of the college might have come to believe that they were in a position to make use of the new assets in undertaking projects. To withdraw the original gift now would leave the college liable for debts it might not be able to honor. Or, it may leave the workmen uncompensated, after they had passed up other employments and committed their efforts to this project.

Marshall recognized, in this case from Georgia, that the same kind of wrong would be done to those innocent buyers of land who now found the title to their land removed, or annulled, by the act of the legislature:

> A law annulling conveyances between individuals, and declaring that the grantors should stand seised [sic] of their former estates, notwithstanding those grants, would be as repugnant to the constitution as a law discharging the vendors of property from the obligation of executing their contracts by conveyances. It would be strange if a contract to convey was secured by the constitution, while an absolute conveyance remained unprotected.[14]

If Marshall were correct in this argument, he would have shown that the revocation of the grant was a species of those acts "impairing the obligation of contracts," and that would have been quite enough to bring the law in Georgia under the proscription of the Contract Clause. And yet, Marshall did not choose to settle the case in that way. Instead, he went on to show that the wrong engaged in this case could be *deduced* from the principle on "ex post facto" laws. Marshall explained that "an *ex post facto* law is one which renders an act punishable in a manner in which it was not punishable when it was committed." But what constituted "punishment"? Here, Marshall separated himself from the understandings of other jurists, who had sought to deal with the puzzle of ex post facto laws by confining the notion to retrospective laws that carried a *criminal* penalty.[15] But *criminal* penalties were not the only penalties administered by the law, and they were not always more serious or astounding than the penalties that were administered through *civil* proceedings. Some criminal penalties may take the form of a fine of $100. In contrast, a "civil" proceeding for defamation may result in a knock-out award of "damages" in the millions of dollars—a penalty sufficiently staggering to put certain newspapers out of business. If a person failed to pay these judgments, he could be confined to jail, and presumably the jails that confined people, in the aftermath of these civil proceedings, could be quite as confining as the jails that confined them at the end of criminal trials.

Marshall understood that so-called civil penalties could be as devastating, to property and reputation, as many criminal penalties; and therefore he recognized that the principle of ex post facto laws could not hinge on such a tenuous distinction. Marshall thought that punishments could be constituted by "penalties on the person" in the form of "pecuniary penalties." That is, when the law assesses a fine, or an award of heavy damages, it makes a claim on the property of an individual, and on the assets that sustain his life. As Marshall reasoned, a legislature could not properly act with an ex post facto law that penalizes a man by removing him from his job or applying the kind of fine that forces him to sell his business or his home or strip his family of his assets. As Marshall put it, a legislature would be "prohibited from passing a law by which a man's estate, or any part of it, shall be seized for a crime which was not declared, by some previous law, to render him liable to that punishment." But Marshall then asked, What would be the distinction between that arrangement and one in which the legislature claims the power of "seizing, for public use, the estate of any individual in the form of a law annulling the title by which he holds that estate?" He saw, in fact, no distinction:

> This rescinding act [in Georgia] would have the effect of an *ex post facto* law. It forfeits the estate of [the buyer] for a crime not committed by himself, but by those from whom he purchased. This cannot be effected in the form of an *ex post facto* law, or bill of attainder; why, then, is it allowable in the form of a law annulling the original grant?[16]

Let us assume, in a slightly different example, that a local legislature passes a law that declares it an offense to public decency for anyone to own an apartment building and charge more than $500 for an apartment with less than two bedrooms. Let us assume that the legislature applied the law to rents that were in effect for the preceding year before the law went into effect. If the landlords guilty of this new "offense" were given, as a punishment, a term in jail, the statute would be branded instantly as an ex post facto law. But what if the legislature had provided, instead, that anyone guilty of this offense would forfeit his apartment building and his assets? That arrangement might be challenged under the law, but our jurists would be convinced that it does not exhibit the properties of an ex post facto law, because the landlords were threatened only with "pecuniary fines" and not with the prospect of jail. And yet, in Marshall's understanding the difference could not turn on a distinction so wanting in moral significance.

Again, we should remind ourselves that Marshall had not been obliged, by the case, to flex his genius in this way and cast his argument in this form. He might have rested the "wrong" of the case on the provision in the Constitution dealing with the obligation of contracts. Instead, he sought to show that *the provision on contracts in the Constitution claimed its authority because it could be deduced from a deeper principle of law*, which did not need to be set down within the text of the Constitution. The principle on ex post facto laws had been understood by the Founders as one of those necessary principles bound up with the notion of lawfulness itself. And in fact, it was so widely understood as a principle of law, before the framing of the Constitution, that a serious question arose as to whether there was any need to mention it within the body of the document. When the question had arisen, during the debates at the Constitutional Convention, James Wilson and Oliver Ellsworth expressed deep reservations over this exercise of naming one or two principles of law in the text of the Constitution. They found something artless, even embarrassing, in the prospect of mentioning ex post facto laws, along with one or two other principles, and omitting, by implication, any reference to other principles, which could be quite as necessary to the character of a constitutional government. Ellsworth thought that the point on ex post facto laws was too obvious, that "there was no lawyer, no civilian who would not say that ex post facto laws were void in themselves." Therefore, he saw no need to prohibit them explicitly. Wilson, too, was "against inserting anything in the Constitution as to ex post facto laws. It will bring reflexions on the Constitution—and proclaim that we are ignorant of the first principles of Legislation, or are constituting a Government which will be so."[17]

These urbane men were sensitive to the perils of mentioning the obvious, but on the question in principle the Founders suffered no divisions: it is clear that they regarded the principle on ex post facto laws as a proposition that had standing, as a necessary principle of law, regardless of whether it was mentioned in the Constitution. When Marshall sought to derive his conclusion *deductively* in *Fletcher v. Peck*, he was calling into play the logic of a syllogism. If his conclusions were drawn, validly, through the form of a syllogism, they would have the force of *logical necessity*. Of course, the propositions drawn through a syllogism may claim that formal validity, even if the original premises are fanciful (e.g., "All Irishmen are leprechauns," "Harry is an Irishman"; therefore, "Harry is a leprechaun"). But when the power of a syllogism is attached to premises that are *substantively* true, the conclusions drawn through the syllogism have the sovereign attribute of being substantively, as well as formally, true.

Marshall began with the premise that the principle on ex post facto laws was a principle of law that was necessary and true. I leave aside here the task of weighing, in a careful way, whether the principle on ex post facto laws could in fact claim that standing as a real "principle" or an apodictic truth.[18] Let us simply take for granted, for the moment, that Marshall and other jurists of his time did accord, to that principle, the standing of a necessary axiom in the law. If Marshall could show, then, that the statute in Georgia was really a species of ex post facto laws, he had every reason to be confident that the conclusion he drew, about the wrongness of the statute, was not merely defensible, but compellingly true. And in that event, the wrongness of the statute would not hinge in any way on the question of whether contracts, or grants, or rescinding laws, had been mentioned in the text of the Constitution. On this point, Justice Johnson was even more emphatic in his concurring opinion in *Fletcher v. Peck*. "I do not hesitate to declare," he wrote, "that a state does not possess the power of revoking its own grants. But I do it on a general principle, on the reason and nature of things: a principle which will impose laws even on the Deity."[19] Johnson wished to have it "distinctly understood that my opinion on this point is *not founded on the provision in the constitution* . . . relative to laws impairing the obligations of contracts. It is much to be regretted that words of less equivocal signification, had not been adopted in that article of the constitution."[20]

Marshall drew out the import of this point with a further, and novel, recognition. He remarked that Georgia was "part of a large empire; she is a member of the American union," and the Union had a Constitution that was supreme over its separate parts. But as a result of the argument that Marshall and Johnson had made here, Marshall could point out that the rescinding act passed by the legislature of Georgia "might well be doubted, were Georgia a single sovereign power."[21] That is, even if Georgia had not come under the Constitution and the restrictions of the Contract Clause, the action of the legislature would still have been wrong. For the legislature had violated a principle that did not depend, for its validity, on the explicit provisions of the Constitution, or on the membership of Georgia in the American Union.

· · · · ·

In the Chisholm case, James Wilson had appealed, as jurist, to the principles of "mind," and to the first principles of practical judgment. He had written of the need to draw out the principles of law through "fair and conclusive deduction." In *Fletcher v. Peck*, Marshall had taken the point notably further by actually going on to offer lessons: He furnished nothing less than a demonstration of the way in which a cultivated mind went about the task of drawing principles through deduction. If we sought to account for the manner in which he carried through the demonstration, we would find ourselves reproducing the inventory of axioms that Marshall had evidently absorbed when he had been tutored in logic. He understood, as Wilson had understood, the difference between *principles* and the *instances* in which principles were manifested. He understood, then, as Wilson had remarked, that a certain fact, "uncontrovertibly established in *one* instance, proves the *principle* in *all other* instances, to which the facts will be found to apply."[22] Once one understood the critical properties of a rescinding act that made it an ex post facto law, it did not matter whether the rescinding act applied to real estate or carriages or grants made to colleges.

In our own time, jurists would condemn the wrong of racial segregation in public schools, and then puzzle over the question of whether the wrong in that case was really bound up with the injuries produced in schools and the special place of education in a republic. In that event, the same principle, or the same wrong, would not appear to be engaged in the problem of segregation in public swimming pools or private clubs. Would the courts require, then, the invention of more refined principles to explain the wrong in these separate cases? Our first generation of jurists might have taken this puzzlement as a sign that these men of the law had not apparently become clear, in the first place, on the principle that defined for them the wrong of racial segregation.

Wilson and Marshall took it for granted, of course, that a case would become part of a *class*, that it would come under the principle that applied to that class, only if it bore the similarities that were critical, or the features that were essential, to the definition of the class. If the legislature of Georgia moved to terminate, or withdraw, a *renewable* grant—if the recipients of the grant knew that the grant could be withdrawn at the end of any year—then that act of the legislature would not have been critically "similar" to the rescinding of the grant in *Fletcher v. Peck*. Wilson and Marshall understood that "like cases had to be treated equally." Cases could be brought within the same class, or family of cases, *if* they bore critical resemblances. But the corollary of that understanding was that jurists were not free to invent spurious classes on the basis of attributes that were *not* critical or relevant. The genius of judges could often be expended then on the task of explaining just which attributes were relevant or irrelevant to the question of principle posed in any case. Marshall was writing in this vein, in *Fletcher v. Peck*, when he rejected the conventional view that "criminal penalties" were decisive in distinguishing ex post facto laws from other, legitimate laws, which applied retrospectively. What he sought to show was that the ingredient of "criminal penalties" was not, in the end, *relevant* to the problem of principle engaged here. It could not be critical in defining—and limiting—the "class" of cases that came under the principle on ex post facto laws.

But that point merely draws us in more deeply, to the layers of logic that have been folded into our jurisprudence. Some of them have been folded in so seamlessly that we scarcely have the sense, any longer, of discrete layers. We readily assume, for example, that "like cases should be treated equally." But why does that proposition have the standing of an axiom of moral and legal reasoning? We may not be aware that we are drawing, at this point, on a critical property of moral reasoning, namely, the attribute of "universality": If we say that it is "wrong" for owners of public accommodations to discriminate on the basis of race, then we imply that the act is wrong for "all persons similarly situated"—that is, all persons who are owners of public accommodations. We treat "like" cases in a "like" fashion; we address them with the same rules. But why are we *obliged* to use the same rules? Because we are pronouncing a judgment on the things that are morally right or wrong, just or unjust. When we speak in a moral vein, we purport to speak about the things that are generally or universally right or wrong—which is to say, right or wrong for others as well as ourselves. When we cast a moral judgment, when we condemn racial discrimination as a "wrong," we mean to say that it is wrong for anyone, for everyone, engaged in the same act. The commitment to "equality" in the law is rooted, then, in the logic of morals, in the logic we are invoking when we judge certain acts to be right or wrong:[23] When we say that people have a right to be treated equally, we are really saying that they have the right to be treated morally or justly; for when they are treated morally, they are treated with standards that happen to apply equally *because they apply universally.* It is that connection to the logic of moral judgment that invests the notion of equality with its moral significance. It also furnishes a moral ground of judgment in distinguishing between the legitimate and the spurious claims of equality. For example, we may all have an equal claim to be judged and certified by the same standards that are used to measure the competence of surgeons; but we do not all have an "equal" claim to practice surgery on the public.

We are obliged, then, to treat equally all cases that fall into the same class. But how broad is that class? That depends on the maxim that defines the nature of the wrong and the sweep of the principle. If we are dealing with racial discrimination in places of "public accommodation," we may find that the breadth of the principle moves us to abstract ourselves from the specific character of the enterprise: We may be entirely indifferent, then, to the question of whether the discrimination takes place in a hotel, a restaurant, a cinema.

But then the sweep of the principle may properly move us even further. Once we understand the principle that defines the "wrong" in cases of racial discrimination, it becomes proper to ask just why that wrong would be confined to places of "public accommodation"? In principle, we could identify the same kinds of wrongs in settings that are private and intimate: Black people may be excluded from membership in a private club. A man provides, in his will, that he will disinherit any of his children who marry a black. A private, religious college accepts men and women of both races, but it confines its membership to students who share the opposition of the school to dating and marriage across racial lines. We are inclined right now to assume that these cases lie beyond the reach of the law, but we seem to have in mind the "law" that condemns in criminal statutes or provides for penalties in civil suits. That does not mean, however, that these cases are removed from the arenas of legal judgment. Courts of law or administrative agencies may still pass judgment on these practices, and affect them with the kinds of disabilities that amount to penalties. And so, the Bob Jones University loses its tax-exempt status because of its official position on interracial dating. A private club is threatened with the removal of its liquor license. A court may decide that it cannot enforce the terms of a private will that runs counter to public policy. In all of these ways, people in positions of authority cast a judgment on the practice of private discriminations. To say that these cases stand for the moment beyond the reach of the criminal law is not to say that they stand beyond the domain of legal judgment—or beyond the burden of legal harassment, legal inhibition, legal disabilities.

What we may see here, of course, is the willingness on the part of politicians to use the levers of harassment that come into their hands. And yet, we ought to be aware that these reflexes of people in authority are shaped in large part by the logic of moral judgment itself. These forms of legal harassment mark the rough awareness of politicians that the wrongs they are addressing are not really confined in principle to public settings. I have had the occasion to explain, in another place, that the logic of a moral principle will be utterly indifferent to the distinction between the public and the private. Once we understand, for example, the attributes that mark an act of killing "without justification" as a wrong, we would realize that a murder staged in a private bedroom is every bit as wrong as a murder taking place in the public streets. The distinction between the public and the private may be convenient on many occasions, and it may supply a serious concern of our law; but that distinction simply has nothing to do with those fundamental postulates, those "laws of reason," that supply the ground of our moral judgment.[24]

In *The Importance of Being Earnest*, the governess directs her young charge to resume her reading in Political Economy, but to omit the chapter on "The Fall of the Rupee" as "somewhat too sensational." We may be inclined, in the same temper, to omit this point on the "laws of reason," as "somewhat too sensational" or distracting; but it does command a word or two of explanation, since it bears, importantly, on the understanding of Marshall and the first generation of our jurists. Fortunately, the point has already been explained more fully in another place,[25] and there is no need to stage the explanation again in these pages. The main point here simply involves a recovery of the ancient recognition that the "moral laws" are really a subset, a part, of the "laws of reason" (or what we have called, at different times, the "laws of logic"). Take, as an innocent example, the "law of contradiction"—the understanding that two contradictory propositions both cannot be true. That happens to be a necessary axiom of reasoning; some commentators would even argue that it is the ultimate ground of our reasoning. There may not be any peculiar moral significance that attaches to the "law of contradiction" in any case. It may be violated by a schoolboy doing his sums, or by an accountant adding up a ledger, without any sense that the "mistake" has a moral overtone. But consider another case: A judge says, "Smith, you have been acquitted; therefore I sentence you to twenty years in prison." The judge has violated the "law of contradiction," and on that basis, we could say, compellingly, that he has made a "mistake," that his judgment is "wrong." The mistake absorbs the significance of a moral wrong because the judge is inflicting a punishment, or a harm, on another person. And since the harm is inflicted on the basis of a mistake, the harm is inflicted "without justification." The harm also occurs here through the action of a "free agent," a judge, who had the freedom to impose the punishment or hold back. That makes the harm notably different from the kinds of hurts produced through the force, say, of falling rocks. As I have had the occasion to put it elsewhere:

> [P]ain and destruction may be wrought by falling bodies propelled by the laws of nature; it is not in the moral realm alone that harms are produced. But we are drawn, rightly, by a different fascination, to those acts of harming or helping that are produced by intention, by the fuel of motive, and by the conscious tailoring of means to ends. No falling rock reveals to us an incorrigible path of "cruelty"; but the world of cruelty and wickedness, of bravery and admiration, excites a different kind of wonder and engages a different part of our souls. And yet, that is all. The difference between our knowledge of moral and nonmoral things may ignite different passions and call forth different talents; but it does not remove us to a place beyond the axioms of understanding or the laws of reason, where we have no hope or prospect of "knowing."[26]

What might be said for the "law of contradiction" could be said, with the same force, for the proposition that Thomas Reid once described as a necessary "first principle" in moral judgment: that "what is done from unavoidable necessity . . . cannot be the object either of blame or moral approbation."[27] This proposition may stand simply as a law of reason, without seeming to bear, on its surface, any special moral significance. And yet, from this simple proposition or its variants, we can extract propositions of moral consequence that have claimed a prominent place in our law.[28] We may derive the "insanity defense," and we may recede from the willingness to punish people when they have lacked control over their own acts. We may also be led to the recognition that it is wrong to draw adverse judgments about people solely on the basis of attributes, such as race, which they are powerless to affect.

Again, I mention these things for the sake simply of recovering a critical point in the understanding of Marshall and the jurists of his time. When Marshall applied the logical rule of treating like cases alike, he did not have any evident sense that he was crossing an invisible threshold that separated propositional logic from something we would call "moral reasoning." For Marshall, for Wilson, and other jurists of their age, the two were indistinguishable. By the same token, they did not seem to suffer any doubt that the laws of logic they engaged, in applying their reason to the facts of cases, were bound up with what Wilson called the "general principles of right."[29] As we have seen, Marshall made use of that logic when he connected the Contract Clause of the Constitution to the principle on "ex post facto laws." He was willing to draw, that is, on the "universal" properties that may connect certain "wrongs" to one another, even though we may find them, in the Constitution, placed in separate sections. But in this way, Marshall was able to explain the deeper wrong in principle that lay behind the clause on "impairing the Obligation of Contracts." He brought the reader from the provision in the Constitution to the groundwork of moral principles that underlay the legal document. He connected passages in the text to principles of right and wrong that did not depend, for their authority, on their mention in the Constitution. And in making that transition, he apparently thought he was explaining, far more fully, why the passage in the Constitution deserved to be treated with the solemn authority of the fundamental law. The section in the Constitution did not mark off merely a convention or understanding established in this country—an understanding of what we, in this particular tribe of Americans, regarded as a wrong. But rather, Marshall amplified the text, and in his hand, the provision on "the Obligation of Contracts" was made to alert us to the uses of law that were in principle wrong in all places.

· · · · ·

Almost sixty years later, another chief justice offered a similar exercise in reasoning, in a rather different kind of case. I would recall that case for a moment for the sake of making the point that Marshall was not employing, in *Fletcher v. Peck*, canons of reasoning that were accessible only to his own genius. Chief Justice Chase, in the *Legal Tender Cases*, showed a similar facility in illuminating, or recasting, a provision in the Constitution, by bringing the canons of moral reasoning to the reading of the text. During the strains of the Civil War, it seemed to be expedient to meet the heightened demands for currency with the printing of paper notes. It was one thing, however, to print the notes and make them available for people to hold and use. But as the Court pointed out in *Hepburn v. Griswold*, it was quite another matter for the Congress to insist that those notes should be acceptable as legal tender in discharging debts that were made before 1862, before the advent of the paper money.[30] Congress had issued several series of paper notes without making them compulsory as legal tender, and those notes had circulated without "unfavourable discrimination." They were not discounted in relation to other currency; they had substantially held their value. In contrast, the paper notes that were made compulsory as legal tender suffered an early and marked depreciation. Two years after they were issued, it required $2.85 in these paper "dollars" to buy a dollar of gold at a free market price.[31] In other words, these dollars had lost almost two-thirds of their value in two years. If a debt of $100 had been contracted before 1862, and if that debt could be redeemed now in these paper dollars, the creditor would receive a payment that was worth no more than about $35 in real terms. When these facts were put in place, the Court could tenably raise the question of whether the policy on legal tender did not in fact impair the obligation of contracts.

And yet, the Contract Clause figured, in the Constitution, as a restraint on the power of the *states*. Strictly speaking, from the text of the document, this provision did not bind the national government. But if that maxim on contracts was thought to express a principle of lawful government, the chief justice thought it plausible to ask just why it should not apply to the federal government as well. "[W]e think it clear," he wrote, "that those who framed and those who adopted the Constitution, intended that the spirit of this prohibition should pervade the entire body of legislation."[32] Still, the chief justice would not settle on that particular argument. He went on to suggest, with a broad construal, that the Legal Tender Acts would violate other parts of the Constitution, including the Due Process Clause of the Fifth Amendment. But he managed to summon the jural imagination of his audience more fully when he brought forth another part of the Fifth Amendment—the provision that "private property shall [not] be taken for public use, without just compensation." There was, of course, no "taking" of property in this case, no transfer of ownership from a private owner to the public authorities. Chase suggested, however, that with a modest engagement of the moral imagination, the principle behind this provision would plausibly extend beyond the narrow terms of the text.

> [The provision on the taking of property] does not, in terms, prohibit legislation which appropriates the private property of one class of citizens to the use of another class; but if such property cannot be taken for the benefit of all, without compensation, it is difficult to understand how it can be so taken for the benefit of a part without violating the spirit of the prohibition.[33]

I would not claim, just yet, that Chase said enough in this passage to settle a rather tangled issue.[34] But I think he was quite warranted in reaching out to the canons of moral reasoning and annexing them to the reading of the text. If we return for a moment to an earlier example, let us assume that the government seizes an apartment building from an owner, without compensation, and transfers that property to the ownership of the government. Would it be a different case, in principle, if the government seized the same building, without compensation, and transferred ownership to one of the tenants? The requirement of paying compensation is a part of a constitutional discipline: When the government is compelled in any case to pay compensation, it may come under a stronger demand to justify its measures to the public, to the people who will have to be taxed in order to raise the needful money. But may this discipline of justification be evaded so easily—may the requirement of compensation be avoided altogether—through the simple device of transferring ownership to a private party? Would the distinction between public and private ownership really be one of those "relevant" differences in marking off the limits to the principle engaged here?

There was nothing alien to the law in Chase's move in this case. He was simply applying the standard of "universality," which came into play as a necessary part of the discourse on moral and legal judgment. In this respect he was drawing upon canons of reasoning that were a familiar part of the tradition of philosophy, running back two thousand years. But even if a jurist had been untutored in Aristotle and Aquinas, Blackstone and Grotius, Reid and Kant, he would have been introduced to this style of reasoning in the Old Testament. In 2 Samuel, the story is told of King David and his infatuation with Bathsheba. David seeks to dispose of Bathsheba's husband by arranging to have him placed in an exposed position in battle. In this way, David manages to rid himself of Uriah. But David is confronted by Nathan, who poses a problem to David in the form of a parable. He tells the king the story of a man rich with many flocks and herds. When a traveler came, the rich man did not draw upon his own cattle or sheep for the provision of the guest. Instead, he took, and offered for his guest, the only lamb owned by a poor man living near him. When he heard this story, "David's anger was greatly kindled against the man; and he said to Nathan, As the Lord liveth, the man that hath done this thing shall surely die." But then, "Nathan said to David, Thou art the man" (2 Sam. 12:7).

The "wrong" of the case was put forth by Nathan in *impersonal* terms, and in those terms the wrong was recognized by David. His outrage formed in response to the story, even without knowing the name of the rich man or his victim. And in that recognition he made his telling concession to the "universal" quality of moral judgments. He showed his recognition that the wrong of the case could be identified as a wrong for anyone, for everyone, who performed the same act. Hence, the telling point made by Nathan when he merely informed the king that his own acts fitted the description of the wrong. The story would have had no point unless this logic of a moral principle had been grasped by David as well as by Nathan.

In the tradition of moral reasoning, that logic of a principle is nowhere conveyed more dramatically than in the famous fragment written by Lincoln on the question of slavery. I have had the occasion to cite this fragment in other places, but it is an example that bears recalling. Lincoln imagined that he was engaged in an argument with a proponent of slavery, and he questioned the grounds on which the slavery of black people could be justified.

> You say A. is white, and B. is black. It is color, then: the lighter having the right to enslave the darker? Take care. By this rule, you are to be slave to the first man you meet, with a fairer skin than your own.

> You do not mean *color* exactly?—You mean the whites are *intellectually* the superiors of the blacks, and therefore have the right to enslave them? Take care again. By this rule, you are to be slave to the first man you meet, with an intellect superior to your own.

> But, say you, it is a question of interest; and, if you can make it your *interest*, you have the right to enslave another. Very well. And if he can make it his interest, he has the right to enslave you. [35]

With this understanding of the properties of a moral argument, Lincoln was able to expose the logical sleight of hand performed by Stephen Douglas during their classic debates in 1858. Douglas had persistently refused to pronounce a judgment on the rightness or wrongness of slavery. In that respect, as Lincoln aptly noted, Douglas was virtually alone in the public life of America. "He has the high distinction, so far as I know, of never having said slavery is either right or wrong. Almost everybody else says one or the other, but the Judge never does." [36] Douglas pretended to hold back his endorsement from either side of this grave dispute, because he was, in the politics of his day, "pro-choice." He insisted that his personal views on morality had to give way in the face of a more fundamental principle in democracy, namely, the right of the majority, in the separate territories, to vote slavery up or down. But Lincoln managed to bring out the logical contradiction that stood behind this staging of political cleverness.

> [W]hen Judge Douglas says he "don't care whether slavery is voted up or down," . . . he cannot thus argue logically if he sees anything wrong in it; . . . He cannot say that he would as soon see a wrong voted up as voted down. When Judge Douglas says that whoever, or whatever community, wants slaves, they have a right to have them, he is perfectly logical if there is nothing wrong in the institution; but if you admit that it is wrong, he cannot logically say that anybody has a right to do a wrong. When he says that slave property and horse and hog prop-

erty are alike to be allowed to go into the Territories, upon the principles of equality, he is reasoning truly, if there is no difference between them as property; but if the one is property, held rightfully, and the other is wrong, then there is no equality between the right and wrong; so that, turn it in any way you can, in all the argument sustaining the Democratic policy . . . there is a careful, studied exclusion of the idea that there is anything wrong in slavery.[37]

Lincoln expressed, in this passage, the connection that was traditionally understood between the logic of morals and the logic of law. The connection has rarely been made with this explicitness; in the canons of political theory, only Thomas Aquinas and John Stuart Mill have come as close to explaining this cardinal point.[38] I have already explained this connection at length in another place;[39] I would simply recall here the main points in the tradition that Lincoln was representing. The most decisive point, of course, was the relation that was taken for granted between law and moral understanding: The edicts of law had a "binding" force; they overrode the claims of private judgment and personal taste; they replaced private choice with a public obligation. In the tradition coming down from the classics, it was understood that this state of affairs could not be *justified* if the law merely represented the replacement of one set of opinions, or one set of preferences, by another. The law could properly override the claims of personal choice if it could appeal to certain understandings of right and wrong that were in fact, valid or true, for the rulers as well as the ruled. These understandings of right and wrong could claim, far more readily, the standing of "truths" if they were grounded in the "laws of reason"—in propositions that were true universally, true for all persons, because they happened to be true of necessity.

In this vein, Blackstone taught that the law represents "a rule of civil conduct prescribed by the supreme power in a state, commanding what is right and prohibiting what is wrong."[40] Years later, professors of law would sneer at his innocence in assuming that the law bore any "moral" concern of this kind, to command what is "right" and prohibit what is "wrong."[41] Legal judgments were to proceed from some standard of "utility," suitably detached from the measure of what was right or wrong, just or unjust. Judges and legislators would not pretend to speak in the name of a science that claimed to know anything of moral significance. In was in this spirit that Justice Holmes offered up the wish, quoted earlier, that "every word of moral significance could be banished from the law altogether."[42] As I remarked, Holmes expressed here the character of the modern project in law. That project is not only at odds with the tradition of jurisprudence—the tradition shared, by and large, by the Founders—but it also runs counter to an understanding that is commonly grasped by people who are not lawyers. When we hear it said that "there ought to be a law," the phrase marks the recognition that the law is preceded by the awareness of a *wrong*, which deserves the restraint or correction of the law. In the traditional understanding, law exists only because rights and wrongs exist.

The traditional connection between morals and law could be expressed briefly in this way: When we invoke the language of morals, we move away from statements of merely personal taste or private belief; we offer a judgment about the things that are universally right or wrong, just or unjust. When we say, then, that any act stands in the class of a "wrong"—that it is wrong, say, to hold other human beings as slaves—we are saying that it is wrong for anyone, for everyone, to hold slaves; that *no one ought* to hold slaves; that *anyone* may *rightly be restrained* from owning slaves, even if the holding of slaves would serve his interests. We could not say that "It is wrong for people to torture their children," and then say, at the same, that "people ought to be left free to make their own judgments on whether they will torture their children or not, according to their own sense of the things that give them pleasure." Stephen Douglas could not say that slavery is "wrong," and then hold, as Lincoln said, that "whatever community . . . wants slaves . . . they have a right to have them." When we come to the judgment that any act stands in the class of a "wrong," the logic of that *moral* recognition would compel us to remove that act from the domain of personal preference or private choice, and forbid that act generally or universally. We may forbid it, in short, with the force of law.

That is not to say that anything we can plausibly describe as a "wrong" ought to come within the reach of the law. Prudence may rightly make us pause before we bring every dispute, or every villainy, within the jurisdiction of the state. And yet, it is remarkable as to the number of intimate and trivial matters that people are willing to submit to the judgment of juries and judges and authorities outside the circle of their families. A father reneges on his promise to pay the college tuition of his daughter. A woman costs a man expense and inconvenience by forcing him to drive for two hours for a date she did not keep. A husband causes his wife to forget her own name by persistently addressing her in a name not her own. All of these incidents, and countless more, quite as important or trivial, have found their way into legal forums. People aggrieved, people fueled with outrage, have sought to have an impersonal, legal, officer pronounce on the wrong that was done to them, and compel a remedy.[43] But whether it becomes prudent at any time to invoke the law, the case in principle for the law would depend on the prospect of showing, in any case, that a *wrong* has been done. In the chapters ahead, we shall have the occasion to see judges seeking to interpret a clause in the Constitution by appealing to a *structure of moral argument* that lies behind the clause. The exercise would hardly be comprehensible if those canons of reasoning did not exist, outside the text. But the larger design of their work may become ever more intelligible when we understand that the judges are working in the cast of a more ancient understanding: Whether they are conscious of the point or not, they are tracing their judgments back to a groundwork of moral principles, or to the canons of reasoning, which provide the foundation for their decisions in law.

In chapter 5, I shall recall one or two judicial spectacles from our own day in which experienced judges were convinced that they were locked in a serious dispute about the clause in the Constitution that furnished the proper ground of their judgment. On closer examination, we will show that the judgments of all of the judges depended on precisely the same underlying structure of moral argument. Regardless of the clause they invoked in making their case, the properties of their arguments were the same in all of their decisive attributes. The identities in the structure of argument were not obscured; they were simply not as evident to jurists of our own time, who are no longer quite as sensitive to the forms of moral reasoning that stand behind their legal judgments.

But in the next chapter, I would carry forward the understanding that I have unfolded in this section: I would collect a few problems, on a variety of subjects, which were addressed by some of the subtlest of our own statesmen and jurists. In all of these cases, one of our more interesting jural minds was addressing a question of consequence, and in each case, the statesman or judge would find it necessary to move beyond the text of the Constitution for the sake of establishing the meaning of the Constitution and showing, far more clearly, how that document bore on the case at hand. The cast I would assemble for this exercise would include Lincoln, Daniel Webster, Benjamin Curtis, Harlan Stone, Alexander Hamilton, and the first Justice Harlan. With Lincoln and Harlan the argument is taken to a further dimension: In one instance, Lincoln's move beyond the text was so compelling in its argument that we would be tempted to conclude that, if his own construction were not correct, the Constitution itself had to be mistaken.

With Harlan, we find that the Thirteenth and Fourteenth Amendments were not strictly necessary to the case he wished to make against the segregation of black people in passenger trains and public facilities. For Harlan, the original text of the Constitution contained all of the foundation that was required for a national government with the authority to protect its black citizens. But if we annex to Harlan's argument the commentaries of Hamilton in the Federalist papers, we would discover that Harlan's argument could have been made even without the written text of the Constitution. As Hamilton would show us, with an exquisite clarity, the premises that were vital to Harlan's argument were established simply with the decisions, in 1787, that displaced a confederation and constituted, in the territory of the United States, a national government.

THREE

MOVING BEYOND THE TEXT

THE ASCENT of Lincoln, in the troubled politics of his time, required nothing less than that understanding he so distinctly and uncommonly possessed—the understanding that joined a demanding, philosophic sense with a regard, quite as thoughtfully measured, for the political requirements of the Constitution. As Lincoln understood, the Union had existed before the Constitution. For Lincoln, the Union had begun with the Declaration of Independence, with the articulation of the principle—the central "proposition"—that stamped the character of the American republic. That "proposition," as Lincoln called it, the proposition that "All men are created equal," was the father of all principles among us. To the extent that Americans were constituted as a political community, they found their common character in their commitment to that principle of the Declaration. The Constitution was a means, an instrument for conveying, in a legal structure, the principles that marked the character of the American republic. Lincoln recalled the biblical proverb that "a word fitly spoken is like apples of gold in pictures of silver" (Prov. 25:11):

> The expression of that principle in our Declaration of Independence . . . was the word *"fitly spoken"* which has proved an "apple of gold" to us. The *Union* and the *Constitution* are the *picture* of *silver*, subsequently framed around it. The picture was made, not to *conceal* or *destroy* the apple; but to *adorn*, and *preserve* it. The *picture* was made *for* the apple—*not* the apple for the picture.[1]

The American republic was not formed for the sake of the Constitution; the Constitution was designed for the sake of imparting the character of the republic to the ways in which we lived together, daily, in this country, when our relations were touched by the law. And yet, Lincoln also recognized that the Constitution had come to represent those critical compromises that were necessary for the preservation of the Union. The Constitution had thrown a certain protection around the institution of slavery in the states. Without that protection, without that assurance, the Union would not have been formed. But with the Union, the holders of slaves agreed to be governed by a Constitution that never named or endorsed their form of property. At the same time, the Constitution provided for the ending of the trade in slaves in 1808. In that provision, the Constitution seemed to mark the expectation, or at least the hope, shared in the South as well as the North, that slavery, as an institution, would gradually wither. In the meantime, the Union constituted a republican government, founded on the premise that men were by nature equal; and that premise of the political order stood, enduringly, as a reproach to slavery. During the nineteenth century, Whig statesmen of the North could bite their lips and preserve their faithfulness to the constitutional bargain: They could accept their obligation to support, through the laws, the return of fugitive slaves, as the only practicable means of preserving a political order that promised to put slavery, as Lincoln said, in the course of ultimate extinction. In his first inaugural address, Lincoln reflected precisely on the sense of prudence that preserved these arrangements.

> One section of our country believes slavery is *right*, and ought to be extended, while the other believes it is *wrong*, and ought not to be extended. This is the only substantial dispute. The fugitive slave clause of the Constitution, and the law for the suppression of the foreign slave trade, are each as well enforced, perhaps, as any law can ever be in a community where the moral sense of the people imperfectly supports the law itself. The great body of the people abide by the dry legal obligation in both cases, and a few break over in each. This, I think, cannot be perfectly cured; and it would be worse in both cases *after* the separation of the sections, than before. The foreign slave trade, now imperfectly suppressed, would be ultimately revived without restriction, in one section; while fugitive slaves, now only partially surrendered, would not be surrendered at all, by the other.[2]

The obligation to return fugitive slaves was contained in the Constitution (in Article IV, Section 2). And yet, Lincoln appreciated that the obligation did not find its sole support in the Constitution. Were that the case, the Republican party could have sought to remove the obligation by amending the Constitution and deleting the clause on fugitive slaves. But Lincoln warned Salmon Chase in 1859 that "the introduction of a proposition for repeal of the Fugitive Slave law, into the next Republican National convention, will explode the convention and the party."[3] The provisions in the law on fugitive slaves reflected the serious interests that divided the political community. It was not really sensible to dream of changing those laws, in a quick political coup, without coming to a settlement on the questions that vexed the country and found their reflection in these passages in the Constitution. The commitment on fugitive slaves was part, then, of the grand compromise, or the political agreement, that was necessary to the preservation of the Union. The continued faithfulness to that commitment was an exercise of prudence at its highest level: the compromise could be justified only because it promised the best means of advancing the cause in principle and putting slavery in the course of extinction.

Lincoln moved, then, to an understanding outside the Constitution, in order to explain and justify the obligation to respect this clause in the Constitution. But he was also free to move in the same way to establish the limits to that obligation, or the framework in which that obligation would be honored. The provision in the Constitution read in this way:

> No person held to service or labor in one State, under the laws thereof, escaping into another, shall, in consequence of any law or regulation therein, be discharged from such service or labor, but shall be delivered up on claim of the party to whom such service or labor may be due.

As Lincoln noted, the Constitution was silent as to who it was who had the obligation to "deliver up" the slave. He assumed that the federal government absorbed the responsibility to enforce any commitment that was established under the federal Constitution. For the fugitive, it made no difference as to whether it was the state, or the national, authority that presided over his capture and return. But the Constitution was also silent about the procedures that would govern a dispute on these matters. Would it be enough for any slave catcher, roaming in the North, to capture a free black man at gunpoint and return him to another state? Would it be necessary to bring the matter before a magistrate, to prove that the black man was indeed the one who had fled from slavery? And yet, if a cause was heard in a formal way, would the presumption be placed in favor of the freedom of the black man, or in favor of his slavery? That is, if the evidence were uncertain, would it simply be *presumed* that a free black man, newly arrived in town, was probably a runaway slave? Or would the burden of proof be placed on those who would claim that he was anything other than a free man? In his famous speech at Peoria in 1854, Lincoln remarked that he was quite willing to respect the "constitutional rights" of slave owners and give them legislation for the reclaiming of their slaves, but that legislation "should not, in its stringency, be more likely to carry a free man into slavery, than our ordinary criminal laws are to hang an innocent one."[4] In other words, the procedures would contain a presumption in favor of the personal freedom of the person accused of being a fugitive. In his first inaugural address, several years later, Lincoln reinforced this understanding:

> [I]n any law upon this subject, ought not all the safeguards of liberty known in the civilized and humane jurisprudence to be introduced, so that a free man be not, in any case surrendered as a slave? And might it not be well, at the same time, to provide by law for the enforcement of that clause in the Constitution which guaranties that "The citizens of each State shall be entitled to all privileges and immunities of citizens in the several States?"[5]

Clearly, these arrangements were not prescribed in the text of the Constitution. The document was silent about the fundamental premises that defined the cast of the hearing, in which evidence would be taken and a judgment would be rendered. In reaching outside the Constitution, Lincoln had drawn on the analogy of a criminal trial, with its presumption in favor of the accused, but it was no more than an analogy. Years earlier, Daniel Webster had insisted that these proceedings over the return of fugitive slaves were not really "criminal" actions: The fugitive was not being accused of a crime; and therefore, it was not necessary to have, in these hearings, the presence of a jury. Webster himself favored the provision of a jury, but he was careful to explain to his constituents that nothing in the Constitution strictly entailed a trial by jury in cases of this kind.[6] He was moved to favor a jury for the same reason that would later move Lincoln: not for the purpose of suggesting that the man accused in these proceedings should be presumed "innocent" of a crime, but that he should be presumed *free*. Lincoln also suggested that the proceeding should engage the clause on the "privileges and immunities of citizens." He wished to have it presumed, that is, in the first instance, that the black man was a free man, that a free man was a *citizen*, and the burden of proof would be placed then, severely, on those who would prove otherwise.[7] But from what would he derive the premise that any man, including any black man, should be presumed to be free? The answer was of course embedded in the teaching that accounted for his mission in the crisis of his time: "The doctrine of self-government," he said in the Peoria speech, "is right—absolutely and eternally right . . . [but whether it applies to the question of slavery] depends on whether a negro is *not* or *is* a man."

> If he is *not* a man, why in that case, he who *is* a man may, as a matter of self-government, do just as he pleases with him. But if the negro *is* a man, is it not to that extent, a total destruction of self-government, to say that he too shall not govern *himself?* . . . If the negro is a *man*, why then my ancient faith teaches me that "all men are created equal;" and that there can be no moral right in connection with one man's making a slave of another.[8]

For Lincoln, as we know, the "crisis of the house divided" turned precisely on the question of whether the nation was indeed founded on the principles articulated in the Declaration of Independence. As he would later say at Gettysburg, that document brought forth "new nation . . . dedicated to the proposition that 'all men are created equal.' " The Declaration spoke of this proposition as a "self-evident" truth, grounded in the "nature" of human beings; the nature that made men separate from animals. In that ancient understanding, human beings did not deserve to be ruled in the way that humans ruled dogs, horses, and monkeys. Creatures who could give and understand reasons deserved to be ruled through the giving of reasons, by a government that would seek the consent of the governed. It was Lincoln's argument in the debate with Douglas that this "right" of human beings to govern themselves had a *natural* foundation: It would hold true in all places where the nature of human beings remained the same. It would not depend on the conventions that were dominant in one place or another; it could not rest simply on the habits of the local tribe or the sufferance of the local majority.[9]

The ground of right and wrong, then, in regard to slavery, could not depend on any moral judgments stipulated in the Constitution. The wrongness of slavery was rooted in the understandings of right and wrong that *preceded* the Constitution. Indeed, as Lincoln recognized, the right of human beings to be ruled only with their own consent was a necessary part of that moral ground on which the Constitution itself was founded. The Constitution of 1787 represented the *second* attempt to shape a structure of government that would be faithful to the principles of the American regime. But in the crisis of the regime, the crisis inspired by the prospect of extending slavery, the Constitution itself could not provide the rules or means of managing the crisis. Or rather, the Constitution could not provide that guidance if it were read merely as a set of formal rules, disconnected from any substantive understanding of the things that were right or wrong, just or unjust. As Lincoln suggested, in the course of his debates with Douglas, the Constitution would furnish a clumsy means of preserving the Union unless the provisions of the document were understood in the light of the principles that *preceded* the Constitution, the principles that provided the foundation for the Constitution. Without that connection, the Constitution could be reduced to a collection of procedures for holding together an alliance of local despotisms. The Union reshaped as a prop to slavery was not the Union that was fashioned for the purpose of making republican government more secure within the separate states.

Lincoln summoned to this question an uncommon clarity of mind, but his teaching had a certain force for his generation precisely because it was not his own invention. His argument was understandable because it drew on the tradition of jurisprudence. And parts of that tradition had already become familiar to the public as a result of the lessons taught by the statesmen and jurists who had preceded Lincoln in trying to cope with the political crisis of slavery. In the Dred Scott case, Justice Curtis summarized, in his dissenting opinion, the understandings that ran back to the classic teachers of jurisprudence, on the difference between the natural law and the "municipal," or the positive law (the law that was posited, or set down, in a particular place). Curtis understood that the accommodation with slavery was a contrivance of the "positive law." But where that law was silent, the protections of slavery were not to be extended. Where there was no statute that applied exactly to a case at hand, the natural law would resume its sovereign place, and the natural law would come into play once again, to limit the compromises that were fashioned under the Constitution. Curtis's opinion reflected the arguments that were made quite as forcefully by his own mentors, Daniel Webster and Joseph Story. But as Curtis reviewed the cases, he reminded his readers that this understanding had been diffused, quite as thoroughly, in the border states and the South.

In Rankin v. Lydia, . . . the Supreme Court of Appeals of Kentucky said: "Slavery is sanctioned by the laws of this State, and the right to hold them under our municipal regulations is unquestionable. But we view this as a right existing by positive law of a municipal character, without foundation in the law of nature or the unwritten common law." I am not acquainted with any case or writer questioning the correctness of this doctrine.[10]

Slavery, as contrary to natural right, could be sustained only by "municipal law." This understanding, said Curtis, was not only "plain in itself," but it was "inferable from the Constitution."

The Constitution refers to slaves as "persons held to service in one State, under the laws thereof." Nothing can more clearly describe a *status* created by municipal law. In Prigg v. Pennsylvania, . . . this court said: "The state of slavery is deemed to be a mere municipal regulation, founded on and limited to the range of territorial laws."[11]

Several years earlier, in the debate on the Oregon bill, senators from the South had argued once again for the right of slaveowners to carry their property into the new territories of the United States. The redoubtable John Calhoun argued that there was no territory under the governance of the United States that was outside the Constitution. And the Constitution stipulated that persons should not be deprived of their property without due process of law. To which Daniel Webster replied, quizzically, "Their 'property'? What do they mean by 'property?' " The Constitution cast its protection on property, but that constitutional formula would have to be filled in with an understanding of what constituted *legitimate* property.

We certainly do not deprive them of the privilege of going into these newly acquired territories with all that, in the general estimate of human society, in the general, and common, and universal understanding of mankind, is esteemed property. . . . They have, in their own States, peculiar laws, which create property in persons. They have a system of local legislation on which slavery rests; while every body agrees that it is against natural law. . . . The Southern States have peculiar laws, and by those laws there is property in slaves. This is purely local. The real meaning, then, of Southern gentlemen, in making this complaint, is, that they cannot go into the territories of the United States carrying with them their own peculiar local law, a law which creates property in persons.[12]

As Webster explained with some precision, "slavery" in the United States bore no resemblance to slavery as it existed "in any other civilized portion of the habitable globe." It was not "analogous to the case of the *predial* slaves, or slaves *glebae adscripti* of Russia, or Hungary. . . . It is a peculiar system of personal slavery, by which the person who is called a slave is transferable as a chattel, from hand to hand."[13] This kind of slavery, this kind of property, ran counter to the clearest teachings of natural law. It could not be *presumed* then to be a legitimate form of property; it could be established as "lawful" in certain places only through the stipulations of the positive law. Within the territories of the United States, only the Congress could provide the municipal law of property that made this kind of slavery legitimate. And if Congress refused, the formulas of the Constitution could not come into play to confirm a "right" to this species of "property." To understand, then, what the Constitution protected as rightful property, it was necessary to move beyond the muncipal laws of the states, and it was even necessary to move beyond the text of the Constitution. The question could be answered only by establishing, in the first place, just which forms of property were legitimate and illegitimate. And the standards for making those discriminations could be found only in the principles of moral judgment, or what the statesmen of the nineteenth century persisted in calling the principles of natural right.

. . . . .

The understanding I have sought to present here may be taken to a further step of refinement: I have suggested, so far, that an earlier generation of lawyers and statesmen understood the need to trace their judgments back, to the principles of law that existed before the Constitution, in order to establish the meaning of different clauses, and apply the Constitution to real cases. But there have been notable examples in which statesmen have been compelled to move even further: They have had to move, for their guidance, to canons of reasoning outside the Constitution, and when they have measured their judgments with a more strenuous standard of reasoning, they have come to the awkward conclusion that the Constitution itself had to be mistaken. These recognitions have been decorously muffled, and yet the conclusions may be read plainly in the arguments, even if they have not been made artlessly explicit.

The most dramatic example was no doubt furnished, once again, by Lincoln. His administration began with the country on the threshold of civil war; and with the enemy laying plans for war, Lincoln had to take control of the government in a capital city that was itself politically unreliable. The government that Lincoln was seeking to command was threaded with officers who were now bound, in their own loyalties, to a cause outside the Union. The government in which they held official authority, they now regarded as the government of an enemy power. This conspiracy of disaffection reached to the highest levels of the civil and military establishment. Justice John Campbell of the Supreme Court would be revealed, in time, as an agent of the Confederacy, offering advice on strategy to Jefferson Davis, and actively working for the secession. Lincoln later recalled, with particularity, the high officers in the military who deliberately weakened the defenses of the Union and then became, with their defections, notable assets to the enemy.

> Gen. John C. Breckenridge, Gen. Robert E. Lee, Gen. Joseph E. Johnston, Gen. John B. Magruder, Gen. William Br. Preston, Gen. Simon B. Buckener, and Commodore [Franklin] Buchanan, now occupying the very highest places in the rebel war service, were all within the power of the government since the rebellion began, and were nearly as well known to be traitors then as now. Unquestionably if we had seized and held them, the insurgent cause would be much weaker.[14]

But as Lincoln also noted, none of them had committed, at the time, "any crime defined in the law. Every one of them if arrested would have been discharged on Habeas Corpus, were the writ allowed to operate."[15] In short, it was precisely the kind of emergency, of war or insurrection, in which constitutional governments have found a justification for suspending the Writ of Habeas Corpus: not for the purpose of confining people indefinitely, as prisoners, without formal charges; but for the purpose of removing enemy agents, depriving them of their effect, at a moment that may be critical in breaking the success of the enemy.[16]

The Constitution itself provided that these steps could be taken legitimately. In Article I, Section 9, it was stipulated that "the Privilege of the Writ of Habeas Corpus shall not be suspended except when in Cases of Rebellion or Invasion the public Safety may require it." Even Rousseau had argued, in *The Social Contract*, that a republic may suspend, in times of danger, the conventions of law that are more appropriate to times of peace: "The very fact that the laws are inflexible, and are not, therefore adaptable to the movement of events, may, in certain cases, render them pernicious, and the cause, in times of crisis, of the State's destruction."[17] Even a republic could face mortal dangers, which could justify, as a temporary measure, the concentration of executive powers. When those powers of emergency were claimed by Lincoln, in defense of the Union, the president did indeed seem to be moving "beyond the Constitution" in an almost literal way. Scholars would later say that Lincoln moved outside the law, for the sake of preserving the law. And this construction did find a minor echo in Lincoln's own words: "The whole of the laws which were required to be faithfully executed, were being resisted, and failing of execution, in nearly one-third of the States. . . . [A]re all the laws, *but one* [the provision on Habeas Corpus], to go unexecuted, and the government itself go to pieces, lest that one be violated?"[18]

But of course Lincoln was not really going beyond the law or the Constitution, since the provision for the suspension of Habeas Corpus was contained within the Constitution. The provision was found, however, in Article I, which set forth the powers of Congress. From this arrangement of the text, some lawyers would draw the inference that the power to suspend the writ was assigned exclusively to Congress. And yet, within the same article, Section

10 established prohibitions on the states, and it was not clear that Section 9 was addressed, at all points, to the Congress. Along with the provision on Habeas Corpus, that section contained features which seemed to mark off the principles or character of republican government in the United States. When it stipulated that "no Title of Nobility shall be granted," or that "no Money shall be drawn from the Treasury, but in Consequence of Appropriations made by Law," that section in the Constitution might have been addressing officers within the executive, as well as the Congress. But Lincoln took the argument to a deeper, more compelling ground.

> Now it is insisted that Congress, and not the Executive, is vested with this power. But the Constitution itself is silent as to which, or who, is to exercise the power; and as the provision was plainly made for a dangerous emergency, it cannot be believed the framers of the instruments intended, that in every case, the danger should run its course, until Congress could be called together; the very assembly of which might be prevented, as was intended in this case, by the rebellion.[19]

A moral philosopher might outline Lincoln's argument in this way: The Constitution had supplied the decisive moral premise, that a constitutional government may be justified in suspending the Writ of Habeas Corpus during an emergency. It would fall then to someone in authority to establish why the suspension was justified in the case at hand. But no question of principle here could possibly *pivot* on the question of whether Congress happened to be in session, or out of town. If a constitutional government would be justified in preserving itself in this way, by suspending the Writ of Habeas Corpus, this justification could not vanish simply because Congress was out of town when the emergency took place. It was far more plausible to suppose that this constitutional power could be exercised by the one part of government that is never out of session or never "out of town."

The president may be absent from Washington, but the administration of the laws is never suspended. The protection of the country may reasonably fall then to the executive, invested with his own standing as an officer under the Constitution. He may act, in the absence of Congress, to preserve the whole system of laws so that the Congress, when it assembled, would have something left to act upon. Lincoln's argument acquires its force when it is drawn back—as he properly drew it back—to the moral premises that stood behind the provision in the Constitution, and to the moral reasoning that rightly flowed from those premises. At that level, Lincoln's argument was so compelling that we may be moved to this judgment: If his construal of the Constitution was not correct; if the Founders did indeed think that the power of suspending the writ belonged exclusively to Congress—that the power could not be exercised when Congress was out of session—then we would have to conclude that the Founders themselves had been gravely mistaken.

Four score and one year later, in the time of another, fearful war, the Nazis landed two parties of saboteurs on the east coast of the United States. One group, armed with explosives and American currency and equipped with a change of civilian clothes, was landed on Amagansett Beach, on Long Island. Another party was delivered, by submarine, to Ponte Vedra Beach, Florida. When they were caught, President Roosevelt appointed a military commission to try these men for offenses against the laws of war. The men had switched to civilian clothes, but the president would not permit this case to be tried within the civil courts. In effect, the president brought forth a different kind of court to try this cause, under procedures that he himself would put in place. The defendants charged that the president was without any statutory or constitutional authority to order their trial in a military court. They were liable to prosecution by the federal government, and they claimed the constitutional protections that would have to attend trials conducted by the federal government. Most notably, they sought a trial by jury. That arrangement was guaranteed by the Fifth and Sixth Amendments in federal trials for criminal offenses, especially when the charges encompassed "capital" crimes.[20] The only exception was provided, in the Fifth Amendment, for "cases arising in the land or naval forces, or in the militia." The exception was meant to cover proceedings directed, in courts martial, against members of the American military. But since the defendants were not part of the American armed forces, they claimed that they were not subject to this exception.

Chief Justice Stone pointed out for the Court that the law recognized a class of "lawful belligerents entitled to be treated as prisoners of war," but it also recognized a class of "unlawful belligerents" who could not claim those protections. These people do not wear military uniforms, and they may not attack military installations, and yet they may engage in sabotage and destruction and make war on the civilian population. Stone insisted that these "belligerents" could come under the jurisdiction of military courts, even though they did not have the standing of prisoners of war. For neither did they have a claim to a trial by jury in "cases in which it was well understood that a jury trial could not be demanded as of right."[21]

And yet, apart from the provision for members of the military services, the Constitution was silent about the exceptions to a trial by jury. The question might seem artless, but someone who read the text in a literal way could reasonably ask: Why would the protections of the Fifth and Sixth Amendments not apply presumptively in all other cases? Stone argued that "petty offenses triable at common law without a jury may be tried without a jury in the federal court, notwithstanding Article 3, Section 2, and the Fifth and Sixth Amendments." Article 3, Section 2 read: "The Trial of all Crimes, except in Cases of Impeachment, shall be by Jury." That language was unequivocal. But apparently, Stone and his colleagues did not think it could sensibly control the case at hand. Which is to say: the Constitution was not to be taken literally. It was not to be taken to mean precisely what it said.

There was the example, as Stone said, of "petty offenses," and there was the trial of "criminal contempts," in which juries may "constitutionally be dispensed with in the federal courts in those cases in which [the cause] could be tried without a jury at common law." As another example, there were actions for debt, to enforce a penalty imposed by Congress, and those actions were not held to require the presence of juries. The language of the Constitution was sweeping and clear, but these provisions on trial by jury were evidently applied with an understanding that certain exceptions were sensible and necessary; that certain kinds of causes simply did not merit a trial by jury. And now, in the light of this "long-continued and consistent interpretation," Stone denied the claim for a trial by jury. In this judgment he was joined unanimously by a Court that included Hugo Black, that self-proclaimed "literalist" in the reading of the Constitution.[22] Without a dissenting vote from his colleagues, Stone explained that the explicit provisions of Article III, and of the Fifth and Sixth Amendments, "cannot be taken to have extended the right to demand a jury to trials by military commission, or to have required that offenses against the law of war not triable by jury at common law be tried only in the civil courts."[23]

In other cases over the years, the judges have been inclined to insist that when the Founders assigned powers and marked off "exceptions," the powers set forth in the Constitution must be presumed to cover everything that had not been "excepted." But here the Court could be taken to mean that the Framers were being "suggestive" rather than "exhaustive" in marking off the exceptions: The Founders merely suggested the nature of the exceptions, and left it to the judgment of statesmen to consider other cases of a similar nature, which could reasonably be added to the list of exceptions. Under this interpretation, the Founders could not have been expected to mark off every variety of case that common sense would remove from the requirement of a jury. If the intentions of the Founders were not to be read in that way, we would have to infer that, in the judgment of Stone and his colleagues, the Founders had been clumsy, inattentive, or too elliptical, too careless in their drafting. But with either construal, *the explicit terms of the Constitution were not to be taken as controlling*. In reaching a judgment, the Court would have to disregard even the explicit provisions of the Constitution. The judges would have to look to the traditions of the common law; and in gleaning the lessons contained in the cases, they would have to extract some understanding, disclosed in our experience, about the kinds of cases that "deserved" or "merited" a trial by jury. But that is to say, they would look to that experience to reveal a *moral* understanding—an understanding of when a trial by jury was deserved or undeserved, justified or unjustified. They would have to look once again to principles of moral judgment that were never registered in the text of the Constitution.

. . . . .

Certain wrongs were known to the judges, as John Marshall observed, because they were rooted in "the general principles of our political institutions," as well as in the words of the constitution."[24] I would switch the scene one last time, to the most notable, overlooked example of a jurist working in this fashion, moving, that is, beyond the words of the text, to the "general principles of our political institutions." John Harlan's dissenting opinion in *Plessy v. Ferguson* (1896)[25] has become more familiar in law and literature than the words of the decision he so powerfully opposed. In that signal case, the Court upheld a law in Louisiana that prescribed "separate accommodations" for the races in passenger trains. Harlan predicted that the judgment of the Court in this case would prove as "pernicious as the decision made by this tribunal in the *Dred Scott case*. . . . The thin disguise of 'equal' accommodations for passengers in railroad coaches will not mislead any one, nor atone for the wrong this day done."[26] The grand passages in Harlan's opinion are not surpassed by any others found in the reports of American cases, including the grandest passages written by John Marshall. But those sentences have rarely been read with a concern for how they were attached, precisely, to any clause in the Constitution. Harlan's words have lingered, but there is curiously little recollection of the ground, in the Constitution, on which he finally settled his judgment about the law in Louisiana.

Harlan acknowledged that the races did not stand at that moment, in America, on a plane of social equality. The "white race," he said, was dominant "in prestige, in achievements, in education, in wealth, and in power." But Harlan insisted on a distinction between social equality and civil equality—that is, the equality of treatment under the law. This sense of the problem seemed to place the decisive accent on the claims of black people as "citizens," and it brought forth the most quoted passage in Harlan's opinion.

> [I]n view of the Constitution, in the eye of the law, there is in this country no superior, dominant, ruling class of citizens. There is no caste here. Our Constitution is color-blind, and neither knows nor tolerates classes among citizens. . . .
> The arbitrary separation of citizens, on the basis of race, while they are on a public highway, is a badge of servitude wholly inconsistent with the civil freedom and the equality before the law established by the Constitution.[27]

In Harlan's understanding, the separation of the races by law placed the stamp of inferiority on a whole class of citizens. The arrangement implied that "colored citizens are so inferior and degraded that they cannot be allowed to sit in public coaches occupied by white citizens."[28] The ingredients in this critique suggested that the Fourteenth Amendment might supply the ground of judgment: The citizenship of black people was established in the Fourteenth Amendment, after the Thirteenth Amendment had removed the legal ground for "involuntary servitude." The Fourteenth Amendment was also addressed to the action of states ("No State shall make or enforce any law which shall abridge the privileges or immunities of citizens of the United States . . . nor deny to any person within its jurisdiction the equal protection of the laws"). If the wrong in the case lay in the separation of races *prescribed and enforced by the law*—not the separations brought about by private discrimination and social conventions—then the injury seemed to mesh with the provisions of the Fourteenth Amendment.

And yet, Harlan also suggested that the wrong of the case represented a lingering "badge of servitude": The inclination to treat blacks as a degraded caste was rooted in the history of slavery. The Thirteenth Amendment swept away the legal supports to slavery, but in Harlan's understanding, it also established an authority for the government to root out the lingering badges and incidents of slavery. That amendment, he said, "decreed universal civil freedom in this country." And with this understanding, he could write, with a knowing precision, that the kind of legislation offered in this case by Louisiana was "inconsistent not only with that equality of rights which pertains to citizenship, National and State, but with the *personal liberty* enjoyed by every one within the United States."[29] The state of Louisiana had created disabilities for black people, and those disabilities would be wrong then even in relation to blacks who were *not* citizens. Those disabilities were incompatible with the "natural liberty," or the natural rights, that inhere in human beings as "persons" or moral agents. Those rights grounded in nature had been acknowledged again in the Thirteenth Amendment. But of course those rights could not have been invented or created or "established" in the Thirteenth Amendment. As Lincoln had understood, those rights existed before the Constitution, and the principle of "natural equality" supplied the founding principle of the American republic. The Thirteenth Amendment merely reflected, in this respect, the understanding of Lincoln and his party, that the principle of natural equality did indeed apply to the question of slavery.

In Harlan's understanding, then, the "rights" that were violated in this case swept well beyond the rights of citizenship mentioned in the Fourteenth Amendment. Indeed, they swept beyond the Constitution itself. But within the Constitution those rights were acknowledged, on behalf of black people, in the Thirteenth Amendment; and the Thirteenth Amendment was not cast in the form of prohibitions on the actions of states. In that respect, it was notably different from the Fourteenth Amendment. That difference could be taken to mean that the protections offered by the Thirteenth Amendment were not confined to the wrongs done by states. And by that reading of the amendment, the federal government would not be confined to the mission of checking the unlawful "laws" of the states. As Harlan understood, the Thirteenth Amendment empowered the government to reach directly to the "badges of servitude" that were imposed even by private conspiracies. By casting his argument in this form, Harlan raised this interesting possibility: The federal government might have been able to reach this arbitrary separation of the races even if the arrangement had not been prescribed by the laws of Louisiana. The federal government might have been able to reach this case even if the arrangement had been imposed simply as the policy of the private railroad. Or at least, that became a more plausible construction of federal authority when the discrimination took place in an enterprise that Harlan thought was affected with a "public character": "[A] railroad," said Harlan, "is a public highway, and . . . the corporation which owns or operates it is in the exercise of public functions."[30]

For the sake of vindicating the civil equality of black people, Harlan was evidently persuaded that the national government bore an authority that ran well beyond the confines of the Fourteenth Amendment. Could we say, then, that it was the Thirteenth Amendment that provided, for Harlan, the sweeping authority of the national government in this field? As Harlan closed his opinion, he felt obliged to make a final reference to the statute in Lousiana, but as he did, he also made a final, surprising turn in his argument. In this closing statement, he did not mention *either* the Thirteenth or Fourteenth Amendment, and he suggested that neither one was strictly necessary for the judgment he was reaching. The statute in Louisiana, he said, was "hostile to both the spirit and letter of the Constitution."

> Such a system [of laws] is inconsistent with the guarantee given by the Constitution to each state of a republican form of government, and may be stricken down in congressional action, or by the courts in the discharge of their solemn duty to maintain the supreme law of the land, anything in the Constitution or laws of any state to the contrary notwithstanding.[31]

Harlan relied here on a conjunction of two clauses in the Constitution: the Guaranty Clause [Article IV, Section 4] and the Supremacy Clause [Article VI]. Those passages were part of the original Constitution; they antedated the Thirteenth and Fourteenth Amendments, and it might be said that they expressed the logic of the decisions of 1787: The Union was aimed at securing or strengthening republican government for the nation, and therefore for all parts of the Union. The principles of the Union would of course claim a sovereignty or supremacy over policies in the separate states that were incompatible with the principles of the national republic. If Harlan were to make his argument within this cast, he had to show that the premises of racial segregation were incompatible with the fundamental principles of republican government. Harlan had sought to supply that connection when he suggested that these policies of segregation created "badges of servitude," the signs of a caste system, which were incompatible with the notion of free men in a republic, equal under the law. I put aside for the moment any elaboration or testing of this argument. I think, myself, that the argument in principle here was even more compelling than the argument offered by Harlan. I would simply note, however, that if his argument on this point were valid, then the constitutional argument would in fact be completed within the cast that Harlan recognized: The Guaranty Clause and the Supremacy Clause would be sufficient to carry the constitutional argument. If racial sergregation were incompatible with the principles of republican government, then the Guaranty Clause and Supremacy Clause would make that judgment binding on the separate states, and that would be enough to overturn the law in Louisiana. And in that event, there would be no need to invoke the Thirteenth or Fourteenth Amendments.

For Harlan, then, the national government would not require the "new" authority conferred in the Civil Rights Amendments before it could reach the wrong of racial segregation in Louisiana. The authority for this jurisdiction was contained in the original Constitution, in the original logic of a government that was both "national" and "republican."[32]

But we could amplify Harlan's opinion here with some of the arguments offered by Alexander Hamilton during the debate over the Constitution; and when we connect the two, we can take Harlan's argument a decisive step further. In the *Federalist* #33, Hamilton addressed the concerns that were raised over the Supremacy Clause and the "necessary and proper" clause in Article I, Section 8 (that Congress would have the power "to make all Laws which shall be necessary and proper for carrying into Execution the foregoing powers"). These clauses were taken, accurately, as marks of a strong national government. But they also inspired, as Hamilton remarked, much "virulent invective and petulant declamation." These clauses were represented, by Anti-Federalist writers, in "exaggerated colors" as "the pernicious engines by which their local governments were to be destroyed and their liberties exterminated." And yet, as Hamilton managed to show, the new government would have borne these attributes even if these provisions had not been made explicit, even if they had not been incorporated in the text of the Constitution. "The intended government would be precisely the same," he wrote, "if these clauses were entirely obliterated. . . . They are only declaratory of a truth which would have resulted by necessary and unavoidable implication from the very act of constituting a federal government, and vesting it with certain specified powers."[33]

Hamilton moved along this chain of considerations: A "political association" is marked by the presence of "law." It is the distinct nature of law that it forms "a rule which those to whom it is prescribed are bound to observe." It is the nature of law, then, that it implies *supremacy*: it must displace personal choice; it may properly override the policies of subordinate associations.

> If individuals enter into a state of society, the law of that society must be the supreme regulator of their conduct. If a number of political societies enter into a

larger political society, the laws which the latter may enact, pursuant to the powers intrusted to it by its constitution, must necessarily be supreme over those societies, and the individuals of whom they are composed. It would otherwise be a mere treaty, dependent on the good faith of the parties, and not a government, which is only another word for POLITICAL POWER AND SUPREMACY.[34]

The decision of 1787, the decision in favor of a *national government*, was a judgment to move away from the arrangements of a confederacy. Under the Articles of Confederation, the "federal government" acted only upon the states that composed the Union. It might have been said that the states alone were the "citizens" of this federation. The measures of the central government were addressed only to the states; the federal government would not act directly on individuals to vindicate any rights of federal citizenship. The central government did not have the capacity to coerce states that were not honoring their obligations to the confederacy. The central government was dependent then at all times on the sufferance and "good faith" of the states, without the capacity to enforce, in its own name, a national policy, with a national law. The government under the Confederacy did not really have the authority to make "law" in the strictest sense, which is why it had the character of a confederation rather than a real government. The decision of 1787 marked a willingness to replace the confederacy with a real government: As a government, it would bear the attribute of law. And it was, after all, the very logic of law that it claimed a critical supremacy over the policies of individuals, families, states, when those policies were in conflict with the commands of the law. Hence, as Hamilton remarked, "the clause which declares the supremacy of the laws of the Union . . . only declares a truth, which flows immediately and necessarily from the institution of a federal government."[35]

In *Plessy*, Harlan suggested that neither the Thirteenth nor the Fourteenth Amendment was necessary to reach a judgment on the constitutionality of the statute in Louisiana. In his understanding, the Civil War Amendments added nothing, in this respect, to the principles that were already supplied, in the original text of the Constitution, by the Guaranty Clause and the Supremacy Clause. And if we follow Hamilton, the Supremacy Clause did not have to be made explicit: Once the decision was made to create a *government* at the national level, the logic of the Supremacy Clause would always be present, even if the clause itself were "entirely obliterated." Harlan was compelling, and Hamilton irrefutable. Had the Court adopted, in *Plessy*, the argument offered by Harlan, it would have added to our jurisprudence a momentous judgment. And if the Court had absorbed, at the same time, the understanding of Hamilton, it would have been clear, to later generations, that the judgment in the case finally turned on a set of propositions so necessary, and so fundamental, that their force would not have been diminished, in any degree, even if they had not been mentioned in the Constitution.

. . . . .

The pattern has become familiar: We appeal to the text of the Constitution, but then we find it necessary to consult the understanding of the Founders, and the Founders seek to make their work more comprehensible to us by explaining the logic, or the principles of law, that guided their judgment. What the Founders did not think it necessary to explain, in the text of the Constitution, may be far more decisive than many of the things they set down. And those omissions are ever more to be missed in a time when lawyers and judges no longer know, uniformly, what the Founders assumed that any literate man of the law would know. In a curious way, that question was posed precisely by the debate over the Bill of Rights, in the first year under the Constitution. That debate did not have the benefit of the most systematic, extended argument. Some of the most important arguments against the appendage of a Bill of Rights were not even offered in the form of arguments, but in the cryptic style of Talmudic questions. As a result, time has dimmed the recollection of what was exactly at issue in this original debate about the Bill of Rights. Indeed, it has dimmed the recollection that there *was* a debate, or even a serious question about the Bill of Rights. The public men who opposed the Bill of Rights had been part of a revolution animated by a concern for the natural rights of men. They were not hostile to republican government or to the notion of rights. But rather, they saw, in the Bill of Rights, a grand device of civic education that would misinstruct the American people about the ground of their rights, and therefore about the ends or purposes of the government under the Constitution.

The people who were reserved about a Bill of Rights were skeptical about the prospect of reducing our rights to a compressed inventory. But beyond that, they were dubious about the kind of legal sensibility that would be shaped by a Constitution that marked off rights in this way. They were concerned, to put it briefly, that the Constitution would beget citizens and lawyers who trained themselves by memorizing pat slogans or formulas. What would be lost was the capacity to deliberate about rights by appealing to those standards of moral judgment that could not be summarized, or set forth with any adequacy, in a Constitution. The Constitution defined the legal structure of a republic; it could not be converted into a handbook of moral philosophy. But without making that effort to teach something more fully about the principles of judgment, the items listed in the Bill of Rights would appear as an inventory of objects ("speech," "press," "searches," "seizures") cut off from the underlying principles that gave them substance. In order to determine just which "searches" were legitimate, which restrictions on the press justified or unjustified, it would be necessary to move beyond these terms, beyond the inventory of objects set down in the first eight amendments.

Some uses of speech, some activities of the press, could be claimed, quite properly, as "rights." But some of them would mark abuses of speech and the press, and they would not come under the protection of the Bill of Rights. The distinction would have to pivot on the understanding of just which uses of freedom were legitimate or illegitimate, justified or unjustified. The judgment would turn, in any case, not on anything written in the Bill of Rights, but on the canons of reasoning that typically guide our judgment when we make discriminations between the things that are justified or unjustified. This much was understood by the proponents of the Bill of Rights, as well as by those who expressed skepticism about these amendments. But what they grasped then, without putting too fine a point on it, was that the catalogue in the Bill of Rights did not even define itself: Every instance of speech or assembly could not mark a "right," which the Constitution was bound to protect. The understanding that was decisive in identifying these the rights could be found only in the canons of moral judgment. They would have to lie, then, outside the Bill of Rights, and outside the Constitution.

FOUR

ON THE DANGERS OF A BILL OF RIGHTS:
RESTATING THE FEDERALIST ARGUMENT

THE PHILOSOPHER Wittgenstein reminded us that certain questions may best be answered by the asking of another question. The style of argument here may be identified as Talmudic, and when it is applied artfully—when the question is properly pointed—it is possible to reconstruct, quite tenably, the understanding that lay behind the question. Several years ago, before he had become prime minister of Greece, Andreas Papandreou was the leader of the Socialist opposition within the national assembly, and he offered up one day a long, tedious denunciation of NATO and American imperialism, which he flavored with praise of the Soviet Union. The prime minister at that time, Mr. Karamanlis, endured this tirade, and he finally responded with one short sentence, which brought laughter from the house. "When you left Greece," he asked, "where did you go?"[1] Under the regime of the colonels, Mr. Papandreou had exposed himself to the ravages of capitalism by settling as a professor in Berkeley, California.

The prime minister's gentle question could have been replaced, rather plausibly, by a fuller commentary which ran along these lines: However much Mr. Papandreou esteemed socialism, he apparently attached a more decisive importance to the security that was afforded by a regime of law; or he apparently thought that a nonsocialist economy had been far more successful in providing those material comforts that could soften, for him at least, the rigors of life. And if it were indeed more important to Mr. Papandreou that a country be "free" before it were "socialist"—that its government be subject to constitutional restraints and the consent of the governed—then the absence of those features had to imply an objection in principle to the Soviet Union that ran far deeper than any objection he could have to the United States.

All of this might have been offered, as I say, as an implication that arose from the prime minister's question. I mention this incident because I think that some of the most telling parts of the original argument against a Bill of Rights were locked away in this manner, in understandings that were evidently present, but which were never filled out or even adequately stated. They were implied, rather, in a number of Talmudic questions that were posed by different writers or speakers in the course of the original debate about the foundations of the new government and the need for a Bill of Rights. I would suggest that these rhetorical questions, posed at strategic moments in the debate, would lead us back along the paths of reason that must have produced them. And if we trace back these threads or fragments of argument, we could reconstruct the understandings that lay behind these questions. When we did, I think we would fill in some of the deeper arguments against a Bill of Rights, which were never made explicitly as arguments.

. . . . .

The case against the Bill of Rights was offered mainly by the men who were known as Federalists, while the arguments in favor of a Bill of Rights were pressed mainly by the men we identify as Anti-Federalists. It is only in recent years that an attempt has been made to recover the Federalist argument or to remind us that there had indeed been a serious dispute.[2] And yet, a certain enigmatic quality still attaches to the argument drawn by the Federalists. My late professor, Herbert Storing, was one of the most thoughtful defenders of the men who led the movement for a stronger national government. But in his last work (published after his death) Storing reviewed what he took to be the main arguments made by the Federalists in resisting a Bill of Rights, and he found those arguments unpersuasive.[3] After all, the Founders had already incorporated in the text of the Constitution prohibitions on ex post facto laws and bills of attainder. If the framers were willing to descend to these particulars, how could there have been an aversion in principle to setting forth several more restrictions on the power of the government? Beyond that, these provisions could be reassuring to many people who were doubtful about the new government, and they could even be useful in defining, with more detail, the restraints of the Constitution. Storing was disposed to join the Anti-Federalists in asking, What would be the harm? As Patrick Henry tauntingly put it, Would this project have taken too much paper?

One Anti-Federalist writer set forth his case in this way:

> We do not by declarations change the nature of things, or create new truths, but we give existence, or at least establish in the minds of the people truths and principles which they might never otherwise have thought of, or soon forgot. If a nation means its systems, religious or political, shall have duration, it ought to recognize the leading principles of them in the front page of every family book.[4]

Herbert Storing thought that this statement, with its sober and measured claims, conveyed the best case that the Anti-Federalists could make for their position: namely, that a Bill of Rights could be "a prime agency of that political and moral education of the people on which free republican government depends.[5] I think the Federalists did understand that the Bill of Rights would find its main effect in teaching, but they were convinced that it would teach the wrong lessons: that it would narrow our understanding of the rights that government was meant to protect; that it would misinstruct the American people about the ground of their rights; and that it would make it even harder then to preserve republican government.

As the Federalists understood, the very notion of a "Bill of Rights" imparted the wrong cast to our conception of "rights," because it drew on the wrong analogies. Hamilton remarked in the *Federalist* #84 that

> bills of rights are, in their origin, stipulations between kings and their subjects, abridgments of prerogative in favor of privilege, reservations of rights not surrendered to the prince. Such was MAGNA CHARTA, obtained by the barons, sword in hand, from King John. . . . Such was the *Petition of Right* assented to by Charles I. . . . Such, also, was the Declaration of Right presented by the Lords and Commons to the Prince of Orange in 1688, and afterwards thrown into the form of an act of parliament called the Bill of Rights.[6]

These arrangements bore the solemnity of a fundamental contract, but as James Wilson and Oliver Ellsworth pointed out, a contract implies two parties equally competent to contract. The metaphor of the contract would suggest then that the government and the people stood on the same plane, with two distinct interests of a comparable dignity. But that notion would be wholly out of keeping with the character of a republic or a popular government, in which authority emanated from the people, not from the government, and in which the government stood, in relation to the people, as an agent in relation to its sovereign.[7] As Hamilton remarked on this point, Bills of Rights "have no application to constitutions, professedly founded upon the power of the people, and executed by their immediate representatives and servants."[8]

For the critics of the Bill of Rights, this was not merely a talking point, but a sign of mistakes that ran deep in the argument for a Bill of Rights. If the Bill of Rights represented a certain reservation of natural rights to the people, the implication would quickly arise that the government may exercise all of those powers which had not been explicitly withheld. The paradoxical result was that this reservation of rights might actually enlarge the total powers of the government. It would remove from the government the burden of justifying its use of authority in a wide range of cases in which its measures were not explicitly forbidden. But as Herbert Storing pointed out, the Founders had not been loath to specify, in the body of the Constitution, that the Writ of Habeas Corpus should not be suspended (except in cases of rebellion or invasion), or that no state may grant any title of nobility. Why had it been necessary, he asked, to make *these* prohibitions explicit? Why should anyone have supposed that the Congress had the authority to suspend the Writ of Habeas Corpus or that the states might grant titles of nobility? In their willingness to make these singular provisions within the text of the Constitution, the Founders had not betrayed any fear that they were conceding to the government, through indirection, all of those powers which they had not explicitly forbidden. Still, if they did suffer those apprehensions, why were their concerns not dispelled finally by the passage of the Ninth Amendment? That amendment read: "The enumeration in the Constitution of certain rights, shall not be construed to deny or disparage others retained by the people." Why did that provision not resolve the matter? Altogether, then, Herbert Storing was moved to conclude that the Federalist argument on this point was rather "sophistical."[9]

And yet, as Storing must have known, the Founders had not shown a uniform enthusiasm for specifying principles, or making prohibitions explicit, within the body of the Constitution. On this matter they were affected by the same apprehensions they would later suffer over the wisdom of making stipulations in a Bill of Rights. It is curious, in this respect, that Storing chose to pass over the reservations expressed by Oliver Ellsworth and James Wilson when the proposal was brought forth, at the Constitutional Convention, to prohibit "ex post facto" laws. As I recalled earlier, Ellsworth remarked that "there was no lawyer, no civilian who would not say that ex post facto laws were void in themselves. It cannot be necessary to prohibit them." Wilson, too, was "against inserting anything in the Constitution as to ex post facto laws. It will bring reflexions on the Constitution—and proclaim that we are ignorant of the first principles of Legislation, or are constituting a Government which will be so."[10]

To pretend to the project of articulating the first principles of lawful government, and to mention only bills of attainder and ex post facto laws, was to run the risk of suggesting, to those tutored in law, that these were the only first principles that the American Founders knew. Or it would suggest at least that, among the first principles of law, the items set forth in the Constitution stood on a higher plane of importance than the principles that the Founders had neglected to mention. And that sense of the matter would only confirm again the understanding that Hamilton feared was simply implicit in a Bill of Rights. With all respect for my late professor, Herbert Storing, I would suggest that the concerns expressed by Hamilton have been borne out quite tellingly in our experience. That they have been borne out even in the presence of the Ninth Amendment may be a deeper confirmation of his argument: For in spite of the avowals in the Ninth Amendment, we have seen, in a number of signal cases, the casual denial of freedom and the cavalier destruction of certain rights precisely because these freedoms and rights were not apparently mentioned in the Bill of Rights or its sequelae. In other words, what has taken hold in practice is the state of mind—or the peculiar logic—that Hamilton thought was contained in the Bill of Rights; and that logic has not been overcome by the Ninth Amendment.

. . . . .

It was possible to add to the Bill of Rights many artful, pointed words to disclaim and reassure, but they could not easily dissolve the logic that was contained within the cast of this instrument: The Bill of Rights bore, ineffaceably, the character of a charter, which listed the terms of an agreement or contract—in this case, the terms on which the American people agreed to be governed. The Bill of Rights would be seen as a list of reservations or stipulations about the rights that the people had not surrendered when they had tendered their obedience to the new government. The Bill of Rights drew, then, on the understandings associated with a "social contract." This metaphor lent itself to a number of variations, but it always assumed that individuals had stood, at one time, with certain natural rights, in a state antecedent to civil society. Some writers have been pleased to refer to this condition as the "state of nature," and it has usually been conceived as a hazardous place: No one, in the state of nature, was restrained or protected by law, and as consequence, any man could be warranted in regarding every other man as a potential enemy. This was, as Hobbes described it, the "war of every man, against every man." Under these conditions anyone would be justified in carrying out preemptive attacks on his potential enemies: as Hobbes put it, "every man [would have] a right to every thing; even to one another's body."[11] These prospects were thought sufficiently frightening that people would be impelled to move from the state of nature to civil society: They would be willing to surrender the rights they possessed in the state of nature for a more limited set of "civil" rights, which would be rendered more secure, however, by the advent of a government that could make those rights enforceable at law.

Of course, not all political philosophers assumed that political life found its origin in a contract. Aristotle had argued compellingly that the notion of "contract" is radically unsuitable in accounting for the foundation of "law" and the justification of polity.[12] And yet, even among philosophers who have favored the analogy of a "contract," there has been a subtle, but critical difference that has turned on the question of whether human beings possessed moral understanding *before* they entered civil society. The most notable denial on this point was offered by Hobbes. As he wrote in the *Leviathan*, "the desires, and other passions of man are in themselves no sin. No more are the actions, that proceed from those passions, till they know a law that forbids them: which till laws be made they cannot know."[13] That is, before the existence of law and civil society, we cannot expect men to know the difference between right and wrong, or to treat that difference as one they can afford to respect.

But this understanding was rejected at the root by James Wilson, who stood, even among the Founders, as one of our preeminent juristic figures.

And the ground on which Wilson rejected that argument made a profound difference for the understanding of the Bill of Rights and the kind of government to which a Bill of Rights would need to be attached. Wilson's rejection of the Hobbesian view was conveyed in one of those Talmudic questions I alluded to earlier. The question was offered, in his classic lecture on "Natural Rights," in response to an argument by Blackstone, and the query was followed by no further commentary. But it left no possibility of mistake about the understanding behind the question. Blackstone had remarked, in Book 1 of his *Commentaries*, that "the law, which restrains a man from doing mischief to his fellow citizens, though it diminishes the natural, increases the civil liberty of mankind."[14] To that observation Wilson responded with a simple question: "Is it part of natural liberty," he asked, "to do mischief to anyone?"[15]

That was all he said, and yet the question placed him in a tradition of understanding that ran back to Aquinas and Aristotle, and which would later be reflected in Abraham Lincoln, in his rejoinder to Stephen Douglas: "When Judge Douglas says that whoever, or whatever community, wants slaves, they have a right to have them, he is perfectly logical if there is nothing wrong in the institution; but if you admit that it is wrong, he cannot logically say that anybody has a right to do a wrong."[16] By this logic, which is nothing less than the logic of morals, we could never claim a rightful "liberty to do mischief." Apparently, for Wilson, it was possible, even in the state of nature, to recognize the difference, say, between an assault that was provoked or unprovoked, justified or unjustified. The inflicting of a harm without justification could be judged, quite clearly, as a wrong, even before the existence of government. In that sense Wilson separated himself decisively from Hobbes: The advent of government did not mark the advent of morality. Even in the state of nature men did not have a natural right to assault or rape or commit injustice of any other kind. And obversely, even people in the state of nature had a right not to suffer these wrongs.

As it turns out, we are not left entirely to inference in discovering the understanding among the Founders on this cardinal point. Over a dozen years before the controversy over the Bill of Rights, a precocious Alexander Hamilton saw the need to address Hobbes's argument explicitly as he sought to appeal to natural rights and vindicate the rights of America in relation to Britain. The nineteen-year-old Hamilton understood the matter quite precisely when he offered this account: "[Hobbes] held . . . that [man in the state of nature] was . . . perfectly free from all restraints of law and government. Moral obligation, according to [Hobbes], is derived from the introduction of civil society; and there is no virtue, but what is purely artificial, the mere contrivance of politicians, for the maintenance of social intercourse." And the young Hamilton was no less precise in grasping, at once, the central point of corruption in the argument.

[T]he reason [Hobbes] run into this absurd and impious doctrine, was, that he disbelieved the existence of an intelligent superintending principle, who is the governor, and will be the final judge of the universe. . . . Good and wise men, in all ages, have embraced a very dissimilar theory. They have supposed, that the deity, from the relation we stand in, to himself and to each other, has constituted an eternal and immutable law, which is, indispensibly, obligatory upon all mankind, *prior to any human institution whatever.*[17]

Some writers recently have sought to build an understanding of the Founders and the Constitution on the assumption that the Founders had accepted the "modern" notion of natural rights put forth by Hobbes, and that understanding encompassed the notion that rights were in fact surrendered in entering civil society. But not the least of the difficulties, passed over in this interpretation, is that it fails to take seriously the Christianity of the Founders. With men like Wilson and John Jay, the understanding of Christianity pervaded their writings and sustained their convictions about natural rights: The Author of the Universe, the Author of the laws of physics, was also the Author of universal moral laws. Any serious believer in a single, universal God, would of course understand that the God of the Universe would not create a separate moral law for New Jersey and France. These moral laws, then, were immanent in the universe. They did not spring into existence at those odd moments, when civil administrations were founded in new lands. And if that was the case, then there was in fact an understanding of right and wrong that preceded civil society. On that point, men like Wilson, Hamilton, and Jay did not show so much as a tremor of doubt. It would simply be untenable, therefore, to identify these men with the notion that civil society marked the advent of morality. And if this understanding cannot be attributed to Wilson and Hamilton, it is hard to see how the same understanding could be attributed, with any plausibility, to "the Founders."

But beyond that, if we did not understand that men like Wilson and Hamilton were rejecting these Hobbesian notions of natural rights, we could not explain the objections they were raising against the movement for a Bill of Rights. Indeed, we could not offer a coherent account of that original argument—or explain just why there was an argument in the first place. The opposition of the Federalists makes sense only when we understand, again, their radical denial of the proposition that there was no sense of right and wrong before the advent of civil society. To repeat: Even in the state of nature men did not have a natural right to "do mischief" or inflict injuries; and on the other side, even in the state of nature people had a right not to suffer these wrongs. It was not the existence of the government that created these rights; it was the existence of these rights that called forth and justified the existence of the government. Wilson was quick to note then that the purpose of government was not to create "new rights by a human establishment," but rather "to acquire a new security for the possession or the recovery of those rights" we already possess by nature.[18]

At the same time, the advent of law marked no diminution of freedom. The law that forbids a man to rape or to steal does not restrain him from doing anything he was ever rightfully free to do. And so if the question were put to Wilson, What "rights" do we give up when we leave the state of nature and enter civil society, the answer, unequivocally, was: None. Since we never had the right to do a wrong, even in the state of nature, the law that restrains us from doing wrong deprives us of none of our rights. And since no rights are surrendered in joining civil society, *nothing needs to be reserved* in a Bill of Rights. Hamilton made the point explicitly: "Here, in strictness [i.e., under the new Constitution], the people surrender nothing; and as they retain every thing they have no need of particular reservations."[19]

But if the concern for rights were merely tacked on to the end of the Constitution, in a list of "reservations," this understanding of Wilson and Hamilton would be overturned. We would indicate rather dramatically that the protection and enlargement of our rights is not in fact the central and animating purpose of the government. We would seem to suggest that the main purpose of the government must be found elsewhere: Perhaps the polity would be seen largely as an alliance for the protection of property or for the cultivation of a manly, military honor. Or, it might be seen far more modestly, as a government dedicated to the protection of certain minimal rights; a government that would secure its citizens mainly in their liberty to pursue their own, private interests.[20] And yet the Founders were clear that the mission of the political order was nothing less than the protection of natural rights, and as Wilson described them, with a sober precision, they seemed to take in the full sweep of those rights. Man has, he said, "a natural right to his property, to his character, to liberty, and to safety"[21]—which is to say, that he has a right to be protected, so far as practicable, from virtually all species of injustice.

That understanding of our "natural rights" extended well beyond any list that could be set down in a Bill of Rights, and one concern of the Federalists was that the understanding of rights would indeed be narrowed to the list of things that the First Congress thought to mention in the Bill of Rights. But the concern ran even more deeply, and it touched, as I have suggested, our understanding of the source and logic of these rights. When the Bill of Rights was brought forth in the First Congress, it encountered the irascible dubiety of Theodore Sedgwick of Massachusetts, who responded to this project with another set of Talmudic questions. Sedgwick first expressed his impatience by wondering just why the House was descending into such trifling details: If people have the right to speak, they must surely have the right to assemble for the purpose of speaking. But then why was it even necessary to specify that, in a regime of law and constitutional liberty, people had the right to speak? Sedgwick was moved to ask sardonically: Why not also specify that "a man should have a right to wear his hat if he pleased; that he might get up when he pleased, and go to bed when he thought proper?"[22]

The questions were artfully placed, but in his impatience Sedgwick did not bother to fill out the understanding that lay behind the questions. Without that statement of his argument, Sedgwick's criticism was likely to be misread as a concern mainly for redundancy. And yet, once again, I think the questions implied an understanding that reached more deeply. I think Sedgwick was suggesting, first, that the people who produced this list of rights did not apparently understand the difference between a principle and the instances in which a principle may be manifested. They revealed the state of mind described by a colleague of mine when he referred to the people who would apparently believe that the series of positive integers were discovered *one at a time*. These people could go on forever, listing the variety of circumstances in which our rights could be violated, but without understanding the logic that stands behind the list of rights. And so, to the current list contained in the Bill of Rights, we could conceivably add the right not to be stopped and searched in our automobiles; the right not to have our briefcases and luggage examined without our consent; the right not to have blood removed from our arms in the search for legal evidence. These kinds of provisions would be no less plausible than many of the items already contained in the Bill of Rights. And at the same time, they would be no more illuminating.

When the Founders spoke of our "natural right" to life, liberty, and property, they never meant to suggest that the government could secure to us life everlasting, or that the government would never be warranted in restricting our freedom or taking our property (in the form of taxation). If there is a fire on a nearby street and the fire department closes off the street to pedestrians, the pedestrians are restrained in their freedom, but their natural rights have not been violated. For this restriction of freedom was made for a justified end, and as we have seen, when freedom is restricted justly, people are not deprived of anything to which they have a "right." It might be said then, more precisely, that we have a natural right to be treated justly: We have a right not to have our lives taken, our freedom restricted, our property extracted, *without justification*. The problem in all instances will pivot on the question of whether the government is restraining our freedom for reasons that are justified or unjustified; and it adds nothing to our understanding of the problem merely to elaborate, in a Bill of Rights, a somewhat fuller list of the kinds of cases in which we are apt to face this question.

For example, if we consider the right to "assemble" that was mentioned in the First Amendment, it should be apparent that the right is not defined as soon as we identify a group that gathers in the street and fits the description of "assembling." They could be assembling with burning crosses outside the home of a black family. They could be assembling without violence, but in the middle of the main intersection in town at the height of the rush hour. The critical question is not whether a group meets a description of "assembling," but as Congressman Page said in the First Congress, the question is whether people are assembling "on their lawful occasions," for legitimate ends.[23] The issue turns then on whether people are assembling reasonably or unreasonably, for purposes that are justified or unjustified. In the same way, the Bill of Rights does not bar *all* searches and seizures, but only those which are "unreasonable" or unjustified. The same qualification would have to attend all of the rights mentioned in the Bill of Rights, because any "right" would have to pivot, as I have said, on a moral judgment, and not merely on a factual description of bodily movements. For that reason it would be equally useless or unilluminating to add to the list by providing, say, for our "right" not to be stopped *without justification* in the street, to have our automobiles searched *unreasonably*, to have our suitcases inspected *without cause*. We could go on endlessly listing the kinds of cases in which our freedom may be restricted wrongly. And we could do that without clarifying anything more about the matter that is truly decisive—namely, the grounds on which we are able to distinguish between rightful and wrongful ends, between restraints on our freedom that are justified or unjustified.[24]

Theodore Sedgwick recognized the mindless quality of laying out an inventory of cases when he asked his colleagues, Why not specify that "a man should have a right to wear his hat if he pleased; that he might get up when he pleased, and go to bed when he thought proper?" His colleagues felt the sting of his humor without understanding his point, and so Congressman Page remarked that Sedgwick's proposal might not be entirely inapt. He observed, rather portentously, to Sedgwick that "a man has been obliged to pull off his hat when he appeared before the face of authority."[25] Let us assume for a moment that Page managed to express here a plausible concern—that the abuse of legal authority might express itself in unjust, peremptory orders to a citizen to remove his hat in the street. There is a point to be made in considering just how a problem of this kind might have been addressed through the Bill of Rights. A passage might have been added, perhaps in the Second Amendment, stipulating that "the government may not require people unreasonably to remove their hats in public or to wear them under compulsion." Two hundred years later this scene would have been predictable: We would have found lawyers and judges straining their arts of argument over the question, Is a motorcycle helmet a "hat" within the meaning of the Constitution? When a legislature requires motorcyclists to wear hats, would that provision violate the understanding expressed in the Bill of Rights?

This kind of exercise has become all too familiar, and it is worth noticing the nature of the shift that has taken place: Instead of deliberating about the question of whether the regulation of headgear may be justified or unjustified—instead of focusing, in other words, on the substantive moral question—lawyers and judges often spend their genius on empirical puzzles. Is a motorcycle helmet a hat? Are movies and peep shows "speech"? If we can subsume peep shows under "speech" we can bring the peep shows under the protection of the Constitution—but without addressing the substantive question of whether the law can reasonably ban peep shows, even if they are a form of "expression."

In the same way, the question we would not face on the matter of motorcycle helmets is whether the government would be justified in restricting personal freedom and compelling people to wear protective covering for their heads. But we need not depend any longer on the example of motorcycle helmets. Since the time I began to write on this question, a case arose over the wearing of a yarmulke in the Air Force, and that case makes the point here as tellingly as any other example. The case of *Goldman v. Weinberger* (1986) involved an Orthodox Jew who practiced as a clinical psychologist in the Air Force.[26] Goldman wore his yarmulke in the health clinic, and he had made a practice of wearing his service cap over his yarmulke when he was out of doors. The "case" over Goldman arose only because he had testified at a court-martial, wearing his yarmulke but not his Air Force cap. The opposing counsel in the case noticed the yarmulke and filed a complaint. Goldman was accused of violating the regulations that prescribed "uniforms" in headgear and provided that "[h]eadger will not be worn . . . [w]hile indoors except by armed security police in the performance of their duties."[27] The colonel in command of the hospital held that there had been a breach of regulations, and he ordered Goldman not to wear the yarmulke outside the hospital. Since Goldman spent almost all of his time within the hospital, the order became trivial. Still, Goldman decided to challenge the regulations as a point of principle; and on that point of challenge, he eventually lost before the Supreme Court.

A look at the case will readily show that it was generated, as a controversy, by no lofty motives. And it could have been resolved in a workable fashion with a modest show of prudence on either side. But when the cause was converted into a case in principle, there were plausible concerns on both sides. On the one hand, the government had an interest in avoiding the kind of headgear or apparel that may introduce sectarian symbols. As the questioning ran, if the military could permit yarmulkes, why not dreadlocks, or swastikas, or Ku Klux Klan hoods? Of course, it was possible to make reasonable discriminations between the different kinds of headgear, but it might have been thought unreasonable to place, upon administrators in the Air Force, the burden of making these vexing discriminations. On the other hand, the Air Force did not apparently interfere with the inclination of its members to wear crosses or stars of David. And once these symbols were allowed, the service would be saddled with the same problem of forming distinctions and enforcing limits on the use of sectarian symbols.

But as the case was framed for the judgment of a Court, it should have been clear that the issue would have to turn precisely on considerations of this kind. Whether Goldman had a "right" to wear his yarmulke in the military would depend on whether there was a compelling, or even plausible, interest on the part of the government in preserving uniforms and avoiding the use of sectarian symbols. However the case is rightly judged, my point is this: The way in which we deliberate about the "rights" of Goldman in this case would be exactly the same, even if a "right to wear a hat" had been incorporated in the Bill of Rights. We would still find ourselves weighing the question of whether the army could have a justification for imposing restrictions on certain kinds of headgear. The nature of this problem was not likely to have been altered in any way, even if there had been a provision in the Bill of Rights on the wearing of hats. And to this exercise of judgment, the Bill of Rights would add nothing. It would furnish no guidelines; it would not augment in any way our means of gauging the difference between restrictions that are justified or unjustified.

Just to test this argument, we might consider two kinds of cases. In one, a man makes harassing, obscene phone calls in the middle of the night, and the question is whether the government may restrain this use of "speech." In another case, the government announces that people should go to their homes and not venture out into the streets without the permission of the authorities.

The first case arises over the use—or misuse—of speech, and so it appears to many people that it involves the preeminent freedom mentioned in our First Amendment. In the second case the government would restrict a rather elementary freedom to move about in the public streets and engage in commerce outside the home. In effect, it would impose a kind of detention or house arrest; and yet it does not touch any freedom that was mentioned specifically in the Bill of Rights. The question may be put: Must the government carry a heavier burden of justification in the first case than in the second? Must it come forth with a far more compelling justification when it restricts a freedom that was mentioned in the Bill of Rights? And yet it is hard to see why the government should be allowed to confine us to our homes for reasons any more casual or less compelling than the justifications it would be obliged to offer before it restrains our speech. For it would be hard to argue that our freedom to venture into public, to engage in a world—including a political world—outside the household would be any less "fundamental" than our right to speak.

But if there is no difference in the kinds of justifications we would demand in these cases, we would have to reach the sobering recognition that the Bill of Rights would make no difference in guiding our judgment. Regardless of whether the freedom involved in any case was mentioned in the Bill of Rights, the questions we would have to pose, the tests we would have to apply, would be exactly the same. Those questions, or those tests, would not be furnished to us by anything written in the Bill of Rights. In both of the cases I have described here, we would ask whether people were inflicting a harm without justification, and whether the government would be justified in restraining these unwarranted acts.

In the case of the phone calls, we have no problem in distinguishing between the caller who torments people for his own pleasure and the caller who phones in the middle of the night to convey news of a death in the family. In both cases speech becomes the cause of hurt, but we can distinguish between a hurt that is inflicted for the pleasure or benefit of the assailant, and a hurt that is inflicted as a regrettable part of a decent and legitimate purpose. In the case of confining people to their houses, it would make a difference if the government were acting for the public safety in a time of riot or insurrection, or if the government were alarmed at the prospect of the Republicans winning elections, and it was trying to keep people safely at home on election day.

Differences of this kind are not inscrutable. They form the ground of judgments we have to make every day, and they reflect the kinds of questions we would have to bring to these judgments in the law even if there were no First Amendment—and *even if there were no written Constitution.* These questions are simply built into the logic of legal and moral judgment, and so they were the questions that were brought to these cases before we had our current Constitution. The men who founded this republic and framed our second Constitution knew a world of law that antedated the Constitution. They had experience in reflecting on legal questions and reaching legal judgments before they could appeal to the Constitution and its amendments. They understood then that they possessed sources of judgment outside the Constitution, which they often referred to simply as "the principles of law." Their singular advantage was that the advent of the Constitution did nothing to disturb their confidence that they already possessed, in ample measure, as many principles of judgment as they required.

As we have seen in the case of "ex post facto" laws, these principles were taken as so evident to the tutored mind, so necessary in logic, that the writers of Constitutions would be almost embarrassed to make them explicit. For the Founders would suggest, in this gesture, that other people were so benighted or unlettered that they should need to have these principles explained. But if questions were raised, the principles of law could be explained by showing that they were indeed "necessary"—that the law could not be conceived coherently without them, even if they had not been written down in the Constitution. We might take, as an example, the most notable case: No maxim in our law has become more familiar than the notion that persons accused of crime must be presumed innocent until proven guilty. This aphorism comes readily to the lip of every schoolchild, so widely has it been absorbed in the public understanding. And yet, it is nowhere set down within the Bill of Rights or within the main text of the Constitution. What is our ground of surety then that this cardinal maxim will be preserved in our law? Could it be anything other than the conviction, rooted in the understandings of lawyers and citizens, that this maxim is bound up with the logic of constitutional government itself; that it would be incoherent for any government of law to arrange its trials on a radically different premise? To ask how confident we are that this maxim of the law will be preserved, is to ask how likely it is that our legislators could replace this maxim with a contradictory premise, namely, that people may be presumed guilty of virtually any crime until they carry the burden of establishing their innocence; that in the absence of clear proof of innocence, any person may stand in peril of legal punishment.

There has been no panic, abroad in the land, that we are in danger of seeing such a premise installed in our law. Evidently, we have retained our confidence that we will manage to preserve the principle of "innocent until proven guilty," even though that notion has not been set down in the Bill of Rights. But then, how have we managed to preserve it? The maxim has been sustained, in the public awareness, through its frequent mention by lawyers and judges as an axiom of the law. And of course, it has been incorporated as a working principle in the administration of the laws. But that is to say, the place of this maxim has been secured because we have come to regard this proposition as one of those necessary axioms, or "first principles," in our law.

In our own day, of course, the willingness to speak seriously of "first principles" and necessary truths is bound to be regarded as quaint. And in a jurisprudence that has suffered the ravages of positivism, along with other varieties of philistinism, the notion of extracting principles through the syllogism is likely to inspire a round of derisive mirth. But the curious concession that the new jurisprudence must make to the old is that it cannot reject as implausible the project of reasoning that Marshall and his colleagues inscribed in the law with such a large hand. For the modern exponents of the Bill of Rights persistently resort to a style of argument that must move within that same cast: There is surely nothing in the First Amendment that marks off the burning of draft cards, or the pitching of tents outside the White House, as forms of "symbolic speech" that the Constitution was meant to protect. And yet those who would protect these acts of "expression" would have to imply that there is something contained in the character of the First Amendment that could be connected, not frivolously or arbitrarily, but plausibly and logically, to these odd instances, which are nowhere specified in the First Amendment. The exercise in reasoning commanded by this enterprise could hardly be less extravagant than the project described by Marshall—the project that is widely regarded today as illusory by conservatives as well as liberals: In that project, the judges deliberate about the restrictions of freedom that are justified or unjustified, and they draw their standards of judgment from the principles that mark the logic or the character of a free, lawful government.[28]

. . . . .

The men who were tutored in this discipline of jurisprudence had access to an understanding of law that was not rooted in the Constitution. For that reason, the Bill of Rights would not make a profound difference for the jurisprudence of the founding generation. The phrases contained in those amendments would not cause John Marshall to alter his understanding of the principles of law. Rather, it was the other way around: Marshall and other jurists would read the Bill of Rights in the light of their understanding of the principles of law or (as Marshall suggested in *Fletcher v. Peck*) "the general principles of our political institutions." In that perspective, he could consider restrictions on speech—or restraints on any other kind of freedom—with a mind that had not been distracted yet by the clichés that would grow out of the Bill of Rights. And so Marshall could proclaim, without a hint of apology, that anyone who writes or publishes a libel in this country "may be both sued and indicted":[29] he may be subject to the judgment—and punishment—of the law in both civil and criminal actions. Marshall evidently understood that speech could be an instrument of wrongdoing quite as much as any other medium by which human beings were able to carry through their acts. Speech could be used to assault and terrorize—it could be used, in other words, to inflict harms without justification; and when it was, the law could judge and restrain these assaults carried out through speech, as it could judge any other species of assault.

Marshall and the jurists of his generation were quite far then from the disposition, found in our own day, to confuse "speech" with a "principle": They knew that speech could not be *categorically* innocent and good, and therefore they could not regard speech as categorically more important, or more deserving of protection, than any other uses of personal freedom. One man could engage honestly in the legitimate trade of a tailor; another man could use his speech viciously, for illegitimate ends. For jurists such as Marshall it was hard to see why the freedom to engage in a legitimate calling did not deserve the same concern and security as the freedom to engage in acts of speech. And here, one might say, was the obverse side of the skepticism borne by the Federalists toward the Bill of Rights. They did not regard speech as sacrosanct, but neither did they think there was anything trivial about other uses of our personal freedom, which placed them beneath the concerns of the law. They were not persuaded that the freedoms mentioned in the Bill of Rights stood on a higher plane than others, but neither were they willing to narrow the protections of the Constitution to the freedoms that could be set down in a

Bill of Rights.[30] In his tart comments on the Bill of Rights, Theodore Sedg-wick suggested that we have a claim to all aspects of our freedom—not merely to our freedom to speak and assemble—so long as our freedom is not being used to inflict harms without justification. As a literature would come to ac-cumulate over the First Amendment, it would become common for scholars to insist that the amendment meant to protect mainly *political* speech and discussion—not tawdry displays in the street, not the crass speech by which vendors seek to hawk their wares in public. It was not until the 1970s that the Supreme Court came to the recognition that a public interest could be served by certain kinds of commercial advertising on the part of pharmacies and other establishments offering services to the public.[31] With that step, the judges came to the threshold of recognizing that if people are engaged in a legitimate calling, they should have a presumptive right to use any decent speech that becomes useful to their practice of a lawful business.

And yet why should that have come as such a momentous surprise? That understanding was contained in Theodore Sedgwick's rejoinder to his col-leagues on the Bill of Rights: Why should there be any ground for doubting that, in a constitutional order, in a regime of liberty, we have a right to speak, just as we have a right to any other form of our personal freedom, so long as that freedom is not used for a wrongful end? And if the speech used to pro-mote a legitimate business is not used maliciously, to injure without warrant, this speech should be no more open to restriction than any other innocent act.

. . . . .

To pick out certain uses of freedom, such as speech and assembly, for a special mention in the Constitution, runs the risk then of disparaging, by implica-tion, the freedoms that have not been mentioned. That was the warning posted by the Federalists, and we would be obliged to consider seriously whether their fears have not in fact been borne out. Has there not been cul-tivated within us a sense that the rights mentioned in the Bill of Rights are more fundamental than others? Are we not more inclined to notice the vio-lation of those "rights," and at the same time have we not blocked from our view whole classes of rights—and whole classes of victims—which have not been mentioned in the Bill of Rights, but which may be quite as deserving of our concern? The Bill of Rights says nothing, for example, of the right to practice a legitimate calling. In many states people who have been trained as physicians, lawyers, optometrists, and whose competence can be certified, are nevertheless barred from their professions by barriers of "licensing." The aim of these procedures is to restrict the number of professionals for the sake merely of propping up the income of the people who are already in the field. There is, in nature, no "principle" that establishes the correct price for a pair of pants; nor is there a principle that can establish the right or "just" income for lawyers and optometrists. No guesses, then, about the level of incomes for lawyers and optometrists could possibly establish a justification for barring people from the practice of a legitimate profession in which they have been properly trained. To an earlier generation of jurists, these arrangements in licensing would have been recognized as a patently arbitrary use of the law in restricting personal freedom.[32]

The right to practice a legitimate business cannot be reckoned as any less fundamental than the right to speak, and yet it is not a right which seems to excite the concern of our jurists or civil libertarians (unless the business in question happens to be an abortion clinic). When John Marshall stated the logic of an ex post facto law, that logic was not confined to laws that carried *criminal* penalties. His understanding could encompass laws that acted retrospectively in imposing penalties on people in the form of heavy fines or ruinous confiscations of their property. In this respect Marshall's understanding was shared by Madison, Oliver Ellsworth, Roger Sherman, and others among the Founders, who thought that the logic of ex post facto laws extended to the field of commercial relations.[33] From this perspective, the concern for ex post facto laws could very plausibly embrace the kinds of penalties and confiscations that come along with wage and price controls. But the civil libertarians of our own day have not been much excited by the serious restrictions of freedom—or even the denial, in effect, of the right to earn a living—that may be imposed through controls on wages and prices. The civil libertarians will quickly concede that they are less interested in these "regulations of the economy" than in the protection of what they call "fundamental freedoms." But in that admission they confirm one of the main points in the argument of the Federalists: The celebrants of the Bill of Rights would actually protect a range of rights far narrower than the rights that the Founders thought they were protecting under the Constitution.

What I am suggesting is that this floundering, this difficulty in identifying the rights engaged here, is not an accident. We encounter this problem because there has been a masking of the jural landscape. Certain kinds of rights have been made indistinct to us, or placed outside our vision, and this masking effect has something to do with the way in which our jural vision has been formed by the Bill of Rights. In spite of the Ninth Amendment, the rights mentioned in the Bill of Rights have in fact made a stronger impression on our legal sensibilities, and they have commanded a larger measure of our concern than the rights that were not named in the first eight Amendments.

That difference could be seen rather dramatically, several years ago, when a small band of American Nazis sought to stage a march through Skokie, Illinois. The location was no accident: The self-advertised Nazis chose a community that contained a large concentration of Jews, including about seven thousand who were survivors of the Holocaust. The incident offered what should have been a minor crisis, but it was converted into a major crisis for judges and libertarians, who suffered the most grievous puzzlement as they seemed to grope for standards of judgment.[34] The source of the strain for them was evident: There was a vivid sense of the "rights" that were engaged on the side of the Nazis. Those were the rights of speech and expression that seemed to be elevated, by many judges, to a place of preeminence in the inventory of our rights. But no label came readily to mind in describing the rights that were engaged on the other side, the rights of the potential victims.

And yet, those rights have not gone unrecognized or unnamed in the traditions of our law. We have long understood a certain right not to be subjected to acts of assault or intimidation, carried out through the use of speech or public displays.[35] Very recently, the Supreme Court has sustained the prospect of a suit brought against people who had sprayed the outside walls of a synagogue with "large anti-Semitic slogans, phrases and symbols."[36] The action here was not reduced to the charge of trespass or the destruction of property. The definition of the wrong included the traditional understanding of an "intentional infliction of emotional distress." When the law awards damages, it pronounces the judgment of a wrong. In this case, the court had to recognize a wrong that was constituted simply by the use of threatening symbols and words, even without the presence of a material injury. In that respect, the judges had to restore an older understanding, which has been undermined by the Supreme Court in recent years.[37] In that older understanding, judges and juries had the wit to tell the difference between a burning shoe box and a burning cross. There is little material difference between the two, but even people without layers of formal education can grasp the difference. They understand that certain words or symbols have been fixed, in our experience and our language, as symbols of assault. They have little trouble then in recognizing that the painting of a swastika on a synagogue represents an attempt to shock or assault, to inflict a hurt, without justification. If all of these things have been intelligible to judges, it should not have required any special exertion of wit in order to understand the nature of the event that was being staged when a band of Nazis promised to march, with uniforms and banners, through a community of Jews.

Still, there was a noticeable imbalance in the public presentation of the "constitutional" issue in the case. The "rights" that were supposedly engaged on the side of the Nazis had a ready name. The rights engaged on the side of the Jewish victims had been recognized even longer in the law, and yet they did not have a ready name—or a comparable place of standing within the protections of the Constitution. How could one account for the difference, except in these terms?: The Nazis seemed to have a more urgent claim to the protections of the Constitution because their "right" to speech and assembly found an explicit mention in the Bill of Rights. But the Jews in Skokie could enlist no slogan from the Bill of Rights to establish, quite as vividly, the substantial rights of their own that were threatened in this case.

If we would merely look about us, with a new willingness to see, we would notice that other examples are not wanting. We may find, every day, fresh evidence of the casualties produced by the legal perspective I have described here. If anyone would ask just where this understanding has made a practical difference in our law and in the lives of our people, we could hardly offer an example more dramatic than the juridical reasoning of Mr. Justice Blackmun in *Roe v. Wade*.[38] As Blackmun understood the problem of that case, the question was *not*: On what grounds would we be justified in regarding the human fetus as less than a human being? And on what grounds would we be justified in removing the protections of law from children before they were born? The problem was not set forth in this way, in a manner that would focus on the substantive moral justification for the taking of fetal life. Justice Blackmun argued, rather, in this way: the Constitution protects the lives of "persons," but it is nowhere specified in the Constitution that the term "persons" refers to people *before* they were born.[39]

Blackmun noticed that whenever the Constitution referred to "persons," it was to persons who were engaged in activities such as voting or migrating or escaping or being extradited—activities that were evidently possible only for people outside the womb. From those clues he concluded that "persons" did not refer to people before they were born and mobile. By the same reasoning, of course, "persons" would probably not refer to people who were crippled or retarded, confined to their beds or wheelchairs. And indeed it turns out that these inferences are now being made about people who are retarded. These handicapped people are now being drawn into that class of beings who are thought to lack what Justice Blackmun refers to as "meaningful life." Their diminished intellect is taken as a justification for abortion in unborn children, and for the withdrawal of feeding and medical care from children who are newly born. Before the passage in 1984 of the legislation on Baby Doe, the burden in the courts was placed on those who would treat retarded infants as "persons" within the protection of the law. And even now, after the passage of legislation, the courts may still resist these efforts to invade the "privacy" of parents for the sake of protecting infants who are retarded. For these children, inside or outside the womb, the Constitution has not been the source of a legal discipline which requires lawyers and parents to justify the destruction of their lives. Instead, the Constitution has been the container of a formula that allows these people to be removed from the protections of the law if they are not *explicitly listed* among the "persons" that the Constitution would seek to protect.

. . . . .

It is arguable, then, that the warnings raised by the Federalists were not rendered "academic" by the passage of the Ninth Amendment. But rather, that amendment was overborne by the logic that was embedded in the Bill of Rights. Our absorption of that logic may be seen today in the language that now reflects the staples of our thought on these matters. Is it not common to hear people speak of that "freedom of speech we possess *through* the First Amendment"? And do we not hear even lawyers speak of our "First Amendment rights"? But the sense in both cases is that these rights flow to us distinctly through the First Amendment. The necessary implication is that, in the absence of the First Amendment, we should not have these rights. There is, in this outlook, a libel on the Founders and the most curious understanding of the Constitution they produced. If the Constitution was not made, as James Wilson said, for the purpose of securing and enlarging our natural rights—*all* of our natural rights—for what purpose was it made? Is it really conceivable that the Constitution framed so carefully by the Founders did not encompass the recognition that citizens had the right to speak and assemble and to be free from unreasonable searches? Were these rights never imagined until they were added, as an afterthought, in amendments to the Constitution?[40] In Theodore Sedgwick's tart remarks to his colleagues we find this understanding: that in a regime of liberty, we have a presumptive claim to all aspects of our personal freedom, not merely to our freedom of speech. Any one of our freedoms may be restricted when there is a justification, but the burden of justification falls to the government. And with a government founded on those premises—founded, that is, on the premises of personal freedom—why should we ever have reason to doubt that our freedoms encompass the liberty to speak and assemble?

But the state of mind that Sedgwick found so unaccountable, in the proponents of a Bill of Rights, has now been spread more widely in the land, and it shows itself even in places quite removed from constitutional law. Several years ago there was a public "Appeal to the Government of Vietnam," signed by Staughton Lynd, Joan Baez, Aryeh Neier, and many others who had been active in the antiwar movement. These people were repelled by the evidence of "systematic violations of human rights" in Vietnam—most notably, the holding of prisoners, without charges or trials, because of their political or religious convictions. The signers of the Appeal were apparently surprised to discover that the Communist regime in Vietnam had no commitment to the notion of habeas corpus or to any of the other, more refined conventions that arise, for defendants and prisoners, in a regime of law. What was strange about the "Appeal" was that the signers seemed to expect the refinements that emerged from a constitutional government, but without the underlying structures from which those refinements emanate. There were, in Vietnam, no free elections and no independent courts of law in which the government could lose cases. In short, there was, in Vietnam, no government restrained by law. Why should the signers of the Appeal ever have supposed, then, that a Communist regime would respect these rights, which grew distinctly out of a government of law?

The answer, apparently, is that they had been given assurances on these points by the Communist leaders of North Vietnam during the war. That they were gullible is quite clear, but their gullibility cannot be attributed merely to personal sources. It is worth considering, after all, just why these children of America thought it was possible to speak of human rights in the abstract, detached from the legal institutions which reflect the moral premises behind those rights, and which furnish, in turn, the most favorable structure in which those rights can be secured. Is it not at least politically interesting that the signers of the Appeal did not understand "human rights" in the way those rights were understood by the men who drafted the Declaration of Independence: They did not understand that, as soon as we begin speaking of rights natural to human beings, the most fundamental of those rights were the rights of human beings to be ruled only by their consent, in a government of free elections, a government restrained by law. The signers of the Appeal had not thought it fitting or practicable to demand of the leaders of Vietnam a government of free elections and constitutional restraints. They were prepared to treat, with a certain tolerance, the unwillingness of the rulers in Vietnam to incorporate, in a Leninist regime, these institutions of a constitutional order. They were willing to scold the rulers of Vietnam over issues of "human rights" that they regarded as more fundamental. What they taught, by implication, was sobering: The right to be governed by consent, in a regime of free elections and constitutional restraints, was desirable, but not strictly necessary for any political order that we would regard as a decent and legitimate regime. But to point these things out is virtually to restate Hamilton's argument about the understandings that had to be passed by in the "injudicious zeal for bills of rights." Staughton Lynd and and his friends failed to understand that the most fundamental human rights, the most critical premises of personal freedom, were already reflected in the very structure of a constitutional government. And for that reason, they failed to understand what the partisans of a Bill of Rights had failed, before them, to grasp: They failed to understand, as Hamilton said, that "the Constitution is itself, in every rational sense, and to every useful purpose, A BILL OF RIGHTS."[41]

There is a point in posing the question: What led these earnest people to believe that fundamental rights could be secured through a separate stipulation of rights, as though the task had no connection to the project of securing, in the first place, the structure of a constitutional government? What part of their civic training could have been the source of this grave mistake? It is, of course, a speculation, but did their mistake not arise, plausibly, from a civic teaching that has been part of the Constitution almost from the beginning? Staughton Lynd and his friends might have been confirming, dramatically, the warnings that were offered by Hamilton and the Federalists: They had evidently absorbed, quite thoroughly, the teaching that was contained in the very logic of the Bill of Rights.

. . . . .

Anyone who contemplates the mind and sensibility reflected in the opinion of the Supreme Court in *Roe v. Wade*, anyone who measures the understanding contained in the "Appeal to the Government of Vietnam," may grasp the dangers that the Federalists saw in a Bill of Rights. It might be said that the concerns of the Federalists, at their deepest level, were with the lessons that would be taught, with the kind of legal sensibility that would be cultivated, by the Bill of Rights. The teaching of the Bill of Rights threatened to affect the citizens of this republic with a brittle, almost childish literalism. It would misinstruct them about the grounds of their rights and the breadth of those freedoms that were protected under the Constitution. It would produce, in later generations, lawyers and judges who no longer knew how to deliberate about questions of justice. These men and women of the law would lose the aptitude for deliberation because they would have forgotten the main questions of jurisprudence, and they would no longer know the difference between a principle and the *instances* in which a principle may be manifested. And so, two hundred years later, we find judges confronting a private college that rejects, in its code, dating and marriage across racial lines. The judges deny a tax exemption to this school, but they still cannot come to a judgment on whether racial discrimination is *wrong in itself*, wrong in principle, regardless of whether it takes place in the choice of housing or of sexual partners. If it is, then discrimination in the domain of sex would be quite as wrong when proclaimed by the Bob Jones University or by the "personal ads" in the *New York Review of Books*. But the judges were not entirely resolved on that point. Most of them still seemed inclined to believe that the wrong of racial discrimination was to be found only in some material harm that was inflicted on black people in *schools*.[42] Judges who suffer these confusions will of course find it hard to establish the principled ground for their judgments, since they are not entirely sure that they can recognize a principle when they see it. The life of the law, for them, will be found in the memorizing of slogans and formulas, and since they know no ground of judgment outside these formulas, they can only convert the task of judging into a game of making ingenious connections between new cases and old descriptions. (Are movies "speech"? Are infants in the womb "persons"?)

Whatever can be said about lawyers of this type, it must be said that they will have become notably different, in their cast of minds, from the men who created this political order. Ironically, we know it was the aspiration of the Founders to make themselves, as a class, dispensable. They sought to fashion a government that would not depend on having at its head, at all times, statesmen who were philosophers, or men, like themselves, who could reason about first principles. They hoped to create a system of institutions that could survive even bad times and venal men. But through the agony of our Civil War—and through the example of Lincoln—we came to learn a different lesson: that the polity may be corrupted to the point of dissolution if states-men and their constituents are not schooled to understand the principles on which their constitutional freedom is ultimately founded. When Stephen Douglas said that he didn't "care" whether slavery was voted up or down; when Senator Pettit of Indiana declared that the proposition "all men are created equal" was not a self-evident truth, but a "self-evident lie"; it was clear that a large portion of the political class no longer understood the prem-ises on which their own, free government was founded. Those men could not be relied on to preserve republican government for the next generation.

What Lincoln represented was the reappearance of a man of the same stat-ure as the Founders, a man who was able to preserve this political order be-cause he could do—and do even better—what the Founders sought to do, and that was to trace his judgments back to the first principles of lawful govern-ment. Sober men may have to acknowledge that the legal culture fostered by the Bill of Rights is more likely to produce a Justice Blackmun or the typical lawyers of the American Civil Liberties Union, and that it is less likely to produce lawyers like Abraham Lincoln and John Marshall.

Of course, no man of prudence would urge us to repeal the Bill of Rights. But we might seek to free ourselves from the constricted vision of the Bill of Rights by restoring to our jurisprudence the understanding of our first gener-ation of jurists. And yet it must be admitted that this task of restoration has been made far more difficult with a legal profession that has been shaped, in its sensibilities, by the formulas of the Bill of Rights. The most damning thing that might be said then, finally, about the Bill of Rights is that it has been part of a curriculum of civic education in this country that has made it far less likely that we will bring to positions of authority people with the same fur-nishings of mind—with the same capacity to trace their judgments back to first principles—as the men who founded this republic.

FIVE

LIFE AMONG THE CLAUSES

HOW OFTEN HAVE we heard the expression, cast off in conversation, about the rights we enjoy "under the First Amendment"? Expressions of this kind may enter the conversation of lawyers and judges, as well as citizens with no particular training in the law; and they reveal just how widely we have absorbed now, in our conventional understanding, notions that the Founders would have regarded as fearful. To say that we claim certain rights "under" or "through" the First Amendment is to suggest that the amendment itself is the source of these rights. In this manner, ordinary citizens have come to speak the language of "legal positivism." Their language carries the implication that our rights have the standing of rights, not because they emanate from enduring principles of law, but because they were "posited" or set down by particular men in a particular document. Of course, most of the people who speak this language would not know the difference between legal positivism and vegetarianism, but the logic behind the language may nevertheless be absorbed. The people who think they have rights "under the First Amendment" are very likely to believe that they would lose those rights if that amendment disappeared.

In the understanding of the Founders, of course, those rights would still be there even if the whole Constitution disappeared. To recall James Wilson again, the object of the Constitution was not to create new rights, but to secure or enlarge the rights we already possessed by nature. The principles of right and wrong, the principles of moral and legal judgment, existed antecedent to the Constitution; it was the existence of those principles that enjoined us, in the first place, to arrange the governance of ourselves under a Constitution rather than a despotism, or an "arbitrary government." But our current language of the law makes sense only when this understanding of the Founders has receded. If we assume that our rights arise only because they have been set down or stipulated, the First Amendment takes on a vaster importance. Our jurists often flex their genius in extracting from the First Amendment—or from other sections of the Constitution—implications that they regard as no less momentous. The right to speak and assemble may be taken to imply a right to engage in associations without revealing lists of members. And so the NAACP may be sheltered from a legislative inquiry into its membership.[1] This "corollary" of the First Amendment is treated as important as anything written down in the Constitution, even though it may be at odds with other implications of the First Amendment—as, for example, the right of the public to get access to information, including the names of people who contribute large amounts of money to political candidates.[2] The rights are drawn from implication, but in a curious inversion, their standing as rights still seem to be rooted in the "positive" law of the Constitution and the First Amendment. Again, the simple question may be put: If we had the wit to extract these implications from the First Amendment, could we not have extracted them from the Constitution itself even without the presence of the First Amendment?

But what has been said here in relation to the First Amendment could be said quite as well in regard to other sections, or even clauses, of the Constitution. With a liberal regimen of interpretation over the last forty years, some of these clauses have been treated as though they bore a significance quite detached from the Constitution itself. And the philosophic leap has been marked, in our language, with the capitalization of these clauses: We now refer quite commonly in print to the Equal Protection Clause or the Due Process Clause of the Fourteenth Amendment. Vast new bodies of "rights" have been created under rubrics marked by these clauses. Many lawyers and judges have come to see them as the names of whole subsets or sections of our jurisprudence, as though these clauses bore entirely separate logics and gave rise to distinct lines of juridical construction. Lawyers speak commonly of an Equal Protection "analysis," or the specialized "tests" spun off through refinements of Equal Protection.

But these clauses of the Constitution may offer, at most, a framework in which to set forth the problem in a case; the clauses become important only as they lead the judges, in any case, to settle a judgment. That is to say, they must lead the judges to get clear on the kind of decision that could be "justified." In setting forth a justification, they must appeal finally to *principles of justification*; and if they are reasonably clear in their account of those principles, the decision they announce in the current case will suggest the grounds of judgment that would come into play in other cases as well. In short, the separate clauses of the Constitution should lead the courts back to the same point: They should bring the judges back to the same logic, or the same core of principles, that help them explain in any case what is "justified" or "unjustified."

The matter may be seen more easily if we draw on one or two notable cases, and I would suggest that the depth of the problem would become more apparent in a case with these features: The judges themselves are unanimous in their sense of how they wish to dispose of the case—they suffer no disagreement in deciding just which side deserves to prevail in the cause; but they fall into a serious dispute over the precise clause in the Constitution that would furnish the ground for the judgment. There would be no disagreement about the result the court was reaching, but the judges would break off into factions, with separate, concurring opinions, attended often with an edge of sarcasm.

For the judges, it seemed to matter profoundly as to whether the case was settled on grounds of Equal Protection, Due Process, or the Privileges and Immunities Clause. In fact, the judges appeared to be astonished, or even offended, by the dimness of mind shown by their colleagues in failing to see that their favored clause—say, the Due Process clause—may be wholly inapt, while another clause, like the Equal Protection Clause, happened to be so cleanly and singularly right for the case at hand.

A telling, benign, example on this head may be found in the case of *Edwards v. California*,[3] decided in 1941. The example is benign, because no grievous injury was done through the confusions that distracted the minds of the judges. Everyone on the Court agreed with the decision that had to be rendered, and no one looking at the case today would imagine that anything but the right judgment had been reached. The case began in 1939, when Edwards, a resident of California, drove to Spur, Texas, with the intention of fetching his wife's brother, Frank Duncan, and bringing him to California. Edwards was apparently aware that his brother-in-law was unemployed. When he arrived in Texas he learned that Duncan had last been employed by the Works Progress Administration (WPA). He became aware, that is, that his brother-in-law had been hired under a program of "public works," which was a part of a larger program of "welfare" and "relief" inspired by the depression. Edwards had become aware then that his brother-in-law would have met the definition of an "indigent" or unemployed person. Duncan had $20.00 in his pocket when the two set out for California, and by the time they arrived, the money had all been spent. Duncan lived with Edwards and his wife for about ten days until he could qualify for a program of public assistance provided by the Farm Security Administration. Once again, his support was furnished by an agency of the federal government, and apart from that aid, Duncan had no employment, and no other means of support.

With these facts defining the case, a complaint was filed against Edwards under a law in California that barred people or corporations from bringing into the state "any indigent person who is not a resident of the state, knowing him to be an indigent person." Edwards was convicted and sentenced to six months imprisonment, but the sentence was suspended. It would not appear that the authorities in California were lusting to imprison people under this local statute, and they might have been contriving a test of the law. On the other hand, they might have been willing to use the occasion for the sake of teaching a public lesson, without actually meting out punishment to a person on relief.

The case was taken on appeal to a higher court in Yuba County, and the statute was upheld as "a valid exercise of the police power of the state." The case made its way into the federal courts, and when it reached the Supreme

Court, the decision below was reversed, the conviction overturned, with a unanimous judgment.

But there the agreement ended. The opinion of the Court was written by James Byrnes, one of the few noticeable opinions he authored during his short stint on the Court. Byrnes managed, however, to induce a state of puzzlement among several of his colleagues when he sought to settle the judgment of the Court on the Commerce Clause. California had punished Edwards for driving his brother-in-law across the lines of a state for the purpose of establishing residence in California. From the brute facts of the case Byrnes abstracted these ingredients: A state attached legal penalties to the transportation of persons across the boundaries of the state. This was not, of course, a massive interference of the state with the flow of goods and persons, but in the phrases made familiar in the courts, the law in California had cast up a certain "barrier" or imposed a "burden upon interstate commerce."

As Byrnes conceded, the states had traditionally exercised an authority, under the "police powers," to carry out the inspection of goods and persons in entering the state. Those regulations would often have an incidental effect on interstate commerce, but so long as the effect was modulated and the purpose legitimate, the Congress and the courts were willing to accommodate these regulations. The question then was why this regulation in California was not fully as legitimate as the other kinds of regulations that the courts had been willing in the past to uphold. The further complication for Byrnes was that the barring of "paupers" and "vagabonds" had been explicitly endorsed by the Court in a string of cases that ran back to *City of New York v. Miln* in 1837.[4] The Court proclaimed, in that earlier case, that it was "as competent and as necessary for a state to provide precautionary measures against the moral pestilence of paupers, vagabonds, and possibly convicts, as it is to guard against the physical pestilence, which may arise from unsound and infectious articles imported."[5]

The challenge for Byrnes was to show why this purpose was no longer legitimate. Eventually, he would say something apt on the point, but he sought to address this moral question in the first instance by casting a grand, hazy theory about the "national" character of poverty, and the futility of "parochial" legislation. Byrnes found in the legislation of California an attempt on the part of a "single state to isolate itself from difficulties common to all of them." The depression did not originate in California, and its effects were not confined to any one of the states. Duncan had moved from Texas to California, but he had never been removed from the jurisdiction and support of the federal government. The provision of relief had long been the responsibility mainly of local government, but Byrnes thought that history itself had now furnished a more recent revelation, namely, "that in an industrial society the task of providing assistance to the needy has ceased to be local in character."[6] With the New Deal, Byrnes and his party had expanded the responsibilities—

and the patronage—of the federal government in providing welfare and affecting, in a clumsy way, to "manage" the economy. Now, he took that expansion of the federal government as the predicate for a moral, or juridical
decision: The expansion of the federal government could be seen as a development sprung from the logic of History, and it would furnish, in turn, the
ground on which to say that the legislation in California was unjustified, because it interfered with the movement of people in a "national" economy. In
this way, a factual proposition without any evident moral properties would be
taken to supply the ground of a moral judgment.

But even in its own terms, this part of Byrnes's argument simply turned in
upon itself: For it was quite arguable that, in an integrated world economy,
the sources and effects of the depression were international, and not merely
national. And Byrnes did not treat that fact as a predicate on which to argue
that the authority to regulate the American economy should be shifted from
the United States to a supranational government. When seen against the
panorama of an international depression, the regulations of the American
government could be seen as decidedly "parochial," especially when those
regulations inhibited the movement of persons and investments across the
borders of nations. But Byrnes did not suggest that it was improper for the
American government to use its control over its borders to bar from the country indigent people who could not establish the sources of their financial support. As Byrnes recognized, those indigent persons who were not yet residents
of California lacked the political leverage to force a change in policy within
the state. Still, the same point could have been made quite as emphatically
for those indigent persons who were barred from entering the country.

But beyond that, Byrnes's argument invited this plausible "thought experiment": What if the national government had sought to respond to the depression with a regimen of planning even more ambitious and severe? What
if the authorities had sought to assign the unemployed to the states in which
investments were channeled by the national government? During the Second
World War, certain workers were prevented from leaving their jobs, in fac-
tories, without the permission of the federal government. Franklin Roosevelt
had proposed to treat the depression as something equivalent to the emergency of a war, and it is not hard to imagine this modest addition to the early
experiments of the New Deal. People might have been barred from moving
to states in which the levels of unemployment were already among the highest, and they might have been restrained from leaving their states without the
permission of the federal planning authorities. If the critical problem in the
Edwards case involved the freedom of persons to move across the lines of the
state, that freedom would have been even more seriously restricted under this
scheme of federal control. But this system of restraint would surely not have
been "parochial."

The problem for Byrnes could have been restated in this way: If the statute in California was invalid because the effects of the depression extended beyond the jurisdiction of any state, the same argument would establish that the federal authority over commerce was invalid and parochial in the same way. At the same time, there did not seem to be anything in the Commerce Clause that prevented Congress from restricting the entrance of indigents into the United States—or even from barring the movement of indigents between the states. But if it were legitimate for Congress to legislate in this way, even when its own responses to the depression were local and parochial; and if it were legitimate for Congress to bar the immigration of indigents; why didn't these same propositions make it legitimate for the state of California to legislate in the same way?

Byrnes was still left then with the moral question that had to remain the decisive question in the case: On what ground, finally, could he explain why it was not *justified* to restrict the movement of indigents? In reaching that question, Byrnes had to move beyond anything that was contained, distinctly, in the Commerce Clause. He had taken note of the earlier commentary of the Court in the Miln case, that it was quite as legitimate for the state to deal with the "moral pestilence of paupers . . . [as it was] to guard against the physical pestilence, which may arise from unsound and infectious articles imported." Byrnes's achievement in the case came with his recognition that his judgment had to turn, in the end, on denying that analogy, or that isomorphy, between poverty and "moral pestilence." It was therefore necessary to break from the language and the moral understanding of the earlier Court.

> Whatever may have been the notion then prevailing, we do not think that it will now be seriously contended that because a person is without employment and without funds he constitutes a "moral pestilence." Poverty and immorality are not synonymous.[7]

Byrnes announced what he had grasped, correctly, with his moral intuitions, but it required the commentary of a moral philosopher to fill out the explanation that lay behind the conclusion. What was engaged in this point was one of the most elementary implications to arise in moral reasoning. Rousseau had drawn upon the principle involved here when he declared, in the opening pages of the *Social Contract*, that physical power could not be the source of moral obligations. The fact that some people succeed in overcoming others by force of arms does not establish, in itself, that they were justified in overpowering and ruling, as though Might made Right, as though power were the source of its own justification. I have sought to explain, in a more extended work, that the same understanding is present when we refuse to draw moral conclusions from attributes that are wholly wanting in moral significance—attributes such as height, weight, social cohesion, color, or even race. Simply by knowing a person's height or the color of his hair, we cannot draw any inferences about his moral character. We cannot infer that the person is good or bad, that he deserves reward or punishment, benefits or disabilities. Precisely why this should be the case still requires a fuller explanation, which would bring us back to the "logic of morals" itself and the ground of our moral judgments.[8] But for the moment, for the purposes of this case, the moral understanding sufficient to the problem would encompass this point: On the basis of poverty alone, we cannot say that we are dealing with a good man or a bad man, with a man whose presence, in a family or a community, would be benign or malevolent. Experience has amply confirmed the truth contained in the nature of human beings as moral agents. The reflexes that mark a selfless, conscientious parent may be found in the poor as well as the rich, and they may be altogether missing in members of either class. The measure of riches provides no measure of the willingness of any person to prefer some other interest to his own, or to subordinate his wants to the needs of others. The gauge of poverty may not even be reliable in marking the person who is shiftless and irresponsible (the man who fits aptly into that class described by Mr. Alfred P. Dolittle as the "undeserving poor"), as against the person who is industrious but unlucky. None of these inferences could be drawn or ruled out on the basis of poverty alone. And for that reason, "indigence" could not furnish a ground of justification for barring people from the territory of the state on the supposition that their presence would degrade the moral climate or place an unwarranted burden on the economy of the state.

Justice Byrnes was not evidently prepared to fill out this explanation. It could be said for him that he saw precisely the right point and he wrote as much as he knew. But the slenderest explanation in the opinion was devoted to the point on which the judgment finally rested. While that part of the argument remained unembellished, Byrnes could not relieve the puzzlement experienced by some of his colleagues, who were still not clear about the reasons that were controlling in the opinion of the Court. Justices Douglas and Jackson were moved, then, to offer separate opinions. Both judges were noticeably uncomfortable with the Commerce Clause as the ground of justification for the judgment in this case. "I am of the opinion," wrote Douglas, "that the right of persons to move freely from State to State occupies a more protected position in our constitutional system than does the movement of cattle, fruit, steel and coal across state lines."[9] As usual, Jackson was even more stylish and cutting: "[T]he migrations of a human being, of whom it is charged that he possesses nothing that can be sold and has no wherewithal to buy, do not fit easily into my notions as to what is commerce. To hold that the measure of his rights is the commerce clause is likely to result eventually either in distorting the commercial law or in denaturing human rights."[10]

Both Douglas and Jackson found a more compelling ground for this case in the Privileges and Immunities Clause and the rights that attended "citizenship" in the United States. Still, Jackson was moved to write an opinion separate from that of Douglas because he found Douglas's writing here no more illuminating or satisfying than the argument of the Court, even though Douglas had found, in his estimate, a sounder ground for the judgment.

There were, of course, two clauses on Privileges and Immunities. The first was in the original text of the Constitution, in Article I, Section 2, and it provided that "the Citizens of each State shall be entitled to all Privileges and Immunities of Citizens in the several States." The emphasis of that clause was on citizenship *in the states*. That clause was compatible with the Jeffersonian theory of citizenship, which held that persons became citizens of the United States only through their citizenship in one of the separate states. That theory of citizenship was displaced with the Fourteenth Amendment, which made explicit the understanding that persons could be citizens of the United States if they were born or naturalized in this country, quite apart from their citizenship in one of the states. With the Fourteenth Amendment, the clause on Privileges and Immunities was recast to read in this way: "No State shall make or enforce any law which shall abridge the privileges or immunities of citizens of the United States." The earlier clause on Privileges and Immunities had been embroiled in the controversies over slavery: Lincoln thought that this clause gave, to the free black man, the right to preserve his freedom even as he crossed the border into states that incorporated slavery in their laws and forbade the presence of free blacks.[11] On the other side, the defenders of slavery thought that this clause assured, to the owner of slaves, the right to cross into free states without being deprived of his property in slaves. Both interpretations were still compatible with the understanding that the right to freedom, or the right to own slaves, originated in the laws of the separate states.

And yet, it was arguable that even the old Privileges and Immunities Clause contained, in its essential logic, a notion of "national" rights that were not reducible simply to the rights that were created in the separate states.[12] Justice Douglas drew on this understanding and claimed that both versions of the Privileges and Immunities Clause supported the freedom of Edwards in this case. Douglas sought to show that even the older clause on Privileges and Immunities recognized, as one of the minimal rights of national citizenship, "the right to pass freely from State to State." This right he regarded as "fundamental." It was bound up with the notion of national citizenship, even though it was never set down in the text of the Constitution. "That the right was implied did not make it any the less 'guaranteed' by the Constitution."[13] Of course, it was conceivable that an exception could be made for those people who would make themselves a burden on the taxpayers of another state. The states might restrict the migrations of the indigent without affecting in any appreciable way the volume of traffic across the borders of the states. But to admit an exception of that kind, said Douglas, would be "to contravene every conception of national unity."[14]

Justice Jackson shared the conviction that the right engaged in this case was somehow rooted in the notion of national citizenship. In an earlier decision of the Court, Chief Justice Hughes had recognized that an alien who had the privilege of entering the United States would have the privilege then of "entering and abiding in any State in the Union."[15] Jackson thought it ironical that an alien would apparently have the freedom to move across the boundaries of the states, but that the same freedom could be denied—as it was in this case—to a citizen of the United States. But the comparison should have inspired more than irony. It should have alerted Jackson to the point that the case could not really have turned on the rights of *citizenship*: Would the problem in the case have been different, in any significant way, if the state of California had barred the immigration only of *resident aliens* who were indigent? The state would still have been casting up barriers to the movement of persons, and there would have been, equally present, the same false tendency to equate the poor with "moral pestilence." The judges who recoiled from these features of the Edwards case were not likely to find their objections dissolved if the state had imposed its restrictions solely on aliens.

More vital than the notion of *citizenship* was the recognition, in the first place, of the logic of a "nation." Regardless of whether the persons in motion were citizens or aliens, the idea of the nation implied a territory in which people were free to move without encountering barriers cast up without warrant by the separate states. But to back into this point was to discover, again, the understanding of nationhood that was marked in the Commerce Clause. The shift from the Articles of Confederation to the Constitution was a shift from a confederation to a real national government. The provisions on Commerce were the centerpiece of the new Constitution, and they expressed, in operational terms, the logic of that change: States could not impose tariffs on goods that came from foreign countries, or from other states; they could not enter into compacts with other countries or other states in the Union; they could not make war; they could not coin money or make anything other than gold or silver coin a payment for debts. The authority of Congress over commerce was dominant, and that dominance marked the supremacy of a national government, which could act directly on individuals without depending on the agency of the states. Quite apart from the rhetorical flourishes of Douglas and Jackson, "commerce" was never understood by the Founders to refer merely to the movement of cattle, fruit, or iron. In Black's Law Dictionary, "commerce" comprehended the movement of persons and ideas as well as goods. That was the understanding of commerce held by the Founders, and it was the understanding that Byrnes meant to draw upon in the Edwards case.

The advent of national government, with a plenary authority over commerce, marked the recognition of a nation, or a national community. And one of the rudimentary implications of that national community was that citizens, residents, even sojourners, would not suffer customs barriers or political impediments from the separate states as they traveled from one part of the nation to another.

The Commerce Clause already contained, then, in its logic, a conception of freedom quite as broad as anything that Douglas and Jackson could call up by invoking the Privileges and Immunities Clause and appealing to the rights of citizenship. But at the same time, the Privileges and Immunities Clause brought the judges no nearer to addressing, or settling, the point that had to remain pivotal in the case. Jackson himself recognized that problem when he was moved to supply, in his separate opinion, the notable omission contained in Douglas's argument. Jackson agreed with Douglas that citizens had a right to migrate from one state to another, but it was necessary to recognize that this right was not "unlimited." Citizens may have a right to travel freely among the states, but that right was not incompatible with an authority on the part of the states to impose *some* legitimate restrictions. Even if a man were a citizen, "he may not, if a fugitive from justice, claim freedom to migrate unmolested, nor may he endanger others by carrying contagion about." Jackson thought the states had ample grounds then for interfering, justly, with the movement of a citizen, "for arresting his progress across a state line quite as much as from place to place within the state."[16]

The recognition of that point brought Jackson to recognize, at the same time, just where the pivot in the argument really lay. "It is here," he noted, "that we meet the real crux of this case. Does 'indigence' as defined by the application of the California statute constitute a basis for restricting the freedom of a citizen, as crime or contagion warrants its restriction?" Jackson was brought, then, precisely to the same point that Byrnes finally recognized as decisive. His commentary on this point offered further reinforcement or embellishment to the argument produced by Byrnes, but it must be said that he added nothing to the logic, or the understanding, which Byrnes had been able to grasp. Jackson formed his explanation in this way:

> We should say now, and in no uncertain terms, that a man's mere property status, without more, cannot be used by a state to test, qualify, or limit his rights as a citizen of the United States. "Indigence" in itself is neither a source of rights nor a basis for denying them. The mere state of being without funds is a neutral fact—constitutionally an irrelevance, like race, creed, or color. . . . I think California had no right to make the condition of Duncan's purse, with no evidence of violation by him of any law or social policy which caused it, the basis of excluding him or of punishing one who extended him aid.[17]

In other words, as Byrnes had said, "poverty and immorality are not synonymous." From the condition of Duncan's wealth or poverty—from "the condition of [his] purse"—one could not draw any inferences about his guilt or innocence, his worthiness or unworthiness. Therefore, one could not rightly draw any inference on the question of whether Duncan *deserved* to be excluded from the state. Jackson apparently thought that his argument had taken a different path, but it moved—as it was compelled to move—to the identical point that had been decisive in Byrnes's opinion. And the under-standing Jackson brought forth to settle the point could not be distinguished in substance from the explanation that was finally put forth by Byrnes.

For some reason, Jackson did seem to think that he was supplying what was absent from Douglas's opinion, but he was surely only supplying what Douglas had neglected to make explicit: We must suppose that Douglas recognized, no less than Jackson, that the states might properly arrest the movement of per-sons who were fleeing from crimes, even if they were citizens of the United States. Presumably, he would have recognized, also, that if the restrictions imposed by the states were justified, they could not be unconstitutional. But by failing to make this point explicit, Douglas had blocked himself off from the recognition that did make its way to Jackson, namely, that the formulas of Privileges and Immunities, or the "rights of citizenship," were no more capable of settling the critical point in the case than the metaphors of the Commerce Clause. Jackson at least had recognized that he had to be carried beyond the rights of citizenship in order to explain "the real crux of the case": Indigence could not be equated with "crime or contagion," and therefore, it could not provide a justified ground for restricting movement into a state.

As I have pointed out, there was no difference in substance between the ex-planation that Jackson and Byrnes offered on this question. We may be for-given then for wondering: Why did these judges write separate opinions? Why did they think that there was any real dispute separating the three men who wrote in this case? We would be obliged to take seriously the explanations offered by Douglas and Jackson: They were evidently put off by the metaphors of trade associated with the Commerce Clause. But from their unease they were moved to indulge an extravagant, implausible claim: that the Commerce Clause was radically inapt as the constitutional ground for the rights engaged in this case; that the Privileges and Immunities Clause, or the rights of citi-zenship, offered a more illuminating set of metaphors. Or at least, Douglas and Jackson must have believed that the clause on Privileges and Immunities could be the source of a more precise logic, which could settle more cleanly the issues posed in this case.

But my argument here is that the judges were distracted by false formulas, laden with their own fictions. And with these formulas, the separate clauses of the Constitution could be invested with a significance, in rhetoric, that could not really be borne out in their substance. My deeper point, however, is that even seasoned jurists could suffer these distractions of mind because they were not alert to *the structure of the moral argument* that had to underlie their arguments in this case, quite regardless of the clause of the Constitution they happened to invoke. No matter where they began, their arguments had to move along the same path and reach the same terminal point if they were to address the case in terms that were even remotely apt. The structure of the moral argument might have been mapped out by beginning in this way:

A. The framework of the American Constitution creates a presumptive "right" on the part of persons to travel freely within the territory of the United States without being restrained at the borders of States, except for reasons that are compelling and justified. This "right" arises distinctly from the character of the American polity in the same way that rights are created in other, special situations, by the "rules of the game" (such as the rules of baseball) or the rules that define the character of different associations (such as the American Association of Pediatricians).

This is the only part of the argument that depends on the character of the American Constitution. The rights that are drawn here are analogous, as I say, to the rights that are created under special frameworks or regimes with distinctive rules. Under the rules of baseball, for example, a batter who receives four pitches outside the strike zone (four "balls") has the "right" to advance to first base. A person walking down the street, who suddenly found that a hostile mob was throwing stones or balls at him, would not have a "right" to proceed to first base when four of those missiles moved quite wide of their mark. This "right" can arise, only through stipulation, within the game constituted by "the rules of baseball." But the same person would nevertheless have a "right" not to be assaulted in this way, without justification, by a mob in the street. This latter right, however, would not depend on whether he was a visitor or a citizen; it would not depend on the peculiarities of the American Constitution, or the "rules" that are created through positive law in any place. It is a right that would arise anywhere, in all places, from the logic of morals or the notion of lawfulness itself. Whether the right is respected depends entirely on the question of whether the local government respects the commands of lawfulness.

Statement A incorporates the recognition that this right to pass freely among the states may be restricted at times *with justification*. This reservation would be recognized even if the United States were a unitary state, administered from the center, without the presence of what we have become accustomed to calling "states." Justice Byrnes had invoked the Commerce Clause, and that clause brought into play the sense of a truly national authority that swept past the borders of the states. Still, the courts had long conceded that the authority of the Congress over commerce would have to accommodate a variety of legitimate local regulations.[18] A harbor, in a particular port, may be especially tricky to navigate, and the local government may have an interest in assuring that the captains of incoming ships have the guidance of helmsmen who are trained in the hazards of negotiating the approaches to the port. And so, as Byrnes made his argument for the dominant authority of the national government, he acknowledged that, even under the Commerce Clause, "the States are not wholly precluded from exercising their power in matters of local concern even though they may thereby affect interstate commerce."[19] Jackson was not the only justice, then, who acknowledged that the states could rightfully impose, at times, barriers to movement. Byrnes had been able to see that point even though he did not view the case with the conceptual lens of the Privileges and Immunities Clause. That insight was just as readily available for anyone who conceived the case, as Byrnes had, from the perspective of the Commerce Clause.

It bears repeating that these provisions for local restraints would very likely have been made even if the American territory had not been divided into states, with political jurisdictions. For the sake of administrative convenience, the police in the street, the teachers in the public schools, would not be required to await, each day, their instructions from Washington. The territory would be divided, more likely, into towns and administrative regions. If the police in any town became aware of a person in their jurisdiction who was fleeing from the authorities in another part of the country, they would probably impede his travels and hold him in custody. They would find themselves imposing the kinds of restraints that were recognized as legitimate by both Byrnes and Jackson. In other words, *the argument could not have been affected, on any decisive point, by the presence or absence of states.* Whether the nation was conceived as a single community, bound up in a flow of commerce, or as a nation that was still divided into local jurisdictions, it was understood in both instances that (1) people had a presumptive right to travel freely within the territory of the United States, but that (2) local jurisdictions may rightfully impose restrictions at times on the movement of persons. Whether or not there were states, the judges would have to encompass the same understandings, and they would have to be brought, finally, to the same point of judgment:

> B. The issue would have to turn, in every case, on the question of whether the restriction that is imposed by the local administration is "justified." But that understanding could not arise from anything contained explicitly in the Constitution. That question can be judged only by consulting the "canons of justification"—the standards that we use more generally when we try to distinguish between the justified or unjustified reasons for restricting personal freedom.

The properties of the problem, as a problem in "justification," might have stood out more clearly if California had blocked the immigration of colored people into the state. For we might have been drawn more readily to this comparison: We would have recognized that the difference between restricting the movement of felons and restricting the movement of black people turned solely on the explanation of why one restriction was justified and the other not. The man accused of a crime could not coherently claim a "right to do a wrong and escape from justice." But in the other case, we could not equate a black man with a felon; we could not regard race as a measure of criminality. At this point, we would need merely to draw on the understandings we have accumulated over the years to explain why it is wrong to impose penalties or disabilities on the basis of race.[20] But once the explanation was set forth in these terms, it might be clearer to lawyers and judges that the ground of the rights and wrongs in the case would not depend on anything that arises from the Commerce Clause or the Privileges and Immunities Clause, or even from the Constitution itself. The understanding that finally proves decisive in settling the constitutional question is an understanding of the "principles of moral judgment"—the standards by which we judge between the ends that are justified or unjustified. In this case, they are the principles that finally explain to us why "poverty and immorality are not synonymous"; why certain restrictions based on poverty cannot be justified.

. . . . .

But even if the case involved distinctions based on race, some lawyers still might not have been drawn to the groundwork of moral understanding, or to the principles of moral judgment, in resolving the case. For some lawyers, the familiar terms of racial discrimination would have triggered an association with another formula, or another clause, in the Constitution. A discrimination with a racial cast may immediately suggest to them that they are dealing with a problem that falls under the Equal Protection of the Laws. This is the clause in the Fourteenth Amendment that has been used most often in striking down racial discriminations that have been fostered in the separate states "under the color of law." And if the restriction on immigrants came, as it did in California, from the laws of the state, then the terms of the Fourteenth Amendment would be apt. Once again, a clause would be invoked as though it were the source of a formula that could settle the case. But even in this case, the Equal Protection Clause would offer no insight, it would supply no principle, that is not available to us through the Commerce Clause, or through the provision on the Privileges and Immunities of Citizens of the United States. And it would not bring us, in the end, to any point but the one we would have to reach, regardless of the path of argument we traversed.

In *Edwards v. California*, Justice Douglas suggested the ingredients of an argument cast in the familiar terms of the Equal Protection Clause, and it is curious in retrospect that he did not make use of that clause, which he and his colleagues would find so serviceable on so many other occasions. Douglas remarked that if California were permitted to exclude from the state people who were poor, the measure would "introduce a caste system utterly incompatible with the spirit of our system of government."

It would permit those who were stigmatized by a State as indigents, paupers, or vagabonds to be relegated to an inferior class of citizenship. It would prevent a citizen because he was poor from seeking new horizons in other States. It might thus withhold from large segments of our people that mobility which is basic to any guarantee of freedom of opportunity. The result would be a substantial dilution of the rights of *national* citizenship, a serious impairment of the principles of equality.[21]

A "caste system"; a stratifying of the population with a superior and an "inferior class" of citizens; a violation of the "principles of equality"—these were the familiar terms and images that attend the grand arguments on the Equal Protection of the Laws. The notion of a "caste system" fits the conception of stratifying that comes along with this analysis. The claim is that the law stratifies the population; it creates a "classification," it marks off classes. One of those classes will have access to the rights and privileges that flow to citizens; the other class will not. *The ground for the denial is the ground of the classification.* If groups are classified, or distinguished, on the basis of race, then race supplies the ground of justification for treating one group differently from another. Let us suppose that the state of California had barred the immigration of black people. The argument, on grounds of Equal Protection, would have arranged itself in this way:

> The State of California has created two classes or tiers of citizens. One is composed of citizens who have the freedom to move in and out of the State without restriction, and the other is constituted by "black persons," who are denied that freedom. The difference in the classes is marked by race; and race is taken as the attribute that justifies the denial, to black people, of the rights that are available to everyone else.

Setting up the problem in its proper cast may help us to notice the ingredients that are critical; but it is necessary to remind ourselves that the problem of the case is not settled once it has been arranged in this cast. To notice a discrimination, to notice that two classes are being treated differently, is not to show that there has been a denial of the Equal Protection of the Laws. There is a need to remind ourselves that the judgment in the problem still finds its pivot elsewhere, and that point may be more evident if we keep the same cast of analysis and simply replace "black persons" with "people fleeing criminal charges." It would read then in this way:

> The State of California has created two classes or tiers of citizens. One is composed of citizens who have the freedom to move in and out of the State without restriction, and the other is constituted by "people fleeing criminal charges," who are denied that freedom.

Faced with this construction, we would not automatically conclude that persons fleeing the law had been denied the Equal Protection of the Laws. The law would have created, in this case, tiers or classes of persons, with different rights. But we would not establish the presence of a wrong merely by establishing the presence of these tiers, with unequal rights. If the ground of restriction is justified, then the distinction between the two classes of persons is warranted. It cannot be wrong or unjustified to restrain the flight of people fleeing criminal charges; therefore the discrimination in the law is a justified discrimination. In that event, no wrong has been done. And if no wrong has been done, there has been no denial of the Equal Protection of the Laws, no violation of the Constitution. The Equal Protection Clause cannot bar, then, *all* discriminations in the law, but only the discriminations that are *unjustified.*

The problem in *Edwards v. California* could have been cast as a problem in the Equal Protection of the Laws just as plausibly as it was cast as a problem of the Commerce Clause or the Privileges and Immunities Clause. But it would not have made the slightest difference in the substance of the argument. The charge could have made been that the state of California created two classes of persons; that it marked off "indigents" as a class of persons who would not have the freedom enjoyed by other persons to move freely in and out of the state. In order to show that there had been a violation of the Equal Protection Clause, it would have been necessary to show why it was not justified to impose, on the indigent, the kinds of restrictions that would have been justified for people who were fleeing criminal charges or carrying contagious diseases. The problem would have come to a focus, once again, on the task of explaining why we may not draw moral inferences about people on the basis merely of their wealth or poverty.

Behind the notion of "equal protection," we are really asked to judge the ground of the classification: When we judge the justification for marking off classes and treating them differently, we are being asked to judge whether the attributes that mark these classes (e.g., race, contagion, the commission of a crime) would justify the imposition of special restrictions or disabilities. But once we are clear on this point, we may be in a position more readily to see how a claim under the Equal Protection Clause can be translated into a claim under the Due Process Clause.

There are, of course, two clauses on the Due Process of Law, and they both bar the government from denying to any person "life, liberty, or property, without due process of law." One clause occurs in the Fifth Amendment, as a restraint on the federal government, and the other was added to the Fourteenth Amendment, as a requirement that may be enforced against the states. Both clauses would appear to be the same, however, in their essential logic. In our own day, jurists of all political persuasions have denounced the tradition of "substantive due process," which flourished in the Court at the end of the nineteenth century and the beginning of the twentieth. And yet, it has become evident by now that the logic of the Due Process Clause goes beyond the provision of ample process or procedure. As the Court recognized in the celebrated case of *Yick Wo v. Hopkins*, it is not enough that a statute be passed with all the formal trappings of legality. At a certain point, the authority of the Court in reviewing the legislation must encompass the question of whether the restrictions or the penalties imposed by the legislation can be substantively justified.[22]

In the case of *Skinner v. Oklahoma* (1942),[23] the legislature marked off certain crimes of moral turpitude, and it was willing to take a record of recidivism as a sign that the tendency to criminality was not merely incorrigible, but genetic. A record of three convictions was taken as the sign of an irremediable criminal bent. After the third conviction, the felon was scheduled for sterilization. In the case of Skinner, the pattern of moral turpitude was described in a record that contained two robberies, including one theft of chickens. The authorities were careful to hold hearings for the sake of establishing that the offender had indeed been convicted of the crimes set forth in the statute, and that the operation would be performed on the right subject. The law provided, in other words, that the offender would have as much "process" as might be "due" him. But in a concurring opinion for the Court, Chief Justice Stone pointed out that the elaboration of procedure did not touch the one point that happened to be critical: The subject was never given the possibility of establishing that he did not in fact belong to a class of offenders whose criminal natures were inheritable.[24]

But to require that kind of procedure was virtually to commit the legislature to a rigorous procedure of science. It would have been necessary to spell out, in operational terms, the evidence that had to be assembled in showing that Skinner's criminal tendencies were genetically transmissible. As Stone must surely have appreciated, the legislature could not have done that without establishing, in turn, the evidence (*a*) that would justify its own surmise that certain kinds of criminality were genetically transmissible, and (*b*) that would justify the finding of the legislature, that chicken-thieving fell into that class. For Stone, it was not enough that the legislature acted in a formally legal way, with a surfeit of procedures. The legislature also had to establish the grounds on which it claimed to know that the punishment of sterilization was relevant and justified. In the absence of that demonstration, Stone was willing to conclude that Skinner had suffered a violation of his person and his liberty without justification—and therefore, "without due process of law."

In that same case, Justice Douglas had been content to settle the judgment on the grounds of the Equal Protection Clause. Douglas thought that the statute revealed its constitutional flaws by inflicting a severe penalty on the chicken thieves, while it left unsterilized the embezzlers, who might be engaged in stealing property worth far more than a few chickens. Stone was moved, however, to point out to his colleague that the statute would hardly have been cleansed of its moral defects if the legislature had gone on, with a proper sense of symmetry, to provide for the sterilization of the embezzlers as well as the chicken thieves.[25] The Equal Protection Clause could not settle the case until the judges had gone on to explain why it was not justified to pick out a certain class of offenders for sterilization. But once the Court did that, there would no longer be any need for the Equal Protection Clause. It would be quite as plausible to say that Skinner, and people like him, were picked out for a special degree of punishment, which could not strictly be justified, and therefore they had suffered a punishment "without due process of law."

To say that the punishment was wrong or unjustified in the case of Skinner was to draw upon the logic that attaches to moral terms such as "justification." A "justification" implies a *principle of justification*, and a principle covers not merely one person but a whole class of people who come within its terms. We can render a judgment then in a particular case, but the decision also implies a judgment on the claims of a whole class of people, who would be covered by the principle contained in the judgment. If it was unjustified for the state of California to bar the entrance of Frank Duncan, the wrong done to Duncan was merely the instance of a wrong *in principle*—the wrong of drawing adverse moral inferences and imposing penalties on people as a result of their poverty. The judgment pronounced by the Court in the case of Duncan or Skinner may settle the claims of these two people, but we understand that the Court has articulated a principle it is willing to honor *in all similar cases*. For that reason, we can move quite as easily back, in translation: from the individual, to the class that the individual represents. And with the same logic, we can translate our argument quite as easily from Due Process to the Equal Protection clause. To say that it was unjustified for the state of Oklahoma to pick out Skinner for the added punishment of sterilization may be the equivalent of saying:

> The State of Oklahoma has created two classes or tiers of people in its system of criminal justice. One class will not suffer any punishment beyond confinement, but another class will suffer the additional penalty of sterilization if its criminal natures are thought to be incorrigible and inheritable.

In this manner, an argument cast in the terms of Due Process is easily translated into an argument under the Equal Protection Clause. I think the point may be confirmed even more compellingly for us if we consider a brace of examples in which the Supreme Court itself has engaged in the translation I have described here. But the judges did not explain, in these cases, the translation they were making. They did not exactly go out of their way to draw the attention of their readers, or to let the public in on the secret of how portable, in fact, these clauses may be.

·   ·   ·   ·   ·

In 1971, in *Reed v. Reed*, the Court encountered the case of a minor who had died intestate in Idaho. The adoptive parents of Richard Reed had been separated before his death. About seven months after his death, his mother, Sally Reed, filed a petition to act as the administratrix of her son's rather modest estate.[26] But a competing petition was filed by the father, Cecil Reed, who sought to have himself declared the administrator of his son's estate. A probate court heard the petitions and discovered that its judgment on the matter was controlled by the Idaho Code, which commanded a preference in these cases for the father. The statutes in Idaho listed the classes of persons who were entitled to administer the estates of people who had died intestate (i.e., without wills to apportion their estates). Among those classes was "the father or mother." But another section of the laws stipulated that "[o]f several persons claiming and equally entitled to administer, males must be preferred to females, and relatives of the whole to those of the half blood."[27]

This curious provision found its place in a set of statutes that recognized the competence of women, along with men, to act as administrators of estates. In the case of a married man who died intestate, the law assigned the authority of administration to the wife, over the claims of a son, father, brother, or any other male relative. When a designation was made in favor of parents over siblings, the authority was accorded to both parents. Nevertheless, when the parents fell out of accord, or the administrators came into conflict, the law fixed a preference for males over females. As the Supreme Court of Idaho understood the law, the concern had been to reduce the delay and expense of hearings, and to diminish the load on the probate courts. That end would be accomplished by settling the authority on one of the two parties who were competent to administer the estate. In this perspective, there was no harm to the interests of the estate, and the procedures could help avert that melancholy situation in which the expenses of litigation could exhaust the assets of a modest legacy. On this basis, the court in Idaho came to the judgment that the ends of the legislation justified the preference that was assigned to males.

But the Supreme Court reversed the judgment. Chief Justice Burger held, with his colleagues, that the interests of the state in reducing litigation could not justify this "mandatory preference to members of either sex over members of the other." The ends of the legislation were plausible, but the preference assigned on the basis of sex represented "the very kind of arbitrary legislative choice forbidden by the Equal Protection Clause of the Fourteenth Amendment."[28]

As the problem arranged itself under the Equal Protection Clause, the state had established the categories of persons who were entitled to act as the administrators of estates. But it then proceeded to create two classes or tiers among the people who were presumably qualified to administer. If those classes had been defined by attributes such as "training in the law," or "closeness to the deceased," the basis of the classification might have borne a faintly rational connection to the legitimate object of the law in finding administrators who were competent to their tasks and sympathetic to the wishes of the deceased. But the difference between the classes in this case was marked solely by sex. That arrangement invited the kind of errant commentary brought forth by the counsel for Cecil Reed, when he argued that the law was predicated on the assumption that "men [are] as a rule more conversant with business affairs than . . . women."[29] Even if that proposition were true most of the time, it was not true in all cases, and there was no consideration of whether it happened to be true in this particular case. In fact, if the Court had not been drawn to the discrimination between men and women, the case could have suggested itself as a classic example of "due process." The precise purpose of the legislation was to foreclose hearings or procedures. And yet, if the law had simply permitted the probate court to hold hearings, to weigh the claims and gauge the competence of the contending parties, there would have been no need to legislate a preference for men, as a class, over women as a class. Under the familiar terms of the Due Process Clause, the Court could have held that the law created a disability for a person on the basis of sex; that the attribute of sex could not justify the disability; and that the state had provided no hearings to determine whether the assignment on the basis of sex really served the interests of the estate in selecting the most competent administrator. Burger and his colleagues took the same ingredients, but simply arranged them to fit the terms of a judgment based on Equal Protection:

> [D]ifferent treatment [was] accorded to persons placed by a statute into different classes on the basis of criteria wholly unrelated to the objective of that statute. A classification "must be reasonable, not arbitrary, and must rest upon some ground of difference having a fair and substantial relation to the object of the legislation, so that all persons similarly circumstanced shall be treated alike." . . . The question presented by this case, then, is whether a difference in the sex of competing applicants for letters of administration bears a rational relationship to a state objective that is sought to be advanced by the operation of [the statute].[30]

A little more than a year later, the Court leaned on its holding in *Reed v. Reed* when it encountered a case arising from the Air Force. Once again the Court found an arrangement that created a stratification of sorts between men and women. In this case the legal procedures worked, overall, to confer benefits on women as a class. But they worked, nevertheless, by imposing, on women, burdens of litigation that were not imposed on men. Sharron Frontiero was a lieutenant in the Air Force, and she had claimed her husband, Joseph, as a "dependent." She sought then the enlarged allowances for housing and medical benefits that would be granted without question to any male in the Air Force who listed his wife as a dependent. In the case of a woman, however, there was a need to demonstrate that her spouse was actually dependent on her for more than half of his support. This degree of dependency Frontiero failed to demonstrate, and her claim was denied.[31] The awkward result was that benefits were withheld from Frontiero that were not withheld from male members of the Air Force, who provided no larger support to their wives than Frontiero had furnished to her husband. And the men could receive these benefits precisely because they were not compelled, in the way that women were compelled, to demonstrate their need.

The Court recited no evidence to show that there were in fact such men, with wives no more dependent than Frontiero's husband. But the government did not pretend to deny that there very likely *were* such men. The government contended, rather, that it was simply not worth the expense of holding hearings that would mainly confirm what was, after all, a plain fact rooted in our conventions—namely, that there were more wives "dependent" on the incomes of their husbands than husbands dependent on the support of their wives. As Justice Brennan summed it up,

> [T]he Government argues that Congress might reasonably have concluded that it would be both cheaper and easier simply conclusively to presume that wives of male members are financially dependent on their husbands, while burdening female members with the task of establishing dependency in fact.[32]

But the Court was no more disposed to honor the claims of "administrative convenience" in this case than it was in *Reed v. Reed*. Burdens of litigation were being assigned or withheld here solely on the basis of sex, and from these different burdens different benefits flowed. Officers with similar relations to their spouses were nevertheless separated into different classes and treated differently for no reason other than their sex. Justice Brennan was willing to invoke the language and the line of argument in *Reed*: the arrangements created "dissimilar treatment for men and women who are . . . similarly situated." Brennan went on to his culmination: "We therefore conclude that, by according differential treatment to male and female members of the uniformed services for the sole purpose of achieving administrative convenience, the challenged statutes violate. . . ."—what part of the Constitution? Brennan had drawn, from *Reed*, the notion of "dissimilar" or "differential treatment" for men and women. The language was identified with the Equal Protection Clause. Brennan cited *Reed*, and he professed to be following precisely along the lines of the argument in that earlier case. As the language rolled on, the reader might have expected that Brennan would finally invoke the clause on which the decision in *Reed* had been based—the Equal Protection

Clause of the Fourteenth Amendment. But in the Supreme Court Reports, the page turns, and the clause we find standing at the end of the text is . . . the Due Process Clause of the Fifth Amendment.

One sentence earlier, Brennan had quoted from *Reed* that the discriminations based on sex involved the "very kind of arbitrary legislative choice forbidden by the [Constitution]." Brennan had removed, from the original passage, the "Equal Protection Clause of the Fourteenth Amendment." In its place he had put, in brackets, the "[Constitution]." Precisely why he had to make this shift should be clear: The Equal Protection Clause is found in the Fourteenth Amendment, which is addressed to the action of states. But the policies that were challenged in *Frontiero* were established by the *federal government.* There is no Equal Protection Clause that is addressed to the federal government. Brennan had to reach for a serviceable clause, which could be a vehicle for the same reasoning that was used by the Court in *Reed v. Reed*, and what came plausibly to hand was the Due Process Clause.

As I have tried to show, this kind of translation was quite legitimate. To show why sex could not be a justified ground for a classification in the law in a case at hand is to show why it cannot be a ground on which to justify the imposing of burdens or the assignment of disabilities. And if the state imposes a restriction on grounds that cannot be justified, we might as readily say that the state is imposing restrictions without "due process of law." The translation is readily made, and Justice Brennan, in this case, readily made it. But what I take as critical here is the silent admission by the Court and Justice Brennan that little of this argument over clauses makes any substantive difference. When the Equal Protection Clause was not available, an argument which had been formed explicitly to fit the cast of the Fourteenth Amendment was simply replicated, without change, and offered under the Due Process Clause of the Fifth Amendment. The grafting was done, the shift was made, without anyone sensing the need to offer even the hint of an explanation.

Of course, the maneuver invited another interpretation: The Court remained silent while it performed this jural shell game because the judges still did not know how to explain this translation they were making. By now they had become used to treating these clauses in the Constitution as though they were interchangeable. Still, they could not offer an account as to why these clauses should be treated, on certain days, as though they were freighted with a special juridical significance, and then treated, on other days, as though they were merely labels, which could be attached to any case as it suited the needs of the judges. The telling event here was the most dramatic occasion in which the Court was compelled to make the translation, and it became plain, to every onlooker, that the judges could not really offer an account of what they were doing. That occasion arose in the aftermath of *Brown v. Board of Education*. The Court had just declared that the racial segregation of children in the public schools violated the Equal Protection Clause of the Fourteenth Amendment. But in a companion case, the Court considered a comparable scheme of segregation in the schools of the District of Columbia. The District was administered, however, under the authority of the federal government, and so the Fourteenth Amendment could have no bearing on the case. Chief Justice Warren was sufficiently candid to admit this point of awkwardness. The Court would have to make use of the Due Process Clause of the Fifth Amendment—but how would the translation be made? The Court had already explained that the wrong in segregation inhered in the violation of the principle of "equality," marked in the Equal Protection of the Laws. But where was the denial of "due process" in these cases? The chief justice apparently preserved a straight face and pushed on with the insistence that the two clauses were "not mutually exclusive": that somehow, at some place, for some reason that remained inexplicable, the Equal Protection Clause and the Due Process Clause faded into one another. What the chief justice offered as an explanation was evidently lame, but it was, quite as evidently, the best he could manage.

> The "equal protection of the laws" is a more explicit safeguard of prohibited unfairness than "due process of law," and therefore, we do not imply that the two are always interchangeable phrases. But, as this Court has recognized, discrimination may be so unjustifiable as to be violative of due process. [33]

It was, in short, an explanation that did not explain. The judges were apparently aware that the critical standards of judgment in these cases were not contained in the clauses of any of these amendments. They would persist over the years in citing the clauses; they would keep up the charade, since it was a ritual that would seem at least familiar and intelligible to their audience. But if they could have commanded the kind of philosophic understanding that was needed to explain, at the root, their real principles of judgment, they could have done far more than spare us a generation of play-acting in the training of new lawyers. They could have explained, with far more coherence, how they would move, in succeeding cases, from segregation in public schools, to segregation in swimming pools and parks and places of public accommodation. At the same time, they could have avoided the massive distractions they would weave into their jurisprudence with "reverse discrimination" and the racial assignment of students in the schools. [34]

．　．　．　．　．

It is a modest blessing that the work of the judges has not yet attracted the attention of those new Hegelians in the academy, who have carried their arts of interpretation to literature and aesthetics, as well as to politics and history, and who have sought to make every subject more deeply comprehensible by making it more enduringly inscrutable. The Hegelians might be tempted to suggest that the course of the judges here reflects an unfolding logic of which the judges themselves are unaware: The judges may be impelled, by a force of Reason inaccessible to them, to move along novel paths and make apt translations, which they themselves, however, seem incapable of understanding. Hence, Justice Brennan and his colleagues continued to shift from one clause in the Constitution to another, as it suited their needs. And yet they persevered in disputing over the fitness of these clauses in any case, as though the difference bore a vast, juridical significance.

I have already noted the confusions on this point that could distract even a judge as urbane as Robert Jackson. But the puzzlement suffered by Jackson in *Edwards v. California* did not abate with the years of his seasoning as a jurist. Eight years later, Jackson flexed his considerable wit in pleading with his colleagues that they use the Equal Protection Clause rather than the Due Process Clause when they presumed to strike down the ordinances of local governments. In the aftermath of the war, Jackson had become more acutely aware of the responsibilities borne by local governments in furnishing the most immediate protections of the law. He became ever more concerned then about a Court that would intervene too casually and remove, from local officials, the authority they required in coping, directly, with the threats to civic peace.[35] Jackson finally persuaded himself that the Equal Protection Clause was a far more benign instrument for the Court in this respect: Far more than the Due Process Clause, it would permit the Court to check the abuses of law at the local level without depriving local governments of the authority they needed to govern.

Jackson was inspired to these reflections by a case involving the regulation of traffic in New York City. For the sake, ostensibly, of reducing the distractions for drivers, the city had passed an ordinance that forbade the operation of what was called an "advertising vehicle." The statute provided an exemption, however, for vehicles used in making deliveries, so long as the owners of these vehicles were advertising only their own businesses. A suit was brought by Railway Express, which deployed about 1,900 trucks in New York City. Railway Express augmented its earnings by spreading, on the sides of its vans, posters that advertised other businesses. The company was convicted and fined for operating in violation of the local ordinance, and when the company challenged the ordinance on appeal, the Supreme Court upheld the local ordinance in a unanimous decision.[36] The company had challenged the ordinance in the familiar terms of the Equal Protection Clause, and that challenge was not without merit. Even as Justice Douglas dismissed the claim, his partial recitation of the argument revealed its strands of plausibility.

Is is said . . . that one of appellant's trucks carrying the advertisement of a commercial house would not cause any greater distraction of pedestrians and vehicle drivers than if the commercial house carried the same advertisement on its own truck. Yet the regulation allows the latter to do what the former is forbidden from doing. It is therefore contended that the classification which the regulation makes has no relation to the traffic problem since a violation turns not on what kind of advertisements are carried on trucks but on whose trucks they are carried.[37]

If a sign on a truck was sufficiently attractive to catch the eye and cause a hazard in traffic, it is hard to fathom why the danger should be diminished in any way if the sign was advertising the business of the carrier. But the argument in the cast of Equal Protection could surely have been pressed further: Could we be warranted in assuming that any signs on moving vehicles would always be more distracting in traffic than signs that are stationary? Would a sign for a local florist, displayed on a truck, be more likely to arrest attention and cause necks to turn than a mammoth pair of lips, emitting smoke in Times Square? To the plausible questions unfolding along these lines, Douglas was content to "answer" by confessing his want of "omniscience."

> The local authorities may well have concluded that those who advertise their own wares on their trucks do not present the same traffic problem in view of the nature or extent of the advertising which they use. It would take a degree of omniscience which we lack to say that such is not the case. If that judgment is correct, the advertising displays that are exempt have less incidence on traffic than those of appellants.[38]

No one familiar with the works of Justice Douglas would have supposed, even at the time, that he would have professed the same want of competence if a local government had "concluded," in a similar way, that it could ban only the leaflets passed out by certain political or religious sects, since the leaflets were far more likely to be thrown on the street and cause a problem of littering. A different reflex would have been triggered: Douglas and his colleagues would probably have demanded that the local authorities find a less restrictive means of achieving the same ends, or that they act with a statute that applies far more evenly across the wide range of groups that distribute leaflets and inspire litter.

Justice Jackson was willing to uphold, in this case, the restraints that were imposed on people who engaged in advertising "for hire." But he thought there was considerable force to the arguments that were being raised by Railway Express in the cast of the Equal Protection Clause, and he took the plausibility of those arguments as the ground for pointing up, to his colleagues, the useful discipline that came into play with that clause.

> [T]here is no more effective practical guaranty against arbitrary and unreasonable government than to require that the principles of law which officials impose upon a minority must be imposed generally. Conversely, nothing opens the door to

arbitrary action so effectively as to allow those officials to pick and choose only a few to whom they will apply legislation and thus to escape the political retribution that might be visited upon them if larger numbers were effected. Courts can take no better measure to assure that laws will be just than to require that laws be equal in operation. . . .

Even casual observations from the sidewalks of New York will show that an ordinance which would forbid all advertising on vehicles would run into conflict with many interests, including some, if not all, of the great metropolitan newspapers, which use that advertising extensively. Their blandishment of the latest sensations is not less a cause of diverted attention and traffic hazard than the commonplace cigarette advertisement which this truck-owner is forbidden to display. But any regulation applicable to all such advertising would require much clearer justification in local conditions to enable its enactment than does some regulation applicable to a few. I do not mention this to criticize the motives of those who enacted this ordinance, but it dramatizes the point that we are much more likely to find arbitrariness in the regulation of the few than of the many.[39]

Perhaps the framers of the local ordinance really did believe that the hazards created by advertising were far graver when the advertising was carried on vehicles—and for products other than one's own. It is more likely, however, that the local councilmen were not really keen on pushing an ordinance that would cut against the interests of the *New York Times* and the *Daily News*. The delivery trucks of those enterprises were very much in evidence, as they sped through the city, blaring on their sides a late headline, or bearing, in bold letters, advertisements for themselves. Nor could we imagine that the councilmen were very anxious to take on the owners of commercial real estate in Manhattan. These merchants had made a considerable business, after all, in renting spaces for garish, outsized signs, designed precisely for the purpose of grabbing attention from the passing traffic. In short, the local politicians were probably willing to go as far, in dealing with the distractions to traffic, as they could politically afford.

But as Justice Jackson understood, this is where the Court could make a contribution to the discipline of legislating. By holding local government to the requirements of the Equal Protection Clause, the Court could force the authorities to face the principled implications of their own policies. For Jackson, the Equal Protection Clause seemed to engage the logic of what philosophers would understand as the test of "universalizability."[40] Once the local councilmen defined the terms of the legislation, were they willing to apply those terms universally, to everyone who fell within their categories? If their concern was with the distractions to traffic produced by advertising, were they willing to apply the proscription to all advertising that posed these dangers? Of course, the test of "universalizability" merely expressed the logic of a moral principle, the logic that was contained in Kant's categorical imperative. That imperative has been expressed with several variations, but it may be para-phrased in this way: Act only on that maxim which you could will at the same time as a universal law.[41] Part of the salutary discipline in making use of this device is that it may alert the practitioners to the fuller implications of the policy they are proposing. In the case of the legislators in New York, it would put the question of whether they are really willing to honor the full sweep of the policy and apply it to all persons, to all interests, who fall within the terms of their legislation. If they are reluctant, their hesitation may reveal that they are not entirely confident that they could justify a policy of that breadth. They may be encouraged then to reflect more searchingly on the problem, and to consider again whether they could really supply, for their policy, a compelling justification. That discipline may move them in two directions, both legitimate, both wholesome: They may, in fact, become clearer about the principle that justifies the legislation. In that event, they may find their way to a policy that stands, with a clearer justification, in reaching the fuller range of its objects. On the other hand, they may discover that they cannot really justify their policy if it were applied consistently, to every case that came within its terms (e.g., to all signs that created distractions in traffic). They may come then to the judgment that they should recede: that they should not impose laws when they cannot define a principle they are willing to apply in its full logic.

There has been no more dramatic example of this exercise than that frag-ment written by Lincoln, in which he imagined a conversation with an owner of slaves about the justification for holding men as property. I had the occa-sion in chapter 2 to cite at length from those notes Lincoln had set down for himself. ("You mean the whites are *intellectually* the superiors of blacks, and, therefore have the right to enslave them? Take care again. By this rule, you are to be slave to the first man you meet, with an intellect superior to your own."[42]) That fragment stands as a model of "principled reasoning," or the application of the "universalizability" test. As Lincoln deftly argued, there was nothing that could be said to justify the enslavement of black people that could not be applied to whites as well. His purpose in this fragment was not to argue for a *broader* policy of enslavement, which could take in whites as well as blacks. His object, rather, was to show that there was no defensible principle that could justify the enslavement of blacks, or any other race of human beings. Again, he made use of what the philosophers would call the "universalizability principle" or the categorical imperative. Justice Jackson correctly understood that this logic of moral reasoning was reflected in the Equal Protection Clause, but somehow he had come under the curious per-suasion that this device always worked in favor of broadening or expanding a policy that was found defective. But as Lincoln managed to show, this exer-cise of moral reasoning may be used quite as aptly to encourage people to back away—to abandon altogether a policy that is indefensible.

For some unaccountable reason, this use of the categorical imperative, this property of moral reasoning, seemed to be lost upon Justice Jackson. It was nowhere incorporated in his understanding as he sought to make his case for the special utility of the Equal Protection Clause. Jackson noted that the dominant inclination of the Court at the time was to use the Due Process Clause when striking down a local ordinance. He found a need, however, to remind his colleagues that there were two clauses on Due Process, one bearing on the states and the other on the federal government. If the Court held that a certain local statute violated the Due Process Clause of the Fourteenth Amendment, then by a parity of reasoning, a similar statute in the federal government would violate the Due Process Clause of the Fifth Amendment. Therefore, when the Court struck down a local ordinance on the basis of the Due Process Clause, it was not restraining only the local government: implicitly, it was barring the federal government from using the same statute or enforcing the same policy.[43] But in contrast, Jackson thought that this vast disarming effect could be avoided through the use of the Equal Protection Clause: "Invocation of the equal protection clause . . . does not disable any governmental body from dealing with the subject at hand. It merely means that the prohibition or regulation must have a broader impact."[44]

In this rare case, Jackson's subtlety was apparently founded on a serious misunderstanding: He earnestly seemed to believe that if the Court had used the Equal Protection Clause to strike down the ordinance in New York, the city would have been far less disabled, or constrained, in its authority to legislate on the hazards caused by advertising. As he imagined the legal scene, the city would have been encouraged, rather, to broaden the coverage of its law. But if the Court had used the Equal Protection Clause for the purpose of introducing the legislators in New York to the discipline of the categorical imperative, it is not at all clear that the legislators would have returned with a new, broader statute. They might have receded from the project altogether. In that case, the result could have been the reverse of what Jackson had anticipated. If the Court had struck down the local statute on the ground of Equal Protection, it might have discouraged the legislators from passing any new law on the subject. In effect, it could have disarmed the legislators, as surely as any judgment handed down under the Due Process Clause.

But did the Due Process Clause really disarm? When the Court used the Due Process Clause on behalf of Sharron Frontiero, it did not strike down the entire policy of the government in supporting the dependents of people in the armed services. It left the rest of the policy standing, and it merely compelled the government to revise its regulations in dealing with the dependents of women. In the famous *Slaughter House Cases* (1873), Justice Field was willing to use the Due Process Clause and deny to New Orleans the authority to create a monopoly in the slaughtering of animals. But Field did not think that the Due Process Clause would bar the state from regulating the slaughter houses in the interest of public health.[45]

To say, with the voice of the Due Process Clause, that the authorities have legislated, in one field, in an unwarranted way, is not to prevent them from legislating again, on the same subject, with a law cleansed of its previous defects. In that respect the Due Process Clause is not in any way more restrictive for local governments. Nor is the Equal Protection Clause the only clause that can offer instruction to a local government in the requirements of moral reasoning. The Due Process Clause may serve quite as well in leading the judges or the legislators to the question of whether freedom is being restricted in any instance, whether a penalty is being imposed, without a demanding justification.

One clause does not guide us more surely along this path than another. To ask whether a statute treats like cases equally; to ask whether the law honors the logic of a principle by applying universally, to all cases that come within its terms—to engage these properties of moral reasoning we do not require the Equal Protection Clause. When Kant articulated the categorical imperative in Germany in the eighteenth century, he did not have the benefit of the Equal Protection Clause of the Fourteenth Amendment. As we have already recalled, the same logic of principled reasoning was exemplified in the Old Testament in the story of David and Bathsheba. Nathan appealed to this logic of moral reasoning when he reproached David over the killing of Uriah and the stealing of his wife.[46] In the *Republic*, Plato had Socrates observe that there was, of course, a "natural" difference between a bald man and a man with hair, but nothing in that natural difference bore on the competence of the bald man to be a shoemaker. Socrates went on to say, in the dialogue, that it was necessary to pay heed "solely to the kind of diversity and homogeneity that was pertinent to the pursuits themselves."[47] If the presence or absence of hair bore no relation to the making of shoes, it could not be justified to bar any man from the trade of making shoes because he happened to be bald. And of course, the analogy that Plato offered here was applied to the differences in "nature" between men and women; the differences that were regarded, in common opinion, as a justification for excluding women from the sharing of political authority.

Evidently, Plato was able to grasp these points without the benefit of the Equal Protection Clause or the Fourteenth Amendment. He could grasp them because they were simply bound up with the logic of moral reasoning. Anyone tutored in the rudiments of moral reasoning would be able to raise the question of whether privileges and disabilities were being assigned on the basis of attributes (e.g., baldness, sex) that bore no rational relation to the end in view (the making of shoes, the governance of the state). One would understand the question of whether a penalty was being inflicted on the basis of a reason that could not justify the inflicting of a harm. And even without much formal instruction, one could be led easily to understand why "like cases ought to be treated alike." That may explain why the British have been able to enact laws barring discrimination based on race, even though they have not had the guidance of a Fourteenth Amendment or a written Constitution. Charles Black once remarked, quite aptly, that "there are fifty-two words which we come close to using for everything. . . .[the fifty-two words that make up] the three celebrated prohibitory clauses of the Fourteenth Amendment. . . . Where would we be, I wonder, if it had happened that these three clauses were not there?"[48] Is it really conceivable that we could not have recognized and justified those rights we have been able to draw out as implications arising from the Fourteenth Amendment? Or might we have discovered those rights, as Black suggested, by deliberating along other paths? We might have established the ground of our judgment in those deeper principles that were simply implicit in the structure of the Constitution, in the most elementary logic of that decision in 1787 to replace a confederation of states with a *national government*. But we might have found some of those rights contained, where the British and others have found them, in the very logic of acting "justly": We treat like cases alike. We do not draw adverse judgments about people on the basis of attributes, such as height or color, which are wholly wanting in moral significance. We do not hold people blameworthy for acts they were powerless to affect. For these understandings we do not require the Fourteenth Amendment. As I have tried to show, the situation is rather the other way around: We manage to apply the Fourteenth Amendment to practical cases because we can appeal, at the point of judgment, to the canons of moral reasoning.

G. K. Chesterton once sketched out a work of science fiction in which a group of earnest explorers sail off from England in the hope of reaching and surveying an unknown country. They finally sight land, they are filled with excitement as they arrive on the beach, and find that they have landed at . . . Brighton. The judges of our own day have set off to create a radical expansion of constitutional rights and the Fourteenth Amendment, and they have landed persistently on a ground of moral argument that is virtually indifferent to clauses, or to any of the provisions in a written Constitution. But they are unwitting explorers. They cannot quite give an account of their travels or the wondrous things they have discovered. They have acted in the style of men who have rediscovered natural law, and yet they themselves can speak only the language of legal positivism. They have helped to spin out a jurisprudence that depends on conversations or deliberations, which can be resolved finally by appealing to the principles of moral judgment. And yet almost all of these judges have been taught to doubt there are in fact such knowable principles of right and wrong, which may furnish a discipline of judgment. The result is that our jurists have reached decisions untethered by the traditional formulas in the Constitution, but without having the least comprehension, themselves, of the moral philosophy that would render this whole enterprise intelligible.

I have concentrated, in this chapter, on cases in which there was no serious division in the Court about the proper outcomes. The disputes were focused entirely on the question of just what clause in the Constitution would provide the most illuminating ground for the judgment at hand. These simpler cases helped to reveal then, in their simplicity, the rather more tangled confusions that affected the judges on the meaning of the constitutional text and the import of the most notable clauses. In the next chapter I would carry the problem into a field in which the Court has been strained, once again, by a serious division over the meaning of the clauses and amendments, but in cases of far graver consequence. Those cases have involved the constitutional ground for the Civil Rights Acts, the limits of jurisdiction under federalism, and the reach of the national government. With a short glance back in history, the problem begins with the competence of the federal government to protect black victims at the hands of the local police. But as the question advances to our own day, it involves the problem of whether the federal government may legislate directly to protect retarded children from the withdrawal of medical treatment at the hands of their own parents. The question becomes entangled in the coils of the Constitution and in the straining over the statutes, but the question, reduced to its essential parts, will remain: Is there a class of wrongs, within the reach of the law, but outside the reach of the national government? Are there wrongs that the federal government may reach, but not in the first instance? The problem obliges us to consider whether the national government must wait upon the action of the states, or whether it may act directly, on its own authority, in the first instance, in reaching serious wrongs regardless of whether those wrongs are committed by policemen, doctors, or parents.

SIX

THE SWEEP OF CIVIL RIGHTS AND THE MAZE OF
FEDERALISM

THE POLICE DEPARTMENT in Chicago has suffered, in its history, curious moments of inattentiveness, but it has rarely been accused of being sissified. In a department so constituted, Detective Frank Pape still managed to stand out as a buccaneer, without many redeeming, romantic features. One of his escapades in the 1950s ended up in a federal court, with litigation under the Civil Rights Acts. The most vivid account of the case was offered, in the Supreme Court, in the dissenting opinion. It was offered, that is, by the judge who was willing to withhold, from Pape, the punishment of federal law, because he was anxious not to make the adventures of Detective Pape the business of the federal courts. Justice Frankfurter set forth this stark account of the facts:

> The complaint alleges that on October 29, 1958, at 5:45 a.m., thirteen Chicago police officers, led by Deputy Chief of Detectives Pape, broke through two doors of the Monroe apartment, woke the Monroe couple with flashlights, and forced them at gunpoint to leave their bed and stand naked in the center of the living room; that the officers roused the six Monroe children and herded them into the living room; that Detective Pape struck Mr. Monroe several times with his flashlight, calling him "nigger" and "black boy"; that another officer pushed Mrs. Monroe; that other officers hit and kicked several of the children and pushed them to the floor; that the police ransacked every room, throwing clothing from closets to the floor, dumping drawers, ripping mattress covers; that Mr. Monroe was then taken to the police station and detained on "open" charges for ten hours, during which time he was interrogated about a murder and exhibited in lineups; that he was not brought before a magistrate, although numerous magistrate's courts were accessible; that he was not advised of his procedural rights; that he was not permitted to call his family or an attorney; that he was subsequently released without criminal charges having been filed against him. It is also alleged that the actions of the officers throughout were without authority of a search warrant or an arrest warrant.[1]

Monroe and his family sought damages, under the Civil Rights Acts, against the City of Chicago and the police officers who engaged in this escapade. By the fullness and vividness of the account, we may readily infer the judgment that Justice Frankfurter had reached about the conduct of the police.[2] But here, as in a series of similar cases, Frankfurter forcefully held to the judgment that the wrongs displayed in the case were beyond the reach of the federal government. In Frankfurter's view, the wrongs of the case found their proper—and fuller—vindication under the laws of the state and the city. Frankfurter well understood that, with the mandate of the Fourteenth Amendment, the federal government could intervene in the separate states to protect people in their civil rights: The national government could vindicate certain wrongs that were suffered at the hands of local figures who were clothed with the authority of law. But it could also protect its citizens from the assaults that were launched by private persons, with the purpose of intimidating people in the exercise of their rights. The authority of the federal government could be flexed in the form of criminal prosecutions, or the sanction of the law could be applied simply by having the federal courts open to civil suits, to private actions for damages that were brought by the victims. The provision on civil suits was added in 1871; and since that time, also, the statutes on criminal and civil remedies have been further divided into two sections, conveying two descriptions of the offenders who inspired the concerns of the law. The enduring question has been whether the two sections have sought to protect the rights of different groups of victims, and whether the "rights" they would protect are essentially the same. These sections have retained their distinctive cast over the years, through several incarnations and revisions. In our current statutes, the sections are marked with the designation of 18 U.S.C., Sections 241 and 242 (criminal prosecutions) and 42 U.S.C., Sections 1983 and 1985 (civil suits). One section refers to any person who acts "under color of any law, statute, ordinance, regulation, or custom" and "willfully subjects any inhabitant" of the country to the "deprivation of any rights, privileges, or immunities secured or protected by the Constitution or laws of the United States, or to different punishments . . . on account of such inhabitant being an alien, or by reason of his color, or race, than are prescribed for the punishment of citizens" (18 U.S.C., Section 242; or its equivalent for civil suits, 42 U.S.C., Section 1983).

The other section does not refer to people bearing a connection to official authority. It speaks, rather, of "two or more persons" who "conspire to injure, oppress, threaten, or intimidate any citizen in the free exercise or enjoyment of any right or privilege secured to him by the Constitution or laws of the United States." An additional paragraph in this section mentions "persons who go in disguise on the highway, or on the premises of another, with intent to prevent or hinder his free exercise or enjoyment of any right or privilege secured" by the Constitution (18 U.S.C., Section 241; and see its equivalent for civil suits, 42 U.S.C., Section 1985). Evidently, the Congress did not have in mind trick-or-treaters. This passage in the law was brought forth by the experience with the Ku Klux Klan in the 1860s, and it persistently alerts us to this possibility: Certain groups may operate outside the law, under "pri-

vate" organization, but they flourish in some instances with the active collab-
oration of the local authorities. Or, they succeed because they have managed
to intimidate the local police into a complaisant weakness.

In *Monroe v. Pape*, Detective Pape and his band carried badges; they were
all agents of the city, clothed with the authority of law. Pape had acted "under
the color of law," but still, Frankfurter was not persuaded that the case came
within the terms of the federal statute. For reasons that were rooted in the
logic of federalism, Frankfurter had separated himself from his colleagues on
this question in two other, notable cases. Fourteeen years earlier, in *Screws v.
United States*,[3] Frankfurter had been convinced that the Civil Rights Acts
could not be applied in a criminal prosecution against a sheriff and two of his
deputies, who had beaten and killed a man in their custody. Sheriff Screws
had arrested Robert Hall, a young black man, about thirty years old, on the
charge of stealing a tire. With this charge, Hall was taken in handcuffs to the
courthouse, but as he emerged from the car, the three officers began to beat
him with their fists and a blackjack. As the Court recounted the facts, Hall
was beaten until he was unconscious and then he was "dragged feet first
through the court-house yard into the jail and thrown upon the floor dying.
An ambulance was called and Hall was removed to a hospital where he died
within the hour and without regaining consciousness. There was evidence
that Screws held a grudge against Hall and had threatened to 'get' him."[4]

Justice Frankfurter joined his colleagues, Jackson and Roberts, in declaring
that "this brutal misconduct rendered these lawless law officers guilty of man-
slaughter, if not of murder, under Georgia law." And it was under the laws of
Georgia that they ought to be tried, for they could be tried in Georgia for
murder. Under the Civil Rights Acts, Screws and his henchmen could be
tried only for the "deprivation" of civil rights, an offense that could bring a
penalty, under federal law, of one thousand dollars or one year in jail, or at
most, both. The disparity between the two levels of punishment marked the
traditional understanding of where the primary responsibility lay in addressing
the most familiar, serious crimes of the common law. The main concern of
Frankfurter, Jackson, and Roberts was not with the trivial penalty administered by the federal law, but with the prospect of rearranging, in a vast, portentous way, the assignments of legal and moral responsibility in the federal
system. As the jurists noted, "Instead of leaving this misdeed to vindication
by Georgia law, the United States deflected Georgia's responsibility by insti-
tuting a federal prosecution."

> The only issue is whether Georgia alone has the power and duty to punish, or
> whether this patently local crime can be made the basis of a federal prosecution.
> The practical question is whether the states should be relieved from responsibility
> to bring their law officers to book for homicide, by allowing prosecutions in the
> federal courts for a relatively minor offense carrying a short sentence.[5]

Six years later, Justice Frankfurter managed to assemble three other colleagues in support of his position, and in a rare, fleeting moment, he was finally able to make a case come out his way. In the case at hand, a firm in Miami, discreetly referred to as "a Florida corporation," hired a private detective to investigate the persisting theft of its property. The detective was joined in the project by two of his employees and a member of the police in Miami, who was assigned to help in the investigation. Suspicion fell on a few employees of the corporation, and the team of detectives soon settled on this speedy, economical procedure: The suspects were taken, one at a time, to a shack owned by the company. There they were subjected to the classic "third degree," and as Justice Frankfurter noted, this regimen of "blows, kicks, threats, and prolonged exposure to a brilliant light, yielded 'confessions.' "[6]

The director of this production, Williams, was subsequently indicted, along with other members of his crew, under the criminal provisions in the Civil Rights Acts. Williams was convicted under the section that proscribed acts carried out "under color of any law, statute, ordinance, regulation, or custom." The other defendants were acquitted under that section. The group was prosecuted, also, under the other part of the statute, which dealt with the conspiracies of private persons to deprive citizens of their constitutional rights. All of the defendants were convicted, but the convictions were overturned in the court of appeals. With Justice Frankfurter writing the opinion, the Supreme Court sustained the judgment of the appellate court, namely, that the Civil Rights Act was wrongly applied to the conspiracy of private persons, and to the abuse of rights, which had taken place in this case. The involvement of a policeman had furnished a slender thread of connection to the police department in Miami. And that thread was used to bring Williams under an indictment for acting "under the color of law," even though he was acting as a private detective. But Frankfurter took the occasion to explain, again, why neither section of the Civil Rights Acts could be used as the basis of a prosecution in a case of this kind.

Sheriff Screws in Georgia and Detective Pape in Chicago had carried the badges of authority, but even where the defendants were agents of the state, it was still not clear that all acts of official lawlessness came within the reach of the Civil Rights Acts. As Frankfurter conceded, these acts were not models of careful phrasing.[7] The frequent essays into the legislative history would find the supporters of the law offering accounts of their work that were maddeningly imprecise, and at times even at odds with one another. And yet, one modest point seemed plainly to arise from the modifications and redrafting in the legislation: It was hard to command a majority in the Congress for legislation so broad in its reach that the federal government would virtually displace the states in taking on the main responsibilities for the enforcement of law. During the debate on the bill, Senator Thurman had expressed his incredulity over the notion that the federal government might reach a conspiracy of private persons "which is their individual act and which is a crime against the State laws themselves." To enact a measure of that kind was "simply to wipe out all the State jurisdiction over crimes and transfer it bodily to the Congress."[8] Even the most advanced supporters of the Civil Rights Acts sought to assure their colleagues, at length, that the law could not support that kind of construction. Senator Trumbull of Illinois offered this account:

> If an offense is committed against a colored person simply because he is colored, in a State where the law affords him the same protection as if he were white, this act neither has nor was intended to have anything to do with his case, because he has adequate remedies in the State courts; but if he is discriminated against under color of States laws because he is colored, then it becomes necessary to interfere for his protection.[9]

On the other hand, Trumbull noted that the law would indeed make officials of a state vulnerable to prosecution in performing their legal duties—if they were acting as the agents of the state in enforcing laws that imposed discriminations based on race. That was precisely what the Civil Rights Acts were meant to reach: not the private villainies performed by agents of a state, animated by their private passions, but the acts that were carried out as part of their official responsibility in *enforcing laws, ordinances, or customs* that were unconstitutional under the Fourteenth Amendment. In this understanding, the Civil Rights statutes would be deployed properly if they were used, say, to prosecute a judge who followed the local law in refusing to enroll blacks as jurors, or in refusing to allow blacks to testify as witnesses in trials. In the Screws case, Frankfurter sought to restate the original understanding in this way: "Federal law . . . was directed against those, and only against those, who were not punishable by state law precisely because they acted in obedience to unconstitutional State law and by State law justified their action."[10]

But what of the other section of the statute? What of the part that dealt with "two or more persons" who conspired to injure citizens and deprive them of their constitutional rights? Frankfurter conceded that this section of the statutes had to run well beyond the acts of officials in enforcing the laws of a state. Clearly, the statute had to encompass here the private acts of lawlessness that were not sanctioned by the policies of a state. And if the statute covered the lawless acts of "persons," it presumably covered, quite as well, the lawless acts of those "persons" who happened to be placed in positions of official authority. In this phase, the statutes were extending well beyond the class of official agents, enforcing the laws; still, the legislation did not expand, in its coverage, to take in all wrongful acts committed against anyone, by anyone, in the country. As Frankfurter argued, the legislation still carried a more precise focus, which supplied a discipline for its use. The concern of the law was not to strike at every instance in which a band of private thugs sought to carry out an unjustified assault. Nor would the law reach every case in which people were denied the protection of lawful procedures at the hands of state and local governments. The statute spoke of a denial of the rights or privileges "secured . . . by the Constitution or laws of the United States." Reading the statute against the logic of federalism, and scanning the precedents of the Court in applying the statute, Frankfurter suggested a confined, and more finely etched, reading of the law. The act sought to protect citizens in those rights that arose distinctly from their relation to the federal government.[11] In this construction, the law was properly applied when it was used to protect a citizen from being assaulted while he was in the custody of a *United States* marshal (*Logan v. United States*.[12]) But when a mob had seized a black man from the custody of a *local* sheriff and lynched their victim, the Court had held that the killers could not be indicted under the Civil Rights Act (*United States v. Powell* [1908].)[13] It was, after all, a local jail and a local sheriff. The right of the victim not to be lynched did not arise from any right that was peculiar to his relation to the federal government.

With the same logic, Frankfurter recalled that the Civil Rights Act was used to protect people from threats and intimidation as they sought to inform on a violation of *federal* law;[14] to vote in a *federal* election;[15] or to file a claim under the *federal* Homestead Acts.[16] But presumably, the Civil Rights Act would not offer a comparable protection against the gangsters who would seek to intimidate people from voting in *local* elections, or informing on a violation of local laws. When a group of private gunmen forced black workers to leave their jobs at a lumber mill in Arkansas, the black victims were denied a right to engage in a legitimate occupation without suffering the threat of lawless violence. But over the vigorous dissent of Justice Harlan, the Court found here no right that arose distinctly from the federal government. Therefore, the judges saw no wrong that could find a remedy under the Civil Rights Acts (*Hodges v. United States* [1906].[17] Frankfurter pointed out, also, that the judges had been inclined to read the statute quite strictly when they referred to the categories of people protected by the law. Against the wrongs that were committed "under the color of law," the statute offered protections to "any inhabitant" of any state or territory. But against the conspiracies carried through by private persons, the statute secured the rights of "citizens." It is arguable that both statutes refer, in the end, to the same kinds of rights, but the Court, in an earlier day, was disposed to take these provisions quite literally. Over the dissent, once again, of Justice Harlan, the Court held, in 1887, that the Civil Rights Acts would not apply when a group of Chinese *aliens* were driven, at gunpoint, from their homes and their jobs in Sutter County, California.[18]

Frankfurter recognized that the results were, at times, uncongenial and even unsettling, but he had to remind his colleagues that the thugs in these cases would not necessarily go "unwhipped of justice." The wrongs would not go unvindicated merely because the federal government was holding to a more tempered view of the reach of its own authority. As we have seen, Frankfurter and his allies pointed out in the Screws case that the penalties administered under the Civil Rights Acts were symbolic and modest. The serious harms described in these cases could be met with far more serious and astounding penalties when they were treated under the local laws as the crimes they were: when they were treated, that is, as crimes of murder and assault. But of course, if the local authorities had shown a serious interest in dealing with these crimes, the Justice Department might not have felt impelled, in the same way, to take on the prosecution in these cases. It was Frankfurter's melancholy sense, however, that this engagement by the federal government would not offer a wholesome corrective. To be sure, this policy of intervention might produce a satisfying result in a handful of cases. But the good to be done in this way would be overborne by the vaster number of harms that would be left unaddressed if the interventions of the national government induced officials at the local level to recede from their responsibilities. As Frankfurter understood, the protections offered by local government were often far more comprehensive than "those minimal guarantees" of "due process and equal protection" that the federal government sought to vindicate. [19]

If officials at the state and local levels began to back away from their responsibilities, they would leave their citizens exposed to a host of serious harms, too local to engage the interest of the Justice Department, and too numerous for any distant authority to cope with in their plenitude. Would it make a difference, for example, if the local authorities lost their interest in coping with the local hoodlums who extorted "protection" money from local businessmen? Would the police lose their interest in intervening in those vexing disputes within families, which often flare into violence and produce a high portion of the murders in the country? Might the authorities even become collaborators with the vendors of prostitution and pornography? These kinds of matters do not typically excite the interest of the federal authorities, and there are enough tendencies already for politicians at the local level to slip into patterns of indifference and corruption in turning aside from these cases. But there was no reason to suspect that the authorities would back away only from the matters of interest to the federal government once they were encouraged to back away from cases that might be politically risky or personally dangerous.

What Frankfurter feared was nothing less than a "debilitation" of local responsibility, a consequence that could follow in quick, short steps as a result of altering the political incentives that bore on officials at the local level. In *Screws v. United States*, Frankfurter took note of the argument that the "local authorities cannot be relied upon for courageous and prompt action, that often they have personal or political reasons for refusing to prosecute." If serious crimes at the local level could not be prosecuted locally, that was an "ominous

sign," but the situation could not be improved by encouraging the local prosecutors to recede even further. "The cure," said Frankfurter, "is a reinvigoration of State responsibility."[20] He left himself open to the facile, evident re-
tort, that this "reinvigoration" of local responsibility could not be supplied
through mere exhortation. But his critics were apt then to miss the stronger
argument contained in Frankfurter's commentary: The case for federal intervention was predicated on the assumption that local officials would be unwilling to act against notable characters and groups, which commanded a
political presence in the local community. But if this predicate was true, if
local officials were especially sensitive to certain political forces at the local
level, this new regimen of intervention from Washington promised to make
them even more sensitive yet, and it would remove whatever incentive they
might have had to resist these forces. For if the federal government is ready
to deal with the prosecutions that are politically troublesome for officials at
the local level, why should those local officials—political animals to begin
with—go out of their way to court political trouble? A district attorney may
face the possibility of pursuing investigations of corruption in unions, the evasion of taxes by fashionable auction houses, or the less refined operations of
the Mafia. In all of these instances, the district attorney may encounter families that are well-connected politically, or groups that can displace a considerable political weight in the local community. And if a local sheriff is elected
by the local yahoos, he may be less than anxious to take on a group, like the
Ku Klux Klan, if they command a following among those same local yahoos.
Over the last twenty years, we have seen political men and women cultivate
the habits of leaving difficult political questions to the judges, who may be
sheltered from the need to run for reelection. The same habits may easily
become engaged as officials at the local level decide to concentrate their legal
genius—and their arts of public relations—in prosecuting the more popular
cases, against groups that are isolated, small, or politically weak. At the same
time, they may be more than content to leave the more vexing cases to the
attorneys in the Justice Department, who are more safely distant from the
local scene.

Frankfurter's vision here of the politics of the federal structure required no
refined theory, no chains of tenuous assumptions. His argument moved
through short steps, immanently plausible, and it was rooted in the understanding, shared by the Founders, of the incentives that would come to bear
on political men as they enlarged the range of their constituencies, from the
local to the national level. But what Frankfurter offered, in the domain of
jurisprudence, were at best rules of statecraft or prudence. He suggested, with
a bundle of plausible reasons, why it could be quite salutary, in the long run,
if people in positions of local authority were encouraged to take their responsibilities seriously. He recognized that there was no infallible rule for marking
off, in our federal system, those matters so distinctly of "local" concern that

they could never become the business of the national government. But a decent respect for the federal system could enjoin the national government not to act too quickly or too casually in snatching any case from the jurisdiction of local authorities. For the common protections of the law, people should be encouraged to seek their remedy "in the first instance" from the hands of local government.[21] It should not be assumed at the outset that the officers of the law at the local level were wanting in the motive or the competence to administer justice.

But as I have suggested, these were at most rules of prudence or statecraft. None of these maxims offered any "apodictic" or necessary truths, and therefore nothing in this inventory of considerations furnished "principles" of law in the strictest sense.[22] To put it another way, acting on these rules did not invariably produce a just decision in any case. Nor did it guarantee that local officials, accorded a proper deference, would actually take their responsibilities and act justly.

Hence, the irony in Frankfurter's argument that I may take now as a pivot in my own: Frankfurter's perspective on the Civil Rights Acts retains a certain plausibility for us because it is drawn from an understanding of the political incentives that were built into the structure of the federal system. I have already suggested—and I have hardly been the first to urge the point—that we may find the foundation for some of our judgments in the law by tracing those judgments back to the logic that was contained in that "structure" established by the Founders in 1787.[23] But if we set about that task with a philosophic seriousness, we would discover that this logic, woven into the Constitution, yields far more than certain contingent rules of prudence. It may yield real principles, with a necessary force. In the end, those principles would override the teaching of Frankfurter; and they would displace his maxims of prudence with doctrines that are neither contingent nor problematic.

·　·　·　·　·

Frankfurter himself marked the paths that lead out from his own argument and point to a different resolution of the problem. As we have seen, Frankfurter found an apt use of the Civil Rights Act when the federal government sought to protect prisoners who were in the custody of United States marshals.[24] To be held in custody by a federal agent was to be in a relation, distinctly, to the federal government. But then what about an attack on the marshal himself—or on the officer who stands, at the apex, as the chief of all officers who execute the laws under the authority of the United States? What about an assault on the president of the United States? At the end of the nineteenth century, the Court recognized that there was an implied authority, under the Constitution, to protect justices of the Supreme Court. In one celebrated case there had been an attack on Justice Stephen J. Field when he was riding on circuit in the West. The Court recognized an inherent power of the executive to assign a marshal and protect Justice Field, even if Congress had not stipulated, in a statute, that it was a federal crime to assault a federal judge.[25] Still, the experience did not inspire a statute. It was not until the shooting of President Kennedy that Congress enacted a statute and made it a federal crime to assassinate the president of the United States. Apparently, it was taken for granted that a murder could be prosecuted under any jurisdiction. If Lee Harvey Oswald had not been shot, he could have been tried in Texas for the murder of the president. Since murder is a crime under all jurisdictions in the United States, it was not obvious to earlier generations that a federal prosecution was necessary.

But if we applied the interpretation suggested by Justice Frankfurter, we would have inferred that, in the understanding of those earlier generations of American legislators, the president did not bear any peculiar relation to the federal government, which might have justified a distinct federal authority to protect his life. Of course, we would recognize that the president is often endangered precisely because he holds that office. By the time Congress provided a federal statute for the protection of the president, there were no inhibitions about this expansion in the criminal jurisdiction of the federal government. No one suggested that the killing of the president was merely another local murder, with nothing more than a local significance. The assault on the president may have the intention of destabilizing the government and inflicting a trauma on the political community. It may be a gesture of grand arrogance, for one man with a gun to sweep away the result produced by millions of citizens in casting free ballots. In a single stroke the assassin may override the sovereignty of a free people. In a word, the assassin constitutes himself, at that moment, as a despot. And even where the motive to a killing may spring from a deranged mind, or from an intensely personal animosity, it may not be stripped of political significance. For why does the deranged mind settle on this particular target rather than the chairman of the local zoning board? And if the violence were inspired by a personal animus, why is it not directed to people who are known personally by the assassin, who might have been the cause of a more direct, personal offense?

But as the motives for a killing become more explicitly political, they are clearly fed by causes, and by currents of belief, that are not confined to the perimeter of local politics. The motives may be fed by interests that are national in character, and the planning for an assassination will almost certainly require the concerting of movements across the lines of a state. I do not mean to suggest that it is necessary to gauge, in any case, whether an attack on the president was really affected by these political motives, or that the aptness of a federal prosecution should hinge, in any way, on the degree of movement in "interstate" travel. I mean to suggest, rather, that there are ample reasons to believe that the attack on the person of a president is inspired by the office he holds within the institutions that define the federal government. It requires no special strain to suggest that these attacks absorb a significance that is "political" and "national," even if they are animated in part by sentiments that are personal and local. It should require no strenuous effort to justify a federal statute and a federal prosecution in these cases, even though the cases could be prosecuted quite as diligently at the local level. The justification for using the federal authority in these cases would not depend, then, on the assumption that the local authorities were wanting in the motive or the competence to vindicate the wrongs that are engaged here.

And yet, if we could justify a federal prosecution for assaults on the president, wouldn't the same reasoning argue for the protection of a person who has not yet been invested with the authority of the office, but who is now a serious candidate for the presidency? Governor George Wallace of Alabama was shot in 1972, when he was campaigning in Maryland in the Democratic primary for president. Was that shooting an affair that was formed out of the life of Maryland? Neither the assailant nor the victim was a resident of Maryland. The motive for the attack sprang from the tensions and issues that defined the presence of Wallace as a figure in national politics. But if a candidate for the presidency could become the focus of these passions drawn from our national politics, it should be evident that the same passions could find a target in certain public figures, who are very much part of our national politics, even if they are not candidates for office. How else to account for the assassination of Martin Luther King? His killing could not be attributed to any disputes arising out of his church in Atlanta. Nor was it, like the killing of Malcolm X, a murder arising out of a war of factions, over the control of a national religious organization. Whatever we may yet come to know about the motives and interests behind the murder of Dr. King, we may readily surmise that the killing was affected by the angers he aroused in his public career, as he challenged the laws and customs of racial discrimination, and pressed the claims of his race.

But if the killing of King could have been seen as an attack motivated by the animus of race, and fueled by the passions of political warfare, it would be hard to draw a distinction between that case and a series of attacks carried out against black victims who were not public figures. Some of these attacks have reflected a hatred cast in a sweeping way against blacks as a racial group; others have been staged precisely for the purpose of intimidating blacks in the exercise of their lawful freedoms. For a while the serial murders of young black men in Atlanta were thought to have that character, and no puzzlement was stirred, on constitutional grounds, when the plea was made to bring in the Federal Bureau of Investigation. Of course, the assumptions proved mistaken; there was no racial motivation for the killings in Atlanta. But other assaults have borne that character, and when they have, the assumption has been engaged—quite tenably, I think—that the federal government may rightly become involved, through the concerns that have been reflected in the Civil Rights Acts. The Supreme Court managed to grasp the essential point of recognition here in a case coming out of Mississippi in the late 1960s. A small group of whites, their sensibilities joined to the power of an automobile, had stopped and harrassed a group of blacks driving on the highway. The blacks in the car were unknown, personally, to any of the assailants. The fact that they were black was sufficient to mark them as targets of brutishness. [26]

The case illustrated the lesson taught many years earlier by the first Justice Harlan, when he argued that the Thirteenth Amendment was not aimed solely at the purpose of removing slavery as a legal institution. That amendment was, as Harlan said, a charter of civil liberty, and its deeper purpose was to strike at those lingering "burdens and disabilities that constitute badges of slavery or servitude."[27] The blacks in the car, in 1966, were marked as targets through the animosities that lingered from the past. Those hostilities were preserved through the abrasions of the races, but the reflex of putting blacks "in their places" had to be understood as part of that history in which blacks were assigned by law to slavery and stamped by convention as an inferior, subject caste. To deal with the injustices borne of that experience was the continuing work of the Thirteenth Amendment, as Justice Harlan understood the ends of the Civil War amendments. The Thirteenth Amendment was not addressed to states; it could be used directly against individuals. In Harlan's understanding, that amendment could justify the use of federal authority in reaching private persons who would try to block, through private acts of violence, the civic equality that was now acknowledged for black people in the laws. And that was the understanding that the Court adopted, in the late 1960s, as it revived the Thirteenth Amendment, with the breadth of concerns, and the reach of authority, that Harlan had found in it. [28]

As we advance along the chain of these cases—as we move from the protection of the president, to the protection of presidential candidates and former presidents, to public figures engaged in politics, and finally, to private persons who become targets of assault—the sense of a "relation" to the federal government becomes more and more tenuous as the ground for a federal jurisdiction. Martin Luther King was a visible figure in national politics, but he held no office and he was not in the custody of a federal marshal. If it is legitimate to use a federal prosecution in dealing with assaults on the president, I would argue that the justification for federal authority may be equally plausible with all of the other cases I have described. That does not mean that we would need legislation to cover all of these cases, any more than we seemed to "need" legislation to protect the president before 1963. But if any of these problems suddenly became more acute, and Congress was moved to legislate on them, I would suggest that there is nothing in the Constitution, or in the logic of federalism, which would put this authority outside the province of the federal government.

In this construction, certain black victims could be protected through a federal prosecution even though they were not on their way to apply for a grant from a *federal* agency or to vote in a federal election. If they had a "right," nevertheless, to be protected from assaults, it was not a right that arose out of a "relation" to the federal government. Or at least, that right did not arise out of a "relation" cast in the narrow terms that Frankfurter had taken as his standard in these cases. But if we returned to an older understanding, we would discover that there may, indeed, be a "right" engaged in these cases; a right that depended for its vindication on the federal government. In fact, as the Founders understood, the defense of these kinds of rights formed the distinct mission of the federal government and the rationale for the Constitution. In the discussions that took place at the Constitutional Convention, Roger Sherman of Connecticut had insisted that the defects of the Union could be treated mainly by strengthening the hand of the Congress in these discrete areas: defending the country against foreign enemies; overcoming the factions that threaten domestic violence; and conducting commercial relations with other countries. James Madison acknowledged these concerns, but he argued that they did not exhaust the concerns of the Convention. For the remedies marked off by Sherman were still designed to treat the problems of the Union in its character as a *confederation* or a league. But the crisis of government at the time was occurring *within* the separate states, in the breaches of justice that were moving beyond the competence of the local authorities, or taking place, in some instances, with the acquiescence of the local government. Madison suggested that Sherman's view of the problem had to be enlarged to include:

> the necessity of providing more effectually for the security of private rights, and the steady dispensation of Justice. Interference with these were the evils which had more perhaps than anything else, produced this convention. Was it to be supposed that republican liberty could long exist under the abuses of it practiced in some of the States.[29]

What Madison had in mind, of course, was Shays's rebellion in Massachusetts and the "abuses" of which it was an example: Factions of debtors, who could command a decisive influence—and perhaps even a majority—at the local level, could use the levers of the law to serve their own interests at the expense of a minority and the detriment of the commonwealth. It was the example of the demos corrupted, and as the Founders understood, a majority that uses its numerical dominance mainly to satisfy its interests was no less a "faction," and no less corrupted, than any oligarchy that would exploit public authority for its private ends. Madison would later explain, in the *Federalist*

#10, that governments at the state and local level were especially vulnerable to this rapacity of dominant, local factions.

> The smaller the society, the fewer probably will be the distinct parties and interests composing it; the fewer the distinct parties and interests, the more frequently will a majority be found of the same party; and the smaller the number of individuals composing a majority, and the smaller the compass within which they are placed, the more easily will they concert and execute their plans of oppression. Extend the sphere, and you take in a greater variety of parties and interests; you make it less probable that a majority of the whole will have a common motive to invade the rights of other citizens; or if such a common motive exists, it will be more difficult for all who feel it to discover their own strength, and to act in unison with each other.[30]

This offering of Madison found expression, also, in the writings of David Hume[31] and Alexander Hamilton,[32] and it has been taken as one of the principal contributions of the American Founders to political theory. It has also been one of the most durable, accurate guides to American politics. A racist party may find it easier to establish a constituency and rise to power within the confines of a smaller state. But it is much less likely to assemble the support of a majority as it is forced to appeal, beyond the perimeter of the state, to an electorate far more diverse in its racial and religious composition, and far more hostile politically to these local eccentricities. A dominant corporation, such as Prudential in Newark, or DuPont in Delaware, may exercise far more political influence over the city and the state than it could possibly command in the wider field of national politics. The question was once raised: Whom would we expect to restrain the local lynch mob? The sheriff who was elected by the members of the mob, and who may need to run for reelection by earnestly seeking their franchises? Or could we have more confidence in the protection offered by a more distant central government, which is not under the thumb of the local yahoos? As the Founders understood, the national government would be more detached, far less dependent on the forces that were dominant in local politics. That disengagement put the officers of the national government in a far better position to intervene in the separate states, to protect a minority whose interests may be threatened, unjustly, by the majority that now controls the government and annexes to its own enthusiasms the force of law.

To vindicate these interests in justice, to defend the right to be treated justly at the hands of local government, was the distinct mission and rationale of a national government. In the recent season of celebrations over the Bicentennial of the Constitution, we have been reminded, from strange quarters, that this character of the Constitution was appreciated by the Founders for the protections it would offer to the rights of "property." It has been a strange commentary, first, because the Founders did not identify property merely with goods or real estate, but with the full domain of personal liberties. As Madison remarked, we might as aptly say that we have property in our rights as rights of property.[33] Beyond that, the implied "criticism" has been hard to comprehend on the part of critics who have made full use of these same features of the American Constitution, for the defense of personal liberties that cannot be equated, very readily, with the defense of "property." And so, a local majority in Akron, Ohio, secures the passage, in the city council, of an ordinance that requires "informed consent" in abortions. Another local government tries to make use of the zoning laws for the purpose of keeping abortion clinics out of town—a device that effectively makes the performance of abortions illegal in the local community. In these instances, the people who have claimed a right to an abortion have sought to secure that right through the courts that created this "constitutional right" in the first place. In other words, they have appealed to the more "distant" federal government in order to protect them, as a minority, from the moral perspective that the dominant majority at the local level would enact into law.

We have seen the same processes at work in the censorship of pornography, the assignment of students to schools, and in countless other policies of state and local governments, which have come under the challenge of the Fourteenth Amendment and the restraint of the federal courts. The fact that embattled minorities are going into courts and seeking injunctions, rather than petitioning the president and the Congress to send troops, should not blind us to the fact that these political happenings have been shaped precisely by the structure created by the Founders. After all, if a minority loses in a local forum, it will have a motive to appeal to a different forum, if there is one available. The Constitution itself offers the incentives to the local losers to make these appeals. As they raise the challenge and make these appeals, they are moved to claim new "rights" for themselves that merit protection. At the same time, they invite the federal courts to expand the authority of the federal government for the sake of protecting these new species of rights. It should come as no surprise, then, that the experience has borne out the anticipations of the Founders as arrangers of new institutions: For the securing of their rights, many groups have indeed cultivated a firmer confidence in the national government, rather than in those local governments that seem to be closest to them.

But if this understanding makes sense—as it made eminent sense to the Founders—the notion of "rights" here must be coextensive with the range of wrongs that may be suffered at the hands of state and local governments. In the section on the Bill of Rights we have already seen that, in the understanding of the Founders, the purpose of the government was to protect people in their "natural rights"; but natural rights could not be marked off in an inventory or list. As James Wilson understood, the protection of natural rights could express itself in the limitless variety of instances in which harms or disabilities are inflicted on people without justification. We may encounter, for example, the case of a photocopying machine that is made available to all members of the public except for blacks. We would not be required, in this case, to articulate a "right to use a photocopier" or to invent any "new" right at all. We would simply see here another one in that numberless variety of instances in which inventive people may seek to create disabilities based on race. What we have here then is merely another instance of the right not to suffer disabilities based on race. We do not require an exhaustive list of all of those contingencies—with photocopiers, tennis courts, delicatessens—in which the same rights may be engaged. Such a list is impossible, and as we have seen, it does nothing to explain the principle that defines the "rights" involved in these cases. We would recognize, then, that the natural rights protected by the government cannot be reduced to a list of the contingencies, or instances, in which wrongs may be committed. We are left with the principles of moral judgment to help us deliberate about the kinds of restrictions or disabilities that may be justified or unjustified, right or wrong. And we are thrown back, also, on our arts of judgment, to consider just which wrongs are practicably within the reach of the law.

If we applied the same understanding to the problem at hand, we would recognize, in the same way, that we could not make an inventory of the rights that the federal government would protect against the states, or against the invasion of local zealots. The right engaged here would have to be understood as a right to be protected by the federal government, as far as practicable, from the harms that are inflicted, without justification, by the agents of local government. That protection may also encompass the harms suffered at the hands of private groups, such as the Ku Klux Klan, which a local government may not have the strength or the political will to resist. We ought not fall into the mistake of an earlier Court, in supposing that we could define these rights according to their material objects, and proceed to set down a list. In 1868, in *Crandall v. Nevada*, the Court sought to explain in this way that a citizen would have the right

> to come to the seat of government to assert any claim he may have upon that government, to transact any business he may have with it, to seek its protection, to share its offices, to engage in administering its functions. He has the right of free access to its seaports, through which all operations of foreign commerce are conducted, to the subtreasuries, land offices, and courts of justice in the several States.[34]

We may find in this passage a continuing reflection of that cast of mind derided by Theodore Sedgwick, when he wondered why the proponents of a Bill of Rights would not wish to specify our right to walk down the street, to awake, without hindrance, in the morning, and to wear a hat. A touch of the same mistake may be found in that inclination, reflected in Frankfurter, to define the rights of United States citizens in terms of their relation to the instruments or offices of the federal government—for example, the right not to be attacked while in the custody of a federal marshal or while enroute to the federal post office. If my own reading of the Founders holds, the national government was invested with a purpose of protecting rights *against* the states, and *within* the states, and those rights could not coherently be confined to the relation between a person and the *offices* of the federal government.

Frankfurter voiced the apt concern of many jurists before him: If the scope of federal rights could not be confined with a formula of this kind, no matter how rough or incomplete, the criminal jurisdiction of the federal government could eventually take in the whole of the common law and displace altogether the governments in the states. At that point, the federal government might as well take on the responsibilities for policing the streets, writing traffic tickets, and fetching stray cats. Of course, it is not inconceivable that the same functions could be performed today by the local office of a Federal Bureau of Motor Vehicles, or Traffic Control, or Humane and Animal Services. And as some close students of the Founding have suggested, there is reason to believe that some of the Founders expected—and welcomed—this withering away of the states. Still, I take the Founders at their word, and I am prepared to believe that most of them would have been appalled by the notion that the states would be entirely displaced by the federal government. I think most of them would have shared the understanding expressed by Justice Sutherland in the 1930s, that "the states were before the Constitution; and consequently, their legislative powers antedated the Constitution":

> Those who framed and those who adopted that instrument meant to carve from the general mass of legislative powers, then possessed by the states, only such portions as it was thought wise to confer upon the federal government.[35]

Contained in the laws of the states were the laws that marked the ancient traditions of polity—the laws on marriage and divorce and the custody of children; the laws that regulated public amusements and displays, and preserved the peace of the community. As far as I know, none of the Founders thought that the federal government would begin to replicate that full matrix of the common law that was present already in the laws of the states. And as I will try to show, the understanding I would put forth here for the reach of the federal government would not require, as its corollary, the atrophy of the states. To acknowledge the fuller reach of the federal government may make us even more alert to the constitutional principles that would discipline and limit the use of that federal authority.

But if we return to the understanding of the Founders, and we begin to appreciate the potential reach of the federal government, we would notice at the same time that the original understanding already contained certain prudent rules of limitation. The need for federal intervention became most compelling when government itself at the local level became the instrument of injustice. The plain recognition here was that it may be vain to seek the redress of wrongs by looking to those same authorities from whom the offense had come. Beyond that, the case for intervention became stronger as it became clear that officials at the local level were not competent to the end of rendering justice. They could be afflicted by a guileless incompetence; they could be intimidated by political factions or powerful families. Or, they could be held back by the force of local customs, which prevented them even from noticing certain wrongs that deserved their interest. But when these ingredients are lacking, when local governments are earnestly attending to the problems within their reach, there may be no pressing need for the federal government to extend its operations. In certain cases, there may be a need only for an intervention well-placed, for the sake of jarring the local officials from the groove of their established habits and teaching some new lessons. In the Williams case, for example, the federal authorities might have detected a cozy arrangement of collusion between private detectives and the police. In that arrangement, the police might provide a sufficient show of authority to bring a suspect into custody. And in turn, the private detectives would be free to use coercion to extract a confession—the kind of coercion that could not be permitted to an agent of public authority, acting under the constraints of public law. The purpose of a federal prosecution in this case might have been to stage a signal prosecution, administer a shock to the local authorities, and draw their attention to a more strenuous sense of legal propriety. And withal, it might have been the kind of intervention that would make other interventions less necessary.

Experience would come to show, in the 1960s and 1970s, that certain legislative interventions were even more salutary in this respect than the interventions of the federal government with the criminal law. The Voting Rights Act of 1965 represented a federal intervention that had the effect of reconstituting the political communities in the southern states. Blacks were incorporated in the community now as citizens with votes, and that brute political fact altered the incentives bearing on local politicians. Careers were not to be made any longer among white politicians by competing in their racial insolence, or in their inattentiveness to the legal treatment of blacks. A fundamental change in the structure of politics brought about a far more dramatic alteration in the legal way of life in the South than anything that might have been accomplished through the intervention of the federal government in a string of prosecutions.

But that is not to say that there is no longer the need at times for the kind of intervention in the states that the Founders anticipated. In the nature of things, there will always be tensions between local majorities and minorities, and there will always be the prospect of an injurious ordinance or statute, which invites the intercession of the national government. Still, those interventions may be made selectively, and when they are made aptly, to teach telling points, they need not lead to an endless stream of litigation. Nor need they result in a deeper involvement by the federal government. The problem will remain, then, as to how those cases are chosen: What causes are sufficiently grave to warrant intervention? And *when*—at what point—should the federal government intervene?

Frankfurter caught the sense of this matter when he remarked, in *Monroe v. Pape*, that the search for a legal remedy must settle "in the first instance, on the States."[36] That simple phrase, offered almost in passing, opened into further recesses in Frankfurter's understanding of the Civil Rights Act and the reach of the federal government. It marked an awareness on the part of Frankfurter that the federal authority might extend to nearly every object within the reach of the law in the separate states. If it were merely a matter of holding back in the "first instance," the inhibition could not arise from anything in the nature of these crimes. If the federal government could prosecute for a murder after the local government had shown its reluctance to prosecute, then clearly the federal government could prosecute for murder. If we followed these implications, it would appear that the jurisdiction of the federal government would not depend, finally, on *the kinds of harms* involved in any case. If the federal government held back, it was merely because of certain rules of prudence, or a certain etiquette of federalism, which encouraged the national government to stay its hand for a while and give the local government a decent chance to demonstrate its competence. In addition, Frankfurter had often pointed out to his colleagues that if he were mistaken in his restrictive reading of the statute, the power remained with the Congress to correct the courts by redrafting the Civil Rights Act.[37] If Congress really wished to give the act the more expansive application that his colleagues were favoring in these cases, Frankfurter left the emphatic impression that the Constitution would pose no serious barriers to this reach of the federal government.

Frankfurter also conceded that the prosecutions directed at local officials were not so easily cabined by that formula he offered in the Screws case: that the prosecutions would be focused mainly on those cases in which officials were acting "in obedience to unconstitutional State law and by State law justified their action."[38] Frankfurter recognized that the statute ran beyond that tight focus to include acts performed "under color of any law, statute, ordinance, regulation, or *custom*" (emphasis added). This provision had been part of the statutes from the beginning, and it did not represent a whimsy in the law. It recognized a profound fact about the origins of law and the climate of opinion that enveloped the laws. The laws arise from the moral sense that is part of the ethos, or the "way of life," in the community. Not all of these moral understandings are enacted into law, and at times the provisions in the statute books become words on dry parchment because they would seem to command, in practice, what the moral sentiments of the community would deeply resist. These sentiments may be even more fundamental and more binding than the law, because they supply the things we take for granted, the notions of right and wrong so settled that we may not even be conscious of making judgments of right and wrong. To make a simple test of this matter, I once called the county building in Northampton, Massachusetts. I asked the clerk a question that had arisen in my class: Would her office issue marriage licenses to couples of the same sex? She thought for a moment, and replied that, of course, they didn't do that. I asked whether there was an explicit statute or regulation that barred that arrangement. She said there was not. It was simply taken for granted that a legitimate "marriage" was constituted by two partners of different sexes. And even if we found one of those rare juris-dictions in the country that issued licenses to couples of the same sex, we might elicit a comparable reaction from the clerk if we called and asked whether licenses were issued to couples of mixed species (for example, a man and his dog). It is taken as an understanding, even anterior to the threshold of a moral argument, that a marriage entails the understanding and commit-ment that are distinct to human beings. It is not as though the matter were beyond argument: it will always be possible, in these times, to find a philoso-pher who is willing to break the bonds of "speciesism" and defend a freedom of human beings to marry their most devoted pets. It is not that arguments cannot be made, but that moral understandings, long settled, prevent most of us even from noticing that there is anything here to argue about.

If we draw, then, on these reflexes, which are quite common in our own time, it may be easier to grasp that the discriminations we saw in an earlier day, in the administration of the law, did not always spring from malice, but from incomprehension. In a celebrated case in the 1870s, a woman trained in the law in Vermont moved to Chicago and applied for membership in the bar of Illinois. The licensing authorities responded with the same incredulity that was expressed by the clerk in Northampton over the prospect of couples of the same sex. There was nothing in the statutes of Illinois, or the regulations of the bar, that explicitly forbade the admission of women to the practice of law. It was simply taken for granted that, for reasons apparently so profound that they could not be explained, this arrangement was beyond consider-ation.[39] And if so much was simply beyond consideration for women of estab-lished families who were trained in universities, it should not require a strain-ing of imagination in order to see why, for certain judges in the nineteenth century, it was beyond reckoning that they would enroll, in a panel of jurors, blacks who were recently delivered from slavery. Even when the prejudices of the South did not come into play, black people could be regarded at the time—and regarded virtually without reflection—as part of a population that was simply not called on for the offices of citizenship.

Frankfurter understood that the Civil Rights Act was enforced in the past in settings of this kind, when the federal government sought to break through the cast of a congealed custom. But then how could one gauge the presence of a custom, which worked with the force of a law, when that custom was not set down in explicit regulations, or even raised to a level of conscious awareness? Would the jurisdiction of the federal government hinge, in any case, not on the acts of officials in enforcing laws, but on the detection of a "custom" observed in the common conduct of unnamed, private persons? And yet, the Civil Rights Act *did* take account of "customs" that held the force of law, and that concern of the drafters remained immanently plausible. After Frankfurter retired from the Court, the Civil Rights Act of 1964 would be tested in the unlikely case of Ollie's Barbecue in Birmingham, Alabama. This was, altogether, an unprepossessing establishment, a small restaurant with a take-out counter, appealing to a local trade. It was the most private and local of establishments, and it provided a stern test of the authority of the federal government to reach private property that was open to business with the public. The Court made an implausible use of the Commerce Clause in this instance, in upholding the federal statute, but a seasoned reader might have noticed an ingredient in the case that would have brought it under the formulas of the old Civil Rights Act. Ollie's Barbecue had confined its main restaurant to white customers since the business was founded, in 1927. But a closer look at the record had to raise doubts as to whether this policy of the restaurant reflected the preferences of the private owners. What came out in the record was that the exclusion of blacks was a practice immured in the conventions and customs of the community in 1927—so much a part of those conventions that any business that ignored it could not expect the patronage of white customers.[40] The government was not really being asked then in this case to respect the sense of a private owner about the decorous uses of his own property. It was asked to uphold, under the claims of privacy, a policy that was adopted by an owner long ago under a custom that had, for all practical purposes, the force of law.

The case of Ollie's Barbecue would have to present a plausible instance, then, of what the drafters of the Civil Rights Act had in mind when they empowered the federal government to strike at the policies of racial discrimination, whether they were enforced in the laws, or whether they were contained in customs that had the force of law. But in that event, we would be driven to the boundary of the problem: the conceptual distinctions contained in the law—the distinctions between laws and "customs"—become ever more plausible, but the distinctions come to dissolve in their significance. We would finally arrive at a point that radically challenges these formulas in the law, and the problem may be shown in the following way.

Let us suppose that we have a restaurant similar in all respects to Ollie's Barbecue in Birmingham, but located in the south of Boston. Let us assume that the restaurant had the same policies of exclusion in regard to black people. We may suspect that the policies of the restaurant reflected the ethos in this section of Boston, which has been mainly one of hostility toward blacks. And yet, we find that other restaurants in the area have not adopted the same policies on race. That may indicate that the prevailing sentiments on race have not exactly acquired the force of a prescriptive rule, which the proprietors of all restaurants feel obliged to obey. And we know that, once we left this enclave in Boston, we would find that other sections of the city did not mirror, uniformly, the attitudes on race that were dominant in South Boston. South Boston is contained in a far more tolerant city, which is in turn contained in a conspicuously liberal state. It would hardly be tenable to argue that the policies of the restaurant reflect a climate of opinion, or a pattern of custom, which has the force of law.

We would have, then, two similar restaurants, with two similar policies. One is located in the South, the other in a liberal state in the North. Both restaurants refuse to accept blacks as customers. And yet, if we were governed by the formulas established in the law, we would have to conclude that the federal government might intervene only in the case from the South; for in the South, the policies of racial exclusion are supported by a custom having the effect of law. But the offense, or the wrong, is in either case the same. Two establishments are the sources of wrongs that are morally indistinguishable; but we are asked to believe that one wrong falls within the reach of the federal government, and the other lies, somehow, outside that jurisdiction. Again, I am not posing a question of prudence. I could readily agree that, as a matter of prudence, there may be far less need for the federal government to prosecute the case in Boston. I am raising a question of how we understand, in principle, the class of objects, or the kinds of wrongs, that come within the reach of the federal government, and the kinds of wrongs that remain outside that jurisdiction.

Of course, any lawyer willing to reach this case for the federal government will not be wanting in arguments, but it is worth noting where the reflexes of argument are likely to move in the first instance. We are likely to hear clever arguments on the point that South Boston is really an insular part of the city; that its residents are not responsive to the climate of opinion in other sections of Boston; that the racial code in the neighborhood has a stern force for businessmen in the area, even if some of them have the nerve, at times, to resist. These arguments would be shaped to the current cast of the law. They accept the premise that the reach of the federal government may hinge upon the showing of a local custom of discrimination. They would simply point us to more subtle ways of redefining a "custom" and proving its influence. They may urge us to consider that a "custom" could be congealed in five or ten years, rather than ten or twenty; that it may be felt more intensely, in a more circumscribed part of the city, even if it is seen only faintly when measured across the community as a whole.

But what I would point out, in these arguments, is *the shift that takes place in our jurisprudence.* We are asked to make a judgment about the *jurisdiction* of the federal government, and yet the analysis does not turn on any point of *jural* significance. We may invite social scientists to gauge whether certain attitudes on race are concentrated or diffused within a city; or we may ponder just how widely and how long an opinion must be held before it may qualify as a "custom." But we are not told just why any of these figures, at any point along the scale, compels conclusions of a jural nature. If 55 percent of the public in a certain state have supported discrimination against blacks for the past ten years, would that fact make acts of discrimination notably more serious, more worthy of federal jurisdiction, than the same acts of discrimination in another place, animated by the same malice—but by a malice only recently settled? When I say that none of these points bears a jural significance, I am saying that none of these points: (*a*) illuminates anything in principle about the nature of the "wrong" in the case; or (*b*), explains anything about the nature of the national government, which would show why this wrong comes properly within the reach of that government.

. . . . .

We would be left, in short, in a condition quite familiar to our own time: law without a moral foundation; an extension of jurisdiction without any distinctly jural rationale. Stripped to its root problem, we find that our law on this subject has shown an affable willingness to live with distinctions that bear no significance and supply no rationale. Hence: Let us suppose that we have a man who possesses a collection of critical photographs and documents, which expose the operations of a drug ring in New York City. Let us suppose that he becomes nervous about his possession of these documents, and he does not wish to be seen visiting the office of the U.S. attorney. He may decide then to gather these materials in a package and mail them to the U.S. attorney. But as he walks to the local branch of the post office he is shot and killed.

Now, by the formulas shaped over the years, we would gather that this informant could have been protected by the federal government, and his assailants prosecuted in a federal court. After all, he was on his way to the post office, an agency of the *federal* government. But let us suppose that, at the last moment, he recalls that the mail has been unreliable, and he decides instead to ship the package UPS.

For the same reasons, he may still be murdered. His killers would have been wholly indifferent to the question of whether he had chosen to ship the materials through the federal mails or whether he was using, instead, a private carrier. Whatever made this killing a murder in the first instance would make it a murder in the second. Nothing of moral significance in defining the nature of the wrong would be altered between the cases. And yet, we would have to suppose that the wrong, in the first case, was a wrong that the federal government has an interest in vindicating, while the wrong in the second case was beyond the concerns or the competence of the federal government.

Clearly, no jurist would have argued that there was anything in the nature of these wrongs that could have justified the difference in jurisdiction. One crime was not more serious than another, more local or national, more invested with federal significance. The difference could be explained only in terms of a rule of prudence that encouraged us to assign these cases to local or federal authorities for reasons that had nothing to do with the nature of the wrongs or the question of just which authorities might be more competent in investigating the case at hand. At their best, as I have acknowledged, these rules of prudence drew upon a powerful motive to preserve the responsibility of officials at the local level by enjoining them to take the case, *in the first instance*. But now the question must be put, in a more demanding way, of whether that rule of practice can really claim the support of any principle bound up with the character of the Constitution.

If there really was a principle that barred the federal government from taking any case in the first instance, it seems to me that a principle of that kind would have to imply either one or both of the following arguments:

1. A subject is placed outside the reach of the federal government because it is foreign to the nature of the federal government—it is a subject that falls, more clearly, or distinctly, to the province of local government.

2. The federal government should become engaged in that kind of subject only when local governments administer their local functions in an unconstitutional way (e.g., if they refuse to issue marriage licenses to couples containing members of different races), or if the local government proves unwilling or ineffective in insuring, for its population, the protections of the law.

With the arguments under (1), we would discover a certain difficulty in marking off the functions that have been regarded traditionally as "local" in this country. But the historical record is equivocal precisely because it is difficult to form a clear conceptual distinction between the local and the federal; and that difficulty in turn is rooted in the Constitution. It is difficult to form a conceptual distinction because the nature of the American Constitution prevents such a distinction from being made.

Over twenty years ago, the late Morton Grodzins taught a generation of scholars that the constitutional practice in this country has never made a clear distinction between the "local" and "federal." Grodzins rejected the old metaphor of the federal and state governments as parallel wheels, doing a similar kind of work within their own spheres, but never touching. Grodzins suggested that the reigning metaphor should rather be the "marble cake." Instead of a separation of fields, there was a sharing of functions. The federal government would rent local jails rather than build its own. The president would at times "federalize" the national guard, or place under "federal" service the troops that could be collected locally under the authority of the state. Grodzins was one of the foremost connoisseurs and defenders of American federalism, and yet he did not think that the case for federalism was built upon the clarity of any distinction between the local and the national. In fact, Grodzins was moved to argue that, if "functions" were assigned to governments at different levels in this country according to a standard of "naturalness" or fittingness, the local governments would be left with almost nothing to do.[41] When drivers licensed in Rhode Island were causing accidents on the highways in California, a case could be made for a national administration in licensing drivers and applying uniform standards of competence. For the citizen, it may not make a notable difference that he takes his driver's test at the nearest regional office of the Massachusetts Department of Motor Vehicles, or that the local office happens to be a branch of the U.S. Department of Motor Vehicles. And if a man preserved in illiteracy by his public education in Mississippi becomes an illiterate citizen of Illinois, a comparable case might be made for a national administration of public education, which might establish national standards of competence in the licensing of teachers and the instruction of students.

In 1985, in *Garcia v. San Antonio Metropolitan Transit Authority*,[42] Justice Blackmun sought to show, in a similar way, that experience had yielded no clear distinction between local and national functions. Writing over twenty years after Grodzins, Blackmun could take account of the expansion of government with novel subjects of administration. But the survey would confirm the line of Grodzins's argument, as Blackmun compared the functions that have been assigned in recent years to the province of the states or reserved to the federal government. For example, regulating ambulances, licensing automobile drivers, operating a muncipal airport, disposing of solid waste, and administering a highway authority had been treated by the courts as "traditional" functions of local government. On the other hand, the issuing of bonds for industrial development, the regulation of intrastate sales of natural gas, the regulation of traffic on public roads, the operation of a facility for mental health, and the provision of "in-house domestic services for the aged and handicapped," have been regarded as subjects more suitable for the federal government. Blackmun defied his colleagues to find, in these lists, any "organizing principle" that could explain why any of these functions should be placed in one group rather than the other.[43]

But if generations of jurists continue to be baffled by this problem, we are tempted to adapt a line from Henry James and say that they are victims of perplexities from which a single spark of direct perception might have saved them. In the understanding of the Founders, no field of the law was more properly in the province of the states—and removed from the administration of the federal government—than the law of marriage and the family. And yet, in the Dartmouth College case in 1810, Chief Justice Marshall suggested that contracts of marriage might come under the protection of the Contract Clause of the Constitution (Article I, Section 10). Marshall planted this question: What if a legislature "shall pass an act annulling all marriage contracts, or allowing either party to annul it without the consent of the other"? Marshall deferred for another time the question of whether this tampering with the obligation of a contract would properly come under the challenge of the Constitution.[44] But the posing of the question strongly implied the answer. In our own day, of course, the Supreme Court has used the Constitution to strike at the laws on marriage in the states when those laws have restricted marriage across racial lines.[45] We have also seen the Constitution applied to family law, a domain of the law that was previously regarded as quite distant from constitutional law. But within that branch of private law family courts had fallen into the practice of assigning the custody of children in mixed racial marriages by indulging a preference for the white parent. At times they would assign children to the different parents by matching their colors.[46] This part of the law was often administered by liberal judges who fancied that they were operating with considerations quite detached from the principles that were articulated in our constitutional law. They understood that to be black in America was to be affected with disadvantages; and when they were asked to consider "the best interests of the child," they were reluctant to saddle a child with the disadvantage of having a black parent. How else to explain the reflexes of Alexander Holtzoff, one of the most seasoned, liberal judges to sit in the federal district court for the District of Columbia? In one notable case in 1955, *In re Adoption of a Minor*, a child had been born out of a wedlock to a white mother, and the mother had gone on to marry a black man. With the consent of the mother, her black husband sought to adopt the child. But Judge Holtzoff denied the petition, and it was evident that he denied the petition with a melancholy "realism," which had been fed by his liberal recognitions.

> Ordinarily [he wrote,] such an adoption [of a child born out of wedlock] should be not only approved but encouraged. [But here] a problem arises out of the fact that the stepfather is a colored man, while the mother and boy are white people. This situation gives rise to a difficult social problem. The boy when he grows up might lose the social status of a white man by reason of the fact that by record his father will be a negro. I feel the court should not fashion the child's future in this manner.[47]

But the recognition finally penetrated to the courts that they were assigning benefits and disabilities in these cases on the basis of race.[48] In the most visible part of our constitutional law, we had absorbed, quite thoroughly, the understanding of why that kind of assignment was wrong. The question surely had to arise: How could an arrangement that was recognized so thoroughly as a "wrong" in one branch of our law be regarded as quite tenable—as quite compatible with the doing of justice—in another branch of our law? After all, the principles of our constitutional law should establish the first-order principles, the principles that govern all lesser fields of the law. They should apply then as a matter of course to all of those places in which courts of law in our country claim to administer justice.

This understanding, which had to be immanent in our constitutional law from the beginning, finally broke through to an explicit recognition in 1984. In the case of *Palmore v. Sidoti*, the Supreme Court confronted a case in which a woman lost custody of her three-year-old child after she had formed an interracial marriage. The local court was advised by a special counselor that custody ought to be awarded to the father because "[t]he wife has chosen for herself and for her child, a life-style unacceptable to the father and to society." The child would then be subject to "peer pressures" and the "social stigmatization" that was "sure to come" when a child lived in a racially mixed household.[49] The decision on custody was permitted, then, to turn on the race of the new husband. The court had been moved by a concern for the "interests" of the child, but the court had construed those interests on terms that permitted custody to be assigned or withheld on the grounds of race. As Chief Justice Burger remarked, "it is clear that the outcome would have been different had petitioner married a Caucasion male of similar respectability." It merely remained for the Court to apply, to this domain of family law, the principles that had been articulated, and extended, in our constitutional law.[50]

From the example of these cases this general lesson may be drawn: There is no subject in our law, no matter how local, that does not imply an understanding of the principles—the understandings of right and wrong—on which the law has been settled. Some of those "principles" may turn out to be in conflict with the principles of jurisprudence, or with principles that are distinct to the Constitution. When they are, the Constitution may reach even some of the most prosaic and "local" parts of our law. But to say that the Constitution can reach these matters is to say that an agency of the federal government would be justified in applying the Constitution in casting aside these local statutes that run counter to the Constitution. The federal courts, or the departments of the executive, may refuse to apply these local statutes, or they may at times override them. And if these local statutes can be overridden by the courts or the federal agencies, who administer the national laws, it stands to reason that they must also fall within reach of the institution that legislates those national laws. If the federal courts can block regulations that impose racial tests of marriage, it would follow that Congress could legislate directly on these matters. Congress could provide the same protections, but through a general, prospective measure that relieves people of the need to launch their own lawsuits. During the deliberations over the Civil Rights Act of 1964, the point was made clear that Congress could provide a far more powerful remedy than the courts: There was no need to leave the vindication of rights to the courts and to the initative of private parties, who would have to test the Constitution anew under the laws of each state and bear, in each separate instance, the burden of litigation.

The point bears restating: There is no part of our law so prosaic or so local that it may not absorb a violation of the Constitution. ("Public swimming pool: No blacks allowed.") The courts, and the federal government, can vindicate any violation of the Constitution, even if it is contained in the laws on marriage and the custody of children, in the segregation of races in public swimming pools, or in the procedures used for the hiring of police. But if we understand that the Constitution can correct even the most prosaic and local parts of the laws in this country, then we should understand, at the same time, that the legislative authority of the federal government could reach any subject that is now addressed through the laws of the states, if the need should arise. That authority often remains dormant, and even when it is exercised, it is exercised through formulas that conceal the true ground of the law. But we should not blind ourselves to the sweeping nature of the legislative authority that has been applied already by Congress, even while it has been masked under a regimen of "federal aid" for hospitals or schools or fire departments. That federal aid just happens to be attended by "federal regulations," which just happen to displace local policies with the requirements of federal *law*.

As we saw earlier, James Wilson sought to explain the ends of government by explaining the mission of government in securing natural rights. The main business of the government was to do justice by protecting people against assaults on their persons, their property, their reputation; against the lawless restriction of their freedom; against the harms that may be inflicted on them, without justification, in a variety of forms. In this understanding, the government was "limited" in the sense that it preserved its focus on protecting people from these serious harms that may be suffered unjustly, in a lawless way. There were many useful and benign things in life that government might do, but it was not presumed here that this new government was obliged to do them. To some people, for example, it might seem to be useful for the government to furnish housing directly to private citizens. But no one in that founding generation seemed even remotely to imagine that this kind of undertaking could fall within the responsibility of government at any level. Or at least, we might say, there would have been a strong presumption against any project of this kind, which departed rather widely from the principal mission of the government. And yet, within the field of this "limited" mission, the reach of the government could be vast. As Hamilton suggested, the operations of the government may have to be as extensive and varied as the dangers with which it was obliged to deal.[51]

When James Wilson wrote of the mission of government in protecting people in their natural rights, it was clear that he was writing about the purpose of any legitimate government. But if we should say that some subjects lay outside the province of the federal government—if we say, for example, that the local government was the source of protections that the federal government could not provide—we would suggest that the federal government, in that respect, is *that much less of a real government*. If a threatening mob collected outside the home of a family, was it only the local government that could protect the family? If the local government showed no interest in protecting the family, was there no other government within the territory of the United States that could offer protection? Several years ago, a federal court awarded damages to a black family in Maryland when the local police failed to protect the family against the burning of crosses outside their home. Even more recently, the Supreme Court has sustained an action for damages against men who had defaced the walls of a Jewish congregation. With red and black paint, they covered the walls with anti-Semitic slogans and symbols.[52] The victims chose, in this case, to pursue a private action for damages under the Civil Rights Act. But if this statute of Congress may be applied to a case of this kind by a federal court, why could the same statute not be enforced, in its *criminal* sections, by the executive? That is, if the federal courts can reach a case of this kind, why would it not be quite as legitimate to engage the authority of the federal executive much earlier in the case, in supplying the protections of the federal law in a more timely way?

Some local authorities may earnestly believe that they have no authority, under the Constitution, to restrict the freedom of people to burn crosses outside the homes of blacks, or to parade with swastikas outside the homes of Jews. They may have been schooled to look upon these public displays as acts of symbolic expression protected by the First Amendment. In that judgment they may prove to be wrong. They may also prove to be tragically insensitive in gauging the traumas that are threatened for some of their citizens. Must we suppose that those citizens would be exposed now, without recourse to any other protections of the law? Or could they possibly seek the protection of that higher, national government, in which they also happen to be citizens?

To deny that possibility is to say that there are certain wrongs that come within the reach of the law in this country, but not with the reach of the government of the United States. To say that, would be to say that the federal government is less adequate to the most elementary ends of government than the authorities in the separate states. It would be to say, in that respect, that the federal government is less of a real government than the governments in the separate states. But of course, that was not Wilson's understanding, and we know that it could not have been the understanding of the Founders. The decision in 1787 was for the creation, at the national level, of a real *government*. The project of the Founders was to perfect the Union and treat the flaws that weakened the Union under the Articles of Confederation. But to strengthen the Union and overcome the defects of the Articles was to create, at the national level, a government, which was fully competent now to the ends of any legitimate government.

I have drawn out my explanation of (1), above, for the sake of taking the matter to the root. And once we did, we would understand just why we could not establish, in principle, any list of subjects that must fall, *by nature*, outside the authority of the federal government. Could we retreat, then, to the second path of argument I marked off under (2)? Someone might concede that the federal government could reach virtually every subject, or every wrong, that is within the reach of the law; and yet one might argue that the federal government is still compelled to act under this limitation: The government may act only when it becomes clear that the local authorities will not deal with the problem, or that they will not supply an adequate remedy. In this view, the federal authorities might conceivably become engaged to protect a family from a hostile mob burning crosses outside their home. But the argument might be offered here that the federal government should be obliged to hold back, in the first instance, to make sure that the local government is not dealing with the problem. Again, this disposition may be entirely sensible as a rule of prudence, and we may wish to follow it most of the time. But it is nevertheless critical to understand just why this rule cannot be installed as a principle.

The implication arising from this arrangement is that the federal government may act, in these cases, mainly to correct the mistakes or the omissions of the local government: The federal government may protect people against local officials who administer the law with "an evil eye and an unequal hand."[53] Or, the federal government may need to protect people against the wrongs committed by private parties, when the local authorities see no pressing need to act. In either event, the federal government would be placed in the position of *acting upon the states*. Its mission is to vindicate the rights of persons, but it would be forced into a cast in which it appears mainly to be dealing with the misdeeds of local officials. The more that the government moves within this cast, the more it suggests that the "citizens" who compose the national polity—the subjects on whom the federal law operates—are the states. And yet, that is precisely the situation that the Founders meant to leave behind when they made the decisive move, in 1787, from a *confederation* to a real *government*.

A confederation or league was composed of sovereign states. The central institutions in the confederacy would address only the member states, and that was the principal defect of the Articles of Confederation. Under this arrangement, the Union could not lay taxes directly on the people of the United States. It could put out requisitions to the separate states and hope that the states would act in turn to levy the needed taxes on their own populations. But in the face of resistance, there was no means by which a confederacy of states could coerce an unwilling member, save with the threat of expulsion. In the *Federalist #39*, Madison had taken care to explain the distinctions engaged here.

> The difference between a federal and national government, as it relates to the *operation of the government*, is supposed to consist in this, that in the former the powers operate on the political bodies composing the Confederacy, in their political capacities; in the latter, on the individual citizens composing the nation, in their individual capacities. . . . [And this] operation of the government on the people, in their individual capacities, in its ordinary and most essential proceedings, may, on the whole, designate it, in this relation, a *national* government.[54]

The hallmark of a government was that it could act directly on those individuals who constituted its citizens. It could legislate for persons, not merely for states. A national government could enforce the laws against the persons who were expected to obey them, without acting through the agency of the states. Madison pointed out that when the Continental Congress called a Constitutional Convention and framed a mandate for the commissioners, it explained that the purpose of the project was to remedy the defects in the Confederation by "establishing in these States a firm national government," or, as it was put in another passage, to "render the federal Constitution adequate to the exigencies of government and the preservation of the Union."[55]

Madison suggested that the Constitution contained features that were "partly federal and partly national." But Madison understood that the critical difference between a federation and a government could not be so handily compromised. The "federal" features could be seen in such arrangements as the election of representatives from the states, the equal representation of the states in the Senate, and the election of the president through an electoral college constituted by the states. Madison was frank, though, to acknowledge that in "the operation of the government," the Constitution "falls under the *national*, not the *federal* character."[56] The Founders had been aware, at all points, of this distinction. In the instructions that were given to them by the Continental Congress, they were encouraged to make improvements in the Articles of Confederation, and at the same time, to render the Union adequate to the exigencies of government. The Founders understood that, as they imparted to the Union the character of a real government, they were not "improving" the Confederation but superseding it with another kind of government, constituted with different principles. But then Madison framed, with a philosophic aptness, the question they faced.

Which was the more important, which the less important part? Which the end; which the means? Let the most scrupulous expositors of delegated powers; let the most inveterate objectors against those exercised by the convention, answer these questions. Let them declare, whether it was of most importance to the happiness of the people of America, that the articles of Confederation should be disregarded, and an adequate government be provided, and the Union preserved; or that an adequate government should be omitted, and the articles of Confederation preserved. Let them declare, whether the preservation of these articles was the end, for securing which a reform of the government was to be introduced as the means; or whether the establishment of a government, adequate to the national happiness, was the end at which these articles themselves originally aimed, and to which they ought, as insufficient means, to have been sacrificed.[57]

The government created under the Constitution would have to arbitrate, at times, the disputes among states over their lands and boundaries. But that government was not compelled to stand, in relation to its own people, through the agency of the states. In vindicating the rights of its own people, it did not have to act as a government of the second tier, a government of the second resort. As a government of the second resort, it might no longer be dealing with the same crime: Instead of protecting its citizens from a lynch mob, it might be administering sanctions to the local officials who permitted the lynching to take place. When the parts of government were arranged well and administered with the same convictions of justice, the federal authorities might afford to hold back and leave the responsibility in the first instance to officials at the local level. But if there were reasons to expect in any case that the local authorities would not be zealous in protecting some of their citizens, the federal government was not constrained by any principle, rooted in the Constitution, to let the danger run its course. For reasons of prudence, the federal government may be willing to let the processes within a state run as far as they can before the federal courts or the federal attorneys become engaged. But that rule of prudence could never be converted into a *necessary* rule in our law, for the simplest and clearest of reasons: The notion of the federal government as a lesser government, or a government of second resort, is incompatible, at its root, with the logic of the decision in 1787 to replace a confederacy with a national government.

. . . . .

During the debate over the Civil Rights Act of 1866, Senator Trumbull suggested that the federal authority may not have to be used massively in order to reach its ends. A smaller number of prosecutions, wisely chosen, strategically placed, could teach the right lessons and bring about the changes that the law sought to achieve. Trumbull offered then this hope: "When it comes to be understood in all parts of the United States that *any person* who shall deprive another of any right or subject him to any punishment in consequence of his color or race will expose himself to fine and imprisonment, I think such acts will soon cease."[58]

The criminal prosecutions under the Civil Rights Act have been in the hands of the Justice Department, and that power has been used sparely, with a sense of the problems that pose, in any period, the most grievous abuses of the day. But the sections authorizing civil suits have not been subject to a comparable control, and there we have seen the most dramatic expansion of litigation under the Civil Rights Acts. The United States Code Annotated contains paragraphs offering précis of the cases argued under sections of the statutes. As I write, I have in hand a recent edition of the Annotated Code. The separate volumes contain the précis of the cases decided up to the time of publication—plus a supplement that runs up to the current year. A simple comparison of the pages taken up in the summaries reveals the striking differences. The *criminal prosecutions* of people who "act under the color of any statute" are conducted under Title 18, Section 242. The cases arising from that paragraph of the statute were reported, in short summaries, covering twenty-one pages. The *civil suits* for private damages are brought under Title 42, Section 1983 (the section that refers to acts done "under color of any law"). It now requires a separate volume simply to list the summaries of the cases that have been decided under this *one* paragraph in the statutes: The précis of cases springing from this single paragraph took up 1,256 pages in the edition I had in hand, along with 365 additional pages in the supplement. This stark comparison reflects the experience of the last twenty years in expanding the notion of the "rights" that may be protected by the federal government as "civil rights."

Anyone who has scanned the record of these recent cases would have to wonder what Lyman Trumbull and his colleagues would have thought if they could have seen the uses to which their grandest work has been put. The men who framed the Civil War Amendments and the Civil Rights Acts thought they were dealing with the exercise of authority at its gravest and most delicate level. They were seeking to cope with the abuse of authority in the states, in furnishing the cardinal protections of the law to black people. Trumbull and his colleagues were willing to risk a serious expansion of the federal power for the sake of securing this difficult project, this re-founding or reconstituting of the political order, by incorporating blacks as citizens. But in our own day, the most curious assortment of people have been sued as agents acting "under the color of law." That label has been applied to a variety of unlikely characters, because they happen to hold official titles in establishments that come under the authority of the state. One must wonder what the framers of the

Civil Rights Acts would have thought of suits lodged against these kinds of people, brought for these kinds of injuries.

—The football coach at a state college in Arizona is sued by one of his former players. The player kicked a punt that the coach regarded as rather lame, and as a consequence the coach ridiculed and benched the player. The coach did not permit the player to kick another punt for the rest of the season. By the beginning of the next season the player was dropped from the team, and he lost his scholarship for football. Without the scholarship, the player could not continue at the college. He was forced to transfer to another college, in another state, without the benefit of a scholarship. The claim, then, was that the decision to bench the football player was unwarranted; that it deprived him, eventually, of an education in a better school, along with the material benefit of a scholarship (*Rutledge v. Arizona Board of Regents* [1981]).[59]

—Students sue the administrators of a public high school in Columbus, Ohio, because seventy-five youngsters are suspended for ten days as a result of a disturbance in the lunchroom that produced some destruction in the school. One student, Dwight Lopez, claims that he was an innocent bystander. The administrators are challenged because they suspended the students without conducting even a rudimentary hearing to collect evidence and consider what Lopez might have said, from his own side, to rebut the charges. The students are suspended for only ten days, rather than expelled for the term; still, it is claimed that they have been deprived, for ten days, of their "property" in their education (*Goss v. Lopez* [1975]).[60]

—The warden of a prison in Pennsylvania is sued by one of the inmates because the library of the prison receives 123 magazines, but only two of those journals are directed to the interests of blacks. It is argued that blacks represent more than half of the population in the prison, and yet most of the magazines were "catering to the tastes of white inmates." The plaintiff launches his suit when he is denied permission to subscribe to a national black magazine that is not on the list of publications approved within the prison (*Owens v. Brierley* [1971]).[61]

To put it charitably, these cases were quite distant from the kinds of problems that engaged the concerns of Trumbull and the framers of the Civil Rights Acts. As is turned out, the complaint of the students was upheld in the Supreme Court, but the other two cases did not get that far. The claims of the punter and the prisoner were rejected in the federal courts of appeal. And yet, I think we ought to hold ourselves open to the curious possibility that these kinds of claims may not always be implausible. They become notably easier to conceive once we understand a premise contained in the Civil Rights Acts, namely, that citizens might have more confidence in the federal courts in challenging the wrongs that are done by people in positions of authority within the state. Of course, some of these positions of authority are not exactly formidable and threatening, and some of the "injuries" in these cases have been laughable. But any system of litigation will draw spurious cases, and the frivolous cases cannot be taken as proof of the proposition that schools or prisons may not be the scenes of serious wrongs, which deserve a remedy. The problem then is to explain just why that remedy must come from a court within the state, rather than a federal court.

Are certain subjects more properly left to the state courts? Are the judges in the states more competent than federal judges in assessing the subtle wrongs taking place, say, in prisons or in schools? In 1976, Justice Rehnquist managed to persuade most of his colleagues that actions for libel could be consigned, as a class, to the courts in the states. In the case at hand, *Paul v. Davis*,[62] the police in Louisville, Kentucky, provided a service to the local merchants during the shopping season of Christmas. The police assembled an album containing photos of the most active shoplifters. The album included the photo of Edward Davis, who had been arrested earlier on the charge of shoplifting; but Davis had never been prosecuted or convicted. Davis sued the chief of police for libel under Section 1983: Acting with the authority and credibility of the law, the police had injured Davis in his reputation and exposed him to public embarrassment.[63] Justice Rehnquist argued that there was no pressing need to bring actions for libel within the federal courts. And on that point, most of the time, he may be correct. He was on far shakier ground when he sought to argue that injuries to reputation are not substantial enough as injuries to warrant a move into the federal courts. Rehnquist argued that it was necessary to show a more substantial, material injury, apart from the injury to reputation. The difficulty, however, is that some of the most serious concerns of our law—and some of our most important federal statutes—do not involve injuries of a "material" nature.[64] Beyond that, as we have seen, James Wilson understood that injuries to "character" or reputation are indeed part of the natural rights that are protected by the government. Traditionally, these wrongs have been vindicated through the laws of libel in the separate states. But is it beyond our imagination to conceive of some cases of libel that might be handled more appropriately in a federal forum? In *Paul v. Davis*, a local court would not be asked to pass judgment on a claim of libel brought by one private citizen against another. In this case, the source of the libel was an agency of the state. The lawsuit was directed at the chief of police. In some cities the chief of police or the sheriff is elected; and even when he is not, he is often well-connected politically. To sue an official of this kind in a local court was to sue in a forum in which the case would be heard by a judge who was apt to be drawn from the same political circles as the chief of police. I am not alleging these facts in the case of Paul against Davis. I am suggesting, though, that situations of this kind are anything but rare, and a plaintiff with political savvy, with a measure of wit in reading the local scene, may sum up these points and make his calculations: He may reckon that he has a far better chance, overall, in a federal court, where the judges are not dependent for their salaries, and far less dependent for their advancement, on the local political establishment.

In this prosaic case, could we not have had an instance of what the writers in the Federalist papers were suggesting? On one issue or another, people in the local community may come to trust a more distant, federal government for the protection of certain rights. Martin Diamond found intimations, in the Federalist papers, that the writers expected a gradual shift in the allegiance of citizens to the federal government: not as a wholesale rush to the banner of one leader or party, but as an accumulation of many, separate decisions, taken by litigants and private citizens over many years. The design would emerge, after a long season of experience, if citizens were more inclined to seek the protection of their interests in the institutions and forums of the federal government.[65] The result, in any case, will not be so predictable. Most people suing for libel are still likely to sue in local courts. Nevertheless, we may ask: Why should citizens not have the choice? Why should a member of this polity not be free to choose the courts that he thinks are more likely to render justice in his case?[66] If the accumulated pattern of those separate choices reveals a marked preference for the federal forums, would that not tell us something? And may it not bear out, perhaps, the expectation of the Founders?

. . . . .

Through formulas preciously convoluted, recent generations of our jurists have managed to convince themselves that they were working within a jurisprudence of federalism. In fact, the discipline they were affecting had no philosophic or jural substance. Our jurists mainly succeeded in obscuring the full reach of the federal government and the ground of principle on which that authority ultimately rests. And yet, this ritual of pretentious concealment has preserved a curious condition in our law: Our political men and women have been free to act as though the federal government can reach virtually any wrong that seems to lend itself to a legal remedy. But at the same time, they have continued to act with a constitutional philosophy that denies this sense of what they are doing. Still, the beamish, practical characters among us might ask, What difference does it really make? The fictions of the law may be quite benign, after all, if they allow our political leaders to attend to the work of their generation while inducing them to affect, in public, doctrines of law that would seem to limit their own power. There is of course that passion of certain finicky people, who would like to see a coherent relation between their practice and their public justifications. When there is a discrepancy between the two, we find the law giving a false account of itself. As I have tried to show elsewhere, the law can become distorted or deranged when there is a notable divorce between the grounds on which our legislators find the presence of certain "wrongs," and the grounds they set forth in public when they try to explain how the government can reach these wrongs.[67] But along with this exercise in muddling through, there is a distraction of our jural imagination. If we could get clear about the true ground of principle that underlies the law in any case, we might be able to see more clearly then where the true analogies lie: we might begin to notice cases that have previously gone unperceived; cases masked in different settings, disguised by different circumstances, but engaging the same questions of principle. If we understood, for example, the true meaning of "prior restraints" on expression, we may eventually come to see that the principle is not really engaged when the Nazis are restrained from marching through a Jewish neighborhood, but when the Federal Communications Commission engages in the "licensing" of broadcasters.

If some of these distractions were swept away, if it suddenly became clear to legislators that the federal government could legislate directly on any subject, then the fuller discipline of legislation would come into force. I will take up this question more fully in a while, and I will offer, as one case in point, the recent efforts of the federal government to protect retarded, newborn children from the withdrawal of medical treatment by their parents. If the federal government could reach such a private matter only through indirection—only by threatening to withhold federal money—then it need not face a very demanding set of questions. It would not have to face the stern questions of justification that would need to be addressed if Congress were acting directly to forbid doctors and parents from withholding medical treatment from retarded infants, and if Congress were attaching to that ordinance the penalties of law. For politicians, life may be far more agreeable, altogether, if they can produce the effects of the law, in controlling people, without needing to supply the kind of strenuous justification that the law should require. So long as members of Congress can avoid the appearance of legislating, they can also avoid the discipline of justification that would come into play if they were truly legislating.

For eminently sound reasons of prudence, we have failed to claim for the federal government the sweep of authority that could be claimed, in principle as well as practice, under the Constitution. Some of the more fetching attempts to explain the rationales for these limits have been offered by men in judicial authority—by judges such as Cardozo, Frankfurter, and the second John Harlan. These men offered to a generation of lawyers some thoughtful reasons for preserving a healthy federalism and holding back from "incorporating" the Bill of Rights as a set of constitutional standards that may be applied in their full stringency to the governments in the states. But the mistake came in supposing that the rationales offered by these men were anything more than convenient rules of statecraft. When they were treated as principles of the Constitution, they could not finally offer a justification for themselves. Almost as soon as they were articulated, they were displaced in the progressive trend of the time, to bind the states, ever more precisely, to the stipulations contained in the Bill of Rights. And yet, if the matter could have been treated with more rigor, we might have learned more about the fuller reach—and limitations—of the Bill of Rights. We might have learned that a stricter application of the Bill of Rights would not contract the powers of the states. As Plato recognized, a man with the discipline of self-control was not a weak man; a government restrained by a sense of principle is not a weak government. As I will try to suggest, a proper application of the Bill of Rights might actually enlarge the field of legislation open to the states. At the same time, I think we would discover that the principles that encourage the flourishing of the states would not imply the contraction of the federal government. A disciplined application of the Bill of Rights would no more weaken the powers of the federal government than it would weaken the powers of the states. It is conceivable that the powers of both may be enlarged, even while both governments come to understand more precisely the grounds of principle that establish the limits to their authority. This set of puzzles in our law came to the judges in a series of cases involving swallowed drugs and stomach pumps, hidden microphones and intrusive police. The judges reacted with the proper aversions of civilized men, who were trying to reconcile their reactions with what they regarded as the principles of federalism. And with a proper sense of what made the cases vexing for them, I will pursue that puzzle into the next chapter.

SEVEN

ON THE ART OF "INCORPORATING" RIGHTS

I T MIGHT HAVE been said of the second Justice Harlan that his arts of
delicacy, and his modest genius, found their most concentrated power in
retrospection: Harlan possessed a rare perception, which often allowed
him to grasp a case, belatedly, with more clarity and precision than he was
able to summon when the case was first decided. He could understand a case,
after the fact, with a finer sense of where the case fitted, with the mortises
and beams of other cases, forming a structure of precedents accumulated from
the past. In this manner, he could make comprehensible, in a later day, a case
whose meaning seemed to elude him when the fate of the parties hung upon
his judgment.[1] It was his limited misfortune that his work as a judge could not
have been postponed to some time after history, when his powers could have
been expended in summing up or explaining the judges who had preceded
him.

His most memorable opinions came when he could write separately, in a
concurring or dissenting opinion. There, without the encumbrance of mesh-
ing his sentences with the demands of his colleagues, he could offer the finely
spun musings of a judicial mind that sought a level of subtlety several tiers
beyond the sensibility of his colleagues. When he occasionally soared and
carried his colleagues with him, when he spoke, that is, for the majority, and
not in the voice of a scholarly, finicky loner, his novelties in the law could be
embarrassing among those urbane readers whose understanding was not
formed exclusively by writers in law. Harlan has probably been praised in
none of his opinions more than he has been praised for his sweeping protection of political expression in *Cohen v. California*.[2] And yet this, his largest
sensation as a judge, arose from his insight in discovering, in 1971, the doctrines of ethical emotivism and logical positivism, about thirty years after they
had been discredited in the schools of philosophy.[3] Right or wrong, he managed to preserve a scholarly skepticism on a Court that was growing, in his
tenure, ever more impatient with scholarly refinements. But when his offer-
ings are inspected with the kind of closeness and leisure that distance affords,
many of them appear, as the English used to say, too clever by half. Such, I
think, is the judgment that would finally have to be cast on one of his most
thoughtful and remembered contributions to the work of the Court and the
project of federalism, his separate opinions, in 1957, in the cases on pornography presented in *Roth v. United States* and *Alberts v. California*.[4]

The Court upheld in these cases restrictions on pornography that were imposed by a state, and by the federal government, through the regulation of the mails. These cases also provided the occasion on which the Court delivered itself of the words that would soon make their way into the conversation of the public. Justice Brennan wrote, for the Court, of material that appealed mainly to a "prurient interest." For the meaning of "prurience," he was content to draw upon Webster's dictionary, namely, an excitement of "itching; . . . [of] morbid or lascivious longings."[5] In a curious display of refinement, Justice Harlan joined the opinion of the Court in upholding the restrictions applied by the state of California, but he dissented from the judgment of the Court in sustaining the federal prosecution. Harlan professed to see some notable differences between the two statutes engaged in these cases, but those differences were superficial, and they were not, in the end, decisive for Harlan. In identifying pornography, the courts in California sought to gauge whether any book had a "tendency to deprave or corrupt its readers." Under the federal statute, as it was applied by the judges in the trial courts, the critical test was whether a book might tend "to stir sexual impulses and lead to sexually impure thoughts."[6] Harlan suggested (with lame conviction) that the statute in California at least tried to make a connection between pornography and the kind of overt behavior (depraved and corrupt) which the law may tenably seek to restrain. The federal statute seemed to find the offense of pornography in the generation of "impure thoughts." But the statute in California did not mark off any particular acts of behavior that had to arise from the influence of pornography. It did not suggest that pornography was open to restriction only if one could demonstrate a connection between the consumption of pornography and the carrying out of arson, theft, or rape. As we have long understood, connections of that kind may be quite tenuous. In cases on racial discrimination, it may often be impossible to establish that a material harm has resulted from an exclusion based on race. In some cases, in fact, the intended victims have actually stumbled into material benefits as a happy accident, resulting from their exclusion.[7] We are driven to recognize, in these cases, that people may suffer a wrong—they may be treated according to the maxims of an unjust principle—even if they do not suffer a material harm. In cases of libel, we have recognized a class of libel per se, which does not really depend on the measurement of damages, registered in a loss of business. In some instances, the courts have recognized that a wrong has been done—and then gone on to *infer* the injury from the presence of the wrong. But in other instances, judges have become distracted by the exercise, and they have persisted in believing that the wrong of the libel must be gauged through the measurement of material injuries.[8]

The statutes on pornography, in *Roth* and *Alberts*, seemed to be settled, uneasily, on a ground somewhere between these two understandings. The state of California registered a concern that pornography, like any form of entertainment, may affect the tastes and understanding of people. And by affecting character, a form of entertainment may affect behavior. If pornography teaches coarse, corrupting things, the legislators may draw the inference that pornography may beget coarse, corrupt behavior. The federal statute could have been rephrased in the same way, to refer to the cultivation of corrupted sentiments and tastes, rather than "impure thoughts," but the substance of the matter was the same. As Harlan himself recognized, the state was drawing the inference "that over a long period of time the indiscriminate dissemination of materials, the essential character of which is to degrade sex, will have an eroding effect on moral standards." In other words, the inference of a wrong was to be drawn from an understanding of what was offensive in principle in pornography. The test, in either case, was the same. The statutes sought the same ends, and if they were subject to charges of vagueness, the points of vagueness would have been identical.

Nevertheless, Harlan was willing to accord to the states a wider latitude of judgment in dealing with that vagueness than he was willing to indulge for the federal government. With the federal government he was disposed to be far more stringent and demanding, because he was persuaded that "Congress has no substantive power over sexual morality." For some reason that remained unarticulated, Harlan thought that "the domain of sexual morality is pre-eminently a matter of state concern."⁹ Whether that is the case may depend on what we understand more precisely as "the problem" posed by the concern for sexual morality: If it is a concern with the breakup of families, or with the cultivation, in some of our people, of a depraved, lawless character, then some searching questions can be pressed in considering just why these matters should not touch the concerns of the national community. Years later, when the issue of "child pornography" would become a serious matter, there would be no visible trace of these conceptual distinctions. Within the American political class, both liberals and conservatives supported a federal statute on child pornography. Apparently, it occurred to neither faction in our politics that this matter of recruiting small children for pornographic films raised problems that were confined, most aptly, to our towns and states; that the subject of children in pornography could never enter, legitimately, the concerns of our national politics.

But if we put that issue aside for the moment, Harlan was working on the assumption that states had a far more direct responsibility than the national government in dealing with the injuries that were likely to arise from pornography. Harlan found his guide here in Robert Jackson's opinion, five years earlier, in *Beauharnais v. Illinois* (1952).¹⁰ That remarkable case involved the defamation of racial groups, or the stirring of ethnic hatreds. Jackson argued, in his separate opinion, that the local governments had a direct responsibility in dealing with the results of this defamation, in the form of riots, or in the degraded climate of civility in the local community. For these injuries the local governments provided remedies through the laws of defamation, or through the engagement of the police in restraining violence in the streets. On these matters, the engagement of the federal government was remote. And for that reason, Jackson pleaded for a certain caution or restraint on the part of the federal government in intervening too casually or too quickly and undercutting those people in local office, whose authority was immediately necessary in sustaining the protections of the law.[11]

Harlan was inspired to argue now in the same vein in cases on pornography. The Court could tenably hold the federal government to a much sterner standard in the restricting of publications, while at the same time, it could allow a much wider latitude to the states. Harlan filled out his understanding in this way:

> Not only is the federal interest in protecting the Nation against pornography attenuated, but the dangers of federal censorship in this field are far greater than anything the States may do. It has often been said that one of the great strengths of our federal system is that we have, in the forty-eight States, forty-eight experimental social laboratories. . . . Different States will have different attitudes toward the same work of literature. The same book which is freely read in one State might be classed as obscene in another. And it seems to me that no overwhelming danger to our freedom to experiment and to gratify our tastes in literature is likely to result from the suppression of a borderline book in one of the States, so long as there is no uniform nation-wide suppression of the book, and so long as other States are free to experiment with the same or bolder books.
>
> Quite a different situation is presented, however, where the Federal Government imposes the ban. The danger is perhaps not great if the people of one State, through their legislature, decide that "Lady Chatterly's Lover" goes so far beyond the acceptable standards of candor that it will be deemed offensive and nonsellable, for the State next door is still free to make its own choice. At least we do not have one uniform standard. But the dangers to free thought and expression are truly great if the Federal Government imposes a blanket ban over the Nation on such a book. The prerogative of the States to differ on their ideas of morality will be destroyed, the ability of States to experiment will be stunted. The fact that the people of one state cannot read some of the works of D. H. Lawrence seems to be, if not wise or desirable, at least acceptable. But that no person in the United States should be allowed to do so seems to me to be intolerable, and violative of both the letter and spirit of the Constitution.[12]

This construction, so plausible on its face, accounts for much of what is appealing in the arrangements of our communities under the federal structure. People have been attracted to small towns and cities precisely because they have been able to mark off a special character in their public policy. Certain suburban communities distinguished themselves by the quality of their public schools, by the willingness of the residents to tax themselves at a higher rate in order to sustain their schools. Other communities have held out the alternative of very low tax rates, with fewer public services and less intrusive controls on the part of government. Some communities have joined the powers of zoning to a sense of aesthetic standards in preserving a tony style in architecture. If people liked the schools in Evanston, Illinois, but if they were averse to the policies that barred the sale of alcohol, they had their own choices to make. They could drive out of town to buy their liquor, or if they valued the drinks more than the schools, they could move to another place. What was appealing in these local communities was the special character that arose from a certain autonomy in government, and that autonomy could in turn be the source of policies that were uncongenial or even repellent. The question, at all times, was whether the repellent features were merely personal, or whether they reached a plane of principle and threatened "rights." If people seriously thought they had "rights" under the Constitution to read what they wished, even if the books were pornographic, they might not be so content to move, with their rights, to another town. When the powers of zoning were used to prevent abortion clinics from operating as businesses in any town, the people who earnestly believed in a "right to an abortion" preferred to move into a federal court and challenge these decisions that were taken, at the local level, in the name of the autonomy and character of the community.

Harlan's construction, so plausible in its explanation, was built on a mistake grown familiar in our own time, namely, the willingness to detach the notion of "rights" from its moral logic. That confusion was registered in his innocent remark that the imposition of a uniform, national rule would remove "the prerogative of the States to differ on their ideas of morality." What is contained in this passage is the same "positivist" understanding that we saw earlier, in the remarks of Robert Bork, on the "moralities" of judges. "Moralities" were always in the plural because there were as many notions of morality as there were persons to conceive them. As I suggested earlier, this argument dissolved as soon as it came up against the logic of morals, which is built into our language of right and wrong. As Lincoln pointed out, in invoking this logic, it is incoherent to say at the same time that slavery is "wrong" and that the separate territories should be free to vote slavery up or down. We would hardly take it as a measure of vitality in the federal system if the different states were allowed to act as "laboratories," in trying out different "moralities" on the question of slavery. But to return to the issues of our own day, let us assume that the example of pornography were replaced, in Harlan's argument, by the example of abortion. It should be plain that none of the current defenders of abortion could find a shred of plausibility in the scheme put forth by Harlan. No one who seriously thinks that there is a "constitutional right to choose an abortion," is prepared to see that freedom dissolved in any city or state, when a local majority is inclined to "experiment" by abridging or withdrawing that "right." And of course, the same understanding would hold true on the other side. Those who regard abortion as the taking of a life can never be content with an arrangement that merely returns the question of abortion to the separate states. They are not prepared to leave to the judgment of a legislature the question of whether offspring in the womb will be regarded as human beings or as nascent snail darters, and whether those beings may claim the protections of the law.

The two sides in the dispute may disagree on the question of who the bearers of rights are in these cases—the pregnant women or the unborn children. But both sides are convinced that there are moral rights and wrongs at stake. And therefore, both sides would have to reject Harlan's ingenious arrangement as a formal scheme utterly empty of substance. The vacuity of the arrangement may be exposed even more fully if we simply applied the premises in the scheme more consistently: Harlan asks just why we should risk the rigidities that come from imposing a uniform, blanket rule across the states. But why should we accept the same rigidities when they are imposed, say, on Chicago and Cairo, Illinois, merely because they are contained within the same state? Why obliterate, in this way, the diversity of codes and moral textures that we find within the separate states? Why should we forego the possibility of having, not forty-eight or fifty, but hundreds of laboratories within the state, as the towns and counties preserve their freedom to experiment with their own "moralities"? And yet, the application of this argument need not stop there. Why should we risk, within the towns and counties, the contraction of freedom that comes with the legislating of one policy, one rule? Why not leave the matter, finally, to the hundreds of thousands of experiments that may be tried simply by leaving *individuals*, persons, free to test their "moralities" in all their variety?

Harlan's argument must be condemned by its own premises to collapse upon itself. If we are convinced we are in the presence of a "wrong," then we would not be discomfited by the notion of legislating to forbid that wrong generally or universally. We would not be troubled by the imposition, then, of a uniform or blanket rule on slavery or the abuse of children. We would not be unhinged, that is, to discover that nowhere, in the territory of the United States, can parents claim a "right" to torture their children. But if we are not clear that there is a "wrong" we can define in principle, if we think that there is something problematic or murky in the very standards that identify the nature of the wrong in any case, it could hardly follow, as a logical conclusion, that only the *national* government ought to hold back from legislating. Assume, for a moment, that people in government were weighing a policy of price controls on works of art. They think it is obscene and wrong to charge hundreds of thousands of dollars for certain paintings or works of sculpture. But they soon discover that they cannot settle on a schedule that would fix the appropriate prices, say, for oils as distinct from water colors, or bronze figures as distinct from massive, abstract constructions in steel. They finally conclude that they have no prospect of establishing a consensus across the country on a fair and reasonable schedule of prices. But they also reason that this intractable problem of national politics need not hamstring governments at all levels: Within the states and towns, smaller communities may find it far easier to establish a consensus on what a work of art ought reasonably to cost, just as they may claim to act now, under policies of rent control, to make judgments about the kinds of rents that are fair or just for all manners of dwellings.

And yet, I hope it would be plain that the decisive point in this problem is not the presence or absence of consensus, but the question of whether there are any principles that could establish, in the first place, rightful and wrongful prices for works of art. In the absence of those principles, the task of legislating is not rendered more practicable or legitimate simply by transferring that project to a local government. The same doubts that inspire the national government to hold back from legislating should inspire the local governments to stay their own hands as well. If the standards of judgment are in so much question, the moral discipline of law would not enjoin us to fly to the scheme of federalism as an ingenious way around the problem: The discipline of moral judgment would suggest, rather, that the law should recede from this project altogether.

The problem for Harlan, then, was that he could not deny the claim of the federal government to legislate on any subject without in turn raising the most serious doubts about the ground on which governments at *any* level would be justified in legislating. But the same logical problems do not run in the reverse direction. To show that the federal government would be justified in legislating on any subject (e.g., pornography, discrimination in housing) would not necessarily show that the state governments must be incompetent to legislate on the same subject. It is conceivable that both governments may properly legislate. They may be spared the need to do the same things at once, and the arrangment may offer the chance to settle on a prudent division of labor. But at times, it may be a mark of our seriousness in addressing certain urgent problems (such as drugs or pollution) that we are willing to mandate the authorities, at all levels, to use the special arts and levers they have available to them, in serving the same public and addressing our common maladies.

But on this, more later. What must be understood about Justice Harlan is that he was attaching himself to a small college of judges who were leaning against the currents of the time, who were straining to be thoughtful, to post warnings, to suggest to their colleagues that the landscape of American law contained many irregular, curious divisions that eluded their simple formulas, but nevertheless merited their respect. What these judges were resisting was the impulse to bring the states more fully under the review of the federal courts by applying the Bill of Rights to the states in a sweeping, formulaic way. Even after the centralizing revolution of the Civil War, even after the passage of the Fourteenth Amendment, the Court continued to endorse the understanding expressed by Chief Justice Marshall in *Barron v. Baltimore*[13] in 1833: that the restrictions of the Bill of Rights applied only to the federal government, not to the states. The First Amendment stipulated that "Congress shall make no law . . . abridging freedom of speech, or of the press"; but that was not taken to mean that the states were restrained in the same way. With this kind of distinction, Jefferson and his party could resist the federal Sedition Act as an exercise of federal power, but they could still insist that the states preserved a vast power to punish libels. Armed with this serviceable doctrine, Jefferson and his allies felt no inhibitions in using the sedition statutes in the separate states to launch "a few wholesome prosecutions" for libel against the more intemperate critics of the administration.[14]

This understanding of the Bill of Rights was not uniformly followed in the federal courts,[15] but it was not unsettled by the Supreme Court until 1925. In *Gitlow v. New York*,[16] the Court upheld a statute on criminal anarchy in New York, which prohibited the "advocacy . . . of overthrowing or overturning organized government by force or violence." In the course of the opinion, however, Justice Sanford allowed that the freedoms of expression mentioned in the Bill of Rights "are among the fundamental personal rights and 'liberties' protected by the due process clause of the Fourteenth Amendment from impairment by the states."[17] From this modest recognition a new doctrine, or at least a new slogan, of jurisprudence would spring, namely, that the Fourteenth Amendment had "incorporated" or absorbed the full inventory of provisions in the Bill of Rights and made them binding upon the states. Starting in 1947, Justice Hugo Black embraced this position emphatically and made it part of his agenda for the Court.[18] He was resisted at the time by Frankfurter and Jackson, and later by Harlan. But when Harlan wrote his dissent in the Roth case, the Court was at the threshold of change. Beginning in 1961, with *Mapp v. Ohio*,[19] the Court would begin to apply to the states the more stringent rules that the Court had developed over the years in applying the provisions of the Bill of Rights to the federal government. If the local authorities had violated a more exacting reading of the provision, in the Fourth Amendment, on "searches and seizures," there was a willingness now to *exclude* the evidence collected in that way and throw out the convictions. (Hence, the so-called "exclusionary rule.") One by one, the Court would extend to the states the provisions in the Bill of Rights, read in the most restrictive way, and within a decade the coverage would be virtually complete.

In some cases, Harlan found himself agreeing with the result, but denying the theory. He had no doubt that the federal courts could protect citizens if the states restricted, unreasonably, their freedom of expression or denied them the requirements of a fair trial. But that was not because of any stipulation in the First Amendment about the freedom of speech, or any provision in the Sixth Amendment about the right to have the "Assistance of Counsel." With the Fourteenth Amendment the Court had an ample franchise for protecting people against deprivations of "life, liberty, or property, without due process of law." If the Court found, in any case, the denial of a right, it did not have to fit the case under the formulas of the Bill of Rights in order to extend the restraints of the Constitution. "The logically critical thing," said Harlan, "was not that the rights had been found in the Bill of Rights, but that they were deemed . . . fundamental."[20]

The skeptics tended to regard Harlan's protests here as an enduring quibble. What difference did it make if the judges reached the same result in the end? But Harlan did not regard his argument here as a refinement without consequence for the work of the Court. In Harlan's understanding, the Court would be compelled to deliberate on the question of whether there was revealed, in the details of any case, a "right" that claimed the protection of the Constitution. The Court would not be allowed to evade that discipline of judgment simply by invoking a formula in the Bill of Rights—by assuming, for example, that the Bill of Rights was engaged every time that a state restrained public expression or a lawyer was not made available, free of charge, to a defendant. As we have already seen, our first generation of jurists understood that the Bill of Rights itself did not contain formulas of that kind. They did not assume that any instance in the restriction of speech (e.g., the punishment of libel) furnished a case that came under the Bill of Rights. It was still necessary to deliberate on whether the restriction of speech, in any case, was justified or unjustified. For the same reason, it would not illuminate the work of the Court simply to say that the First Amendment was binding on the states. There would still be the need to consider, in the same way, whether any restriction imposed by the state was a restriction of expression that could not be justified. To that enterprise of deliberation, the Bill of Rights added nothing. And the license to engage in this deliberation, in judging the restrictions of the state, was already supplied to the Court in the Fourteenth Amendment (if, indeed, the Court required any such special license). It is notable, in this respect, that even in the Gitlow case, Justice Stanford did not claim that the rights of speech could be protected because the Court could deploy the Bill of Rights against the states. As Sanford explained, the Court simply understood that the right not to suffer restrictions on speech without justification was "among the fundamental personal rights and 'liberties' protected by the due process clause of the Fourteenth Amendment from impairment by the states."[21] What is more telling, the same assumption was made by the dissenting judges. Holmes and Brandeis would have protected, in this case, the right of the Left Wing Section of the Socialist Party to advocate the overthrow of the government. But they did not think that the "right" they were protecting in this instance had to be rooted in the First Amendment or the Bill of Rights. As Holmes remarked, "The general principle of free speech . . . must be taken to be included in the Fourteenth Amendment, in view of the scope that has been given to the word 'liberty' as there used." He was quick, though, to add that "perhaps [this principle of free speech] may be accepted with a somewhat larger latitude of interpretation [in relation to the States] than is allowed to Congress."[22]

Harlan sought to preserve, then, this older understanding: The Court could well protect persons from the denial of "fundamental rights" on the part of the states. It could engage, in that mission, any principles or rights contained in the Bill of Rights; but it would not apply the Bill of Rights in a formulaic way. It would not assume that every provision in the first eight amendments articulated a fundamental right or a principle of law that had to be applied, without qualification, to the states as well as to the federal government. For example, the Second Amendment stipulated that "A well regulated Militia, being necessary to the security of a free State, the right of the people to keep and bear Arms, shall not be infringed." This amendment was understood as a guarantee that the federal government would not have a monopoly on the legitimate use of force. The states would have the means of protecting their citizens from domestic violence, without waiting for federal troops; and they might even have a means of resisting a tyrannical central government. The amendment seemed to embody a policy that was to be applied mainly as a restriction on the federal government. It was not at all clear that it expressed a principle that deserved to be applied to the states as well—as in removing from the states the authority to regulate the use of private guns.

Harlan joined a line of judges who were willing to take up the discipline of a philosophic inquiry and consider, in one case after another, whether any particular provision in the Bill of Rights could plausibly claim the standing of a necessary principle of law. If any provision could meet that demanding test, then it would rightly be applied to the states, as well as to the national government. Harlan and Frankfurter worked at this task over many years without much illumination, and with a diminishing effect on their colleagues. They would take, as their main guide, Benjamin Cardozo's opinion in *Palko v. Connecticut* (1937).[23] That brief, suggestive opinion encompassed the problem, and it marked off the ground that Cardozo's successors would have to explore if they were to advance the understanding of the Court. But the missteps that Frankfurter would later make would also find their origin in the difficulties that Cardozo suffered in that earlier, landmark case in settling his judicial mind.

Frank Palko had been indicted in Fairfield County, Connecticut, for murder in the first degree. He was found guilty of murder in the second degree and sentenced to prison for life. But the state of Connecticut sought an appeal on the basis of several errors at the trial, which prevented the state from making a compelling case for its most serious charge. The Supreme Court of Connecticut agreed, on appeal, that there had indeed been serious errors "to the prejudice of the state." The trial court had excluded testimony on a confession made by Palko, as well as testimony that would have impeached his credibility. In addition, there had been an error in the instruction to the jury on the difference between first and second degree murder. In the judgment of the Supreme Court of Connecticut, these errors warranted a new trial. Palko was tried again, the jury returned a verdict of murder in the first degree, and he was sentenced this time to death.

Before the onset of the second trial, Palko raised an objection on constitutional grounds. To be tried again for the same crime seemed to run against that provision in the Fifth Amendment, that no person shall be "subject for the same offence to be twice put in jeopardy of life or limb." The objection was overruled, and the trial commenced, but it was the question of "double jeopardy" that brought the case on appeal to the Supreme Court. Cardozo condensed the brief for Palko.

> The argument for appellant is that whatever is forbidden by the Fifth Amendment is forbidden by the Fourteenth also. The Fifth Amendment, which is not directed to the states, but solely to the federal government, creates immunity from double jeopardy. . . . [I]n appellant's view the Fourteenth Amendment is to be taken as embodying the prohibitions of the Fifth. His thesis is even broader. Whatever would be a violation of the original bill of rights (Amendments I to VIII) if done by the federal government is now equally unlawful by force of the Fourteenth Amendment if done by a state. There is no such general rule.[24]

Cardozo noted that the Fifth Amendment also provided, in its first clause, that "No person shall be held to answer for a capital, or otherwise infamous crime, unless on a presentment or indictment of a Grand Jury." And yet, the Court had treated this provision merely as a rule that bore on the federal government. The Court found no breach of justice, no denial of "due process of law," when a state decided to dispense with grand juries and hand down indictments in the form of "informations" filed by a public prosecutor. The Fifth Amendment also stipulated that "no person shall be compelled in any criminal case to be a witness against himself." But the Court had found no violation of the Constitution when certain states came to regard the arrangement as a privilege that may be withdrawn, rather than a right which may not be abridged. In a similar way, the Sixth Amendment had provided for a trial by jury in criminal cases, and the Seventh Amendment for a jury trial at common law when the value in dispute exceeded twenty dollars. Still, the Court had not been willing to say that it was unreasonable for any *state* to modify the trial by jury in certain instances, or to displace juries altogether with trials at the hands of judges.[25]

On the other side, Cardozo acknowledged that some portions of the Bill of Rights did seem to be absorbed through the Fourteenth Amendment and applied to the states. In that class he placed the freedom of speech, the right to peaceable assembly ("without which speech would be unduly trammeled"), and the right to counsel. But he strained to make the more refined point that the Fourteenth Amendment did not incorporate these rights merely because they were mentioned in the Bill of Rights. And so, for example, in that signal case on the right to counsel, *Powell v. Alabama* (1932),

> ignorant defendants in a capital case were held to have been condemned unlawfully when in truth, though not in form, they were refused the aid of counsel. . . . The decision did not turn upon the fact that the benefit of counsel would have been guaranteed to the defendants by the provisions of the Sixth Amendment if they had been prosecuted in a federal court. The decision turned upon the fact that in the particular situation laid before us in the evidence the benefit of counsel was essential to the substance of a hearing.[26]

Again, the difference may seem so refined that it may be indiscernible to most onlookers; and yet, if the judges were really fit for these exertions of mind, Cardozo's understanding opened this notable, vast prospect: The judges could have protected the defendants in *Powell v. Alabama even if there had been no Sixth Amendment*. It was open to the judges to discover and articulate a much wider range of rights than anything set down in the Bill of Rights. The recognition of rights depended then on the depths of reflection summoned by the judges as they considered those implications that had to be contained in "the lawful rendering of justice," the implications that could be drawn from the logic of "due process of law."

But how did Cardozo himself understand this discipline of finding the implications of the Fourteenth Amendment? How did he explain the difference between the parts of the Bill of Rights that were absorbed by the Fourteenth Amendment, and the parts that were not considered so fundamental or critical that they had to be binding on the states? Cardozo conceded that "the line of division may seem to be wavering." Still, he thought that, with a strenuous reflection, "there emerges the perception of a rationalizing principle which gives to discrete instances a proper order and coherence." Cardozo allowed, for example, that the right to a trial by jury, or the right to be prosecuted only after an indictment by a grand jury, were features that had "value and importance." But "even so, they are not of the very essence of a scheme of ordered liberty. To abolish them is not to violate a 'principle of justice so rooted in the traditions and conscience of our people as to be ranked as fundamental.' "[27]

This notion of "a scheme of ordered liberty" did not exactly explain itself. As Cardozo roughly recognized, the object was to identify those arrangements that were utterly necessary or essential to the idea of rendering justice. But as Cardozo sought to explain this standard, through a series of examples, he really sketched in two standards, which could point in different directions and imply two radically different methods for extracting our judgments. On the one hand, the standard of judgment was distinctly *logical*, and the enterprise involved here was the discipline of drawing out the logical implications that flow, as I have suggested, from the very idea of justice. Taking again the examples of trial by jury and indictments by grand juries, Cardozo remarked that "few would be so narrow or provincial as to maintain that a fair and enlightened system of justice would be impossible without them."[28] In the seasons of our experience, we have seen juries, grand and petit, animated by prejudice. It could never be said, then, as a categorical proposition, with the force of a true principle, that a jury will always render a verdict more just than any decision that is likely to be rendered by a judge trained in the law. It could not strictly be said then that a trial by jury was absolutely necessary to a just trial. And if we did not recognize the force of that point, we could not justify our willingness to permit many defendants to waive a trial by jury and have their cases tried solely by judges. If these defendants were waiving arrangements that were indispensable to the logic of a just trial, we should be obliged to save them from "alienating" a right that must be "inalienable."

Conversely, when Cardozo set about explaining the provisions that were necessary or essential to a constitutional government, he began with a notion of features so critical "that neither liberty nor justice would exist if they were sacrificed."[29] And here he would move with the shortest of steps, with the care of one who was trying to put in place a modest, but unshakeably logical, train of propositions. He began with freedom of thought and speech: "Of that freedom one may say that it is the matrix, the indispensable condition, of nearly every other form of freedom." As a "logical imperative," then, the liberties protected by the Fourteenth Amendment, against the restrictions of the states, were extended to include "liberty of the mind as well as liberty of action."[30] The notion of acting in a lawful way, in rendering fair and accurate verdicts, was summarized in the notion of "due process of law"; and from that point, as Cardozo suggested, it was a matter of drawing out the *implications that were simply necessary to the rendering of justice.* And thus: "condemnation shall be rendered only after trial. *Scott v. McNeal . . . Blackmer v. United States . . .* The hearing, moreover, must be a real one, not a sham or a pretense. *Moore v. Dempsey . . . Mooney v. Holohan.*"[31] And so on in this vein: Modest steps, with clear connections, and the string of cases in which these logical implications were progressively recognized.

That, as I say, was the first path: We begin with the very idea of "rendering justice" and proceed to draw out its implications. But along with this account of the cases, Cardozo mixed in some other phrases, which suggested a rather different path, and a rather different standard for the recognition of rights. In a passage quoted above, Cardozo referred to principles of justice "rooted in the traditions and conscience of our people."[32] They were the principles that could be "traced in our history, political and legal,"[33] and their standing would be confirmed in the opinions of those who were not "narrow or provincial."[34] With these phrases, Cardozo suggested a standard of moral judgment far more familiar to lawyers trained in the traditions of positivism and legal realism: Judges had long been tutored now to be skeptical of enduring principles of justice, principles that could be valid and recognized in all places. They were far more comfortable with a more modest claim, to discover the principles of moral judgment that were settled within *this community* and preserved in the traditions of *this place*. As Cardozo remarked, the relevant record of experience here was the record of "our history," the "traditions and conscience of our people." In this perspective, the notion of rights would not be drawn from the "logic of morals" or the central idea of rendering justice. It would be drawn, rather, from the conventions that made up *our* traditions, and from the opinions that supported those conventions—the opinions that were dominant among "our people."

A jurist habituated to logic might be inclined to offer a radically different account of his vocation: He might be inclined to explain the rudiments of a just trial by explaining the connection between an accurate verdict and the insistence on weighing evidence and testimony with the canons of reason. To grasp that connection is to understand, at once, why the arrangements of a trial are in principle superior to any system for drawing inferences about innocence and guilt from the performance of a defendant in walking over hot coals. Once that connection is established between the canons of reason and the rendering of an accurate verdict, that connection should be sufficient unto itself. There would be no need to canvass our history to see whether the connection had been noticed in the past. Nor would there be any particular relevance in conducting a survey of the opinions of "our people," to see if they recognized any such requirements of a fair trial. The possibility should not be consigned entirely to the domain of romance that certain notions of justice have become part of the tradition and conscience of our people precisely because they *are* in accord with the reason and logic of justice. But in that event, the appeal to reason should be sufficient—and sovereign. For after all, by the test of "tradition," any novel recognitions, any new interpretations of rights, would have to be invalid. Or at the very least, they would have to come under the most serious doubt. By Cardozo's account, it was not until 1932, in *Powell v. Alabama*, that the Court declared a willingness to review the trials in a state in order to insure that "the hearing . . . must be a real one, not a sham or a pretense." Since the Court had not claimed that mandate for itself in the past, this vindication of a constitutional right had evidently not been part of the legal "traditions" of our people. Its absence had not apparently disturbed any notion of justice "rooted in the . . . conscience of our people." The Court was articulating new rights, arising from the character of the Constitution. Were we to believe that the judges were merely acting now as a band of legal anthropologists? Were they simply unearthing convictions that had been immured in our traditions all along, but somehow never brought to the point of expression? Or would it come closer to the truth to offer this account: That it was precisely the work of the Court to school our people to a more exacting temper of justice by drawing out for us—drawing out, even, for our *new* recognitions—the implications contained in the very idea of doing justice.

But Cardozo's teaching in *Palko v. Connecticut* straddled these two different methods of discovering rights and the requirements of the Constitution. Because he straddled the question, he failed to concentrate the minds of his successors on the kind of philosophic reflection that was indispensable to this calling of jurisprudence. It was only to be expected that many of his successors on the Court would find, in his teaching, the method that was more familiar to them, and their inclination would then be to convert jurisprudence into an exercise in historicism or psychology. Instead of testing any claim against the logic of morals itself, or the logic of "justice," some of the judges would spend their genius in canvassing again the history of our conventions, or gauging the "conscience" of our people by reporting on their own psychological reactions in any case. Years later, in the famous "stomach pump" case, a man suspected of selling narcotics swallowed two capsules when the police forced their way into his bedroom. After the police failed to extract the capsules, they took him to a hospital, where an emetic was forced into his stomach. He vomited two capsules, which were found to contain morphine. On the basis of this evidence he was convicted under a law in California that forbade the possession of morphine. Justice Frankfurter was shaken, in this case, from his legendary restraint in relation to the states. He was also displaced, for this signal moment, from his persistent unwillingness to throw out convictions because the evidence had been collected in a manner that was not strenuously correct. Frankfurter insisted that the grounds of judgment in this case were not merely personal and "self-willed": "the proceedings by which this conviction was obtained do more than offend some fastidious squeamishness or private sentimentalism." And yet, as Justice Black complained in a concurring opinion, the decisive sentences in Frankfurter's opinion seemed irreducibly, impenetrably personal. "This is conduct," said Frankfurter, "that shocks the conscience. . . . [T]his course of proceeding by agents of the government . . . is bound to offend even hardened sensibilities. They are methods too close to the rack and the screw to permit of constitutional differentiation."[35]

Two years later, Frankfurter's conscience would not suffer a comparable shock when police in California entered and reentered the home of a suspect in order to place a microphone, with more advantage, in the bedroom. Or at least Frankfurter was not moved in this case, as he was in *Rochin v. California*, to throw out the evidence and the conviction.[36] For some reason he did not seek to explain, his threshold of outrage was not crossed in this case, as it had been in *Rochin*—all of which made the standards of judgment seem all the more personal and idiosyncratic.

In fairness, however, it must be said that Cardozo had furnished his successors with far subtler guides. And in that respect it is worth recalling the more refined examples he offered as he finally explained the judgment of the Court in the Palko case. The question in the case involved the meaning of "double jeopardy," but in working his way to that point, Cardozo took, as an analogy, the problem of settling the meaning of another provision in the Fifth Amendment, which granted, as he put it, an "immunity from compulsory self-incrimination." Cardozo noted that there was an enduring dispute over the utility, the justification, even the meaning of that provision. There were many students of the law who regarded this convention "as a mischief rather than a benefit, and who would limit its scope or destroy it altogether." For his own part, he thought that the provision stood with an unassailable force when it was understood to offer "protection against torture, physical or mental." But that was quite different from a blanket immunity from answering any proper, pointed question that touched on one's knowledge of a crime. It was not evident to Cardozo that any principle in the Fifth Amendment would cover such a claim to hold back evidence, or that justice would perish "if the accused were subject to a duty to respond to orderly inquiry."[37]

In the same way, it was not apparent to him that the clause on "double jeopardy" would be violated any time a person was tried a second time on the same charges. In *Palko*, the state was not "attempting to wear the accused out by a multitude of cases with accumulated trials." The authorities could not be warranted in snatching a man from the occupations of his private life and subjecting him to a series of trials that would continue until the prosecutors found a suitably credulous jury, willing to convict. But in this case there had been errors that bore a direct relevance to the judgment that a jury could reach. As Cardozo pointed out, "if the trial had been infected with error adverse to the accused," no one would have caviled over the prospect of a second trial. There was no principle that barred, categorically, any second process, any retrying of the same cause, if there were grounds on which to believe that there were, in the first trial, errors that prevented a just verdict. Cardozo raised the question of why the same reasoning would not support a reciprocal claim on the part of the state. After all, an injustice may not come solely with the conviction of an innocent man. It may be found, also, in the failure to punish the guilty and to vindicate the wrong that was done to the victim. In the end, said Cardozo, the state "asks no more than this, that the case against [Palko] shall go on until there shall be a trial free from the corrosion of substantial legal error. . . . There is here no seismic innovation. The edifice of justice stands, its symmetry, to many greater than before."[38]

From these winged words, caricatures would later spring. Commentators in the law would look back to Cardozo and draw, from these phrases, the notion that the Bill of Rights does not bind the states in the same way that it binds the national government. But I think Cardozo's account here lends itself to a far more calibrated understanding. Clearly, Cardozo did not think that all parts of the Bill of Rights expressed principles of law, which had to be respected, in all places, by all governments that presumed to call themselves governments of law. It would become necessary to consider, then, just which parts of the Bill of Rights actually expressed principles of that kind. The critical test is whether any feature in the Bill of Rights would flow, as a necessary implication, from the idea of law itself, or from the very notion of rendering "justice." As Cardozo suggested, the test of any such principle of law is whether *any* intelligible notion of justice is conceivable in its absence or its denial.

But the language of the Bill of Rights is not set forth in this style. The propositions contained there do not reveal just how they were derived, in a chain of propositions emanating from the logic of law itself. For that reason, it is necessary for the judges to supply that touchstone of philosophy: They may begin with the language in the Bill of Rights (e.g., "nor shall any person be subject for the same offence to be twice put in jeopardy of life or limb"), and their task is to consider whether they could trace that passage back to any proposition that arises, as a logical implication, from the idea of law itself. Their discipline is to move, from the language of the Bill of Rights, to the underlying logic, or the first principles, of law. Only if they can make that connection will they be able to find the principle contained in any clause of the Bill of Rights. And if they can discover the principle of law that lies behind any clause, they would have a standard for recognizing the cases that truly offer instances of that principle. They would be in a position then to distinguish those cases from the cases that do not finally engage these principles of law—the cases that raise, in the end, only a spurious claim to a constitutional issue.

In the case of Palko, the difference may show itself in this way: Cardozo did not claim that the provision on "double jeopardy" marked no principle of law; nor did he suggest that the Fifth Amendment, or the principle behind "double jeopardy," would not be binding on the states. He concluded, rather, that the case of Palko simply *did not offer an instance of "double jeopardy."* It furnished no example that came plausibly under the concerns marked in the law by the notion of double jeopardy. But at the same time, Cardozo left the implication that the principle of double jeopardy would indeed apply to the states, in any case in which that principle bore any relevance to the facts at hand.

And yet, if we followed Cardozo this far, the momentum of the reasoning would carry us one additional step further, with this novel result: The whole dispute over the "incorporation" of the Bill of Rights in the Fourteenth Amendment, the dispute that has engaged the most serious minds on the Court for over fifty years, would dissolve as a problem without substance. If we followed Cardozo, we would not enforce the provisions of the Bill of Rights with a mindless literalism. We would establish the meaning of these provisions by seeking the principles that stand behind them, and we would enforce upon the states only the real principles of law that can be found in the Bill of Rights. If Palko's case did not engage the principle of double jeopardy, then the Court would not presume to interfere merely because the state was trying him for a second time. But then the further twist: If the same case had arisen in a *federal* court, presumably it would still not have furnished an instance of double jeopardy. In that event, why should the federal government be restrained, any more than the states, in a case that did not violate the principle behind "double jeopardy"?

The problem might be summarized finally in this way: To the extent that we articulate a genuine principle of law, that principle is bound up with the logic of administering justice, and it would be binding, as a *logical* necessity, on governments at all levels, and governments in all places. From the logic of morals, for example, we could draw as a necessary principle of law that "we ought not hold people blameworthy or responsible for acts they were powerless to affect." If Smith were thrown out of a window, and on the way down landed on Jones, we would not hold Smith responsible for an "assault." From this simple recognition many other corollaries follow, and I have drawn some of them out already in another place.[39] When we grasp the necessary force of this point, we understand that it is *tied logically* to the very idea of justice—that any system of justice would be incoherent if it denied this proposition. We would grasp, then, at the same time, that this proposition would be valid as a principle anywhere in the domain of reason where moral agents were rendering judgments on matters of innocence and guilt. It would be as valid in New Jersey as in Washington, D.C. It would be as valid in the private affairs of a family as in the decisions rendered by a Court. If parents punished a child for a wrong committed before he was born, and which he had been powerless to affect, the injustice of the act would be as plain as any comparable imbecility, applied in a legal forum.

To the extent that the Bill of Rights leads us back to real principles of law in that sense, then those principles must, perforce, be binding on the states, as well as on the national government. And that is why it would be unavailing, finally, to act on the recommendation that has been offered in recent years by some commentators on our law, to restore the holding of Justice Marshall in *Barron v. Baltimore*, namely, that the Bill of Rights shall be understood, again, as a set of constraints that bear only on the federal government.

This proposal has emanated from writers who have seen, in the federal courts, a record of unchecked authority, wedded to an overt political project; of judges who have snapped any tether of discipline that may connect their judgments to the principles of the Constitution.[40] There has been a concern, that is, about judges who deny that there is any such discipline, or any such prescriptive meaning, in the Constitution. These judges have been pleased to regard their commissions, as judges, as a license to shape the Constitution to their own tutored sensibilities. And their notions about the proper ordering of our law has shown a remarkable tendency to coincide with the liberal perspective in our politics. It is that blending of politics and jurisprudence that has inspired, in turn, remedies that are more striking than measured; and included in that number is the proposal to restore the doctrine in *Barron v. Baltimore*.

With this proposal, "activist" judges may be deprived of one of their most potent devices for tying the hands of the local police and undercutting the capacity of local governments to govern. I should say that I am, for my own part, quite sympathetic to the concerns that have brought forth these proposals, and I must note, also, that some of them have been brought forth by my own friends. But if we follow the understanding I have set forth here, in its root simplicity, I think we could see, more readily, just why these proposals could not be sustained in principle. At the same time, though, we would see why they may be unnecessary. If we restored a proper discipline of constitutional judgment, the Bill of Rights would not be used casually to encumber local governments for the morale or recreation of federal judges. The requirements for identifying the "principles" of our law would be suitably exacting. To the extent that any case does not engage an authentic principle of the law, in that demanding sense, the Bill of Rights would simply bear no relevance to the case. But in that event, the fuller meaning of this point should not be obscured: If the case engages no principle of the law, in the deepest sense, then the Bill of Rights should not be invoked, in an artless way, to hamstring the national government, any more than it is used to interfere with the earnest efforts of the states in making laws.

．　．　．　．　．

The point I am urging here is not especially esoteric, but it has been made harder to grasp in a jurisprudence that has suffered from the steady, obscuring effects of third-rate philosophy. An example rather near to us may be helpful, then, in illuminating the point. In 1971, in *California v. Byers*, the Court sustained a statute in California that dealt with hit-and-run accidents on the highways.[41] Anyone involved in an accident that caused damage to property was obliged by the law to stop and disclose his identity to the owner or operator of the vehicle that was damaged. Alternatively, he could leave the information on the damaged vehicle and notify the police about the details of the accident. The law was inspired by an evident concern to furnish timely aid to victims, and to establish an accurate record for the assessment of rights and wrongs. But as with other schemes of "self-reporting," the measure seemed to collide with the protections, in the Fifth Amendment, against self-incrimination. The Supreme Court in California held that the law would violate the Fifth Amendment unless this condition was attached: the driver should be sheltered from any criminal prosecution arising from the information he provided, or from any facts that came to light as a result of this information.

On appeal, the Supreme Court of the United States vacated the judgment of the court in California and upheld the statute. But the Court was closely divided over the central question of self-incrimination, and the opinion of the Court commanded no more than a plurality. Chief Justice Burger lost adherents for the opinion of the Court as he tried to settle the case while evading the issue of self-incrimination. Burger sought to slide around that question by arguing along these lines: The statute was directed in the most general way to "all persons who drive automobiles in California." To be identified as a member of this group was not to be branded as part of a class that was in imminent danger of prosecution. Beyond that, the statute seemed to bear a dominant interest in the fixing of financial responsibility. The law did not seem to have, as its main concern, the prospect of criminal prosecutions.

The majority of the Court received this reasoning with a proper disbelief. People who are responsible for serious accidents on the highways risk far more than financial liability when they identify themselves. They may open themselves to suits for substantial damages, and even to prosecution. Just how serious the risk may be is a judgment that has usually been conceded to the subject himself in gauging his own culpability and making his own judgment on invoking the Fifth Amendment. As Justice Harlan remarked, pointedly, the Court was "indulging in a collection of artificial, if not disingenuous judgments that the risks of incrimination are not there when they really are there."[42]

But from this point of recognition, shared by most members of the Court, the justices then diverged: Justices Black and Brennan thought that the Fifth Amendment was indeed engaged, and that it should work in this case to insulate the driver from prosecution. In contradistinction to Black and Brennan, Justice Harlan recognized that the driver faced a serious prospect of incriminating himself. Still, he was not prepared to abandon the purposes of the statute. Harlan was not persuaded that the Fifth Amendment made it necessary for California to give up either one of the legitimate ends contained in the law—to forego either the prosecution of serious wrongs, or the good to be attained through the timely reporting of injuries. Harlan's unease in this case reflected the bewilderment that has ever attended the provision on "self-incrimination" as a rule of justice. In the Byers case, Harlan had trouble in appreciating just why the good sought by the law—the good of saving lives and fixing responsibility for wrongs—should be overborne by the interest of any driver in avoiding liability for his own wrongs.

Harlan might have been moved then to deny that the provision on self-incrimination was really meant to furnish that kind of a shelter from wrong-doing. But rather than taking that path, he too tried to slide around the problem: He suggested that this case had to be distinguished from those in which people were compelled to report on activities that would make them vulnerable, instantly, to criminal penalties. The events that brought forth these reports on accidents were not "inherently suspect of criminal activities." And the statute demanded only a "minimal level of disclosure of information consistent with the use of compelled self-reporting in the regulation of driving behavior."[43] Such a refined rationale, of course, could not dispose of the fact that the driver compelled to report on himself was still making himself vulnerable to a criminal prosecution. This offering by Harlan was quite evidently an artifice for getting through the day and upholding the statute, while evading the main question in principle.[44] But Harlan supplied the useful office, nevertheless, of raising searching questions again about the rationale or meaning of any principle contained in the provision on self-incrimination. He was apparently willing to endorse lines of reasoning that were immanently implausible, because he was willing to give the states a certain freedom in pursuing their just projects, without the interference of judges, who may be inclined to apply the Fifth Amendment in a clumsy, mechanical way.

If we managed to join Harlan's reservations with a more demanding philosophic temper, we would be brought, I think, to this threshold: We may rightly doubt, with Harlan, that there is any principle in the Fifth Amendment that should prevent California from requiring drivers to provide timely information, rather than flee the scene of an accident. But if this doubt is justified, then our conclusions here about the Fifth Amendment would not apply only to the states: If the Fifth Amendment does not preclude this kind of obligation to report on accidents, then the Bill of Rights *should pose no more of a barrier to the federal government than it does to the states.* If Congress took the legislation in California as a model and legislated the same kinds of obligations for drivers on *interstate* highways, why should that arrangement not be quite as defensible and justified for the federal highways as it is for the highways in California?

But we need not depend on the hypothetical case; once we discover the apt analogy, someone often obliges by supplying the statute that fits the argument: One year after the Byers case, Congress passed the Federal Water Pollution Control Act. That act prohibited the discharge of oil or hazardous materials, in harmful quantities, in the navigable waters of the United States. For the sake of enforcing this policy, the act imposed a requirement of "self-reporting" on companies or persons who had knowledge of these harmful spills. The failure to report, even on one's own violations, would bring a prospect of criminal penalties. But the penalties would be offset by a form of "use immunity." The information supplied by any person could not be used against the reporting person or his company in a criminal prosecution. In that way, the drafters of the law hoped to get around the complications of the Fifth Amendment. And yet, they did not relieve the reporting persons from all penalties. Persons and companies responsible for the pollution might still be liable for a "civil penalty" administered by the Coast Guard.

As we have already seen, Chief Justice Marshall once raised serious questions about the relevance of the distinction between civil and criminal penalties. Certain fines, certain awards of damages in "civil" proceedings, may be far more devastating and punitive than certain fines and penalties administered in "criminal" proceedings. The drafters of the Water Pollution Act evidently thought they were skirting any problems of the Fifth Amendment simply by foreclosing the prospect of criminal penalties. But when the act was challenged in the courts, a federal court of appeals held that the "civil" penalty administered by the federal government was sufficiently punitive to resemble a criminal penalty.[45] And this said nothing, of course, about the liability of the company to civil suits, for substantial sums, brought by private litigants.

On appeal, however, the Supreme Court sustained the government. In writing for the Court, Justice Rehnquist was quite content to confine the Fifth Amendment to cases that involved a criminal penalty, and he was willing to defer to the judgment made by Congress, in labeling the fines assessed by the Coast Guard as "civil penalties."[46] Rehnquist was more inclined to dispose of the case, and uphold the authority of Congress, rather than meditate on a tangled philosophic problem. The Court was willing to settle, then, for distinctions that were good enough to get through the day, even if those distinctions offered little help in addressing the serious problems of principle bound up with the Fifth Amendment. Nevertheless, the Court bore out the understanding I am urging here. If a requirement for "self-reporting" does not seem to violate any principle contained in the Fifth Amendment, then the federal government should be as free as any government of a state to make use of this device.

The main point may be stated again in this way: If any of the sections in the Bill of Rights really reflects a principle of law, bound up with the logic of doing justice, then of course that principle would be as binding on the states as on the federal government. But if we do not find, in any case, the instance of a real principle contained in the first eight Amendments, there is no reason to constrain the federal government, any more than the states, to a mechanical reading of the Bill of Rights, uninformed by a jural or moral understanding.[47]

· · · · ·

To reach these conclusions does not require the application of reasoning that has been entirely novel to the Court. This argument would draw on the strands of recognition that have already been left to us by many of our most thoughtful judges. I would simply seek here to bring these separate recognitions together by incorporating them in a perspective that depends more explicitly on the discipline of moral reasoning. As the jurists of our first generation recognized more readily, that *is* the discipline of jurisprudence. And that is the discipline that our recent jurists have sought, in a rough way, to summon to their aid as they have tried to fathom the meaning of the Bill of Rights on the question of compelling people to yield up, from their persons or their private papers, the evidence of their own guilt. These questions have come to us in cases that often contain, in combination, problems of unreasonable "search and seizure" in the Fourth Amendment, as well as "self-incrimination" in the Fifth. I would extract from these cases a strand of problems that would further illustrate—and, I think, confirm—the project in philosophy that I have sought to map out, for the law, in these chapters. I would take as my point of connection the problem that remained unsolved in Harlan's opinion in the Byers case—the meaning of "self-incrimination." And I would return for a moment to an earlier effort by Felix Frankfurter to unlock that same problem.

EIGHT

INCRIMINATIONS: SELF, AND OTHERS

IN 1956, Justice Frankfurter wrote the opinion of the Court in *Ullmann v. United States*,[1] a case arising out of the investigations into the ties between the Communist Party and employees in the federal government. A grand jury in New York had posed questions to Ullmann about espionage, his membership in the Communist Party, and his knowledge about the involvement of other people in the Communist Party and in projects of espionage. Ullmann refused to testify, and he claimed a right, under the Fifth Amendment, to remain silent. In response, the United States attorney invoked the Immunity Act of 1954. That statute allowed an attorney for the government to declare that certain testimony or evidence was necessary to the defense of the United States against espionage or sedition, and the court would then direct a witness to testify or produce the evidence. The witness would not be allowed to excuse himself on the ground that "the testimony or evidence required of him may tend to incriminate him or subject him to a penalty or forfeiture." But at the same time, the statute also provided that "no such witness shall be prosecuted or subjected to any penalty or forfeiture" as a result of providing this evidence; "nor shall testimony so compelled be used as evidence in any criminal proceeding . . . against him in any court."[2]

Ullmann challenged the constitutionality of the Immunity Act, but the act was sustained in the courts. When Ullmann persisted in his refusal to testify, he was held in contempt of court and sentenced to prison for six months unless he "purged" himself of the contempt by supplying his testimony. For Ullmann, it was insufficient that he was spared a criminal prosecution as a condition for compelling him to render testimony. That shield of immunity would not extend to friends who were incriminated by his testimony; nor would it shelter him from the loss of a job in the government, or from other adverse effects, quite apart from a criminal prosecution. But on appeal, the Supreme Court sustained the government. In the opinion for the Court, Justice Frankfurter professed a willingness to accord, to the provision on self-incrimination, the standing of a "landmark" in our civilization and a necessary place in our law. Time had not shown that the provision was unneeded, and he insisted that the provision ought not be construed in "a hostile or niggardly spirit."[3] Nevertheless, he rejected the interpretation put forth by Ullmann, and as he summed up his account he remarked that "the history of the provision establishes . . . that it is not to be interpreted literally." The historical record also revealed that the "sole concern [of the provision on self-incrimination] is, as its name indicates, with the danger to a witness forced to give testimony leading to the infliction of 'penalties affixed to the criminal acts.' "[4]

The provision in the Fifth Amendment read in this way: "nor shall any person . . . be compelled in any criminal case to be a witness against himself." If this provision were not to be read "literally," then Frankfurter was raising the question of where the accent had to be placed in unlocking the meaning of this provision. For Frankfurter, the accent was to be placed mainly on "criminal"—and perhaps also on the notion of testifying "against himself." For Ullmann, and the dissenting judges in this case (Douglas and Black), the accent was to be placed on "compelled." But on one cardinal point they agreed with Frankfurter: Once they decided just where the accent would properly be placed, they too would ignore the literal meaning of the other critical words that made up that clause. They were prepared to treat, as entirely insignificant—so wanting in significance that their absence would have made no difference—the words "criminal" and "against himself." And there was some force to their argument. If the wrong in principle here was the compelling of testimony from an unwilling witness, then it may be irrelevant in principle as to whether the testimony extracted in that way is used to indict the witness *or other people*; whether the public accusation is made in a criminal or civil proceeding; or whether the penalties come in the form of a legal sentence or the loss of a job.

To support his own reading of the Fifth Amendment, Frankfurter leaned on an earlier precedent of the Court in upholding another statute on immunity in 1896.[5] But in his dissenting opinion, Justice Douglas urged the Court now to revert to an even older precedent, the grandfather of all cases on the Fifth Amendment, *Boyd v. United States* (1886).[6] In that signal case, the Court sustained a defense based on the Fifth Amendment, and the penalty at stake in that case was not evidently a *criminal* penalty. Boyd was an importer who was accused of evading the customs duties on thirty-five plates of glass. The government sought access to Boyd's records, but the statute did not authorize the search or seizure of his papers. Instead, the law required that the defendant produce the documents, and if he failed to produce them, the allegations would be "taken as confessed."[7] In other words, the statute established an inference of guilt from the refusal of a person to yield up his private papers. On the face of things, it seemed to the judges that the government was compelling Boyd to be a witness against himself.[8] But the government argued that the restrictions of the Fifth Amendment did not come into play in this case because Boyd was not faced with the prospect of a criminal penalty. The statute did encompass the possibility of imprisonment, but it provided mainly for a fine or the forfeiture of property, and the government insisted that it was seeking, in this case, nothing beyond those "civil" penalties.

And yet, it did not seem to the Court that the distinction was so unequivocal. Justice Bradley registered the judgment of the Court that the proceed-ings instituted against Boyd, "though they may be civil in form, are in their nature criminal."

> If the government prosecutor elects to waive an indictment, and to file a civil information against the claimants—that is, civil in form—can he by this device take from the proceeding its criminal aspect and deprive the claimants of their immunities as citizens, and extort from them a production of their private papers, or, as an alternative, a confession of guilt? This cannot be. The information, though technically a civil proceeding, is in substance and effect a criminal one.[9]

We may wonder whether Bradley and his successors spent their genius in the most productive way as they strained to show that certain civil penalties were really closer, in their nature, to criminal penalties. But they did see through the charade of using the forms of civil proceedings to disguise a sub-stantial punishment and to cover some novel rules for the inferring of guilt. The judges seemed to recognize, also, that the distinction between criminal and civil did not mark the severity of the penalties. An award of damages in a *civil* action for libel may be in the millions of dollars—enough to put a newspaper out of business or destroy a professional career. Jeremy Bentham once remarked on the same curious willingness to believe that a grand prin-ciple of the law should somehow be cabined, or marked off in its boundaries, by the distinction between civil and criminal penalties.

> Those who are governed by sounds would cry out tyranny and be in agonies at the thoughts of a man's being bound to confess an act for which he would be made to suffer to the amount of five pounds when the payment of that five pounds is called a penalty: at the same time they are perfectly well satisfied at his being made to suffer by the same means to the amount of five thousands when the payment of it goes not by that name.[10]

In the light of these commentaries, it may be all the more revealing to recall that the original clause on self-incrimination contained no distinction between criminal and civil penalties. In the original draft offered by Madison, it was simply provided that "no person shall be compelled to be a witness against himself." But the draft was amended in the House and narrowed, in its coverage, to criminal cases. To the benighting of posterity, this change was made with almost no debate,[11] and so the original decision leaves us with nothing to illuminate the understanding of Madison or the men who altered his draft. A more artless adherent to the school of "original intent" may be tempted to remark that the loss here was regrettable, but beside the point. In fixing the "intent" of the Founders, it may be enough to know that the Con-gress which drafted the Fifth Amendment explicitly confined the provision on self-incrimination to criminal cases. And yet, that willingness to settle the law with a wholesome credulity, with a serene avoidance of vexing questions, cannot finally serve its ends. The law will not be settled on those lines, because the distinction between civil and criminal penalties cannot finally explain anything of consequence here, and it cannot help the judges in finding the principle engaged in these cases. As the judges have worked at the task of practical judgment, they have been drawn back persistently, drawn back to reflect, again, on the logic that stands behind this clause in the Fifth Amendment—just as the judges in the Ullmann case were drawn back yet again to the same problem, as though they were writing about that question for the first time. The Court, in 1886, in *Boyd v. United States*, was hardly composed of giddy men, and yet those jurists could not apparently see that there was any "principle" that confined the clause on self-incrimination to cases in which the convicted are sent to jail. And more recently it has become clear, in the accumulation of our experience, that the courts have not been able to confine the claims on self-incrimination to criminal cases.

Professor Robert Heidt has charted, with more detail than we should ever wish to possess on this matter, the many routes by which the Fifth Amendment has been invoked in civil cases, including cases as private, and as distant from prosecution, as cases on divorce. A husband may be asked to disclose his sources of income, as part of the process of working out a settlement. But if any of these details touch on activities that could even remotely become the object of a prosecution, directed at the husband or his company, he may invoke the Fifth Amendment and shelter these activities from the searching inquiries of the law. Professor Heidt complains that the curtain has been drawn in this way, to block the process of discovery in a host of cases, involving issues as varied as frauds in the sale of securities and suits for damages under the Civil Rights Acts. This extension of the Fifth Amendment to private litigation has seriously undercut the capacity of the complainants in these cases to compel the discovery of facts that are necessary to their cases.[12]

Heidt would seek to confine the claim of self-incrimination to those cases in which the person who invokes the clause is actually the defendant in a pending criminal case.[13] But it is hard to imagine a plausible ground for contracting that freedom in civil cases, which would not apply, even more forcefully, to criminal cases. Is there a concern for the truths blocked from view, the wrongs that may go unvindicated in civil proceedings, because defendants have been accorded a right to withhold evidence? And yet, why are the same defects of justice not as grave in criminal cases? In measuring the quotient of injustice in the country, it is a rare sensibility that would show a more anguished concern over the husband who escapes the just demands of alimony than the Mafiosi who have been preserved, by the Fifth Amendment, in their freedom to pursue thuggery as a vocation.

Still, Heidt thinks this weighting of sympathy is made plausible, in the end, by the disparity in power between the government and the private litigant. That disparity makes it deeply unfair, in his estimate, to impose on the private litigant the same burdens of investigation and proof that may be imposed on the government. But it is not at all clear that this disparity in resources should bear any moral relevance to the deserts of the victims and the good to be attained in a trial. The fact that the government has more resources than a private litigant could hardly establish that the wrongs prosecuted by the government are less serious, or that the injuries suffered by the victims are any less grievous than the injuries suffered by private plaintiffs. In that event, it is less than self-evident that the defendants, in criminal cases, *deserve* a special advantage, in withholding evidence, because they happen to be prosecuted by the government. Surely, they would not deserve *less* protection in the rules of evidence, but on what principle could they claim *more*?

Heidt observes that, when the testimony is extracted by a private party, at least "the government would not be the one seeking to compel self-incriminating testimony."[14] And yet, that complaint summons us to take seriously again the kind of argument made by the dissenting judges in the Ullmann case. If the principle of "self-incrimination" involves the compelling of testimony from an unwilling witness, why should it matter if the testimony is compelled by the government or by private litigants? The Constitution itself is silent on the source from which the compulsion may come. If we were dealing with a criminal case, would anyone seriously believe that we could circumvent the restrictions of the Fifth Amendment simply by having confessions extracted, through torture, by private detectives or vigilantes, and turned over to the government? And if we find that the distinction between criminal and civil penalties finally ceases to matter, we would discover that the distinction between public and private compulsion would also lose its significance: If our concern, in principle, is with the compelling of testimony that could be the ground of a penalty, imposed through the law, then why, again, should it make any difference if the evidence is brought to the court through the compulsion exerted by a *private* litigant?

In the Ullmann case, Justice Douglas recalled a searching, thoughtful opinion in the federal court of appeals by Judge Peter Grosscup, in 1894, construing the Immunity Act of 1893. For Judge Grosscup, the granting of immunity could not dissolve the problem of compelling testimony from an unwilling witness. "[I]f the immunity was only against the law-inflicted pains and penalties, the government could probe the secrets of every conversation, or society, by extending compulsory pardon to one of its participants, and thus turn him into an involuntary informer."[15] With this recognition, it became evident that the clause on self-incrimination had to sweep beyond the penalties imposed by the government.

The stated penalties and forfeitures of the law might be set aside; but was there no pain in disfavor and odium among neighbors, in excommunication from church or societies that might be governed by the prevailing views, in the *private liabilities* that the law might authorize, or in the unfathomable disgrace, not susceptible of formulation in language, which a known violation of the law brings upon the offender?[16]

The law might grant to Ullmann an immunity from prosecution, but it did not offer protection against the loss of his job, or the decline in his business as a result of the notoriety arising from his testimony, or even from the accusation. It seemed clear to Douglas that "when a man loses a job because he is a Communist, there is as much a penalty suffered as when an importer loses property because he is a tax evader."[17] And Douglas was moved now to claim that the Fifth Amendment was meant to offer shelter to people from these "private liabilities"—not merely the loss of a job in the government, but the loss of a job in private business as well. A teacher could lose a job in a school administered by the state; doctors or lawyers could lose their franchise to practice as a result of the decisions made by professional licensing boards, acting with the authority of the law. Beyond that, an actor who is identified as a Communist could be placed on a black list and shunned by private companies.[18]

As it turned out, the Supreme Court in later years would follow in part along the route described by Douglas. In a series of cases, the Court would strike down statutes or regulations that provided a variety of noncriminal penalties for people who invoked their right to silence under the Fifth Amendment. In this way, the Court extended the Fifth Amendment to offer protections against the loss of a government contract,[19] the disciplining of an attorney,[20] and the loss of a job with a sanitation department.[21] But these penalties were imposed, of course, by law. The Court has not offered a sign yet that it may be willing to take the further step and extend the protections of the Fifth Amendment to the "noncriminal" sanctions that are imposed through *private* decisions to deny jobs or withhold contracts. This move would not require a strain of imagination that would be so much out of the ordinary, when judged by the record of the Court in our own time. With a few simple steps, the Court could extend the coverage of the Fifth Amendment in a case of this kind: A man loses his job in a private company because he invokes the Fifth Amendment in a congressional investigation or a criminal prosecution. He then brings a suit under Section 1981 of the Civil Rights Acts and claims that he has been deprived of his job solely because he invoked his constitutional right to preserve his silence in the face of questioning. In order to bring a suit against a private employer, he brings the suit under Section 1981 of the Civil Rights Acts, and he molds his argument to the statute in this way. He argues that, in firing him, his employer has interfered with his freedom to make contracts for employment, and that he cannot rightfully require, as a condition of employment, the surrender of constitutional rights.

The question then is whether the Court would be willing to uphold this kind of suit as a legitimate cause of action under the Civil Rights Acts. By the summer of 1987 the Court had already taken a decisive step. In *Rankin v. McPherson*, the Court upheld a suit under the Civil Rights Acts (42 U.S.C.A., Section 1983) against a constable in Texas who had fired a clerk in his office. President Reagan had been shot on March 30, 1981, and when the news was heard in the office, Ardith McPherson remarked that "If they go for him again, I hope they get him." For this remark, she was fired. But with the disbelief of three colleagues, a majority of the Supreme Court ruled that her rights had been violated. Justice Marshall held that McPherson had been fired for a remark expressing her political opinions, and therefore, as he reasoned, she had been fired for exercising her First Amendment rights.[22] The reasoning, then, is already in place. It would require no new principle, no leap in logic, to extend the same argument to the Fifth Amendment. And with Section 1981 of the Civil Rights Acts, this use of the Fifth Amendment could be extended to the hurts or indignities, the sanctions or rejections, suffered at the hands of private employers. The coverage of the Fifth Amendment could be expanded, then, quite in accord with the imagination of Justice Douglas. What might have seemed unimaginable to everyone else as recently as three years ago, could now be established by the Court without suggesting even a trace of novelty in its jurisprudence.

. . . . .

But in order to give that reach to the Fifth Amendment, the Court would have to explain why people are not entitled, even in private settings, to draw their own, adverse inferences about the refusal of a person to testify about his own guilt or innocence. That is to say, the Court would have to explain—far more clearly than any court has yet managed to explain—just why the clause on self-incrimination can really claim this kind of standing as a "principle" of justice. To face this question in a serious way is to face the gravest doubts that have been registered over many years by some of the most thoughtful jurists in America and abroad. Among those countries in the world today that could be counted as constitutional orders, the United States is virtually alone in finding, in the principles of constitutionalism, the "right" of a witness to remain silent, even when he could furnish vital evidence about a crime. Lawyers and jurists in other countries have often expressed puzzlement over this part of the American law. They have wondered why it is considered wrong or unjust to draw adverse inferences when a man implicated in a criminal project refuses to answer reasonable questions and dispel the accusations of his own guilt. They have wondered just what decent motive would impel an innocent man, in this setting, to hold back from speaking. That sense of puzzlement is rightly deepened when the questions are directed aptly to the end of reconstructing the facts, establishing responsibility, perhaps even disrupting a crime in progress and saving innocent lives. Among our own judges, as we have seen, Justice Cardozo doubted that the clause on self-incrimination would be violated if a person accused of a crime "were subject to a duty to respond to orderly inquiry."[23] In a highly noticed essay, Judge Henry Friendly once raised the question of just how there could be a "right" on the part of an accomplice to refuse to respond to questioning. The responses of the collaborators could establish whether the victim of a kidnapping was dead or alive, and whether his confederates were on the way out of the country.[24] People unlettered in the law, but possessed of moral wit, may wonder what is "rightful" or justified in the claim to preserve silence in this situation. In a comparable way, Judge Friendly was raising the question of just what there was in the logic of "justice," or the principles of the Constitution, that obliged us to accord such a respect to the interests of criminals in completing their projects without detection. What principle would compel us to assign to that interest a higher standing, in the ranking of our moral concerns, than the interest in saving innocent victims and disrupting criminal projects?

But to raise questions of this kind is to recall the puzzlement that has been inspired enduringly by the clause on self-incrimination: Those who are unschooled in law, as well as jurists who are quite accomplished in the science, have failed to see any manifest justice in the claim that it is wrong to compel a person to testify about his own guilt or innocence. Blackstone took, as a grand maxim of the law, that "No man is bound to accuse himself." In his relentless, exacting critique of Blackstone, Jeremy Bentham found, in Blackstone's treatment of this maxim, the smug complacency, the pretentious shallowness of the jurists. They would trumpet, as a grand principle of the law, a proposition that could not withstand an examination affected with any philosophic rigor. They would drape the reverence of tradition around a maxim whose compelling truth—or whose elementary sense—they could not quite explain. What did it mean to say that "No man is bound to accuse himself"?

> To be bound to do a things is to be liable to punishment for not doing it. . . . To accuse one's self is to accuse one's self of something: of having committed something: that something is an offence. . . . To accuse one's self of an offence is to confess the having committed it.

> The maxim, to judge strictly of it, is far from being universally a true one. Deplorable indeed would be the state of our Jurisprudence if it were.[25]

Not everyone accomplished in the law or philosophy has regarded the maxim on self-incrimination as a necessary principle of the law. The puzzlement of the most thoughtful writers and jurists should be sufficient to justify a thoughtful effort, in turn, to explain just why this provision should be regarded, as Justices Bradley and Field, Douglas and Black regarded it, as one of the grandest principles of our law.

Douglas and Black took their guide from Justice Bradley's classic opinion in *Boyd v. United States*, and it is worth recalling the sweep of Justice Bradley's statement. In that case, the federal government had sought the records, held by an importer, on thirty-five cases of plate glass that had been brought into the country. The government sought access to the merchandise and the records as evidence, and under the reigning statute, the refusal to yield up the evidence was itself taken as a confession of the crime.[26] As Bradley conceded, this was not quite the same as a forcible entry into a man's house and the searching of his papers. Still, the case seemed to present a merging of the concerns expressed in the Fourth and the Fifth Amendments. Here, as Bradley said, "the Fourth and Fifth Amendments run almost into each other."[27]

[A]ny compulsory discovery by extorting the party's oath, or compelling the production of his private books and papers, to convict him of crime, or to forfeit his property, is contrary to the principles of a free government. It is abhorrent to the instincts of an Englishman; it is abhorrent to the instincts of an American. It may suit the purposes of despotic power; but it cannot abide the pure atmosphere of political liberty and personal freedom.[28]

In this critical passage, where Justice Bradley delivered himself of his grandest declaration, he notably failed to explain any principle that entailed the judgment he was announcing. Instead, he merely appealed, as Justice Frankfurter would later appeal, to the traditions of "our people." Frankfurter would later add a kind of empirical test of "shocking the conscience" of the judges. Justice Bradley would offer a comparable standard: not that the practice at hand was based on maxims that were incompatible with the logic of justice itself, but rather, that for some unfathomable reason, the practice offended what Bradley was pleased to call "the instincts of an Englishman" or "the instincts of an American." This was quite different from saying that the "wrong" here was grounded in the logic of lawfulness itself; that the extraction of evidence in this way would have to be wrong in all places, for the same reason. The language expressed merely the "habits of the tribe," or the accents familiar in the better clubs ("We just don't do things here in that way"). In the terms offered by Bradley, it could not even be claimed that this compulsion of evidence would be wrong in other countries with constitutional governments. Bradley could not presume to pronounce on the rightness or wrongness of this arrangement, say, in France or Germany, because he did not presume to speak with any authority about the jural "instincts" of Frenchmen or Germans. Whether the practice would also offend the "instincts" of the French and the Germans would have to depend, then, on a survey of opinion.

Bradley evidently thought that he was invoking a principle rooted in the foundations of constitutional law. And yet, he reduced that "principle" to the standing of a mere convention or a local tradition. Once again, that was a startling shift in the standards of judgment in jurisprudence. Whether the compulsion of evidence is right or wrong is something that could be determined, only from moment to moment, as we measured, in surveys of opinion, the sensibilities of the public. But those sensibilities seem to have altered, quite noticeably, even in our own time. In the early 1970s there was dramatic evidence that a large portion of our political class, and a sizable share of our lawyers and judges, no longer shared Bradley's "instincts" on this matter. In the presence of a signal case that excited the interest of the nation, they conspicuously failed to show any sense of outrage or disbelief over the prospect of the "compulsory extortion of a man's own testimony or of his private papers to be used as evidence to convict him of crime or to forfeit his goods." In 1973 lawyers, judges, and journalists were now proclaiming, as a high principle of law, that a sitting president of the United States should in fact be compelled to hand over his private papers and "tapes"—materials that were similar, in many respects, to a personal diary. The tapes contained comments offered under the expectation of privacy and confidentiality; comments that would never have been uttered if the principal were aware that he was speaking for the public record.

When it came to deploying the instruments of the law against President Nixon, many members of the bar apparently failed to remember a "principle" that was supposed to be inscribed, indelibly, in the legal traditions of "our people." The ease with which even the most learned lawyers managed to overlook this august "principle" may confirm some ancient doubts about the principle itself. When it came to the matter of investigating what many members of the political class regarded as a serious crime of state, the interest in securing the evidence apparently struck many lawyers as a higher and more compelling interest than any interest in sheltering this accused man, in his refusal to yield up evidence about himself. There was, after all, nothing novel here to comprehend: The connection between executive privilege and the Fifth Amendment had been made as early as 1842, when President Tyler refused to furnish, to the House of Representatives, certain papers of the executive. "It is certainly no new doctrine in the halls of judicature," he observed, "that certain communications and papers are privileged, and that the general authority to compel testimony must give way in certain cases to the paramount rights of individuals or of the Government. Thus, *no man can be compelled to accuse himself*, . . . or to produce his own private papers on any occasion."[29]

But that claim was majestically ignored by the redoubtable John J. Sirica, judge of the federal district court in Washington, D.C. The political establishment, looking on, found in the words of Judge Sirica the grandeur of the law. President Nixon had invoked the claim of the executive to withhold, from the scrutiny of the other branches, the private papers of the executive. But against that claim, made by many other presidents before him, Judge Sirica posed what he called "the well established premises that the grand jury has a right to every man's evidence." And when it came to the gathering of evidence, Sirica declared that "process may issue to anyone."[30]

The words carried an elementary force, because they seemed to touch the root. They seemed to express one of the rudimentary implications arising from the idea of justice. With the same understanding, the courts would later insist that this obligation to bring forth evidence, to help establish the facts of innocence and guilt, was an obligation that covered journalists as well as presidents.[31] This news was received with a vexed surprise by journalists, as well as by other professionals, who fancied that they were affected with certain critical "privileges" in protecting their clients or the confidentiality of their "sources." The surprise suddenly highlighted the significance of that tendency to speak of a "privilege" to remain silent or avoid self-incrimination. If the law had a "right" to gain access to certain evidence, there surely could not be a correlative "right," on the part of anyone else, to withhold that evidence. If Judge Sirica had touched the most fundamental axioms, or the necessary truths, of the law, then the withholding of evidence was cast in a clearer light. The claim to withhold evidence was at most a "privilege," which may be granted or withheld by the law, as it seems prudently to serve the interests of the public. Lawyers, doctors, and clergy may be accorded a certain "privilege" of confidentiality in relation to their clients. There are ample reasons to believe that, without that assurance of confidentiality, fewer people would seek counseling. The counseling, in turn, may encourage treatment, referrals, even confessions; and in its paradoxical operation, the offer of confidentiality may help bring to light certain wrongs that would otherwise have remained concealed. Still, in certain cases the privilege may be abridged: In cases involving the abuse of children, the authorities in certain states have legislated an obligation for professionals to report the cases. There may be a "privilege" of confidentiality or a privilege to avoid self-incrimination, but quite evidently, we do not attach to these claims the properties of a real "principle." If our reflexes on this question have been accurate, the clause on self-incrimination could not express any proposition that flows, as a *necessary implication*, from the logic of constitutional government. And those who invoke such a claim could not be invoking anything as momentous as a "constitutional right."

Nevertheless, it is arguable that there really is a constitutional principle contained in that passage in the Fifth Amendment ("nor shall [any person] be compelled in any criminal case to be a witness against himself"). I would suggest that the principle would become clearer and more precise if we applied the discipline I suggested earlier for the extraction of a real principle of law.

The task is to consider just which propositions, fitting the language and sense of this clause, can be drawn as implications that arise out of the very logic of rendering justice. If we did that, we would become, as I say, clearer about the principle contained here, and by indirection we would become clearer about the spurious claims made under the "privilege on self-incrimination." But at the same time, to see clearly is to see anew. We would notice, I think, some cases common in our experience, in which the principle of this clause has been engaged, but unnoticed.

In drawing out these propositions, it is necessary, as I have said, to return to the root logic of rendering justice. Judge Sirica touched that root of simple propositions, and he furnished an example that may be readily used in reminding ourselves of the way in which this discipline of jural reasoning would unfold itself. How would we connect, to the logic of rendering justice, the dictum announced by Judge Sirica, that the law "has a right to every man's evidence"?

We remind ourselves first, that by the logic of morals and the logic of law, we are justified in inflicting punishment only in the presence of a wrong. To say that "X is wrong"—and not merely unpleasant or distasteful—is to say that people, more generally or universally, should refrain from the "doing of X." It is to say that people may *justly be restrained* from the "doing of X"; and if they cannot be restrained in advance, they may justly be punished for the doing of a wrong. [32] To speak of rendering "justice" is to speak of settling the cases in which punishment is *justified* or *unjustified*. That is to say, it is to speak of establishing whether someone is guilty of a wrong, and therefore deserves punishment; or whether that person is innocent of wrongdoing, and should therefore be untouched by punishment.

The logic of rendering justice begins by commanding our respect for the moral differences that separate, in this way, the innocent from the guilty. But we respect those differences only when we insist on drawing them in the most solemn and reasoned manner. We do not establish, as a measure of innocence or guilt, the capacity of an accused person to traverse, without harm, a bed of hot coals, or to outrun a mob in the street. We respect the logic of rendering justice when we insist: that questions of guilt or innocence shall be measured only with evidence or testimony that bear a logical connection to the wrong that is charged; that the evidence should be collected and assessed according to the most practicable and exacting standards, governed by the canons of reason. Stray bottles and bullets do not end up in court as "evidence," with no documentation, with no means of establishing their provenance or authenticity. Our preference must run, then, to "trials" that are not trials of strength or combat, but proceedings affected with formal procedures for the assessment of evidence. But that is to say that, immanent in the nature of a formal trial, is the commitment to arrive at a verdict of innocence and guilt that is not merely formally impeccable, but substantively accurate, substantively just. As Max Weber once reminded us, many trials conducted in primitive settings by witch doctors and men of magic may be hedged in with rituals that are exacting and fastidious. It is entirely possible that a trial may be formally correct in all of its arrangements, and yet it may produce results that are substantively wrong or unjust. We should be clear that, in the strictest understanding of a "juridical" proceeding, the purpose of the procedures is not merely to produce verdicts that relieve anxiety in the community or appease a hunger for punishments, but verdicts that are accurate and right.

By the logic of morals, as I have pointed out, we are obliged to do what is right and refrain from what is wrong. We are also enjoined, by the same logic, to forbid what is wrong; to prosecute and punish the people who commit wrongs. But we are enjoined to punish only those who are guilty, and our strenuous effort to make accurate distinctions between the innocent and the guilty expresses another side of the same understanding: The unjust punishment of an innocent man is a wrong, and we would be obliged to do as much as we practicably could to avert that punishment of the innocent. If there is a danger, then, that an innocent man is likely to be convicted, it follows, from this chain of propositions, that anyone with a true knowledge of the crime would be obliged, in principle, to come forth with the evidence. He would be obliged to do whatever he practicably could to avert this miscarriage of justice and the suffering of a wrongful punishment.

We may ask: *For whom*, for which innocent person, would one be obliged to produce evidence and try to avert the miscarriage of justice? I hope it would be clear now that the answer, set in the universal cast of a moral proposition, would be: for anyone, for everyone. The particular identity of the accused person would not matter. The relevant moral facts are in place as soon as we know that there is a person, innocent of the crime, who is falsely charged and threatened with an unjustified punishment. The ingredients of a "wrong" would be present, and the obligation to help avert that wrong would be quite indifferent to such attributes as the height, weight, race, personality, or even the identity, of the defendant.

But the same logic would be attached to the converse of these propositions: If we are morally obliged to offer evidence, where we can, to save the innocent, that service may be rendered at times by identifying the persons who are truly guilty. If we are obliged to help render justice by saving the innocent, the same reasoning would also command us to act, where we can, to assure that the guilty are rightly named. The question may be asked: For whom—for which guilty person—would we be obliged to supply this evidence and see that justice is done? And the answer, once again, would be: for anyone, for everyone. *Anyone* would be obliged to respect this requirement of justice, in regard to *anyone* who is truly guilty of the crime. As a logical matter—and this *is*, I must emphasize, a distinctly logical matter—the identity of the wrongdoer is a matter of irrelevance to the obligation. But then the twist: What if I can supply the critical evidence and save an innocent man only because I know, more accurately than anyone else, the details of the crime, and I know those details because I myself committed the crime? As we have seen, the obligation to bring forth the evidence is utterly indifferent to the identity of the person who holds that evidence. *And it must be indifferent, in turn, to the identity of the person who is incriminated by the evidence.*

This chain of propositions supplies the ground of reason that Judge Sirica drew upon when he announced, quite rightly, that anyone with evidence of a crime would have an obligation to supply that evidence and insure that justice is done. What we may see now is that this chain of reasoning, unfolded with its logical stringency, would oblige any person to come forth with evidence, even when he would be virtually compelled to be "a witness against himself." That was precisely the understanding that Sirica was willing to impose on President Nixon. But the point may seem more startling to us when it is drawn explicitly from its ground of reason: Strictly speaking, there can be no moral "right" to withhold evidence of one's own guilt.[33] There would be an obligation, rather, to bring forth evidence of innocence and guilt, quite apart from whether the person who suffers embarrassment and punishment happens to be oneself.[34]

Viewed strictly, then, in moral terms, anyone who committed a crime would have an obligation to confess, to make restitution, to accept a just punishment, to repent the wrong. There is no "theological" component here. People may feel "purged" of their guilt when they confess, and their confession may help in the preparation of their souls. We are not predicting here whether people are likely to "feel better," or whether they will succeed in the restoration of their souls. We would be stating simply a logical matter: Confession and repentence are logically apt responses flowing from the recognition of a wrong committed. But at the same time, the authorities cannot be obliged to accept just anything that is offered as a "confession." In the major cities in this country, the police encounter every day people who come in off the street and confess to crimes they never committed. They may confess because they have been afflicted by guilt on other matters, or because they are moved, in a perverse way, to attach themselves to a highly publicized crime and draw a new attention to themselves. But the police are not usually so credulous as to accept any "testimony," offered on the strength of personal avowal, without the benefit of supporting evidence. And that critical difference between testimony and evidence, between personal declaration and impersonal proof, may be at the heart of the principle that is finally engaged in the clause on self-incrimination.

Max Weber once pointed out that the "tests" involved in trials by ordeal might be quite empirical and precise.[35] The failure to withstand burning coals or the weight of heavy stones could be manifested rather clearly. Reverence is due, then, to those ancestors of ours who first insisted that this "evidence" did not establish any facts that bore, with relevance, on the commission of the crime and the guilt of the accused. One might as well pound on a stone with a club in the hope that it could establish the truth or falsity of any proposition bearing on a crime at issue in a trial. In place of the stone, we might put the head or shoulders of the accused. We would find, however, that this variation in the exercise would still not alter the epistemic value of pounding with a club. To beat a suspect around the head and shoulders is still not a procedure that is preeminently tailored toward the end of testing the truth or falsity of propositions. Of course, it would not persist as a practice unless it was confirmed, in the experience of the police, that the application of these methods can often bring out useful information. But what may be useful to the police may not always be valid as evidence. In the meantime, the "testimony" extracted in this way must be tainted with an ineffaceable doubt; it must be unsalvageably doubtful as "evidence." To put it more precisely, there must be something immanently suspect about a confession of guilt, *or even an accusation of guilt directed at another person*, if that declaration is extracted under conditions of duress or torture, and the person interrogated is given to understand that the pain will cease, the prospect of further punishment will dissolve, if he merely yields up to the interrogators the testimony they wish to have.

Under those conditions, the search for truth has been alloyed with the understandable interest that anyone may have in stopping the pain. There may be rare characters whose commitment to truth is so disinterested and unshakable that it withstands even the most grievous privations and tortures. We need not suppose that most people will be weak, when measured by that standard. It is enough to know that the procedures geared toward the rational assessment of evidence have been mixed now with procedures that create personal incentives to furnish even false testimony. To state that limited point is to state a point that is sufficiently decisive. It is all that one needs to say, if one recalls that the logic of rendering justice entails the commitment to seek verdicts that are, in their most critical attribute, true. And that is why Justice Cardozo could remark, with assurance, that the clause on self-incrimination would "no doubt [offer] protection against torture, physical or mental."[36]

. . . . .

But is that the only instance that would come under this corollary, or this drawing out of the principle? If we brought this restatement of the problem to our current practice, we might begin to notice a number of other instances in which defendants have been given almost irresistible incentives to provide false testimony about others, as well as themselves. The point merits some accent, lest we pass it by: If our concern is with the contriving of false testimony, it can make no difference to the principle here that the false testimony is offered about oneself *or others*. In that respect, the language of the Fifth Amendment would depart from the demanding requirements of principle when it refers only to the compulsion that may be exerted on any person to be a witness "against himself." In the Ullmann case, the plaintiff argued that the principle of the Fifth Amendment would be subverted if he were granted immunity solely for himself, but then compelled, on that very ground, to furnish evidence that would incriminate others. But we have seen other cases more recently that have displayed even more starkly the concerns that would be covered in my restatement of the principle: We have seen prosecutors offer to drop charges and grant immunity if persons under investigation will furnish the kind of testimony that could be pivotal in convicting a more prominent or visible figure.

Of course, these kinds of arrangements may be vital to the authorities in unlocking a complicated case; they may be a critical help in dismantling the systems of loyalty that work to conceal the facts of criminal conspiracies. But the situation may be altered dramatically when the offer of immunity does not beget real evidence. When the inducement to testify is detached from the tether of documented facts, there is a powerful incentive to incriminate other people as a means of diverting blame from oneself. That incentive may become, as I say, irresistible when the willingness to tell a rich, embellished story can secure, to a vulnerable defendant, the grant of immunity. There has been ample experience by now with testimony of this kind, which could not withstand the rigors of cross-examination. In the fallout over Watergate, it appears that these kinds of pressures were at work in securing testimony against John Connally, the former secretary of the treasury.[37] Mr. Connally was finally acquitted of the charge of accepting bribes from the dairy industry in exchange for the granting of subsidies. Connally was never exactly a frail player of the game of politics, but even he could suffer notoriety, and a lasting damage to his political career, as a result of a criminal trial for corruption.

It became known, in the summer of 1987, that the Department of Justice was maturing plans for a prosecution of Congressman Fernand J. St. Germain (D-R.I.), the chairman of the House Banking Committee.[38] St. Germain had drawn a certain attention in the press for an accumulation of personal wealth that could not be explained by his salary as a congressman or by any sources of income available from his family. In his chairmanship, he had been in a position to shape legislation that mattered dearly to banks and other financial institutions. It was said that an affable commerce arose between St. Germain and the officers in many of these institutions. Allegations began to appear in print that St. Germain had become the beneficiary of generous gifts and even, at times, some profitable counsel on his own investments, from these men of business. The charges were brought before the House Ethics Committee, but the committee found no more serious fault in St. Germain than a failure to report fully on the sources of his income. In that oversight, he had violated some rules of the House and the federal laws on "ethics." Still, the committee recommended no censure or prosecution. But in the summer of 1987, the Department of Justice had offered limited immunity to Mr. James O. (Snake) Freeman, who had been a senior lobbyist for the U.S. League of Savings Institutions. The department had subpoenaed some records of the League that bore on the activities of St. Germain. The government was now offering to Freeman a "limited use immunity," which would shelter him from any criminal prosecution arising from his testimony. In exchange, Freeman would agree to testify.

Even with the aid of this testimony, the government still found it hard to prove that Mr. St. Germain had exchanged "legislative favors" for a generous menu of free meals and other gifts. In the spring of 1988, the prosecution was dropped;[39] but as a result of the notoriety, St. Germain was finally retired that fall, through the votes of his constituents. If the government had managed to secure evidence, independent of Freeman's testimony, it would have been free to overthrow its agreement and seek the prosecution of Freeman as well. Such were the terms—and the perils—of "limited use" immunity.[40] In that event, a paradox comes into play, which must raise suspicions: A person receiving this offer of "limited" immunity would have a stronger incentive to accept the offer when his value to the prosecution arises mainly from his testimony, rather than from any "evidence" that may be uncovered by his testimony. If he leads the prosecution to evidence, it may not take much imagination for the authorities to see the alternate routes that could lead them to the same evidence. In that event, they would be free to evade their bargain with the witness. The witness would be in a far safer position when there is little evidence to uncover—and at that point, he would come under a stronger incentive to bargain for immunity by incriminating someone of more interest to the prosecutors.

It was evident, in March 1988, that calculations of this kind had been made in the office of Lawrence Walsh, the independent counsel who was appointed to investigate the Iran-Contra affair. Walsh arrayed the kinds of threats that finally induced Mr. Robert (Bud) McFarlane to plead guilty to misdemeanors, rather than face the possibility of more serious charges. McFarlane was the former advisor to the president on National Security. It was evidently hoped, by Walsh and his staff, that McFarlane would provide the testimony that could help build a case against McFarlane's successor, Rear Adm. John Poindexter, and Poindexter's former aide, Lt. Col. Oliver North. But it was also apparent, to the reporters covering the story, that the "deal" with McFarlane was struck precisely because Walsh had been blocked in his access to critical documents: twenty-one notebooks, with North's daily notes, were made available to committees in the House and Senate, in exchange for a grant of limited immunity. That grant of immunity was now depriving

Walsh of the documents, or the material evidence, he needed in making his case. The move to McFarlane was an attempt then to supply, through testimony, what was wanting in the evidence.[41] But once again, the testimony was extracted by facing a vulnerable defendant with the prospect of a humiliating, expensive trial, and the risks of a graver penalty. As it happened, the case of the prosecution was rather shaky, and McFarlane stood a decent chance of clearing himself, even on the charges of the misdemeanors.[42] And yet, the risks, concentrated on this one defendant, could still be too intimidating to bear.

When a conviction is secured on the strength of testimony detached from evidence; and when the testimony is extracted in this way from witnesses who are given a powerful incentive to save themselves by implicating others, it is arguable that a constitutional threshold is crossed. The signals of alarm are not usually set off; there seems to be little awareness these days that the authorities are drifting into an arrangement that may raise serious constitutional questions. But I would argue that the authorities would be violating the substance of the real principle that is contained in the Fifth Amendment, in the compelling of testimony from an unwilling witness.

If I am correct, the constitutional principle is violated through an arrangement that creates a compelling incentive for a witness to bring forth false testimony, uncorroborated by evidence, for the purpose of sparing himself or averting a far more severe penalty. Professor John Langbein has found the same connection in principle to the current practice of securing most convictions in criminal cases through the device of plea bargaining.[43] The connection to the Fifth Amendment, or to the principle I have described, would come through these features: The conviction is ordered almost entirely on the basis of the "testimony," or the plea of guilty entered by the accused. That plea relieves the court of any need to examine the evidence in a disciplined way in order to reach an accurate, justified verdict on guilt or innocence. The accuracy of the judgment is now an unresolved matter; the case is simply "settled" through a decision that has the assent of both parties.

The logic of this arrangement, or the coercive effect that produces the result, can be seen in this one case recalled by Langbein. An attorney in San Francisco was called in to defend a man charged with kidnapping and forcible rape. The evidence was weak, and the attorney was confident that his client would be acquitted. The prosecutor seemed to have arrived at the same judgment, for he offered to drop the original charges and accept a plea of guilty for a simple battery. A conviction on this charge would not have brought a more serious penalty than thirty days in prison. The lawyer informed his client of the offer, but he also advised him that conviction on the original charges would be highly improbable. But the defendant felt he had no other practicable choice than to plead guilty to a crime he did not commit. As he explained to his lawyer, "I can't take the chance."[44]

In this arrangement, as Langbein notes, the discipline of constitutional government, and the check of the courts, are removed. Since the courts do nothing more than record the settlement, they do not weigh the evidence and reach a judgment independent of the government. The separation of powers is, in effect, suspended: the prosecutor combines, in himself, the functions of prosecutor, judge, and jury.

As Langbein points out, this procedure accounts for 95 to 99 percent of the felony convictions in our major cities. "This nontrial procedure," he remarks, "has become the ordinary dispositive procedure of American law."[45] It has become the procedure of choice because a trial by jury—the ideal of American law—has been rendered nearly unworkable by the effort to mold its features to the demands of a perfect justice. The administration of justice through a jury has become burdened now with the most exquisite requirements in the selection of jurors, the exclusion of evidence, and the framing of instructions. In England, in the early eighteenth century, a court could administer twelve to twenty jury trials in a day. A single jury might dispatch several cases. But in Los Angeles, in the late 1960s, the average trial for a felony lasted over seven days, and some of the more celebrated trials have drawn on for well over a month.[46] The procedure has become unthinkably long, expensive, and very nearly impracticable.

But this experience is not inherent in the project of rendering justice in a constitutional order. France, Germany, Britain, and other civilized countries have not suffered quite the same obstructions. They have experienced the same pressures of "case load" felt in the United States, and prosecutors have shown a similar inclination to settle for a lesser charge for the sake of disposing of cases more quickly. Still, jurists abroad tend to react with disbelief when they learn of the American way of justice in bargaining over pleas.[47] And yet, this practice, so surprising to the Europeans, has been sustained as the dominant convention in our criminal law by our most seasoned lawyers and judges. Very little in their preparation has alerted them to the possibility that the dominant procedure in our criminal law may be at odds with a critical principle underlying the Fifth Amendment. In order to recognize that point, they would have to understand the principle standing behind the text. But no motive, no interest, nothing in the way they earn their livings, moves them to paths of reflection that could lead them to that principle behind the text. What they know, instead, are the formulas that have been contrived over the years for the purpose of honoring the text in a technical way, while making life a bit less unworkable for those men of the law, on either side, who make it their business to prosecute cases and defend clients.

. . . . .

This understanding of the Fifth Amendment may also help to explain a cluster of modern cases that has inspired a proper degree of bafflement—and no small portion of unwelcome surprise—among commentators on the law. The cases have involved the extraction of evidence from unwilling suspects; they have offered instances, as Justice Bradley said, in which the Fourth and Fifth Amendments run into one another: problems of "search and seizure" merge with questions of self-incrimination. Within this bloc of cases, Justice Brennan has been placed as a pivotal figure. He himself determined the outcome on two signal cases, which seemed to form, for some observers, the phases of a paradox. Within the space of eight days, in 1966, Justice Brennan helped form the majority of the Court in *Miranda v. Arizona*,[48] and he wrote on behalf of the majority in *Schmerber v. California*.[49] Brennan was the only member of the Court who was part of the majority in both cases. Every judge who joined him in *Miranda* was in dissent in *Schmerber*. In *Miranda*, the Court pronounced its legendary judgment about the need to warn suspects of their right to be sheltered from interrogation until they were joined by counsel. In *Schmerber*, the Court sustained the action of the police in Los Angeles in having a sample of blood taken from the arm of a man suspected of driving under the influence of alcohol and causing a serious accident. In upholding the conviction in this case, the Court rejected the claim that Schmerber had been compelled, in effect, to be a witness against himself. Without his consent, his body was made to yield up evidence that bore, in a telling way, on his blameworthiness in a criminal act. All of the judges who had joined Brennan in the Miranda case were persuaded that this unwilling extraction of evidence marked a violation of the Fifth Amendment. If the judgments in *Miranda* and *Schmerber* could be reconciled, the connection could be found only in the understanding of Justice Brennan.

Brennan has never shown a contracted spirit in interpreting the protections of the Bill of Rights. Over thirty years on the Court, his disposition has been to construe these rights in the most generous, expansive way. He has not been disposed to take a view of the Fifth Amendment that is any more contracted; and yet, he did not believe that the Schmerber case disclosed a violation of the principle engaged in the Fifth Amendment. His understanding of the distinction moved along these lines:

> We hold that the privilege [on self-incrimination] protects an accused only from being compelled to testify against himself, or otherwise provide the State with evidence of a *testimonial or communicative nature*, and that the withdrawal of blood and use of the analysis in question in this case did not involve compulsion to these ends.[50]

Not even a shadow of testimonial compulsion upon or enforced communication by the accused was involved either in the extraction or in the chemical analysis. Petitioner's *testimonial capacities were in no way implicated*; indeed, his participation, except as a donor, was irrelevant to the results of the test, which depend on chemical analysis and on that alone.[51]

The accent here was on the nature of the objective, material evidence. The decisive thing to be learned from the sample of blood depended on "chemical analysis and on that alone." There was little room to shade the meaning of the evidence through the interpretation of counsel. Nor could the evidence be rendered obscure through the failures of memory. By the same token, the conviction would not be based on "testimony," which could be distorted or colored as it was extracted with threats of punishment or intimations of reward. To the extent that a conviction depended more heavily on testimony, the extraction of that testimony under compulsion would have to affect that testimony with suspicion. But to the extent that the conviction depended on material evidence, and to the extent that the rendering of justice hinged, then, on any particular piece of evidence, there was a justification for demanding that evidence, even under compulsion.

Brennan offered this gentle challenge to his colleagues: If the Court were not guided by this understanding, how would they explain their willingness to accept, as evidence, many items that depend on the body or person of the accused, and which are typically extracted without his consent? Defendants have persistently invoked the clause of self-incrimination to resist the taking of their fingerprints and voiceprints and samples of their handwriting. They have objected to the demand that they be measured or photographed; that they speak the words spoken by an assailant; that they take a certain stance, make a certain gesture, walk in a particular way. And just as persistently, these claims have been rejected by the courts.[52] But if it were wrong in principle to compel suspects to yield up evidence of their guilt from their own bodies, it is hard to see how any of this evidence could be admissible. In fact, it is hard to see how the law could even compel a defendant to make his body available in the courtroom, so that a jury would have the chance to regard him and estimate his credibility.

Of course, it is but a small, and barely distinguishable step, between the evidence extracted from the body, and the evidence drawn from the most intimate personal effects. Defendants have been convicted on the basis of evidence in the form of dried blood (the blood of a victim) scraped from under the fingernails. Some convictions have turned on traces of paint found in the fibers of a pair of pants. In one notable case, a man named Blackford had sought to smuggle heroin into this country by putting a quantity of the drug in a condom and inserting the condom into his rectum. Blackford drew the suspicions of the agents at the border, and the stains on his body finally led them to the hiding place. But Blackford resisted the attempts to extract the evidence. That resistance led to the involvement of a physician at a Naval Hospital, along with two corpsmen, who held Blackford down while the evidence was removed, clumsily, with an anoscope and forceps. This search was later challenged in the courts, but here, as in other cases involving the smuggling of drugs, the courts upheld the search of bodily cavities. When there were plausible grounds for suspicion, neither the Fifth nor the Fourth Amendments would prevent the authorities from getting access even to the most improbable places and using that evidence in a court of law.[53]

But again, these are cases in which the Fourth and Fifth Amendments "run almost into each other." Schmerber was made to give up evidence from his body, and even if the taking of that evidence did not convert Schmerber into a "witness against himself," Brennan thought that a plausible question could be raised under the Fourth Amendment. That amendment provided that people should be "secure in their persons, houses, papers, and effects, against unreasonable searches." When the question was posed this way, as a problem under the Fourth Amendment, it became legitimate to ask that the police seek a warrant and explain to a disinterested judge why the search they have in mind is not "unreasonable." But as Brennan quickly grasped, a reasonable argument for the government under the Fifth Amendment may satisfy the requirements of the Fourth Amendment as well. The police were justified in extracting the blood because the evidence was necessary to the assignment of responsibility, and the focusing of charges, in a criminal case. Once it is understood that the authorities may have a legitimate claim to the evidence, the barriers of the Fourth Amendment begin to drop away. As Brennan put it, "the Fourth Amendment's proper function is to constrain, not against all intrusions as such, but against intrusions which are *not justified in the circumstances*, or which are made in an improper manner."[54]

Once again, the meaning of a provision in the Bill of Rights would hinge, in any case, on the question of whether there was a legitimate end that justified the restriction of freedom or the abridgement of privacy. In this particular case, Brennan was drawn to a cluster of rather precise features that made the extraction of the evidence both tolerable and justified, even without the presence of a warrant. For one thing, the evidence was perishable: the percentage of alcohol in the blood would diminish rapidly. Brennan thought it was reasonable then for the police to conclude that "there was no time to seek out a magistrate and secure a warrant" without risking the destruction, or loss, of the evidence.[55] But these conclusions were easier to sustain because Brennan did not find anything particularly assaulting (or, in the older version of the word, "insulting") in the procedure for extracting the blood. "Such tests are a commonplace," he remarked, "in these days of periodic physical examinations." The quantity of blood extracted here was "minimal," and "for most people the procedure involves virtually no risk, trauma, or pain." Finally, the judgment was borne out for him by the fact that the "petitioner's blood was taken by a physician in a hospital environment according to accepted medical practices."[56] The decision would not foretell, then, the judgment of the Court on another kind of case, "if a search involving use of a medical technique, even of the most rudimentary sort, were made by other than medical personnel or in other than a medical environment—for example, if it were administered by police in the privacy of the stationhouse."[57]

But in *Rochin v. California*, the case that "shocked the conscience" of Justice Frankfurter, the stomach pump was administered by doctors in a hospital. And for the practitioners in a hospital, the procedure had ceased to be remarkable or extraordinary. The evidence had been removed from Rochin's stomach by "medical personnel" in a "medical environment," according to "accepted medical practices." Still, those features had not been taken by the Court to establish the "reasonable" character of the search. In our own day, nastro-gastric tubes have become more pliable, less irritating, far more routine (or "common"). As one commentator has remarked, every new procedure is of course novel or uncommon, but in a field marked by accelerated changes in technique and equipment, the new quickly becomes routine. We are now in the early seasons of operations performed with lasers, without the need to break the skin. Which is to say, it has now become possible to conduct serious surgery on a person without cutting into the body or using techniques any more "invasive" than those used to remove a sample of blood from the arm of Schmerber.

Brennan apparently thought that his judgment in *Schmerber* could be reconciled with the decision of the Court in *Rochin*. But the comparison merely drew our attention, once again, to the *personal* quality of Frankfurter's reaction in that case, and the distinctly nonjural ground of his judgment. "This is conduct," said Frankfurter, "that shocks the conscience." Frankfurter thought he was invoking here a standard more professional and exacting than "fastidious squeamishness or private sentimentalism."[58] Still, he offered no criteria that could be drawn from the logic of rendering justice. He could connect his reactions with slogans and familiar figures ("These are methods too close to the rack and the screw"), but not with *propositions* that had the standing of real axioms, or principles, in the law.

In contrast, the understanding set forth by Brennan was connected, through several strands, to the logical properties of rendering judgments in matters of right and wrong. That understanding has preserved for the Court a dependable strand of connection to the grounds of practical judgment, and that may explain why it has continued to guide the Court.[59] But how did Brennan manage to reconcile all of this with the famous ruling in *Miranda*? The ruling in that case has become identified over the years with a right to have counsel present, even during the first stages of an interrogation by the police. And yet, as Chief Justice Warren had explained, in the opening paragraph of his opinion for the Court, the central concern of the Miranda case was with the Fifth Amendment and the clause on self-incrimination. Something in the accumulated experience of the Court had moved a majority to conclude that there was a "compulsion inherent in custodial surroundings";[60] that the "atmosphere [of interrogation under custody] carries its own badge of intimidation."[61]

> [W]ithout proper safeguards the process of in-custody interrogation of persons suspected or accused of crime contains inherently compelling pressures which work to undermine the individual's will to resist and to compel him to speak where he would not otherwise do so freely.[62]

For the sake of drawing this conclusion, and pronouncing this judgment, the Court collected four separate cases; but the cases seemed to offer only the faintest illustration of the point the Court was determined to establish. In the Miranda case itself, Chief Justice Warren conceded that "the records do not evince overt physical coercion or patent psychological ploys."[63] Ernest Miranda had been arrested by the police in Phoenix, and after an interrogation of only two hours, he confessed to the charges of kidnapping and rape. In contrast, in one of the companion cases, *California v. Stewart*, the defendant had been interrogated in nine sessions, drawn out over five days.[64] The Court apparently had in mind the prospect of innocent people, worn down by overbearing, manipulative techniques, and induced to confess to crimes they had not committed. But none of the cases in this collection offered such a fetching example. Evidently, the Court had drawn its inspiration for this ruling from something other than the facts that described these cases.

The chief justice cast the argument of the Court against the current operating practice of the police in conducting interrogations. And for that point, he took the leading textbooks on interrogation as a reliable guide to the actual practice of the police. The teaching in those books favored a regimen of isolating the suspect in the setting of the police station, cutting him off from friends, family, or any other sources of support. The object was to enhance the sense of the police as dominant, irresistible, bound to discover the truth. An inventory of techniques was brought forward to disarm and cajole, to evoke, from the suspect, a sense of excuse or even repentence, and bring him to a state of mind in which he becomes willing to confess.[65] Perhaps the Court joined these fragments of evidence to the common experience of the police, in receiving every day "confessions" from people who had committed no crimes. In any event, from these "facts"—which had not been borne out in any of the cases before the Court—the judges now drew the conclusion that there was something immanently coercive in the interrogation conducted by the police.

If the surmises of the Court were warranted, interrogations by the police could only produce confessions that were tainted or suspect, unless the atmosphere of intimidation could be broken. It could be broken only by removing the sense of a closed system dominated entirely by the police. And that state of affairs could be disrupted, quite dramatically, quite simply, by bringing in a lawyer. The Court could mandate the presence of counsel as early as the suspect wished to have the support of a lawyer. The accused could also be informed—and informed as an indispensable part of the procedures of the police—that he had a right to remain silent until he was joined by counsel. Under this new regime, as the Court described it,

> the prosecution may not use statements, whether exculpatory or inculpatory, stemming from custodial interrogation of the defendant unless it demonstrates the use of procedural safeguards effective to secure the privilege against self-incrimination. . . . The defendant may waive effectuation of these rights, provided the waiver is made voluntarily, knowingly and intelligently. If, however, he indicates in any manner and at any stage of the process that he wishes to consult with an attorney before speaking there can be no questioning.[66]

The Court was now prepared, in effect, to legislate these requirements as part of the manual of procedures followed by the police in all parts of the country. And yet, it was not clear from the record that the police had failed to satisfy the standards that the Court was now legislating in this case. The Court was pressed, then, to make a more refined point in the companion case of *California v. Stewart*: As the Court conceded, "nothing in the record specifically indicates whether [the suspect] was or was not advised of his right to remain silent or his right to counsel." The Court had no evidence that the warning had not been rendered, that the protection had not been offered. The Court was articulating, rather, as a point of doctrine, that the warning was so critical that it could not be left to inadvertence: In the absence of any explicit evidence that the warnings had been given, the Court would presume that they had *not* been. The confessions would then be disallowed and the convictions overturned.

In this manner, the Court moved all too easily from a tenuous constitutional argument to an astounding remedy. The Court was prepared now to exclude testimony, even if it turned up valid evidence, and to revoke the conviction that was built upon this evidence. To an argument that was already deeply problematic, the Court added a remedy that was morally dubious.

Justice Harlan was compelled to remind his colleagues of the melancholy fact that the sense of coercion or confinement could not be purged entirely from the interrogation that is carried out while a suspect is in custody. The suspect is, after all, deprived of his freedom to leave custody. The law could not practicably hope to dispel from this setting all traces of coercion and intimidation. But what the courts had done in the past—and done, by and large, successfully—was to review the cases in which the police had gone too far and used methods that were patently coercive. The courts could deal with these cases in all of their variety, and when the canons of lawfulness had been breached, the courts could indicate, very precisely, the points at which the State had lapsed from the requirements of "due process of law." There was no need to legislate a manual of procedures, drawn from the most clichéd readings of the clause on self-incrimination.[67]

I do not wish to obscure my own judgment that the animating concern of the Court had been eminently right-headed. Anyone who understood the most elementary grounds of the law would have to regard it as nothing less than a grave matter if the conditions of interrogation throughout the country really were productive of confessions that were immanently flawed or suspect. On that cardinal point, Justice Brennan furnished the connection between the majority in Miranda and the majority in the Schmerber case: The Fifth Amendment did not rule out the possibility of extracting material evidence, even under compulsion. But it did register an aversion in principle to testimony that might be molded falsely, because it was extracted under conditions of duress.

The matter that had to be judged in any case was whether there really was the kind of coercion that could distort the assessment of guilt or culpability; and then a serious question would be raised as to where the proper remedy would lie. Justice Harlan argued that the remedy could not be found by seeking, in the daily practice of arrest and interrogation, a "utopian" deliverance from every shade of intimidation and moral condemnation. Harlan would have had the judges available to review the cases with tutored suspicions and practiced eyes, ready to remand cases for new trials when the practice of the police was egregious. On the other side, his colleagues in the majority were inclined to cope with the problem with a stern, simple prescription: They would insert a lawyer. They would make the presence of counsel a constitutional requirement at almost every stage of interrogation, once a suspect has been arrested "or otherwise deprived of his freedom of action in any significant way."

But to say that the presence of a lawyer would "mitigate" the problem of coercion was a precious fiction. Justice Robert Jackson once observed that "any lawyer worth his salt will tell the suspect in no uncertain terms to make no statement to police under any circumstances."[68] The policy of requiring lawyers at all stages of questioning would "mitigate" the problem of faulty confessions by discouraging any confessions at all. Regardless of whether the decision of the Court would produce that effect, Harlan's critique was unexceptionable on this point: Implicit in the "remedy" offered by the Court was a willingness to see confessions disappear from the criminal process altogether if that was the only way of insuring that all confessions would be free from intimidation. But as Harlan aptly rejoined, "the Fifth Amendment . . . has never been thought to forbid all pressure to incriminate one's self."[69]

In this observation, offered almost in passing, Harlan wrote even more pre-
sciently than he could have suspected at the time. For he saw the premise that
was taking hold among his colleagues, even though it was only dimly reflected
in the text of the opinion. What Harlan apparently detected in the minds of
his colleagues was this lurking conviction: that it was wrong in principle to
expect any man to incriminate himself, or confess to wrongdoing, even if he
were guilty of the most conspicuous wrong, and even if he thoroughly deserved to incriminate himself. In the curious understanding of the Court, the
human "dignity" protected by the Fifth Amendment was abstracted from the
nature of human beings as moral agents.[70] The dignity of a moral agent arose
from his capacity to give reasons over matters of right and wrong—and to
respect the implications that flowed from this moral understanding. A moral
agent would understand that he was obliged to do what was right and refrain
from what was wrong. But in the understanding of the Court now, it was not
part of the reflexes of a moral agent to repent his own guilt, or to expiate that
guilt by offering a confession. In fact, as the Court began to weave the strands
of jurisprudence that came out of the Miranda case, the defenders of the pur-
est Miranda doctrine would come to this understanding: Any confession offered by a suspect in the absence of a lawyer was itself proof of coercion, for
no rational man, freed from coercion, would have any reason or motive to
confess his own guilt.[71]

Only an understanding of this kind could explain the curious dissents that
would be offered by Justices Marshall and Brennan in these notable cases.

—A man is arrested for committing armed robbery with a sawed-off shotgun, and
he is advised of his "Miranda rights." On the way to the police station the
officers in the car fall into a conversation about the missing shotgun. One
officer notes that there is a school for handicapped children in the area and
"God forbid one of them might find a weapon with shells and they might hurt
themselves." The conversation continues in this way, and it is overheard by
the suspect (as indeed, it might have been staged for his overhearing). The
suspect finally responds to this veiled appeal; he breaks into the conversation
and tells the police that he will lead them to the weapon if they will turn the
car around and return to the scene of the arrest. The suspect is informed once
again that he has a right to remain silent. He replies that he understands those
rights, but he "wanted to get the gun out of the way because of the kids in the
area in the school." With the gun as evidence, the suspect is eventually convicted for kidnaping, robbery, and murder (*Rhode Island v. Innis* [1980]).[72]

—A man suspected of rape is spotted in a supermarket, and he is chased through
the store before he is finally caught. As the police make the arrest, they notice
that the suspect is wearing a shoulder holster, which is now empty. As they
place the handcuffs on the suspect, one officer asks him where the gun is. The
suspect nods in the direction of some empty cartons and says, "the gun is over

there." This action takes place at the spur of the moment, before the police fall back into the rituals of their usual procedures and advise the suspect of his Miranda rights. The police report that they were concerned, at the moment, for the safety of other customers in the store, who might come upon a loaded gun. The trial court excluded the evidence of the gun, because it was found at the direction of the suspect before the police had issued the Miranda warning. But the Supreme Court eventually reversed this judgment (*New York v. Quarles* [1984]).[73]

In both of these cases, a majority on the Court backed away from applying the ruling in *Miranda* with a formulaic stringency. For these exercises of judgment, the Court has suffered the charge, in some circles, that it is engaged in a subtle, reactionary move to roll back the Miranda decision. In the opinion for the Court in the Quarles case, Justice Rehnquist reminded the audience of the Court that the Miranda ruling was, after all, a means tailored to an end; it was not an end in itself.[74] The purpose of the rules announced in *Miranda* was to assure, as much as practicable, that the setting for interrogation would not be marked by compulsion and intimidation. In the cases of Innis and Quarles, no one could plausibly argue that the police had used compulsion in extracting information from a suspect. In the Innis case, as I have noted, the police had even issued the Miranda warning, not once but twice. Still, Justices Brennan and Marshall saw a manipulation at work, which was inconsistent with the doctrine set forth in the Miranda case. If these judges revealed here a rigid insistence on procedure, to the exclusion of discretion and judgment, it happened to be the case that this rigid insistence, this unwavering application of formula, was indeed the essence of the doctrine in *Miranda*. Justice Harlan had made that point plain in his dissenting opinion. To cavil now, to carve out an exception here or there for the "public safety," or for the exercise of sound judgment, was to engage in a misleading ritual. In these recent cases, the Court has in fact been trying to disengage itself from the ruling in the Miranda case. The judges have sought to narrow that decision, and diminish its significance, in a decorous way.

But in this style of revision, the judges have evaded the task of explaining just what there is, in the teaching of the Miranda case, that must be an enduring source of mischief in the law. They have taken what they have regarded as a less vexing path, avoiding a full-scale debate with their adversaries on the bench. But this "easier" path has turned out to be far more laborious and far less convincing. The Court has had the burden then of explaining why the facts of the case at hand would warrant yet another exception from the ruling in Miranda. In the Quarles case, Justice Rehnquist strained to show why it was reasonable to give the police a certain latitude to make mistakes, to part from the established procedures, when there was a concern to find a weapon and remove an imminent danger. To the degree that his argument really hinged on that justification, it was quite vulnerable to the response, offered by Brennan and Marshall, that the police had known, by their own account, that the gun was in the immediate vicinity of their encounter with Quarles: "The police could easily have cordoned off the store and searched for the missing gun. Had they done so, they would have found the gun forthwith."[75]

Passed over in this argument, however, was the question of why it was reasonable to impose this burden of discovery on the police, when it was possible to relieve the danger by a simple query, posed to the suspect. "Where is the gun?," is all that Officer Kraft asked of Quarles. That question was posed without compulsion—and Quarles had been free to ignore the question without suffering a penalty. In the cases of Quarles and Innes, both men answered questions that were asked without the hint of compulsion, and the suspects led the police to real evidence. There was no example, in either case, of intimidating the suspects and inducing them to sign on to implausible stories. One must wonder, then, why Justice Brennan was not able to fashion, in these cases, a meeting of his separate juridical selves. Brennan and the Court seemed to work in separated compartments; one day they would argue about the Miranda doctrine and its implications, and on another day they would construe the lines of law emanating from the Schmerber case. Brennan was willing to have blood extracted from an unwilling suspect because the procedure produced real evidence. But he was moved to see grave breaches of the Constitution when a suspect was induced, without questioning, without solicitation, to reveal the whereabouts of a gun.

Of course, the Court he had joined in the Miranda case had been concerned about the subtler forms of manipulation, as well as the grosser forms of intimidation.[76] But it was not at all clear from the record in the Innis case that the police were doing anything other than expressing the concerns they genuinely felt over the hazards posed to children by a stray weapon. And yet, let us assume for a moment that the conversation was not initiated idly, that it was drawn out, in the presence of the suspect, with the hope of producing an effect. If that was all, the thread of psychological manipulation was to be found in a modest appeal, to the concern or sympathy of the suspect, for the harm he might cause to innocent children. But in the logic that attached to the dissent, that is precisely the kind of appeal that Justice Marshall and Brennan were willing to regard as unseemly and even unscrupulous. With the support of Brennan, Marshall complained that "one can scarcely imagine a stronger appeal to the conscience of a suspect—*any* suspect—than the assertion that if the weapon is not found an innocent person will be hurt or killed. And not just any innocent person, but an innocent child—a little girl—a helpless, handicapped little girl on her way to school."[77]

In their hours off the Court, Marshall and Brennan might have inhabited a world more beamish than the rest of us know; a world in which even hardened gangsters are Damon Runyon types, with a sentimental weakness for stranded women and helpless children. But not all cutthroats can be depended on to respond to the "appeal" that was made in this case by the police in Providence. And yet, if we put aside this reading, offered by Marshall and Brennan, on the moral reflexes that can be found, even among killers, their teaching on the Fifth Amendment stands out as even more striking. Not only is there a constitutional "right" to hold back evidence of one's guilt, but that claim also entails a subsidiary right not to suffer an appeal to one's "conscience" or one's moral sense. Apparently, for Marshall and Brennan, nothing in that moral sense should induce a wrongdoer to confess his crime and bring forth the evidence of his guilt. But this curious moral sense would somehow impel the suspect, irresistibly, to incriminate himself, to yield up the evidence of his guilt, rather than risk an injury to some unknown, innocent person.

As an empirical theory on the operations of the moral sense, this notion, advanced by Marshall and Brennan, could found a new school, and occupy new cohorts of researchers, in the psychology of moral learning. And in the field of jurisprudence this novelty should be startling: As Marshall and Brennan came to understand the clause on self-incrimination, the principle behind that clause stamped the authorities as corrupt, sleazy, manipulative, when they appealed, even in a muted way, to the "conscience," or the moral sense, of a suspect. In the moral world of Marshall and Brennan, a rational man would never respond *rationally* to appeals for repentence or contrition. He would never be moved, by the recognition of his wrong, to confess his guilt and seek to remedy the harm he has caused. If he responds to the commands of a moral sense, or an appeal to his conscience, those entreaties must be the product of psychological manipulation. The chain of reasoning eventually produces this conclusion: Any appeal by the authorities to the moral sense of the accused must, by definition, be a species of manipulation. Therefore, it must be illicit, illegitimate, unconstitutional. In the inversion brought about by Marshall and Brennan, we have been asked earnestly to believe that any appeal to the accused in his nature as a moral agent must offend our deepest sense of right and wrong. And that is the moral understanding that Marshall and Brennan would build into the Constitution now, as they seek to preserve the purity of the doctrine in the Miranda case, and uncover, for their colleagues, the real meaning of the Fifth Amendment.

The Fifth Amendment has curiously brought forth, in our own day, two Justice Brennans. Like the principal characters in Henry James's story, "The Friends of the Friends," they would no doubt bear a fascination for one another if they could ever meet. But one is always out when the other comes to call. Almost as though they were guided by an elegant choreography, the two manage to glide past each other in the arrangement of their lives. Were they to meet, the two Justice Brennans would be compelled to have a conversation that goes to the root. And yet, apart from the range of their differences, they share one critical point of understanding, on the application of the Bill of Rights to the states. That understanding was recorded in the Schmerber case without putting too fine a point on it, but in the proper Jamesian style, that silent turning away from any gesture to summon attention, that holding back of an explanation, may itself summon our attention and lead us back to the muted point that may in fact be, after all, the fine point of it.

Brennan recalled, in the Schmerber case, that the Court had considered almost exactly the same kind of problem nine years earlier in *Breithaupt v. Abram* (1957).[78] Once again, blood had been removed from the arm of a suspect, and the Court denied the claim that this procedure was inconsistent with the "due process" of law. The claim had been rejected, that is, under the Fourteenth Amendment. The argument had been made at the time that the procedure violated the Fifth Amendment, but the Court had not yet held that the Fifth Amendment had been "incorporated" in the Fourteenth Amendment and made binding, in that way, on the states. That step would come in 1964, in *Malloy v. Hogan*.[79] Justice Brennan himself wrote for the Court in *Malloy v. Hogan*, and when he wrote again, two years later, in the Schmerber case, he understood quite well that the Court was not merely upholding, once more, the extraction of blood from the arm of a suspect. If Brennan upheld the extraction of evidence from an unwilling suspect, it was evidently not because the Fifth Amendment applied with less stringency to the states. But rather, it was—it could only be—because this compelling of evidence did not offend any principle contained in the Fifth Amendment. Brennan's presence, as the writer for the Court on both occasions, in *Malloy* and *Schmerber*, made that point ever clearer. The extraction of the evidence was not to be upheld so that the *states* could be freed from a stringent reading of the Bill of Rights. The procedure was upheld because *governments at all levels, federal as well as state*, would be freed from the constraint of a spurious principle. The federal government would be no less free now than the governments in the states to compel the production of material evidence, without encountering constitutional barriers, cast up through false constructions of the Fifth Amendment.

In his opinion in the Schmerber case, Brennan reached back and drew a passage from the opinion he had joined a week earlier in *Miranda v. Arizona*: "the constitutional foundation underlying the privilege [on self-incrimination] is the respect a government—state or federal—must accord to the dignity and integrity of its citizens."[80] When a real principle of law was engaged, the sweep of that principle would of course cover the states, no less than the federal government. What Brennan supplied now, in Schmerber, was the logical corollary of that recognition: When a genuine principle of law was *not* engaged, the Constitution would interpose no artificial barriers. The officers of the federal government would be licensed, no less than the authorities in the states, to draw upon the range of their powers and their judgment in addressing those questions of policy, those questions of right and wrong, that they thought it fitting to reach.

I have traversed, in these pages, a wide terrain; but I have kept in hand the same strands of questions as I have moved over this legal landscape. My hope has been that this style of questioning would allow us to see some parts of this landscape anew. If we trace the provisions of the Bill of Rights back to their tenable grounds of principle, we discover that we have attached importance in the past to events that have not merited our anxiety; while at the same time we have often blocked from our view events near at hand, in which the principles of the lawful government are seriously violated every day, without drawing our notice or stirring our outrage.

As some of the Founders anticipated, our lawyers and judges have fallen out of the practice of deliberating about principles in a demanding, philosophic way, by tracing their judgment back to first principles and testing their propositions against the axioms of moral reasoning. Instead of being tutored in the real principles of law, we have been offered mainly slogans, which have claimed the standing of principles largely through repetition. The tell-tale signs have been found in the appeals to the "legal traditions" of "our people," or in the reflex, shown by Justice Bradley in the Boyd case, when he thought it sufficient to remark that the practice at hand was ".abhorrent to the instincts of an Englishman [and] abhorrent to the instincts of an American."[81]

These grand, hazy appeals to "traditions" or "instincts" come into play when judges are evidently incapable of explaining the logic that imparts, to any maxim, the substance of a principle of law. There is no need to invoke the "traditions" of our people in order to explain why "it is wrong to hold people blameworthy or responsible for acts they were powerless to affect." We can establish the necessity and truth of that proposition, with lines of connection that run back to the logic of law itself. The force of a necessary truth supplies all the justification that is wanted. The "traditions" and "instincts" of Englishmen have encompassed villainy and mayhem and judicial murder. To invoke those traditions is not to explain the parts that are valid and relevant as guides to the rendering of justice. Judges may repeat, in each generation, that it is "cruel" to "compel any person to be a witness against himself." But mere repetition does not itself explain why that compulsion is wrong or cruel—and it certainly cannot identify for us the cases, or the instances, that properly come under this principle.

The burden of my argument here has been that we can illuminate this question only by appealing beyond the text of the Constitution to the principles that stand behind the text. When we do that, as I have suggested, we may find that the Constitution provides us with a different lens. We may then begin to notice the presence of grave, constitutional questions contained in practices or policies that have not ordinarily struck us, in the past, as matters freighted with constitutional problems. And among them we may find such familiar, notable practices as: plea bargaining, the imposition of wage and price controls, the encouragement of testimony from informers. In the final chapter, I would like to draw upon the understandings I have spun out in these pages, and consider, again, just what we may see differently. If we may conceive in a different way the grounds of our rights and the ends of our government, we may open, to governments in this country, some new paths in pursuing their ends. But to open up, in this manner, an understanding of new paths may illuminate the question of ends as well as means.

As the Founders understood, a constitutional government is not a weak government, any more than a man with self-restraint is a weak man. A government may be restrained in its methods and its ends by the discipline of acting in a principled way. A clearer understanding of the principles of lawfulness may constrain the government from touching, with the laws, the subjects that it has no justification in reaching. But in diverting the government from the things it ought not do, that understanding may also direct the government to the subjects that form its rightful, urgent business. And those ends may be reached with the full, moral authority of the law. A national government that can bar private hospitals from turning away patients on the basis of race may have the authority, also, to bar those same hospitals from withdrawing medical treatment from infants who are retarded. If that is the case, there would be no need to conceal the reach of that law with dishonest fictions and distracting formulas: no need to pretend that the government is merely offering or removing federal aid, rather than really "legislating"; no need to furnish a "nonmoral" rationale for a law that addresses a serious matter of right and wrong. In short, the federal government may be enfranchised to act with the moral seriousness of a real government. It may act then with an understanding of its ends that is no longer constricted by slogans dressed up as principles, or by theories of law that pretend to be the fitting surrogates for moral understanding.

NINE

NEONATES AND REPROBATES: THE REACH OF A GOVERNMENT COMPETENT TO ITS ENDS

THROUGH the working of some inscrutable force, Mr. Terry Lenzner found himself, in the early days of the Nixon administration, in an immanently implausible position. Within a conservative administration, he was the lieutenant of a kind of legal combat unit with a radical mission. He was the director of the Neighborhood Legal Services Project in the Office of Economic Opportunity, the agency created under Lyndon Johnson, to wage a "war on poverty." The young lawyers attached to this project could be dropped into local communities as legal paratroopers. After establishing their connections to the natives, they would proceed to wage lawsuits, on behalf of the "poor." The fees would be paid by the federal government, and the "clients" were spared the burden of bearing any share of the expenses. Delivered in that way from the strains that affect more conventional plaintiffs, they could persevere more happily in this program of litigation.

Of course, the targets for many of these lawsuits would be the establishments headed by the local mayors and governors. Predictably, these people would not affably tolerate this state of affairs. They would soon make use of the leverage they could command in Congress and the executive; they would take the steps needed to contain this project, with its promise of endless litigation at limitless expense. There was a move, then, to give governors a veto over these campaigns of litigation. In the face of these moves, Terry Lenzner registered his fierce opposition, and in November 1970 he was fired. Thus ended his improbable alliance with the Nixon administration. It was not, however, an amicable divorce. Less than three years later, he would align himself quite explicitly with the opposition in another legal project, to bring down the Nixon administration: Lenzner would become the assistant counsel to the *Democratic* majority in the Senate Committee on Watergate.

In the late 1970s Lenzner was practicing law in Boston, and his experience in civil rights brought him forward when the city had to deal with a grave racial incident, brought on by local thugs. In 1978, there were threats of violence directed at black people in East Boston with the purpose of driving them out of public housing—and keeping them out of the neighborhood. The state of civility in the city had already been strained by several years of dispute over busing in South Boston, attended at times with outbreaks of violence. The minor terrorism in East Boston may have been inspired by local yahoos, without the benefit of strategy and design, but it was portentous nevertheless, for it was the kind of tactic that could be fed by success, and quickly spread into a pattern of lawlessness. The occasion required a response from the authorities that could be, at once, chilling and decisive. Terry Lenzner was called in to offer counsel, and he offered a plan that seemed, to the mind of lawyers, a suitable mixture of genius and repression. First, the problem would be treated as a "federal" case, a violation of the Civil Rights Acts. The level of engagement would be raised; the local delinquents would learn that the weight of the federal government would be brought in against thuggery of this kind. The private thugs who focused their threats on black people might readily fall under the familiar terms of "two or more persons [who] conspire or go in disguise . . . for the purpose of depriving, either directly or indirectly, any person or class of persons of the equal protection of the laws." But the turn of genius came in the choice of statutes: Lenzner would not have the U.S. attorney seek a criminal prosecution under Section 241. Instead, the defenders of the blacks in East Boston would make use of the civil provisions of the Civil Rights Acts, in Section 1985: On behalf of the victims, there would be a civil suit for damages, directed at a handful of people, who had been indentified as leaders or participants in this campaign of harassment.

Why the civil suit? And where was the genius? If the assailants were subjected to a criminal prosecution, the provisions of the Sixth Amendment would come into play, and the defendants would have a right "to be confronted with the witnesses" against them. But as Terry Lenzner explained, there had been a "problem of obtaining live witnesses to testify in criminal proceedings on acts of violence committed by their neighbors. . . . Many potential witnesses fear retaliation and violence if they testified in an open court." But with a civil proceeding, it was permissible for the court to accept "sealed affidavits as evidence without live witnesses."[1]

When he enforced the Civil Rights Acts, when he served on the Watergate Committee, Mr. Lenzner had identified himself with the cause of a stringent fidelity to the terms of the Constitution. One would gather that he found, in the provisions of the Constitution, principles that merited his reverence, not rules to be invoked or circumvented in a clever way when it suited the interests of the government. Presumably, also, he shared the temper of those lawyers and judges who thought that these principles should be read in an expansive way, true to their fuller spirit, and not construed in a narrow, carping manner. His deepest respect was not apparently drawn to those lawyers for the government who were willing to fasten on the most literal meaning of the text, for the sake of gaining their end in any case, even when the text offered the most constricted view of the principle at hand. If Justice Cardozo's perspective had been applied to this case, Lenzner would have been urged to consider whether the provision on the confrontation of witnesses could really claim the standing of a "principle" of law: Could it be drawn, as a logical implication, from the very idea of rendering justice? Would its omission render any legal proceeding incoherent as a proceeding that pretended to arrive at a *just* verdict? To call back an earlier example, it would be literally incoherent for any system of justice to incorporate in its premises the possibility of holding people blameworthy and punishable for acts they were powerless to affect. That premise would be incompatible with the very logic of establishing a "justification."[2] The acceptance of this proposition would introduce a decisive flaw into any system of adjudication, whether it was a proceeding in a courtroom, a procedure for the expulsion of members from a club, or a rule employed by a parent in disciplining a child. The forum, or the field of law, would be utterly beside the point.

The question for Terry Lenzner was whether the provision on the confrontation of witnesses could really claim the standing of a principle in the same way. Did it arise from the very logic of law; was it necessary to any criminal trial that would even pretend to be just? If it were, then it should have been quite as necessary, as a rule of procedure, in a civil suit. After all, in a civil suit, defendants are subjected to a public accusation, they are tried in a legal forum, and if they are found guilty, they are condemned with a penalty. Lenzner remarked that the stringent requirements of the Sixth Amendment came into play with a criminal prosecution because "the penalty is so high—possible incarceration." And yet, the civil judgment he sought would bring an order from a court to enjoin the defendants from further harassment. If they failed to obey the injunction, they could be held in contempt of court, and in that event, as Lenzner pointed out, "the sanctions can range from fines to possible imprisonment."[3]

Of course, the provision, in the Sixth Amendment, referred only to "criminal" proceedings. Lenzner was not bound by anything in the words of the Constitution to apply the same notion, on the confrontation of witnesses, to civil suits. But if he were convinced that this provision in the Sixth Amendment truly had the standing of a principle, which merited his respect, why would he not respect it even in the places where the Constitution was silent? For the Constitution also left him free to apply a more demanding sense of propriety: He was indeed free to seek a legal punishment for people in a suit that would not require the confrontation of witnesses; and yet he was free, also, to judge that he would rather not gain his ends in that way if he had to circumvent a principle that commanded his respect.

During the 1950s and 1960s, when the country awoke to the problem of racial segregation, the awakening seem to ripple through the country with an ever widening arc. In private universities and social clubs, in corporations and unions, people began to challenge the convention of racial separation, even in places that the courts and the law did not reach. They showed, in other words, an awareness of the principle engaged in racial discrimination; they understood that the principle bore a relevance to their lives, even where the law was silent. A comparison to the case in Boston would suggest that Lenzner was not affected by any comparable sense concerning the provision in the Sixth Amendment on the confrontation of witnesses. That provision did not, apparently, impress him with the sense of a principle that had a claim to guide his moral reflexes in all matters touching the law. I do not make this point for the sake of condemning, but for the sake of noticing, in Mr. Lenzner's reactions, an intuition that might have pointed to a different understanding. If he had read his own reactions in this way, he might have been moved to reflect on the question of why he did not seem to regard the provision on the confrontation of witnesses as a proposition that claimed his adherence as categorically, as unconditionally, as the principle that barred discrimination on the basis of race. He would have been moved, of course, to consider just why he thought it reasonable, in this case, to avoid the provision on the confrontation of witnesses. Evidently, he thought that the avoidance of the rule, in this instance, would help to protect innocent witnesses from harm and secure the ends of justice. The fact that the evidence could still be tested by a judge and jury apparently furnished a sufficient assurance to Lenzner that this arrangement was not at odds with the discipline of rendering justice.

But if Lenzner had moved along this path, he might have opened to himself still others paths of reflection—and still other possibilities for the law. He might have arrived at the recognition that Felix Frankfurter once expressed in regard to the Fifth Amendment: that the words could not be read with a naive literalness. There was a need, still, for judgment and deliberation in deciding just where the accent ought to be placed in this series of words: that a person accused in a criminal prosecution had the right "to be confronted with the witnesses against him." A sampling of our recent experience may be enough to suggest just how problematic these simple words may be, even in criminal cases. A federal court of appeals decided in 1985 that the clause on confrontation did not bear with the same stringency on witnesses who were children. The case involved the charges of sexual abuse on the part of a man in Arizona who lived in a "crisis center" operated by his mother. The center offered a temporary shelter for children, and the charges arose in this case over sexual advances made to two children, ages five and seven, and to a young woman, who had been sixteen at the time. A concern was raised about the capacity of children to deal with the strains of a confrontation in a courtroom, with an encounter that could bring forth again the vivid moments of their experience. The court was willing to settle for an arrangement in which the children were interviewed, in a less portentous setting, and the testimony was recorded on videotape.[4]

The arrangements for taking testimony, and confronting evidence, may be modified, and the pivotal question for the courts is whether any of these arrangements would impair the possibilities for challenging the testimony and gauging the credibility of the witnesses. In a more recent case, in 1987, the

Court allowed a defendant to be barred from a hearing, conducted by the judge, to determine the competence of three small children to testify as witnesses.[5] There were strong dissents in the case by Justices Marshall, Brennan, and Stevens, who feared that the right of the defendant to confront witnesses would be reduced merely to "an opportunity to cross-examine these witnesses *at some point* during his trial."[6]

But for the majority, apparently, the reasonableness of the decision had something to do with the strains imposed on witnesses who might be too vulnerable or too weak to bear the intimidation of confronting the man they were accusing. And yet, if these kinds of considerations may be plausible and legitimate for the Court, they may be quite arguable in other kinds of cases, with witnesses who are not children, but who may be even more acutely vulnerable and face even graver dangers. Terry Lenzner had evidently taken these possibilities seriously in the case in Boston. He recognized, that is, a serious concern for sheltering witnesses from retaliation. But if that concern was plausible, why could it not have been quite as plausible a concern for a *criminal* prosecution? The danger to the witnesses reflected the viciousness of the defendants and the seriousness of the offense: Why should these ingredients in the case finally move Lenzner—or any other lawyer—to *scale down* the charges for the sake of protecting the witnesses, with sealed affadavits?

Why would it not be better to apply the same inventiveness and imagination to procedures that are more in keeping with the gravity of the charges? Is it possible to have judges screen the testimony offered by a witness and recorded in an affadavit? Can the testimony yield evidence, which may be subject to testing? If there is a need for the further questioning of a witness, could the questions be put, in a further round, by the same judge, preserving the same protections to the witness? If these arrangements may be legitimate in civil actions, which can end in a legal penalty and perhaps even incarceration, why would they not be at least as worthy of reflection in criminal actions, where the penalties may be no more astounding than they are in civil actions?

The defendants in Boston seemed to be a handful of local delinquents, without serious pretensions to organization. But the law has been stymied, in even more momentous cases, when it has sought to deal with the syndicates of organized crime, where the gangsters have cultivated a professional competence in savagery. Not merely their personal honor, but their professional interests, bring the threat against witnesses to a level of believable certainty. If the Sixth Amendment can be accommodated to the vulnerability of children, might it not be accommodated, with as much justice, to the vulnerability of people who are threatened by villains far more formidable than the abusers of children?

These questions merited as much reflection, or as much exertion of mind, as lawyers are likely to expend anyway, as they try to find clever ways of steering around the provisions in the Sixth Amendment. It appeared to Lenzner that a literal application of the clause on "confrontation" would not serve the ends of justice; but instead of reflecting on the principle that lay behind his sense of the matter, he chose to steer around the Sixth Amendment in a mechanical way, through the contrivance of a civil suit. Instead of thinking through the question of principle, he chose, in that phrase of Evelyn Waugh, "the low door under the wall."

In fairness to Terry Lenzner, he was trying to cope with an immediate and pressing problem, and a prudent lawyer might not have thought this the best time to offer a novel argument to the courts. And yet, every notable case may require a flexing of the imagination, and in this case, Mr. Lenzner had to summon no small arts of interpretation in order to explain just how these acts of local thugs came within the reach of the federal government. Lenzner was obviously counting on the prospect of chilling the local vandals by facing them with an action in a *federal* court. But the "short run" marked off the epoch in which most of these local hoodlums conceived and acted out their projects. If a court of appeals happened to decide much later that the case did not plausibly fit under the terms of the Civil Rights Act, Lenzner still had the chance of administering the jolt he wished to administer, and accomplishing his "effect." With the same calculation, he might have encouraged the authorities to seek a criminal prosecution in this case, and ask the judge to protect the witnesses. It might have been urged upon the judge that there were dangers to the witnesses here, which justified the same kind of inventiveness that was used in civil cases to examine testimony while sheltering the witnesses. Perhaps a judge might have been persuaded. Or, perhaps the judge would have been persuaded, but this show of inventiveness might have been challenged on appeal. Lenzner could have left it, then, to the courts to ponder whether these arrangements might be compatible, after all, with the Sixth Amendment. In the meantime, Lenzner would have achieved his effect on the local villains and their audience. The fine points of the appeal could have offered them only a faint solace. And Lenzner might have performed the added, enduring service of compelling the courts to reflect on a serious question, which tested the logic of the Sixth Amendment.

But whether Lenzner chose to move with a criminal prosecution or a civil suit, he still had the burden of explaining just how this case fit under the Civil Rights Acts. The government could have applied the modified perspective offered by Felix Frankfurter: The victims of harassment lived in public housing, funded in substantial part by the *federal* government. Read in these terms, the case could fit neatly within Frankfurter's construction. It might have been argued then that the victims were deprived of a right to live in a *federal* housing project—a right that arose directly from their relation to the federal government. Once again: the federal government might protect the person who was shot on the way to the post office, but not the person who had been on the way to the United Parcel Service. By this reasoning, the federal government might protect the person who is threatened with intimidation, and discouraged from living in a federal housing project. But the same reasoning would not protect the same person from the same kind of intimidation, fueled by a racial animus, if his tormentors had sought to discourage him from moving into a *private* apartment building.

The authorities could have settled for a limited reading of this kind, good enough to get through the day. But to his credit, Lenzner did not settle with such a contracted view of the rights engaged in the case. His own explanation cast the rights of American citizens as broadly as the law could practicably reach. The authority of the federal government was accordingly measured, in turn, to the rights that it was meant to protect. Lenzner noted that the federal government had sought injunctions in the past to protect people against "acts of violence which were an attempt to deny minority people of the federally protected right to vote, the right to assemble, the right to peaceably protest, and the right to use lunch counters." But what was the "federally protected" right in this case? Was it a right not to be intimidated, through the threat of violence, from moving into an apartment building? Lenzner thought that the rights engaged here swept even more broadly than that: "We hope," said Lenzner, that "the suit will be perceived as focusing on a relatively few number of people on behalf of all the people of the city—not just the victims of racial violence." And what he hoped to secure, to the people of the city, as a result of this suit, was nothing less than the freedom to "walk safely in any part of the city."[7]

In substance, Lenzner sought to protect a right of people not to be subject to threats of violence, or a campaign of intimidation, as they tried to pursue innocent activities that anyone may legitimately pursue. Between the city of Boston and the federal government, the boundaries of authority remained hazy for him, and he was not overly concerned with the question of how those lines, precisely, would be drawn. Apparently, for Lenzner, the lawyers for the city, and the lawyers in the office of the U.S. attorney, were all agents of the American people, and they were free to use the different levers available to them for the sake of vindicating the same body of rights. Lenzner did not seem anxious to have the federal government displace the city of Boston in the responsibility to police the streets. But neither did he think that the federal government was so distant from the concerns of the city, so concentrated on the remote objects of foreign affairs and commerce, that it could not reach, if it had to reach, the dangers posed to people in the streets of the city.[8] Through experience and indirection, Lenzner and the federal authorities had come to absorb James Wilson's understanding about the objects of the federal government. The government of the United States was no less a government than any other government constituted in the terrritory of the United States. No less than any other government, its purpose was to protect people from the lawless violation of their natural rights at the hands of private felons or public authorities. That government may leave certain matters to the preoccupation of the states, but it preserved a broad concern to secure, for any person, "a natural right to his property, to his character, to liberty, and to safety."[9]

. . . . .

But if this is correct, where would the division of authority finally run between the national government and the states? What is it that marks the distinct work of the states, and supplies the justification for their existence? As we have already seen, we cannot make an inventory of the subjects that fit more "naturally" or distinctively in the sphere reserved to the states and local government, and the subjects that mark off, clearly, the purposes of the national government. Of course, the states were never sovereign in foreign affairs. From the beginning of the nation, the powers of sovereignty in conducting diplomacy and organizing the national defense were the dominant concerns of the *United* States, or the national government. And yet, even in these domains, that authority of the national government has not always been exclusive. John Andrew, the governor of Massachusetts during the Civil War, became active in raising troops and dispatching them to Washington when there was a serious danger that the capital could be cut off from reinforcements by rail.[10] At the same time, the state of New York had to become active in Europe in buying arms for the national government—the state of New York happened to enjoy, at that moment, a higher credit rating than the national government, at the end of the Buchanan administration.[11] No telos of this government, no theory of its ends and functions, can furnish us with a satisfying division of authority. Nor can it supply even a remotely adequate sense of the "rights" that may be protected at the different levels of government.

I would suggest that we may conceive the differences between the levels of government by taking, as our guide to comparison, the difference between the *principles* of law and the *regulations* of the *positive* law. That difference was once understood, commonly, as the difference between natural law and the provisions of positive law; but the labels are not as critical as the differences they continue to describe for us. For example, we could establish without strain that people who describe themselves as physicians would not be justified in luring patients into surgery and putting them at serious risk when the self-described physicians had not been trained in surgery. The principle of the matter would be clear. But our moral judgment, and our imaginations, would have a wide range in reflecting on the precise measures that would be apt and warranted in applying the principle. Would we establish an official agency to test the competence of physicians, to grant and withhold licenses with the authority of the law? What tests could we tenably use in measuring competence? Could we take as a sufficient measure of competence the grades amassed over a program of courses in medical school? Or should there be, in addition, a separate, standard test? Apart from a written exam, should there be a "practical" examination, gauging judgment and maturity?

These are all plausible questions as we try to make the transition between the principles that would justify regulations, and the practical measures that seek to apply those principles in the world of experience. If we understand the difference engaged here, I think that understanding may finally help us make sense of the federal system. I do not mean to suggest anything so gross as, "The national government articulates the principles and the local governments tend to the practical matters of administration." Both governments seek to apply principles to cases. If there is a project that is legitimate for any government to undertake, I have argued here that it may fall, properly, within the concern of any government in the United States, at the national or the local level. But when we understand the difference between natural law and positive law, or the difference between principle and practice, we may understand this cardinal point, which seems to evade the grasp of so many commentators on the law: It is possible that governments at the national and local level may be moved by the same concerns, animated by the same principles, drawn to the same subjects; and yet, when they set their hands to these subjects, the differences may not only be discernible, but dramatic. One state may try to cope with the hazards of drunken driving by having the police stop motorists at random and apply Breathalyser tests. Another state may experiment with forms of "self-reporting" after an accident. One state prescribes a program of intensive counseling for recidivists; another state takes away the driver's license on the first offense and enforces a mandatory term in jail. Still another state uses forms of public humiliation, by forcing people to carry license plates announcing that they have been convicted for drunken driving. Yet another state may be inspired to try again to enforce a modified form of prohibition, to restrain the sale and use of alcohol.

If any of these essays in regulation become so inventive that they become arbitrary, we would remind ourselves that we are finally connected, after all, in one constitutional order, one system of law, with the superintendence of the federal courts and the guidance of a national legislature. But this same scheme of concurrent interest, with a variety of jurisdictions, and an ultimate, constitutional restraint, may be applied to many other domains of public policy. We may engage the same regime in subjects ranging from the protection of infants to the safety of the highways to the use of vouchers in education.

More recently, we have seen Senator Moynihan of New York recede from his lively interest in programs for "guaranteed incomes," mainly on the strength of experiments carried out in a handful of states. And every so often, the peculiar initiative of a state turns up lessons that were unexpected. One such lesson has turned up recently in Minnesota and inspired some new questions. In 1980, the legislature required the permission of a parent before abortions could be performed on minors. By the end of 1982, the law had been in effect for a full year, and it produced some interesting results. It was anticipated, of course, that the need to inform parents would have the effect of discouraging certain abortions. That expectation seemed to be confirmed: The number of abortions performed on minors fell 33 percent, from 2,327 to 1,565. In some cases, the law might simply have encouraged teenagers to drive to another state for an abortion, but it is not likely that the decline could be explained entirely in that way. For at the same time, the figures on abortion were attended by other figures, which had not been expected: The number of births to teenagers showed a significant decline of 13 percent, from 7,033 to 6,125. Those who were familiar with the local scene found some reason to believe that the new law had some bearing on these outcomes. Youngsters were no longer free to "dispose" of their pregnancy without exposing their sexual engagements to the knowledge and censure of their parents. That prospect apparently induced some of them to be ever more careful in their use of contraception, or perhaps even to back away from early sexual involvements.[12]

Whatever the explanation, it is evident that the separate policies legislated in the states can still generate novel results and yield unexpected lessons. And my point is that this variety of experience can still arise while the states and the national government remain free to legislate on the same subjects. During the original debate on the Constitution, Alexander Hamilton was derided by the Anti-Federalists in New York when he made, substantially, the same point I am offering here. The opponents of the new Constitution were convinced that Hamilton was serving up a species of double-talk in his arguments in the ratifying convention. But we may be able to see more clearly now that the paradox he offered to his colleagues was nevertheless, plainly, true:

> That two supreme powers cannot act together is false. They are inconsistent only when they are aimed at each other, or at one indivisible object. The laws of the United States are supreme, as to all their proper, constitutional objects: the laws of the states are supreme in the same way. These supreme laws may act on different objects without clashing, or they may operate on different parts of the same object, with perfect harmony.[13]

As we have already seen, there are powerful reasons, of prudence and statecraft, that would argue for a system of federalism, in which people are encouraged to take a more direct responsibility for the things that are nearest to them. Of course, the Founders also understood that, at certain times, a distant central government may supply a need that cannot be met by a local government. But on the other hand, a certain field must be conceded to the claims of "personal knowledge," the knowledge that arises distinctly through experience, and through an engagement with those real persons who cross our lives. Certain kinds of obligations are enlisted more readily, with a more direct bond of sentiment, when they are tied to a case.at hand, and to a visible person before us. In certain communities, neighbors have acted as occasional guardians of other people's children. They offer warnings, and they may even intervene at times to divert children from harm's way. They may also act as uninvited lecturers, delivering moral lessons that were not solicited. More than once, in my own childhood in Chicago, I was the beneficiary of this officiousness, shown by neighbors who knew me well. The experience has been noticed by observers of the urban scene, who fear for the passing away of this ethic. They have also noticed the palpable ways in which people affect the lives of their neighbors by the kinds of liberties they permit to their children, and by the codes they enforce, informally but emphatically, about the conduct that is fit for a public place. Codes of this kind may be far more critical in shaping the character of a community and our daily lives than the policies administered through distant bureaucracies. And the understanding that sustains them is, irreducibly, local. This ethic depends, as I say, on the bond of direct knowledge, on the kinds of exertions that people are willing to make when they see before them a person, or a need, that engages their sense of personal responsibility.

The character disclosed in this kind of life is not readily manufactured for others. And yet, this kind of ethic may become more pronounced or muted, it may be encouraged or discouraged, by the political institutions that mark, in any country, the character of the regime. Under the arrangements of Stalinist Russia, for example, it could even be fatal to take this kind of responsibility for the condition of neighbors. The memoirs of the period offer us vivid glimpses of people who were compelled not to notice when their neighbors were taken away in the night. Beyond that, the regime virtually created incentives for people to denounce their colleagues and neighbors in a desperate effort to divert suspicion from themselves and protect their own families. As Nadezhda Mandelstam observed, "some people had adapted to the terror so well that they knew how to profit from it—there was nothing out of the ordinary about denouncing a neighbor to get his apartment or his job."[14]

Those rare people who have been the founders of political orders have generally understood that the character of the regime will affect the character of its people. And it must remain an enduring concern, for the people who would be the preservers of political orders, that certain institutions are more likely to cultivate—or retard—the willingness on the part of citizens to take a direct, personal responsibility for others. Observers viewing us from the outside may see the connections more readily, in our own case, than we see them ourselves. It seemed evident, long ago, to Tocqueville that the character of the Americans was bound up with the character of their institutions. The Americans showed a powerful inclination to take their own initiatives on matters that came within their own reach. That civic temper of the Americans could not be detached from a regime of liberty, with flourishing, private associations, and with local governments that could take themselves seriously.

Tocqueville professed surprise, at first, when he heard that one hundred thousand men in the United States "had bound themselves to abstain from spirituous liquors." This public gesture "appeared to me more like a joke than a serious engagement, and I did not at once perceive why these temperate citizens could not content themselves with drinking water by their own firesides." But he came at last to understand that these hundred thousand Americans had made up their minds to "patronize temperance." They had acted in the manner of men of high rank in Europe, who might dress plainly in order to encourage in the public a contempt for luxury. In Europe, these men "of high rank" claimed the attention of the public, and they were in a position, more readily, to teach public lessons. But in America, in a country without an aristocracy, ordinary citizens might supply, in combination, the place held by men of high rank: By joining together in associations, they could patronize a cause. They could teach lessons to the public simply by broadcasting the terms of their associations, or the public purposes that brought them together. In this simple inclination, Tocqueville thought one could see the most striking differences that separated the civic life of America and France. "It is probable," he wrote, "that if these hundred thousand men had lived in France, each of them would singly have memorialized the government to watch the public houses all over the kingdom."[15]

When we ask, who should care for the aged, do we think first of the family or the government? When there is an assault taking place in the street, and a victim in danger, is the inclination of the citizens to go to the rescue themselves? To leave the matter to the police? Or to retreat behind the shades of their windows? The pattern we describe in answering these questions comes to describe our character as a people. In an earlier day, Tocqueville thought he had found, in Americans, a dominant inclination to take responsibility first themselves, for the lives they could touch, for the events that came within their reach. The most compelling case that can be made for a system of federalism and for serious, local government is that it furnishes to our people a persisting practice in the arts of taking responsibility. As Felix Frankfurter understood, this willingness to take on the burdens of responsibility may be easily undermined by a national government that would intervene too readily or reach too widely, and relieve people in local government from the need to make vexing, unpopular decisions. I have tried to suggest that these considerations run deep, and they provide, altogether, a weighty case in favor of an America composed of states. But at the same time I have sought to preserve this case in its proper scale: These arguments for federalism make up a powerful brief; and yet, even at their best, they can offer nothing more than considerations of prudence and statecraft. They cannot supply a principle that would carve up the American polity into islands of jurisdiction, with certain questions of law, certain problems of justice, placed fixedly beyond the reach of the national government. Once again, that does not mean that all questions that excite our interest must come within the reach of the law or the federal government. But if a case properly claims the concern of the law anywhere in the territory of the United States, we have no formula that can stamp it, generically, as a case that can never come within the concerns of the national government. As I have tried to show, we are constrained in principle from saying that there is a serious wrong, within the reach of a legitimate government somewhere in the territory of America, and yet outside the reach of the national government. As James Wilson understood, that is tantamount to saying that the national government is less of a real government. And that kind of answer was decisively foreclosed by the decision, in 1787, to create, at the national level, a real government.

This simple, ineffaceable point has become absorbed in our practice of government since the Kennedy-Johnson administration flexed the authority of the national government to its fullest reach. The commitment of the federal government to "welfare" enlarged the spending of the government in the fields of education, medicine, and the support of the poor. But at the same time, this extension of spending on social projects brought the national government new levers of social control. By threatening to remove federal funds from hospitals and schools, the national government could wield a heavy club over the American South and break down the conventions of racial segregation in these local institutions. To these commitments of social programs, the government soon added another arsenal of controls on industry: controls that were aimed at the restraint of pollution; regulations that would mandate changes in the workplace; guidelines that would bring the federal government into decisions on hiring and firing for the purpose of barring discriminations based on race and sex. By the time that the Johnson administration was at the full brandishing of its strength, men of affairs acted on the practical assumption that any matter that stirred the interest of the country was a matter of national concern. And if that matter lent itself to a public policy—if it could be addressed aptly by the law anywhere in the country—the understanding now took hold that this question of policy could be addressed by the national government.

That, as I say, was the pattern revealed in our practice of government. And yet, we have participated, with a wink, in an artful charade of concealing these premises from ourselves. We have been content to disguise the reach of federal authority by legislating through fictions or formulas that imply layers of limitation on the national authority. Instead of legislating directly against businesses that discriminate on the basis of race, the national government pretends to act, through the Commerce Clause, only on those businesses that may "affect" interstate commerce. Instead of condemning the wrong of discrimination itself, we find ourselves prosecuting businessmen on the strength merely of a conjecture—undocumented, and perhaps even false—that discrimination will discourage black people from traveling between the states.[16] Instead of articulating the nature of the wrong in principle, the legislators offer formulas to gauge businesses that are more or less likely to produce an effect on the stream of commerce. And so, for example, in the statutes barring discrimination in employment, the reach of the law under the Commerce Clause was confined to those businesses with fifteen or more employees.[17] Under this formula, the federal government could prosecute a store run for the Salvation Army, but it could not reach stores that sold package liquors.[18]

Under the formulas of the Fourteenth Amendment, the federal government pretends to wait for "state action." Supposedly, the authority of the federal government will not be brought into play unless an agency of the state acts, through the laws and regulations, to enforce a policy of discrimination. But it turns out that the federal government will not stand by innocently, waiting for that clear threshold to be crossed. The government may use an old subterfuge and find the presence of "state action" in the action of a court or other agency of the state in upholding a private discrimination.[19] If the record is lacking even that degree of "action by the state," the authorities may be clever enough to find "state action" in the sly willingness of the state to hold back, to forbear from acting. And so the failure to remedy a private act of discrimination may be taken as the equivalent of a deliberate decision, on the part of the state, to sustain discrimination with the tacit support of the law.

As it works through these fictions, the national government comes to represent itself, in its official rationales, as a government of the second tier, or a government of *second* resort—not as a government that may act directly, in the first instance, to address a serious wrong. In any of these cases, the interest of the government is drawn by the presence of complaints or the sight of victims, by the sense that a wrong has been committed. But as the government seeks to justify its involvement in the case, it may spend the energies of its lawyers, not in arguing about the nature of the wrong, but in offering a brief about the negligence of the state—the negligence that compels the national government to intervene. With this subtle shift, the original wrong may disappear from view. And its place is taken by the villainies, or the moral defects, of the local government. One might almost imagine, then, that the fecklessness of the local government overshadows the wrong, say, of the private hospital that tries to turn away black patients.

These established rituals of argument are rituals of evasion, and they produce this further charade. Instead of acting directly on private hospitals or schools, instead of addressing the wrong it means to condemn, the government legislates by pretending not to legislate. The government will make generous grants available to private hospitals and schools, but then it will threaten to cut off the funds if these institutions do not comply with the most stringent regulations governing discriminations based on race and sex. As the familiar story now runs, no one is threatened with a prosecution or a punitive fine. No institution can complain of an "injury" if it is denied the largesse of the federal government. And on its own side, the federal government cannot be obliged to extend its grants to institutions that will not align themselves with the commitments of federal policy. If an institution is not entirely comfortable with those regulations, it remains free to sustain itself entirely from private funds. No one is obliged, after all, to accept money from the federal government. But at the same time, the federal government manages to avoid the moral discipline of legislating. The Congress may seek to bar schools from steering their students to careers that are traditional, or even "stereotyped," for men and women. If Congress made that kind of counseling illegal, some demanding questions may be raised as to how Congress could justify reaching, in that way, certain religious schools that favor traditional roles for men and women. But the same problem of justification does not arise if Congress simply attaches these requirements to any school that accepts federal aid. Congress may legislate, in effect, without the need to justify the measures it would impose as law.

And that is the paradox that finally belies all of these fictions of limitation: The formulas of indirect jurisdiction, the fictions of the Commerce Clause and the Fourteenth Amendment, do not in fact serve to limit or restrain. Instead, they permit an even deeper, less disciplined reach of the national authority. By pretending merely to give and withhold grants, the national government becomes free, in effect, to ban a wider range of conduct than it could ever hope to proscribe if it were compelled to legislate directly, and to justify that legislation in a court.

Some of the most striking examples in this vein have sprung upon us now from Title IX of the Education Amendments of 1972, but with this added twist of irony: The bureaucracy and the courts have conspired to fill in, or extend, the legislation provided by Congress, and the political leverage has shifted to the unelected branches of the government. The bureaucracy and the courts have propounded regulations that would not stand a chance of passing Congress; but it is far harder politically for Congress to overrule what the courts have legislated. The result is that the "legislation" of Congress may be extended now to ordain policies that Congress never intended to enact, and to control private establishments on matters that Congress would not presume to reach. As a notable case in point, the Education Amendments of 1972 provided that "No person in the United States shall, on the basis of sex, be excluded from participation in, be denied the benefits of, or be subjected to discrimination under any education program or activity receiving Federal financial assistance."[20] But then, in January 1973, the Supreme Court decided *Roe v. Wade* and established what some of the judges have described as a "constitutional right" to choose an abortion. If abortions were regarded as legitimate medical procedures, there were plausible reasons for asking just why certain hospitals refused to perform them. If the choice of an abortion represented a "constitutional right," there were new grounds for challenging public provisions of medical care or private insurance plans that withheld support for abortions. Some advocates of abortion were willing to take a further leap: The denial of support for abortions marked a refusal to support a medical procedure that could be performed only on women. Therefore, they concluded, the refusal to fund abortions marked a discrimination based on sex—an unwillingness to provide, equally, for the medical needs of men and women.

Up to this time, the most prominent academic writers on behalf of the Equal Rights Amendment—and the cause of sexual equality in the law—had declined to take this path of argument. In a notable essay in the *Yale Law Journal*, Emerson, Freedman, Brown, and Falk acknowledged that a tenable law does not lose its constitutional standing merely because it focuses on activities peculiar to one sex. A law regulating the sale of sperm may indeed be constitutional even though its restrictions are placed wholly on males.[21] The crime of rape is usually defined in a way that requires an act of "penetration"—which is to say, the crime is defined as a wrong committed by men. And surely, the nature of the wrong would not be effaced in any degree by the fact that men seem to be situated, uniquely, to perform it. In the same way, if there is something wrong about abortions—or if that question is at least open as a moral question—then it could hardly erase the wrong, or dissolve the question, if we noted that abortions are performed only on women.

Still, it became harder to raise those questions about the legitimacy of the operations once the Supreme Court decided *Roe v. Wade*. And the administrators in the Department of Health, Education, and Welfare were willing to embrace, in an instant, what the academic commentators were too cautious yet to demand. The premise supplied by *Roe v. Wade* was now read into the regulations of the Department of Education: the failure of any school or college to cover abortions in their private medical plans was now taken as an instance of discrimination on the basis of sex.[22] The courts quickly upheld this effort of the bureaucracy to bring its regulations into line with the temper of the times, or at least into line with the dominant spirit of the federal courts. Schools that refused to cover abortions would now be faced with these possibilities: They could suffer the withdrawal of funds from the federal government, or they could drop all insurance coverage for their employees and their students.

This lever of compulsion became ever more intimidating when the Supreme Court explained, in 1984, just what might be encompassed under the notion of "Federal financial assistance." Grove City College in Pennsylvania made it a point of policy and pride to accept no direct assistance from the federal government. But the students of the college received loans from the federal government, and on that basis alone, the Department of Education insisted that the school file an Assurance of Compliance with federal regulations. Milton Friedman remarked, years ago, in response to a similar argument, that one might as plausibly regard the local supermarket as a federal installation, or an enterprise receiving "federal financial assistance," if some of its customers used food stamps provided by the federal government. But what Milton Friedman discarded as laughable, the courts were now willing to take seriously. Grove City College insisted that the school had never discriminated on the basis of sex or race in any of its programs; but as a matter of principle, as a matter of affirming its own autonomy as a private institution, the college would not file an Assurance of Compliance. In this refusal, however, the college was rebuffed by the federal courts. The Supreme Court finally sustained the judgment of the Department of Education.[23] The result, then, was that a school that failed to comply with the regulations devised by the Department of Education would be threatened with far more than the removal of federal grants. It would be faced, also, with the prospect of having its students deprived of the loans they might need in order to continue their education.

The Supreme Court was strictly required to say no more, but it went on to insist on this limitation on the reach of the regulations: As the Court read the law, the statute required no remedy more drastic than the removal of federal funds from the program that was not in compliance with the federal regulations. Grove City College was asked to file an Assurance of Compliance because its students received loans from the federal government. Justice White concluded, for the Court, that the failure to execute that Compliance would justify no more than the refusal of the government to provide further loans to the students. It would not justify the removal of federal funds from other programs of the college.[24] That seemed an altogether decorous position, especially if there were no reason even to suspect that other programs in a college were failing to comply with federal regulations. Still, that reading of the law would notably diminish the weight of the club that was in the hands of the federal authorities. For that reason, a movement arose almost instantly in Congress to amend the statute with a new measure, which would be called the Civil Rights Restoration Act: Either the Court would be corrected, or the Congress would make clear now its own willingness to see federal funds cut off across the board, if any part of a college failed to comply with the federal regulations. That movement picked up an astonishing support within the Congress, and it was soon apparent that it would easily command a majority in both houses.

But then matters stalled—and remained stalled until March 1988, when the bill finally passed the Congress. And what stalled the bill all this time was the matter of abortion. Under the Civil Rights Restoration Act, the federal regulations, with their provisions on abortion, would be applied to all parts of an establishment that received federal aid, even in the form of loans to students. When the regulations on abortion were combined with a coverage of this sweep, the results were staggering. If some of the students at Georgetown University received loans from the federal government, all parts of the university would come under the regulations, and those regulations regarded the refusal to support abortions as a variety of discrimination based on sex. That not only meant that Georgetown, a Catholic school, would be compelled to cover abortions in its medical insurance; it also meant that Georgetown might no longer refuse to have abortions performed in its University Hospital. The managers of the bill did not deny this implication. Indeed, there was no way of denying it, since the possibility was rooted in the logic of the bill. Senator Weicker of Connecticut confirmed this meaning of the bill during the hearings of the Senate Committee on the Judiciary. "The fact is," he remarked, "that if Catholic University [another Catholic school] wants to take Federal funds they cannot deny—they are not forced to perform them, but they cannot deny an abortion if it is requested"[sic]. [25]

Weicker and his allies claimed that they were simply seeking to restore the administration of the law to its condition before the Grove City case—which meant that they were willing to preserve the guidelines that regarded the refusal to support abortion as a form of discrimination against women. But Senators Graham (Florida) and Durenberger (Minnesota) quickly grasped the fact that this new law would not merely restore the state of affairs before the Grove City case: the regulations on abortion would now be extended to all the relevant parts of an institution, from medical plans to surgical operations (in the case of a hospital). Graham and Durenberger recognized, then, that the Congress would be compelled now to address those original regulations, which had never been passed by Congress: Had Congress really meant to mandate the private funding or performance of abortion when it legislated, in 1972, against discrimination on the basis of sex in educational programs?[26] Or, if Congress had not intended such a policy in 1972, was it willing to impose that policy now?

Anyone remotely familiar with the Congress knew that the question virtually answered itself. For over a dozen years, Congress had acted, through a series of statutes, in a variety of cases, to deny the use of federal funds in supporting or encouraging abortion. The most signal decision came in the Hyde Amendment in 1976, when Congress prohibited the use of federal money to pay for abortions under medicaid unless the mother would be endangered by carrying the child to term. That same refusal to cover "nontherapeutic" abortions would be extended to the armed forces;[27] to international agencies engaged in projects for family planning;[28] and to any program on family planning that included abortion in its methods or its counseling.[29] The Congress had also barred the Legal Services Corporation from using public funds in a program of litigation to compel the support of elective abortions.[30] Senator Hatch (Utah) surveyed this record and noted the curious "irony" in the Civil Rights Restoration Act: For years Congress had withdrawn federal money from any activity that would remotely support elective abortions. Could it really be supposed that, for all this time, Congress had meant to insist that "institutions [receiving] Federal assistance would be required to pay for or provide abortions"?[31] Senator Danforth (Missouri) remarked on the curious prospect offered in this legislation: that "the Senate at this point should force even church-related colleges and hospitals to do what we will not do ourselves."[32]

The very fact that this bill had been stalled for four years over the problem of abortion was itself a sufficient sign that Congress had never imagined that it was legislating, in 1972, an obligation for private schools to fund or perform abortions. In any event, Congress now resolved that question unequivocally in passing, by a large margin, the amendment brought forth by Senator Danforth. The amendment read in this way:

> Nothing in this Title shall be construed to require or prohibit any person, or public or private entity, to provide or pay for any benefit or service, including the use of facilities, related to an abortion. Nothing in this section shall be construed to permit a penalty to be imposed on any person because such person has received any benefit or service related to a legal abortion.[33]

This amendment was meant to be "abortion-neutral": It would not undo *Roe v. Wade*; it would not roll back, at any point, the private liberty of a woman to choose an abortion on the terms that were then available to her in the law—which is to say, the right to choose an abortion, at *any* stage of the pregnancy, for any reason she regarded as sufficient. Those liberties were left undisturbed in the law. The new measure would insure, however, that abortion would not be transformed from the status of a "legitimate, private choice," to a "positive, public good," which could be imposed then, as a matter of legal obligation, on private schools and hospitals.

And yet, the supporters of abortion were warranted in their judgment that this legislation was not fully neutral on the question of abortion. It was pointed out by Molly Yard, the president of the National Organization for Women (NOW), that the Danforth amendment had "put abortion language into civil rights law for the first time."[34] That language rejected the notion that the "equality of women" in the law *entailed* a right to an abortion. But perhaps more important, the language offered another expression on the part of Congress that abortion was not a "positive good" that deserved to be encouraged by the law; that abortions were not exactly like other surgical procedures. In that act of holding back, Congress seemed to sustain the understanding that abortions raised troubling questions of principle that were not raised in the same way by other kinds of surgeries. The bill did not, as I say, diminish in any degree the rights to an abortion. But the defenders of abortion saw a grave symbolic move in this unwillingness, on the part of Congress, to concede the full legitimacy, the full rightness of abortion. In the eyes of NOW, the passage of the bill with the Danforth amendment converted the Civil Rights Restoration Act into a "debacle." But the Civil Rights Coalition would not permit the bill to be stalled any longer for the sake of avoiding this symbolic setback to the proponents of abortion. When the bill was passed with large majorities—and passed again over the veto of President Reagan—the radical feminists found it politic to remain mute: The embarrassment sustained by Mr. Reagan seemed to obscure, to most commentators in the press, the serious defeat that had been absorbed for the cause of extending "abortion rights."

The senators who managed the Civil Rights Restoration Act had sought, strenuously, to resist such a defeat for the cause of abortion. Their strategy in fending off the Danforth Amendment was to argue that the amendment was not needed: The law already contained an exemption for "religious" institutions. Catholic University, in Washington, had received such an exemption, and there was no danger that the university would be compelled to support or perform abortions. But this argument turned out to be altogether too slick and disingenuous. The managers of the bill insisted that the institutions manifested their "religious" character only when they were controlled by churches. And yet, as a number of senators would point out, the rising expense of private education over the preceding twenty years had wrought many changes in the governance of schools with a religious character. These schools had been required to seek funding outside their churches, and they were moved then to include on their boards people who could bring support from new sources, outside the religious community. As Senator Hatch pointed out, there were only two schools that clearly met the tests of the new law—Brigham Young University and Catholic University, "because they are the only ones completely controlled by religious institutions."[35] Georgetown University, one of the most prominent Catholic schools in the country, would not qualify, because its board was dominated by "lay" members. A relaxed Department of Education may be willing to grant a "religious" exemption, but a new administration could quite as readily withdraw that privilege. As Senator Gramm (Texas) pointed out, even under the current law, the exemption had been denied to the Dallas Theological Seminary, Lubbock Christian College, the University of Dallas (a private, Catholic university), and the Concordia Lutheran College.[36]

But even if these institutions had received religious "exemptions," the awarding of that privilege might not have ended their troubles. The government might readily tolerate the unwillingness, say, of Georgetown University to lend an official endorsement to the practice of abortions. But that tolerance would not necessarily spare the University from suits brought by members of its staff, both Catholic and non-Catholic, who bore no reservations about abortion. These members of the staff might concede that Georgetown, as a Catholic school, may properly honor its own objections to abortion, grounded in religious doctrine. But they may argue that, as long as Georgetown is receiving money from the federal government, it should not impose that aversion on members of the staff who do not share the religious commitments of the institution. As the argument might run, Georgetown should not prevent individuals on its own staff from performing operations they are willing to perform—and honoring, in that way, the "constitutional right" of a woman to choose an abortion.

Against these kinds of claims, the safeguard of religious exemptions promised to be a facade with little substance. But beyond that, the policy on religious exemptions could have preserved the misleading notion that the opposition to abortion arises solely from "religious" beliefs. In that respect, it steers around the awkward recognition that an argument could be made about abortion on a distinctly moral ground, without appealing at any point to matters of faith or revelation.[37] The opposition to abortion has not arisen solely from Catholics, or from people animated by religious belief. And within Catholicism, the argument on abortion has not been drawn from theology, but from moral reasoning. On that same ground, private and municipal hospitals have refused to perform abortions, even though their opposition to abortion has not emanated from any religious doctrine. Without an appeal to religious grounds of justification, the city of St. Louis has refused to permit abortions in its municipal hospitals. According to the American Hospital Association, about three-quarters of the "secular" hospitals in the country have refused, for one reason or another, to perform abortions. Senator Heinz (Pennsylvania) pointed out that, within his own state, out of 380 hospitals, 240 were community hospitals, not affiliated with any religion. Of those 240, only 40 performed abortions or provided for their funding. As Heinz noted, most of the remaining 200, like the Scranton General Hospital or the Medical Center in Wilkes-Barre, "have chosen for moral reasons not to perform or fund abortion."[38] An exemption offered merely on "religious" grounds could not protect these institutions. But with the passage of the Danforth amendment, the problem of religious exemptions seems to have been dissolved. On the matter of abortion, at least, it will not make a difference any longer as to whether a school is "controlled" by a religious body, "closely identified" with religion, or wholly removed from any religious definition. During the debates on the Civil Rights Restoration Act, Senator Weicker sounded at times like Claude Rains in *Casablanca*: In this case, Weicker professed to be shocked—shocked—that anyone would take seriously the phantoms cast up by Senator

Danforth and his allies. What administrators would really make use of this legislation for the sake of compelling schools like Notre Dame to perform or support abortions? But here, Weicker was affecting an innocence that could hardly be warranted. In the current legal environment of America, the enforcement of these laws would not always depend on the moderation of administrators. The enforcement of the laws would be driven also by outside groups, with their own agendas and their own strategies of litigation. Some of those groups would have an interest in driving the law to its furthest reach, and testing the radical possibilities contained in the statute. At the time Weicker was affecting his innocence, the Office of Civil Rights in the Department of Education had accumulated nearly 700 complaints, brought by outside parties, over three years. Those complaints were cast in identical style, with the same form letter. And they sought the same end: to compel private schools to cover "elective abortions" in their medical plans. The language in the complaints was in all cases the same, and at the head of the letter there was a blank, which merely remained to be filled in with the name of the school at hand.[39] These complaints began flowing at the same time, in the fall of 1985. They came from different parts of the country, but they were evidently orchestrated according to a common plan. They composed, in sum, a campaign of legal harassment, which was intimidating, cruel—and anonymous: Under the regulations, the complainants were allowed to conceal their identity. In a deceptively broad sweep, some of the complaints were directed at liberal schools in the East—schools such as Amherst, Smith, and Wellesley—which would not offer any resistance to the coverage of abortion in their medical plans. But the real targets of this campaign seemed to be the small colleges with a religious character, which were more likely to be opposed to abortion, and at the same time, too fragile, financially, to withstand the threat of litigation. Among them were institutions like the Eastern Baptist Theological Seminary in Philadelphia, Merrimack College in West Andover, Massachusetts, and Biola University in La Mirada, California.[40]

By June 1987, the box score in this mean contest revealed these results: of 693 complaints that were filed, 486 were "closed" when it was determined that "no jurisdiction existed over the insurance programs of the institution."[41] But that did not mean that the department really bore no jurisdiction. It meant, rather, that most of these schools had caved in to the pressure and removed the ground of complaint. With the dissolution of the complaint, there was, of course, no jursidiction any longer for the Office of Civil Rights. Faced with costs of litigation they dared not risk, many small colleges agreed to cover abortions in their medical plans, even though that arrangement offended their deepest convictions. Others, such as LaSalle University in Pennsylvania decided to drop, altogether, the program of medical insurance for its students. That seemed, to the administrators, the only tenable way to preserve the moral position of the university while averting the crippling expenses of litigation.

This campaign of legal harassment had been launched when the Civil Rights Restoration Act had been stalled. It was evident that Congress would not readily pass a measure that would oblige private institutions to perform or support abortions. And so this campaign seemed to be inspired as a means of accomplishing, through private initiatives, what the Congress would not enact into law. Private parties could put into motion the procedures that activated the authority of the bureaucracy and the courts. Even if Congress did not act, then, to extend the obligation to fund abortions, the same project could be put into place, and it could be an accomplished fact: The policies on abortion, accepted by many private schools, could be impossible to undo if Congress provided nothing more than a "religious" exemption. The strategy made powerful political sense, and it had its effect. It could be undone only by a measure, such as the Danforth amendment, which swept past the exemption for "religious" schools and denied, in a categorical way, the obligation of any school to fund abortions. With that move, the Congress offered a remedy at once to the schools that had been the targets of intimidation. And Congress seemed to offer, at the same time, a shelter that would protect the vulnerable from any similar strategies of harassment.

Yet, this curious moment of resolution on the part of Congress illuminated, with indirection, that irresolution which seems to be planted even more deeply in the institutional character of Congress in our own time. And this signal act of legislating would exemplify, once again, the skewed habits of mind of an institution that typically legislates without legislating. The offending regulations under Title IX had been in place since 1975, when Caspar Weinberger had been Secretary of Health, Education, and Welfare. It should have been as obvious in 1975, as it was in 1988, that Congress would never have enacted into law a measure that required private schools to fund abortions in their medical plans. It should have been evident, also, that Congress would not have regarded the refusal to fund abortions as a species of discrimination based on sex. Why, then, did it take thirteen years for Congress to override regulations that were so cynically at odds with the intentions of the Congress? But the interval of thirteen years may be less surprising than the fact that Congress acted at all: For it is equally obvious that Congress would have done nothing for thirteen more years—or twice thirteen years—had it not been for the crisis precipitated by the Grove City case and the Civil Rights Restoration Act. Congress was perfectly willing to hold back from legislating a requirement, on the part of private schools, to perform or fund abortions. But it was not willing to act gratuitously, in a move that would seem to "dispossess" people of rights that were granted to them by the bureaucracy, even if they were rights to an abortion funded by private institutions. The hand of the Congress was forced inadvertently by the Civil Rights Restoration Act: Inadvertently, because a powerful momentum had been built up in support of the act before most congressmen realized just how gravely this bill would affect the problem of abortion. Were it not for this strange concatenation of issues, brought together in the crisis over the Grove City case, this domain of policy could have been controlled enduringly by an alliance of civil servants and federal judges.

Congress could summon a rare resolution in this case, also, because Congress seemed to be safely absolved from any need to legislate anything more emphatic. After all, it was merely a matter of reinforcing, yet again, the established "policy" of Congress, that it would not legislate any affirmative obligation to perform or fund abortions. More than that, Congress could not do. Or, so at least, most people were content to assume. In *Roe v. Wade*, the Supreme Court sought to remove the subject of abortion almost entirely from the domain of legislatures. The states were still free to enact minor restrictions, mainly to assure the safety of the operations. But it was no longer permissible to legislate on the premise that there was something morally wrong about abortions, which could justify the use of the law in restricting the massive volume of abortions (1.5 million) that were performed every year in this country. Even if *Roe v. Wade* were overturned, it was widely assumed that the subject of abortion would simply be returned to the legislative powers of the states. Even—or especially—among conservatives, it was not assumed that the federal government would have any responsibility for this subject, which had remained traditionally within the jurisdiction of the states. And for that reason, it was taken for granted, with an unseemly serenity, that Congress would have no authority to legislate directly on the subject of abortion.

I think I have said enough, in the course of these chapters, to show that these facile assumptions could not have been warranted. The deeper irony is that Justice Blackmun, the author of *Roe v. Wade*, was also the author of *Garcia v. San Antonio Transportation Authority*[42]: The same man who articulated the right to an abortion also demonstrated that there was no theory of "traditional" functions, no organizing principle, that could tag any subject as a matter that belonged distinctively to the province of the states or the federal government. What proved true for transportation, or the protection of rare animals, would prove true quite as well for abortion, for the commerce in fetal tissue, or the protection of unborn children.

But even if none of these points managed to penetrate the understanding of the political class, even if the matter of abortion were thought to lie wholly within the domain of the states; Congress could still act with consequence on the question of abortion. Congress could legislate in effect to ban almost all abortions, from almost all hospitals in this country, and it could do that even if *Roe v. Wade* were never overturned. It could do it by legislating in the style it has now made a way of life: the artful manner of legislating while appearing not to legislate. Congress need not forbid, directly, the performance of elective abortions, any more than it legislates now to forbid racial discrimination in private schools and hospitals.

In this same style, the Congress could merely take one more, small step in the series of decisions that began with the Hyde Amendment in 1976 and found its most recent expression in the Civil Rights Restoration Act of 1988. In these statutes, Congress has built up a compelling series of precedents for removing public funds from the support of abortion, and from agencies that promote abortions, at home and abroad. In none of these cases has Congress legislated to ban abortion or to interfere with the private liberty to choose an abortion. It has merely insisted on the position that the general public is not obliged to support these procedures through the compulsory levies of taxation; that the public will not be compelled to support, with their taxes, operations that many of them regard as morally abhorrent. In this manner, Congress has thought it reasonable to insure that the money of American taxpayers will not be implicated in the support of abortion through medicare, through the military, and through programs of counseling. And in this course, the Congress has been upheld by the Supreme Court.[43] It would require no leap, then, or no use of novel reasoning, to add this step to the inventory: The American people may not be implicated in abortions as taxpayers by supporting, with public funds, hospitals and other facilities that are performing abortions.

The prospect of removing federal funds would have to be a powerful weapon, and it may be sufficient to induce hospitals to remove, from their premises, a program of operations that did not become legal, in most places, until 1973. Abortions could be thrust out of hospitals, into freestanding clinics. But then, if the Congress applied the understanding of the Grove City case, and the tools of the Civil Rights Restoration Act, it might have, in combination, a powerful new weapon: Congress has established now that all of the federal regulations on discrimination could come into play if the students of a school received federal loans. With the same reasoning, Congress could ban abortions in clinics if *any* patient in the clinic is receiving support from the federal government, in welfare, unemployment, or medical care. And that could indeed mean *any* patient—not merely the patient who is seeking an abortion. In the same measure, Congress could also ban abortions in buildings that were built with federal subsidies. In effect, *Congress could legislate to forbid abortion, even while it is not actually forbidding anyone to choose or perform an abortion.* For that reason, Congress would escape once again from any need to justify its measures, as it might indeed be compelled to justify itself if it claimed to legislate, directly, to forbid abortions.

But would Congress not be forbidding here what the Supreme Court has already established as legitimate? In truth, it would not be. The Court has established that any woman has a right to exercise her choice, as an attribute

NEONATES AND REPROBATES 231

of her personal freedom, to choose an abortion. Congress would not restrict that personal freedom in any degree. As in cases of racial discrimination in private schools and clubs, Congress would say: People are free to choose abortions, and institutions are free to perform them, but they may not claim the support of federal tax money in pursuing those irreducibly private choices.

I hasten to add that I would not endorse the use of these roundabout devices to legislate about abortion in a backhanded way. Congress could legislate directly on the subject, and it could even legislate in a way that challenges the doctrine of the Supreme Court in *Roe v. Wade*.[44] Of course, if congressmen are truly persuaded that they cannot legislate directly on the question of abortion, this indirect style of legislation may be the only path of legislation open to them. But once again, this method of "legislating" would divert the Congress from putting the question to itself, in a demanding way, of precisely why it should be justified—or unjustified—in restricting abortions.

The design I have sketched in here would not come as a surprise to most congressmen. Most of them are no doubt aware that they could legislate on the matter of abortion in the most sweeping way, through the familiar devices that have permitted them, in the past, to legislate without really legislating. In that event, the absence of this "legislation" must be as striking as the notable example, in Sherlock Holmes, of the dog that wasn't barking. How do we account for this absence? Congress has moved along a chain of decisions to withdraw federal funds: Why has it not made the most critical move that would seem to be prefigured in its earlier moves? Why has it not added the item that would bring the chain nearer to completion?

I have put this question to practiced observers of Congress, and the judgment seems to be that members of Congress do not see, in this case, merely another step in a continuous path. They seem to sense that they are near the edge, that they would be crossing a border. They seem to be aware, in short, that they would now be legislating to restrain abortions. Precisely what holds them back from crossing that border is not entirely clear. They may hesitate in a spirit of prudence inspired by politics, or they may be affected by doubts about their own authority. But in either event, they seem to have sensed that this is not the right way to address a momentous question. If they are to legislate on the matter of abortion, they should do it directly and explicitly, and confront, at the same time, the questions of constitutionality, the considerations of policy, that would rightly toughen the task of making laws in this field.

In this reflex, I am bound to think they are right. But it would be quite as important for the coherence of their project that they settle on the reasons that hold them back now from taking the next decisive step, which would seem to follow from the logic of their earlier decisions. If the congressmen hold back now—if they are not really prepared to legislate against abortion as a "wrong"—should they not have grounds, then, to rethink their unwilling-ness, of the past, to support the funding of abortions? And if that is the case, why keep engaging in these symbolic moves, to cast a burden of reproach on people who would seek and perform abortions?

In short, why not be serious—in this, and in all other matters? Why not face the question of whether Congress has the authority to legislate directly on any matter that Congress would presume to reach with its powers of fund-ing and coercion? A Congress that set about to legislate in that way—by pro-scribing certain conduct, by forbidding directly what is wrong—is a Congress that will restrict freedom more explicitly. For that reason, it will excite more opposition and come under a stronger political demand to establish the justi-fication for its measures. I think it should be apparent, then, that if the au-thority of the national government were taken up in this way, the result would not be a continuous extension of the federal authority. My own guess is that we would be more likely to feel the benign restraints of the political process, and we may find ourselves with a Congress that suffers far more strain before it adds to the book of statutes.

I have not been faint in suggesting that this style of backhanded legislation has been attended with rituals of dishonesty: a persisting willingness to em-ploy formulas or fictions that cannot finally explain or justify the authority that Congress is exercising. But I have also tried to show that this style of evasion has been inspired by some earnest, recurring confusions about feder-alism and the reach of the national government. Over the last few years, there has been no more powerful example, combining these confusions of doctrine, these habits of evasion, than the crisis that was posed to us over the "Baby Doe" cases. The problem burst upon us in April 1982 with the celebrated case of the "Bloomington Baby" in Indiana. At issue was the withdrawal of medi-cal care from retarded, newborn children. But as the administration sought to engage the federal authority and protect these children, it encountered in the courts every familiar confusion and every familiar slogan to resist the reach of the federal government. And it encountered that resistance on the part of judges who had rarely shown such an exquisite concern for federalism and the authority of the states. This spectacle was played out, with some embarrass-ment and disarray by the majority of the Supreme Court at the culmination of these cases in 1986, in *Bowen v. American Hospital Association*.[45] In these cases the Reagan administration appealed to a traditional concern, under the statutes on civil rights, as they bore upon the treatment of patients in hospi-tals. The concern in these cases was with the withdrawal of medical treatment from newborn infants who were afflicted with Down's syndrome or spina bi-fida. The statutes on civil rights had already been augmented, in 1973, to include discriminations based on "handicap." Section 504 of the Rehabilita-tion Act of 1973 read:

No otherwise qualified handicapped individual . . . shall solely by reason of his handicap, be excluded from the participation in, be denied the benefits of, or be subjected to discrimination under any program or activity receiving Federal financial assistance.[46]

The question was whether the authors of this legislation had intended the law to apply to the decisions made in hospitals, by parents and doctors. Would the statute apply to the withdrawal of medical care from children who were regarded by their parents as "deformed" or "defective," or having lives that were "not worth living"? But the legislation drew on principles that had a meaning of their own, quite apart from the applications that may be made in one case or another by the people who drafted the statute. To speak about discrimination against the handicapped was to speak, in familiar terms, about the creating of disabilities, or the withdrawal of benefits from people, solely on account of their infirmity. But did this policy on discrimination bear on *hospitals*? On its face, there was no reason to suspect that a "principle" would apply everywhere *except* in hospitals.

If there was ever a serious question about the reach of the federal law, that question seemed to have been settled long ago, when the regulations on racial discrimination had been applied to hospitals, along with the threat to remove federal funds. The reach of the law had been established; the sanctions had become familiar. And in 1973, Congress apparently agreed that discriminations based on handicap should be attached to the body of laws dealing with the violation of civil rights. For its own part, the Reagan administration looked upon this case as simply another instance that engaged the traditional principles on civil rights. Yet, when the matter finally came before the Supreme Court, it produced, among some of the judges, an expression of deep surprise, as though they had heard this reasoning for the first time. And to preserve this sense of astonishment, some of the judges had to invert, for the day, the positions they had marked off for themselves over a career in jurisprudence.

How else to explain that on January 15, 1986, after a long career, Justice Thurgood Marshall now discovered for the first time his reverence for "states' rights." He had spent his career as the bitter foe of every barrier, cast up by the authority of the states, which could shelter the wrong of racial discrimination. His career had been consecrated to the end of removing every inhibition that would prevent the federal government from penetrating the jurisdiction of the states for the sake of vindicating civil rights. But now he turned his outrage upon Mr. Charles Cooper, who was arguing the case for the government. Stripped of its shadings and complications, Marshall thought the plain "truth is that the Federal Government is just taking over the state's function. . . . The only thing that's involved here is the right of the Federal

Government to move into what for centuries has been a state matter, namely how to operate a hospital."[47]

But the shadings had been decidedly important on earlier occasions. The regulation of hospitals had ceased to be a matter exclusively for the states when the federal government had taken on the mandate of extending, to hospitals, the ban on racial discrimination. Marshall wrote as though he had never seen the national government reaching in this way, sweeping past the authority of the states, and applying the regulations on civil rights to hospitals. Had he fallen into a state of jural amnesia? Had he somehow forgotten those historic movements in the law, built up from the 1930s, the movements that he himself had helped to sustain? Or did he affect the style of mockery here because he thought the litigation itself was a mockery. It was brought by an administration that could not claim, in his reckoning, to speak for civil rights, and it was advanced on behalf of persons who did not deserve, in his eyes, the protection of civil rights—or even the standing of "persons."

In the first Baby Doe case, arising in Bloomington, the baby was thought to be afflicted with Down's syndrome and other handicaps. The child needed an operation at once to remove an obstruction in the esophagus, which prevented oral feeding. The parents of the child refused their consent to the surgery. And it appeared that the parents held back their consent because they were reluctant to preserve the life of a child who would be afflicted by retardation and other disabilities. The hospital sought to override the judgment of the parents, but it could gain no support from the courts in Indiana, or from the local Child Protection Committee. Six days after its birth, the child was dead.

The news of the Bloomington Baby made its way to President Reagan, and the interest of the president set off a series of moves within the federal government. The Office of Civil Rights in the Department of Health and Human Services issued a reminder to "health care providers" receiving federal funds that newborn children with Down's syndrome and other handicaps were protected under Section 504. That reminder was quickly followed by a set of federal regulations that announced the engagement of the government on this question, in a "vigorous federal role." Hospitals were required to post "in a conspicuous place in each delivery ward, each maternity ward, each pediatric ward, and each nursery, including each intensive care nursery," a notice that the withdrawal of treatment from newborns could violate the federal law. The notice would also advertise the availability of a "hotline" to report on the violations of the law. There were provisions to hasten the access of the government to the relevant records or files in investigating the treatment of children in any case.

The regulations were challenged by the American Academy of Pediatrics in the District of Columbia, and on technical grounds the challenge was sustained: In the rush to issue the rules, the Department had not followed the

Administrative Procedures Act and solicited public comment before it promulgated the rules. But with some redrafting, and a decorous observance of the timetable, the regulations were issued again in December 1983. In the meantime, another version of the Baby Doe case had arisen in October, in a hospital on Long Island. "Baby Jane Doe" had been born with what were described as "multiple birth defects." The most serious among them were spina bifida, a condition in which the spinal cord and the surrounding membranes were exposed; microcephaly, an unusually small head; and hydrocephalus, the accumulation of fluid in the cranial vault. The spina bifida produced, in turn, other deficits in sensory functions, in the control of the legs and the bladder.[48] Most of these conditions could be remedied or ameliorated through surgery, especially if the operations were performed soon. The child was transferred to University Hospital for corrective surgery, but her parents finally withheld their consent for the surgery, which would prolong the life of the child. A third party sought to intervene to act as a guardian for the child and direct the hospital to perform the surgery. That effort was eventually blocked in the courts of New York. But a complaint was registered with the federal Department of Health and Human Services. The department referred the complaint to the state Child Protective Service, but before the service could act, the federal agency pursued its own course. The department sought access to the records of the hospital, for the sake of determining whether medical treatment was being withheld for reasons that would run afoul of the federal law. The hospital would not accede to these requests, and it reported that the parents of Baby Jane had refused to release the records. Facing that resistance, the government filed suit in a federal district court, in an effort to gain access to the facts.

From this point forward the government would persistently lose in the federal courts. It would lose for reasons that would escape the comprehension of people who are not lawyers. From the beginning, the issue would be framed in a manner so narrowed and artificial that it could have sprung only from the sensibilities of those trained in the parsing of statutes. As Justice White would later show, in his dissenting opinion in the Bowen case, the courts had rendered an implausible account of the facts of the case and the concerns of the federal government in applying the law. But it is also arguable that the curious perspective of the judges reflected the curious construction of the laws themselves. The awkward, implausible construction of the issues may be one of the expectable results when the federal government tries to apply, to the case at hand, legislation that did not really legislate—laws that sought to achieve their ends by indirection, by focusing in any place but the problem they were meant to address.

The courts held that the federal government was "overreaching." The Administration was demanding access to information privately held, but in the opinion of the judges, this information was not relevant to any wrong that the government had the authority to reach under the existing law. The statute was directed, after all, to the acts of discrimination that would be committed by hospitals, or by providers of medical care. But there was no case of a hospital refusing to provide medical care or surgery for a handicapped child *when the parents consented to the operation.* To operate on a child without the consent of the parents was to expose the hospital to legal action for committing a battery or a tort. The real concern of the government was that the parents and their physician had decided to withhold surgery because the child was likely to be retarded. But it was not at all clear to the courts that the Rehabilitation Act of 1973 was really meant to inject the government into these decisions, on the part of parents, in making judgments about the medical care of their children.

During the oral argument in the Bowen case, Justice Stevens posed this question to Charles Cooper, who was arguing for the government:

> Suppose the decision was made by the parents simply because the child had the handicap. That's the reason for the decision by the parents, but the reason for the decision by the hospital was that the parents . . . had refused. Does that violate the statute? . . . What should [the hospital] do absent parent consent if they think the parents have decided for an incorrect reason?[49]

Cooper pointed out, in response, that the hospital may do what hospitals often do when parents seem compelled, by "religious compulsion," to withhold medical treatment from their children:

> If a transfusion is necessary to save a perfectly normal child, a blood transfusion— and this happens not infrequently—then hospitals would not yield to the decision of the parents.

Beyond that, as Cooper reminded the Court, "the state laws in all 50 states would require the hospital in those circumstances to seek review by the appropriate authorities."[50] In the preamble to the regulations put out by the government, the Secretary of Health and Human services had noted that "under every state's law, failure of parents to provide necessary, medically indicated care to a child is either explicitly cited as grounds for action by the state to compel treatment or is implicitly covered by the statute." These laws in the states were attended by suitable provisions for enforcement, including the "access to medical files, immediate investigations and authority to compel treatment."[51] In other words, the controlling law within the states did not confirm, to any hospital, the right to detach itself so glibly from the decisions made by parents.

Justice White pointed out, in addition, that this account of the case offered a misleading fiction: The parents were not usually making decisions on their own. As case studies revealed at the time, parents were usually guided in these decisions by the advice of their pediatricians. White recognized that the crisis had been precipitated by a new willingness on the part of pediatricians to use their influence with patients for the sake of discouraging operations for children who were retarded. He recalled the figures that had made an impression on the administration: In surveys of pediatricians, less than 8 percent of the surgeons said they would acquiesce in a decision on the part of parents to avoid surgery for an intestinal blockage in an infant. But over 76 percent of the surgeons expressed their willingness to acquiesce in that decision if the child were also afflicted with Down's syndrome.[52] Obviously, the difference did not turn on the question of whether it was practicable to treat the blockage in the intestine. The decision to provide an operation that was medically useful for the child would pivot, rather, on the question of whether the child was likely to be retarded. And that was precisely the problem of "discrimination" in these cases—the problem that engaged the concern of the law and brought the administration into the courts in the spring of 1983.

The administration had made it clear from the outset that it had no intention of challenging the advice offered by surgeons on judgments that were "medical" in nature.[53] Nor was the administration seeking to commit doctors and patients to a regimen of "heroic surgery." The administration was not insisting that doctors do everything possible to sustain the lives of patients even when the conditions were hopeless and the operations impracticable. Those judgments on the prospects for surgery were left to the domain of the professionals. The concern of the administration was with the cases in which surgery was indeed practicable, when it would be ordered in any case for a patient regarded as "normal," but when the surgery was held back solely because the patient was retarded or "handicapped."

I was writing on this matter for the *Washington Post*, in April 1983, when the first regulations were challenged in the district court in Washington, and I sought to explain the distinction that guided the administration. A judgment was not a "medical judgment" simply because it was rendered by a doctor. People may believe that a retarded child does not have a life worth living, a life that deserved to be saved, but that judgment did not turn on any issue in the science of medicine. It was, rather, a question of moral principle: Is there something in the very condition of being retarded which establishes that people *deserve* to perish, or that they have a lesser claim to live? Does the presence of infirmities justify a policy of withholding from the "handicapped" services or benefits that should not be affected by their disability? I went on to put this question:

> Suppose for a moment that the new regulations had declared that "it is prohibited by federal law to withhold treatment from infants on the basis of their race." Is it imaginable that the American Academy of Pediatrics would now be in court ar-

guing that rules of this kind interfere with the "medical" judgment of doctors and the privacy of their patients.[54]

This reasoning would find expression in the courts only in the dissenting opinion of Judge Ralph Winter, in the Court of Appeals in New York:

The government has never taken the position that it is entitled to override a medical judgment. Its position rather is that it is entitled under Section 504 to inquire whether a judgment in question is a *bona fide* medical judgment. While the majority [of the Court of Appeals] professes uncertainty as to what that means, application of the analogy to race eliminates all doubt. A judgment not to perform certain surgery because a person is black is not a *bona fide* medical judgment. So too, a decision not to correct a life threatening digestive problem because an infant has Down's Syndrome is not a *bona fide* medical judgment. The issue of parental authority is also quickly disposed of. A denial of medical treatment to an infant because the infant is black is not legitimated by parental consent. Finally, once the legislative analogy to race is acknowledged, the intrusion on state authority becomes insignificant.

The logic of the government's position on these aspects of the case is thus about as flawless as a legal argument can be.[55]

The question of discrimination could be assessed, then, only when it was possible to discover the reasons on which the judgment turned, when the parents and their physician decided to hold back from surgery. That was the sole interest of the government in getting access to the record. But it was a necessary interest. In all strictness, of course, true professionals should never be affronted by any question about the facts or the considerations on which their judgments turned. Their claim to speak with the authority of a professional depends on the capacity to give reasons in any case, and to demonstrate the ground of their competence. What made these cases all the more troublesome was that they were likely to reveal physicians with a rather tenuous command of the research that bore on the advice they were rendering. In the case of Baby Jane in Long Island, the doctors apparently informed the parents that the child was highly likely to be retarded even after the spina bifida was corrected. Precisely how the doctors arrived at that judgment was not revealed, and it is not likely that a review of the record would yield any reliable foundation for a judgment of that kind. Writing at the time, Daniel Robinson described these professional estimates as a species of "oracular medicine." The hidden secret in these proceedings was just how remarkably uninformed the practitioners were of the research, in America and abroad, that overturned some traditional notions about the connection between brain mass and mental capacities. Robinson offered, as but one example, the patients reported in the studies of Dr. Lorber in Britain.

[These patients] were hydrocephalic at birth [as was Baby Jane] and . . . now, as young adults, are indistinguishable from an utterly normal population. While brain scans reveal that these patients' cranial cavities are still filled mostly with fluid, none of them having as much as half of the brain mass of "normal" persons, some can be found programming computers and pursuing advanced degrees. Had oracular medicine been practiced at the time of their births, none of them would have been judged worth saving.[56]

The limited, modest mission of the administration in this case was to get access to the record and bring out the facts that were known. And yet, this was the interest that was finally rejected, by a closely divided Court, in *Bowen v. American Hospital Association.* Only four judges signed on to the inscrutably narrow decision written by Justice Stevens in denying this reach of authority by the national government. The plurality included Justice Powell, and it was joined by Chief Justice Burger, who concurred in the judgment, but not in the opinion. Both judges have now departed the scene. Justice Rehnquist was missing, because he had recused himself. (His son-in-law was a member of the law firm engaged on the side of the hospitals.) Justice Brennan had detached himself from his usual partners and joined the minority in this case. To put it another way, he was willing to hold to his traditional position in cases on civil rights, even when it meant overriding the claims of "privacy" on the part of the parents and sustaining the Reagan administration. Considering the alignments that were revealed here, it is entirely possible that a new case, with the current, reconstituted Court, would yield a notably different judgment. And that is especially likely, because any such case would be litigated under a new statute, the Child Abuse Prevention Act of 1984.[57] That act was passed with bipartisan support in the midst of the controversy over the Baby Doe cases, and the statute made it clear, beyond the aptitude of judges to make unclear, that Congress did in fact intend to protect retarded infants from the withdrawal of medical treatment.

But the act of 1984 was still arranged in the familiar cast. It legislated, once again, through indirection. It did not issue commands, nor did it focus its sanctions on the perpetrators of the wrong. It offered grants. And it contained the prospect of withdrawing those grants. It spoke to states and to the providers of medical care, to the institutions that would act as agents in pursuing the concerns of the national government. But it marked off no procedures for engaging the federal courts and seeking a penalty, in a national forum, for a violation of a national law.

The enduring predicament could be seen, once again, in the oral argument before the Supreme Court in the Bowen case (the case of Baby Jane). Even an advocate as straightforward and as clear-minded as Charles Cooper could not help but get entangled every so often in the coils of the federal legislation. And when a jurist, such as Justice Stevens, was determined to find complications to ensnarl the government, a few questions, placed well, could soon appear to disassemble the case for the government. But it was the form of the legislation that made Stevens's questions quite apt. His questions managed to bring out the layers of complication in the law, and those hedgings in the law reflected an abiding uncertainty about the reach of the federal authority.

Justice Stevens suggested that the hospital itself was not discriminating against the handicapped; it was simply honoring the judgment of the parents.

[JUSTICE STEVENS:] [S]upposing . . . they have a general hospital policy of never allowing surgery absent parental consent? Where is the discrimination?

MR. COOPER: I see your point. . . . There is no discrimination if the hospital would not seek—

[JUSTICE STEVENS:] Even if it's valid—even if medical people could dis-agree on whether it's proper or not.

MR. COOPER: Well, that's right. . . . First, if the hospital has a blanket pol-icy, we do not get involved in court to override parental decisions, no matter how irrational, no matter how inconsistent with the interests of their child it is, then the hospital would not have to just because the child is handicapped.

But the fact is that state laws in all fifty states would require the hospital in those circumstances to seek review by the appropriate authorities, either directly petitioning a court—

[JUSTICE STEVENS:] Well, but I'm asking what is the violation of federal law. We're not concerned with a violation of state law.

MR. COOPER: There would be no violation of federal law under those cir-cumstances.
[At this moment, Justice O'Connor intervened.]

[JUSTICE O'CONNOR:] Well, I thought your position was that the violation was in not reporting it to the state agency. At least that's what you had told me in response to my [earlier] question. Are you saying something else to Justice Stevens?

MR. COOPER: I don't think so, Justice O'Connor. The point is that if the hospital is set up to deal with these kinds of problems for kids who aren't handi-capped, such as—

[JUSTICE O'CONNOR:] You said that the law in all 50 States requires the hospital to be set up to do that.

MR. COOPER: I think that's right, and so therefore I don't think it is possible for a hospital to engage in the kind of policy that has been articulated by Justice Stevens.

[JUSTICE O'CONNOR:] All right, so it's your position that what the hospital must do is refer it to the child abuse agency.

MR. COOPER: That's right.

[JUSTICE O'CONNOR:] And otherwise, and if they don't, it's discrimination because in non-handicap situations they must [refer the case to the agency on child abuse] under state law.

MR. COOPER: I don't know of any state law that makes a distinction between whether the child is handicapped or not. But that's exactly our point.

[JUSTICE O'CONNOR:] And if they treat the handicaps different, your position is that's discrimination [under the federal law]?

MR. COOPER: That's right. If they treat the handicapped child because of his handicap, for the reason that he is afflicted by this handicap—[58]

Thanks to the intervention of Justice O'Connor, she and Mr. Cooper managed to conduct a duet that led away from the trap of Justice Stevens's argument. They were able to show that the hospital could not disengage its own responsibility so easily, by deferring in such a beamish way to the judgment of the parents. If there was discrimination against an infant on account of her disability, the hospital was obliged to report that decision to a committee of review, under the authority of the state. And the prospect of that kind of discrimination had justified the interest of the federal government. But even after the play of this more calibrated analysis, O'Connor still preserved the cast of Stevens's argument: The hospital had the responsibility to review a decision on the part of parents to withhold the medical treatment of their child. The hospital was obliged to consider whether the treatment was withheld for reasons that would violate the federal law. *But the sanction would come from the agencies of the state, enforcing this obligation of state law on the hospitals.* As Justice O'Connor put it, "the violation [of federal law] was in not reporting [the decision of the parents] to the state agency." The hospital had become the proxy for the parents. And in the eye of the law, it was the hospital that was engaging in discrimination against the handicapped. The *hospital* had become the wrongdoer.

The hospital would be pursued, then, with the laws of the state. But in that case, who—or what—would become the target of the federal law, when the powers of the federal government were finally engaged? And the answer, apparently, was: the state! If the state proved to be deficient or unresponsive in dealing with a case of discrimination, *then* the federal government would become involved. To put it another way, the engagement of the federal government would hinge upon a judgment of the rightness or aptness of the decisions taken by agents of the state. Once again, the federal government would act as a government of the second instance, at a later stage of the proceeedings.

And against whom would the judgment of the federal government be rendered? Not against the people who sought to withhold medical treatment, wrongly, from an infant. Apparently, the judgment would be cast against the agencies of the state, for their failure to remedy the wrong of withholding treatment from the handicapped. And the penalty?: *The withdrawal of funds from the agency of the state,* and perhaps also from the hospital that permitted this treatment of infants.

During the closing moments of the oral argument, Justice White strained to sort out these strands in the puzzle. With Charles Cooper, he established the chain of decisions: A committee in the hospital may review the decisions of the parents. If the committee disagrees with the judgment of the parents, if it thinks the federal law has been violated, the committee may then refer the case to the "child protective agency" in the state government.

[JUSTICE WHITE:] All right. And what if they disagree with the hospital, too?

MR. COOPER: If they disagree with the parents and the doctor, then presumably they would undertake those state court procedures necessary to override the decision of the parents and the doctor and have the treatment or the nourishment administered to the child.

[JUSTICE WHITE:] When they go to state court on it, they're applying a federal standard, aren't they?

MR. COOPER: No, sir. . . . The federal standard is what requires them to go to the state court, but it is certainly true that it would be the state child abuse and neglect standard that obtains there in the state court.

[JUSTICE WHITE:] Except that I thought you said if the state child protective services agency did not employ the standard that the Federal Government thinks is appropriate, the Federal Government would then withhold funds from the child protective services agency. So if the Federal Government doesn't agree with what the child protective services agency does, it will try to withhold funds.
. . . So there is a federal standard provided that either must be satisfied or funds are withheld?

MR. COOPER: The federal standard that governs the conduct of the recipient of federal funds, which is the child protective . . . agency. Yes sir, that standard, a non-discrimination standard, would govern.[59]

In this manner, the wrong of the parents has been converted into the wrong of the hospital, and the wrong of the hospital has been converted into the wrong of the state. If the federal government finally comes to the judgment that the federal law has been violated—that medical care was withheld from handicapped infants—then how is that wrong to be vindicated?: By withdrawing funds from the "child protective agency" of the state.

The convolutions have become so familiar to us by now that it may be too much to ask that we try to break away from the tangle of these fictions and notice what has happened. We began with the sense of a wrong, a lethal wrong, done to handicapped infants. That sense of the moral wrong, or the grave injustice, accounts for the outrage felt by the president, along with other people in the country. That moral sense of the problem accounts for the interest that moved the administration into the courts. But then the conventions of our jurisprudence became engaged. The administration had to work with a statute that contained the traditional evasions, as the federal government sought to legislate on a problem, but without touching directly the wrongs it sought to forbid. The result was that the original wrong of the case was finally put out of view. It was not—it could not—be taken up in any of the briefs offered to the courts. Nor could it enter into the oral arguments. The lawyers for the government had to be placed in this implausible position: They had the burden of explaining just how the federal government could reach a case of parents who withhold medical treatment from their child. But at the same time, they had to explain, as eminently sensible, the most tortuous procedures, which could make sense only if there was a serious doubt about the authority of the federal government to reach directly a case of this kind. Charles Cooper's colloquy with Justice White was an artifact of this system of law: It was a conversation made necessary by this tangled system of legislating by indirection. It was a conversation pursued with strain and a sense of duty, but not a conversation that could illuminate any matter of right or wrong that lay at the heart of the case.

And because the conversation had to take place within this mold, no time was left to explain those vexing matters in principle that were indeed pivotal for the case: No one took the time to explain just why the discomfort of the parents, or their unwillingness to keep a disfigured child, could not supply a justification for taking the life of the child or withholding, from the child, the care she needed in order to live. The explanation was not evident to everyone. It was decidedly worth the effort, then, to explain why human beings—even new human beings—do not forfeit their claim to live when they are afflicted by infirmities, when they suffer deficits of intellect, and when they become, perhaps, an aesthetic embarrassment for their families. Many parents had already absorbed the notion that they had a "right" to rid themselves of any unborn child who may be retarded or "defective." Who was to explain to them just what commands of principle suddenly got in the way of these "rights" when they now had the chance to see, even more clearly, the defects of their newborn children?

But consider, in one last, backward glance, the savvy curiosity of Justice White, as he sought to work through the maze of the Baby Jane case. If the committee of review in the hospital disagreed with the judgment reached by the parents, it could refer the case to the "child protective agency" of the state. If the agency concluded that the judgment of the parents had been justified, then it would conclude that there had been no "discrimination," no wrongful withholding of medical care from the child. In that event, how would the federal government know that this judgment, reached by the agency of the state, had been wrong? As White asked Charles Cooper, "how do you tell about discrimination? You are looking over their shoulders as to what standard a doctor uses or the hospital uses for withholding treatment."[60] The federal government could find fault with the judgment of the state only if it had a basis for knowing that the decision of the parents was unjustified. But it had no way of forming that judgment unless it could get access to the record on its own. And yet, it could not claim the authority to get access to that record unless it claimed the authority to inquire into the decisions made by the parents—that is, unless it claimed an interest in protecting *directly*, with its own hand, the victim who is endangered by the decision of the parents. But the government was a bit equivocal, in the Bowen case, in making that claim for its own interest and its own authority. And the Court responded to that equivocation by denying the claim of the government to get access to the record. *Catch-22*: The government can apply its sanctions only by withdrawing funds from the hospital or the state. But it cannot justify the use of sanctions without having access to the records of the parents and the doctor. It cannot have a claim to the records unless it has the authority to reach directly to the wrong done by the parents. And yet, if the government has *that* authority, it has no need to enforce its laws in such a backhanded way, by withdrawing funds from states and hospitals!

What I am suggesting then is that the whole, cumbersome exercise becomes coherent only if we assume precisely the point that we seem driven to deny—namely, that the national government may reach directly to the wrongs that inspire the creation of the law in the first place. If the national government thinks it can address the wrong of racial discrimination, then it should define the acts that constitute the wrong; it should mark off the instances of racial discrimination that come within the reach of its prohibitions; it should condemn, in its statutes, the wrongs it would condemn; and it should make *those wrongs* the focus of its punishments. If the government is moved by the prospect of parents withholding medical treatment from vulnerable, infirm children, then it should address itself precisely to *that wrong*. It should explain why that decision, made in private settings, deserves to be brought within the reach of the law. The drafters of the law may wish to ponder the question of whether the policies of the federal government will be meshed with the the policies of the states, or whether they will supersede the policies of the states. But those questions should not be placed in the center of the problem. Nor should they be confused with the main question of the law, in accounting for its own concern, and justifying its claim to override private judgments in the interest of protecting children.

When lawyers for the government leave their offices, they seem able to explain, in their conversations, just why any matter is urgent enough to justify the engagement of the law. On the other hand, they also seem to have a cultivated sense of why certain matters are best left untouched by the law. They show, in other words, every day, that they regard this brand of discourse as intelligible. But more than that: they regard it as pertinent, accessible, decisive. Why should we think, then, that the life of our law would be diminished if we transferred, from our private discourse, the style of reasoning that we seem to regard as more apt, more readily understood, more responsive to our moral sense, more telling?

I have argued, in these pages, that there is a need to move beyond the text of the Constitution, to the principles of moral reasoning that stood antecedent to the Constitution. Those principles furnished the understanding of the Founders when they framed the Constitution, and I have sought to show just why it becomes necessary to draw on those principles when we seek to apply the text of the Constitution to any case of practical judgment. In the discussion of the Bill of Rights, I suggested that the inventory of objects marked off in the amendments could not possibly supply the ground of our judgments. Speech may have the effect of hurting when it comes in a phone call bearing tragic news, or in an obscene call in the middle of the night. One kind of speech may be punished by the law, and the other may not be. Some restrictions on speech can be justified, and some cannot be. The limits to the reach of the law cannot be found, then, in the text of the Constitution, but in the understanding that enables us, finally, to distinguish between the cases in which the law may rightly restrain the uses of freedom, and the cases that lie properly beyond the reproach of the law. I have sought to show how this same understanding would be applied, in a variety of instances, as I have moved, in these chapters, through a series of problems in our constitutional law. And what I offer, by the end, is drawn from the same understanding: To say that the national government may reach any question that comes within the reach of any government in the territory of the United States is not to say that the national government is licensed to act without limits. Those limits cannot be furnished by the convenient formulas of federalism. We may rightly prize the benefits of federalism, but the arrangements of federalism cannot supply a real principle, which marks off plausible zones of jurisdiction. But to say that federalism cannot supply such a principle is not to say that there are no boundaries, no restraints, to the reach of the national government. It is to say, rather, that the reach of the national government is regulated by the same principles that regulate the reach of the law with the Bill of Rights: The limits to the national government can be found only in the principles that mark off for us the boundary between the subjects that the law would be justified in reaching, and the subjects that could not be brought, with justification, within the control of the law.

That people will disagree, enduringly, about the placing of those boundaries, that they will even disagree about the existence of those principles of judgment, is simply a mark of our lasting condition. But it is one of those "self-refuting" propositions to suggest that the presence of disagreement on any matter is sufficient to establish that there are no right answers. During the period of the Founding, the disagreements touched every part of the Constitution, and the litigation flared over matters that we would regard today as too plain, or too elementary, for any controversy. It is hard to imagine, in this respect, that litigants once argued seriously over the justification for creating lower federal courts, or the authority of the Supreme Court to override the judgment of a state court. And yet, this willingness to argue over everything flourished at a time when the political class in the country had never been more unified in their conviction that there were indeed laws of reason that allowed them to judge the soundness of the arguments. On either side, they were convinced that the arguments of their opponents could be exposed in the end as false, to anyone whose reason was not clouded by passion or partisanship.

Of course, they might have been more successful in conveying their convictions to our own generation if they had taken the trouble to set down some of those maxims, or those laws of reason, in the Constitution itself. They might have left a subtle reminder for their successors that the Constitution required, for its completion, the principles of judgment that could not be set down, in their entirety, in the Constitution. After all, the Founders regarded the Constitution as a frame of government, a legal structure, and not a manual on logic. They trusted that the study of logic was part of the curriculum of the educated, of the people who would ever be entrusted with the instruments of government. And as James Wilson remarked, the educated did not have to be reminded of the laws of reason. They did not have to be told, for example, that ex post facto laws were incompatible with the principles of lawfulness. Still less did they have to be told, as Thomas Reid put it, that "what is done from unavoidable necessity . . . cannot be the object either of blame or moral approbation." They did not have to be told that people should be presumed innocent until proven guilty, or that two contradictory propositions could not both be true. Or at least they did not have to be told in the Constitution. The political men and jurists of that generation could take the occasion to teach those maxims again in the course of their essays or opinions. James Wilson could simply remark, as it were, in passing, in *Chisholm v. Georgia*, that "the fact, uncontrovertibly established in *one* instance, proves the *principle* in *all other* instances, to which the facts will be found to apply."[61] And Hamilton could fill in a preface to an essay in journalism by marking off "certain primary truths, or first principles", for example, that "things equal to the same are equal to one another. . . . that there cannot be an effect without a cause; that the means ought to be proportioned to the end; that every power ought to be commensurate with its object; that there ought to be no limitation of a power destined to effect a purpose which is itself incapable of limitation."[62]

The most cultivated men of this day could be bitterly divided in their judgment of national policy; but they would not divide themselves into parties over any of the propositions contained in this list. Neither the Federalists nor the Anti-Federalists, neither the Hamiltonians nor the Jeffersonians, found anything problematic or divisive in this list of "primary truths, or first principles." They could hardly have imagined that their arguments could have been carried on coherently in the absence of these laws of reason. Hence, the curious spectacle of our own day, when a certain relativism or moral skepticism has found a constituency even among conservative lawyers and jurists. If we ask, What is a conservative in our discourse on politics and law today, the answer comes in this irony: A conservative is one who celebrates Professor Alan Bloom's recent book, *The Closing of the American Mind*, with its attack on moral relativism; and at the same time, a conservative is one who insists that when a judge departs from the text of the Constitution, he has nothing to look to but himself—nothing, that is, but his own subjective judgments on the things that please him. If we take this notion seriously, we are asked to believe that when a jurist leaves the text, he cannot appeal to any moral truths, to any propositions with a validity of their own, which can claim to govern his judgments. Why this moral relativism must be the doctrine of conservatives in our law is one of the puzzles of our own time. The skepticism of some of our "conservative" jurists certainly does not accord with the understanding of the Founders, whose "original intent" is often taken as the touchstone of our jurisprudence. It was not, for example, the understanding of James Wilson, who denounced the "sceptical" philosophy of his own time for its "bold, but false pretentions to liberality." The question may earnestly be raised: Why would American conservatives be disposed at this moment to leave the tradition, or the rhetoric, of natural law to their liberal adversaries? Why do they think it a service to embrace, instead, the maxims of moral relativism, even when they are dressed up in the language of legal "positivism"?

Conservatives have understandably recoiled from the marriage of ideas they have seen taking place in public: The commentators who have made more of a show in appealing to "natural rights" have had a remarkable way of making natural rights coincide with the current liberal agenda, from affirmative action to abortion. And yet why should the conservatives allow this exercise to give natural rights, for them, a bad name? Why not, rather, celebrate this willingness on the part of liberal commentators to accept the tradition of natural rights, and the moral postulates that come along with that tradition? And why not then take it, as the mission of conservatives as well as liberals in the law, to restore the discipline of moral reasoning that has ever been a part of the tradition of natural rights?

It is said that Delacroix, the painter, when he was blocked by a problem, would repair to the Louvre. He regarded the collection at the Louvre as the equivalent of a grand library. He could see, in the paintings, just which of his predecessors encountered the problem he faced now, and he could see just how an earlier master had dealt with the problem. In the same way, we might discover an interest in looking seriously again at the works in jurisprudence left to us by the first generation of our jurists. There is an enduring satisfaction in learning anew of the furnishings of their minds. There may also be a source of comfort in learning again, learning seriously, of the "laws of reason" that guided their understanding and gave them a certain confidence in their judgments. We may even discover then, as a late colleague of mine once put, that we have principles we have not even used yet.

NOTES

CHAPTER ONE

1. See *Daniel v. Paul*, 395 U.S. 298, at 310 (1969).

2. Quoted in ibid., 312–13.

3. See, in this respect, my own discussion of the Supreme Court's use of the Commerce Clause in the cases on "public accommodations," and, in another kind of case, Justice Harlan's rather belated "discovery" of "logical positivism" about thirty years after that doctrine had been abandoned in the schools of philosophy. Arkes, *The Philosopher in the City* (Princeton, N.J.: Princeton University Press, 1981), pp. 243–45, 225–31, 63–74.

4. *Daniel v. Paul, supra*, note 1, at 315.

5. *Bowen v. American Hospital Association*, 476 U.S. 610 (1986).

6. On this connection between the logic of morals and the logic of law, I shall have more to say later. For an extended consideration of this problem, the reader may wish to see Arkes, *First Things* (Princeton, N.J.: Princeton University Press, 1986), chapter 2.

7. *Fletcher v. Peck*, 6 Cranch 87, at 140 (1810).

8. 3 U.S. (Dallas) 386 (1798).

9. Ibid., at 388, 391.

10. I put aside here that handful of redoubtable characters who would seek to restore the tradition of "natural rights" and moral truths against the bafflement of their colleagues. And I place, in a class by themselves, the Marxists, who skillfully attack the liberals for their moral relativism, but then encounter the grievous burden of their own reluctance to concede the existence of "autonomous" legal principles, which may have a standing of their own as truths, quite apart from the interests of "classes." For reflections of these problems, see Hugh Collins, *Marxism and Law* (Oxford: Oxford University Press, 1982), especially pp. 61–76, 124–46; Hans Kelsen, *The Communist Theory of Law* (New York: Praeger, 1955); and Eugene Kamenka, "Law and Morality in Soviet Society," in *The Ethical Foundations of Marxism* (London: Routledge and Kegan Paul, 1972), pp. 168–87.

11. See the two notable pieces by Thomas C. Grey, "Do We Have an Unwritten Constitution?" 27 *Stanford Law Review* 703 (February 1975) and "Origins of the Unwritten Constitution: Fundamental Law in American Revolutionary Thought," 30 *Stanford Law Review* 943 (May 1978).

12. Sanford Levinson, *Constitutional Faiths* (Princeton, N.J.: Princeton University Press, 1988), p. 175. Professor Gary Jacobsohn has marked out a different ground of "faith" in the Constitution, based on a notably different conviction about the kind of regime that must be described and deepened when the implications of the Constitution are unfolded. See Gary Jacobsohn, *The Supreme Court and the Decline of Constitutional Aspiration* (Totowa: N.J.: Rowman and Littlefield, 1986).

13. Levinson, *supra*, note 12, p. 69.

14. The final irony for my colleague, Sanford Levinson, is that he was constrained from making even the modest claim that his own argument deserved at least to be

taken seriously. As he wrote in his concluding passage: "Whether constitutional faith
maintains itself depends on our ability to continue taking it seriously. I have tried to
show that this is no easy task" (ibid., p. 194). That is: If "nothing interesting can be
said about truth," then we say nothing interesting when we claim that our own argument is true or even plausible. Levinson, a model of scrupulosity, holds back then
from claiming that his own teaching is sufficiently plausible that we ought to be "taking it seriously." Instead, he claims only that "answers can emerge, if at all, only out
of conversation." But the ground on which we can claim to know even *that* point
would have to be—on his own terms—the subject of the most earnest questioning.

15. Grey, *supra*, note 11, 717–18.

16. Hence, Professor Dworkin's persistent references to "a nation's political
traditions and culture" as the ultimate foundation of jurisprudence. In this vein,
Dworkin would explain, say, that racial segregation is wrong because it "offends principles of equality that are accepted over most of the nation." He goes on: "[L]aw as
integrity is sensitive to a nation's political tradition and culture and therefore to a
conception of fairness that is fit for a constitution." Dworkin, *Law's Empire* (Cambridge: Harvard University Press, 1986), pp. 404–5, 377–78. Dworkin is drawn to the
notion of "integrity" as an "adjudicative principle" in the law precisely because it is
needed as a surrogate for moral truth. It is the expedient offered by a commentator
who cannot finally credit any understanding of right and wrong grounded in "nature"
or in "the laws of reason." In Dworkin's account, the notion of "integrity" serves as
the "basis for claims of political legitimacy in a community of free and independent
people who disagree about political morality and wisdom" (p. 411). That is, his notion
of "integrity" becomes necessary, as the substitute for moral truth, because the writer
begins with the premise that there is no truth that retains its validity, and its authority,
in the presence of disagreement. By this point, it is hard to see what can separate
Dworkin, in any decisive respect, from the collection of legal positivists, historicists,
and skeptics that he has taken so much care to deride. See also, Dworkin, *Taking Rights
Seriously* (Cambridge: Harvard University Press, 1977), pp. 106, 122, 124, 125.

But what can be said here about Dworkin could be said, with a comparable force,
about any of the recent, liberal commentators on the law. John Hart Ely has been most
explicit in rejecting natural rights while affirming, at the same time, a mandate for
judges to seek the deeper meaning of the Constitution; a meaning that will not be
anchored either in the text or in any discipline of "moral judgment." Ely, *Democracy
and Distrust* (Cambridge: Harvard University Press, 1981). And, of course, there is
Professor Tribe:

> Even if we could settle on firm constitutional postulates, we would remain inescapably *sub-
> jective* in the application of those postulates to particular problems and issues. . . . For me
> [the hard cases of constitutional interpretation] seem basically unanswerable; theories that
> offer or presuppose answers to them—*any* answers—seem not worth pursuing with passion
> or even worth criticizing in great detail. . . . [W]henever I suggest . . . for want of space or
> of humility, that one or another decision [of the courts] seems to me "plainly right" or
> "plainly wrong," or that some proposal or position is "clearly" consistent (or inconsistent)
> with the Constitution, I hope my words will be understood as shorthand not for a conclu-
> sion I offer as indisputably "correct" but solely for a conviction I put forward as powerfully

held (emphasis added). (Tribe, *Constitutional Choices* [Cambridge: Harvard University Press, 1985], pp. 5, 6, 8.)

No one who has encountered these writers could suppose for a moment that they suffer even the slightest doubts about the truth of their own arguments. But the affectation of humility has become a necessary part of the posture of moral skepticism, and it retains its appeal even when it moves estimable writers to say what they could not possibly mean, namely, in the case of Professor Tribe, that his arguments would claim our serious attention, not because of the force of their reasoning, or their correspondence to the truth, but merely because they are "powerfully held."

17. See Bork, "Neutral Principles and Some First Amendment Problems," 47 *Indiana Law Journal* 1 (1971), at 30.

18. Bork, "The Struggle Over the Role of the Court," *National Review* (September 17, 1982), pp. 1137–39, at 1138.

19. For an extended explanation, see Arkes, *First Things, supra*, note 6, pp. 51–52 (and chapter 4, more generally), 132–33, 134–37.

20. Holmes, "The Path of the Law," in *Collected Legal Papers* (New York: Harcourt Brace and Co., 1920), p. 179.

21. William H. Rehnquist, "The Notion of a Living Constitution," 54 *Texas Law Review*, 693, at 705 (1976).

22. See *supra*, note 6.

23. *Supra*, note 21, at 704, emphasis added.

24. Ibid., at 705. Compare, in this vein, Robert Bork: "Truth is what the majority thinks it is at any given moment precisely because the majority is permitted to govern and to redefine its values constantly." Bork, *supra*, note 17, at 30; and see also 31.

25. There is of course no example more powerful in connecting Lincoln to the tradition of political theory, or more elegant in imparting the writings of Lincoln, than Harry Jaffa's book, *The Crisis of the House Divided* (New York: Doubleday, 1959).

26. See *First Things, supra*, note 6, pp. 36–50.

CHAPTER TWO

1. Herbert J. Storing, ed., *The Complete Anti-Federalist* (Chicago: University of Chicago Press, 1981), vol. 2, p. 419.

2. Ibid., pp. 419–20.

3. Quoted by Brutus in ibid., p. 420.

4. Blackstone, *Commentaries on the Laws of England* (Oxford: Clarendon Press, 1765), book 1, p. 91. I am using here the edition published by the University of Chicago Press in 1979, with a copy of the original plates and preserving the same pagination.

5. Ibid., book 4, chap. 5, p. 67.

6. Ibid., book 1, p. 91.

7. Ibid.

8. See *Franz v. United States*, 707 F.2d 582 and 712 F.2d 1428 (1983).

9. 2 Dallas 419, at 453 (1793).

10. Ibid., at 453–54.

11. Ibid., at 464, 465.

12. *Fletcher v. Peck*, 6 Cranch 87, at 139.

13. A rich account of the background, and details, of this case was provided by Albert Beveridge in his *Life of John Marshall* (Boston: Houghton Mifflin, 1919), vol. 3, chap. 10.

14. *Supra*, note 12, at 137.

15. See, for example, the opinions of Justice Chase and Justice Iredell in *Calder v. Bull*, 3 Dallas 386 (1798).

16. *Fletcher v. Peck, supra*, note 12, 138–39, emphasis in original.

17. Max Farrand, ed., *The Records of the Federal Convention of 1787*, [rev. ed. 1937] (New Haven: Yale University Press, 1966), vol. 2, p. 376 [August 22].

18. For an explanation of the character and properties of real "principles" and "necessary truths," see Arkes, *First Things* (Princeton, N.J.: Princeton University Press, 1986), chaps. 4 and 5.

19. *Fletcher v. Peck, supra*, note 12, at 143.

20. Ibid., at 144, emphasis added.

21. Ibid., at 136.

22. See Wilson on this point in *Chisholm v. Georgia, supra*, note 9, at 464.

23. For a fuller explanation of this point, see *First Things, supra*, note 18, pp. 68–71.

24. On this point, see *First Things*, chap. 15.

25. See *First Things*, chap. 4, especially pp. 78–84, and chap. 5, pp. 87–88.

26. Ibid., p. 83.

27. Thomas Reid, *Essays on the Active Powers of the Human Mind* (Cambridge: MIT Press, 1969 [1788]), p. 361.

28. See *First Things, supra*, note 18, pp. 92–99, 159, 167–68.

29. See *Chisholm v. Georgia, supra*, note 9, at 456.

30. *Hepburn v. Griswold*, 8 Wallace 603, at 616, 619 (1870).

31. See ibid., at 608, 619.

32. Ibid., at 623.

33. Ibid., at 624.

34. In ibid., at 624, Chase takes account of a serious challenge made to his argument by the judges in the minority. It would require a more extended treatment to consider whether these objections could be defeated, or whether Chase's response offers the ingredients for the refutation.

35. Roy P. Basler, ed., *The Works of Abraham Lincoln* (New Brunswick, N.J.: Rutgers University Press, 1953), vol. 2, pp. 222–23.

36. Lincoln, Speech at Quincy, Illinois (October 13, 1858), in ibid., vol. 3, p. 256.

37. Ibid., p. 257.

38. See Aquinas, *Summa Theologiae*, 2a2ae, 57, 3; and John Stuart Mill, *Utilitarianism* (Indianapolis: Bobbs-Merrill, 1957 [1861]), p. 61.

39. See my book, *First Things, supra*, note 18, chap. 2, especially pp. 24–30.

40. Blackstone, *Commentaries on the Laws of England, supra*, note 4, book 1, chap. 2, p. 44.

41. See, for example, the commentary of Professor William Draper Lewis in his

1897 edition of Blackstone's *Commentaries* (Philadelphia: Rees Welsh and Co.), sec. 2, p. 44.

42. Oliver Wendell Holmes, "The Path of the Law," in *Collected Legal Papers* (New York: Harcourt Brace and Co., 1920), p. 179.

43. For some examples on this head, see Arkes, *The Philosopher in the City* (Princeton, N.J.: Princeton University Press, 1981), pp. 357–58 and *passim*, and *First Things*, *supra*, note 18, pp. 327–41.

CHAPTER THREE

1. Roy P. Basler, ed., *The Collected Works of Abraham Lincoln* (New Brunswick, N.J.: Rutgers University Press, 1953), vol. 4, p. 169.

2. Ibid., vol. 4, pp. 268–69, emphasis in original.

3. Ibid., vol. 3, p. 386 [June 20, 1859].

4. Ibid., vol. 2, p. 256 [October 16, 1854].

5. Ibid., vol. 4, p. 264.

6. Letter to the Citizens of Newburyport, May 15, 1850, reprinted in George Ticknor Curtis, *The Life of Daniel Webster* (New York: Appleton, 1870), pp. 423–26, and see also p. 422.

7. Daniel Webster often remarked on the understanding that arose here from the tradition of jurisprudence: "It was a maxim of the civil law," he remarked, "that, between slavery and freedom, freedom should always be presumed, and slavery must always be proved. If any question arose as to the *status* of an individual in Rome, he was presumed to be free until he was proved to be a slave, because slavery is an exception to the general rule. Such, I suppose, is the general law of mankind." Speech on the Exclusion of Slavery from the Territories, made in the Senate of the United States (August 12, 1848), in *The Writings and Speeches of Daniel Webster* (Boston: Little, Brown and Co., 1903), vol. 10, p. 41.

8. Lincoln, *supra*, note 1, vol. 2, pp. 265–66, emphasis in original.

9. For an elaboration of this argument, see Harry Jaffa's classic book, *The Crisis of the House Divided* (New York: Doubleday, 1959), and my own *First Things* (Princeton, N.J.: Princeton University Press, 1986), chap. 3.

10. *Dred Scott v. Sandford*, 19 Howard 393, at 624 (1857).

11. Ibid.

12. Webster, *supra*, note 7, p. 40.

13. Ibid., p. 37.

14. Letter to Erastus Corning (June 12, 1863), in *The Collected Works of Abraham Lincoln*, *supra*, note 1, vol. 4, p. 265.

15. Ibid.

16. For a more recent discussion on these issues, which helps to strengthen the case for Lincoln's course, see Alan Dershowitz, "Terrorism and Preventive Detention: The Case of Israel," *Commentary* (December 1970), pp. 67–78.

17. See *The Social Contract*, book 4, chap. 4 ("Of the Dictatorship").

18. *Supra*, note 1, vol. 4, p. 430 (Message to Congress, July 4, 1861), emphasis in original.

19. Ibid., pp. 430–31.

20. See *Ex parte Richard Quirin*, 317 U.S. 1, at 21, 24 (1942).

21. Ibid., at 39.

22. Over the years, Justice Black would suffer many embarrassments to his claims as the Great Literalist of the Court, even though he professed to carry with him, at all times, a copy of the Constitution. But his copy must have been an abridged version, which omitted Article I, Section 6, paragraph two, which should have been sufficient to bar his own appointment to the Court. See *Ex parte Levitt*, 302 U.S. 633 (1937).

23. *Supra*, note 20, at 40–41.

24. *Fletcher v. Peck*, 6 Cranch 87, at 139.

25. 163 U.S. 537.

26. Ibid., at 559, 561.

27. Ibid., at 559, 562.

28. Ibid., at 560.

29. Ibid., at 555, emphasis added.

30. Ibid., at 553. For an extended commentary on these points in the Plessy case, see my own book, *The Philosopher in the City* (Princeton, N.J.: Princeton University Press, 1981), pp. 227–28, 240–41, 351.

31. Ibid., p. 564.

32. For an argument that is strikingly similar in its cast—and deft in its exposition—see Charles Black, *Structure and Relationship in Constitutional Law* (Baton Rouge: Louisiana University Press, 1969).

33. Hamilton, the *Federalist* #33, in *The Federalist Papers* (New York: Random House, n.d.), pp. 198–99.

34. Ibid., p. 201.

35. Ibid., p. 202.

CHAPTER FOUR

1. Walter Laqueur, "Euro-Neutralism," *Commentary* (June 1980), pp. 21–27, at 25.

2. For this recovery of historical memory we must be obliged most notably to Gordon Wood for his engaging book, *The Creation of the American Republic, 1776–1787* (Chapel Hill: University of North Carolina Press, 1969), especially pp. 536–43.

3. See Storing, *What the Anti-Federalists Were For*, Vol. 1 of *The Complete Anti-Federalist*, ed. Herbert J. Storing (Chicago: University of Chicago Press, 1981), pp. 64–70.

4. Quoted in ibid., p. 70.

5. Ibid.

6. *The Federalist* (New York: Modern Library, n.d.), p. 558, emphasis in original. See also the remarks in this vein by James Wilson at the ratifying Convention in Philadelphia, in Jonathan Elliot, *The Debates in the Several State Conventions on the Adoption of the Federal Constitution* (Philadelphia: J. B. Lippincott Co., 1836), vol. 2, pp. 434–35.

7. On this point, see Wilson's remarks in the ratifying Convention, in Elliott, ibid., pp. 454, 497.

8. Hamilton in *The Federalist, supra*, note 6; and see Gordon Wood, *supra*, note 2, pp. 540–42.

9. Storing, *supra*, note 3, p. 67.

10. Max Farrand, ed., *The Records of the Federal Convention of 1787* [rev. ed. 1937]

(New Haven: Yale University Press, 1966), vol. 2, p. 376 [August 22]. And see above, chap. 2, note 17.

11. Thomas Hobbes, *Leviathan* (Oxford: Basil Blackwell, 1960; originally published in 1651), pp. 82, 85.

12. See Aristotle, *Politics*, 1280a–1281a, and my extended discussion of this point in *First Things* (Princeton, N.J.: Princeton University Press, 1986), chap. 2.

13. Hobbes, *supra*, note 11, p. 83.

14. William Blackstone, *Commentaries on the Laws of England* (Chicago: University of Chicago Press, 1979; originally published in 1765), vol. 1, book 1, chaps. 121–22.

15. Wilson, "Of the Natural Rights of Individuals," in *The Works of James Wilson* (Cambridge: Harvard University Press, 1967), vol. 2, pp. 585–610, at 587.

16. Lincoln, Debate with Douglas at Quincy, Illinois (October, 1858), in Roy P. Basler, ed., *The Works of Abraham Lincoln* (New Brunswick, N.J.: Rutgers University Press, 1953), vol. 3, pp. 256–57.

17. "The Farmer Refuted" [February 1775], in Harold C. Syrett, ed., *The Papers of Alexander Hamilton* (New York: Columbia University Press, 1961), vol. 1, pp. 86–87, emphasis added.

18. Wilson, *supra*, note 15, p. 585.

19. Hamilton, *supra*, note 6, *The Federalist* #84, p. 558. In the same vein, Dr. Benjamin Rush commended the framers for avoiding the incoherence of attaching a Bill of Rights to the Constitution: "As we enjoy all our natural rights from a pre-occupancy, antecedent to the social state," it would be "absurd to frame a formal declaration that our natural rights are acquired from ourselves." Quoted in Herbert J. Storing, "The Constitution and the Bill of Rights," in *How Does the Constitution Secure Rights?*, ed. Robert A. Goldwin and William A. Schambra (Washington, D.C.: American Enterprise Institute, 1985), pp. 15–35, at p. 30.

20. This understanding of the American founding has indeed been offered in a celebrated essay by Martin Diamond, "Democracy and the Federalist: A Reconsideration of the Framer's Intent," *American Political Science Review* 53 (1959), pp. 52ff.

21. Wilson, *supra*, note 15, p. 592.

22. Sedgwick, *Annals of Congress*, 1st Cong., vol. I, p. 731 (August 15, 1787).

23. See Page, in ibid., p. 732.

24. The point would seem to be embarrassingly evident to anyone who has spent any time reflecting on the grounds of our practical judgment on matters of right and wrong; and yet Blackstone once reminded us just how venerable is the tradition, among doctors of law, of overlooking this simple point. Blackstone recalled an ancient law in Bologna, which proclaimed "that whoever drew blood in the streets should be punished with the utmost severity." But after further reflection, the experts on the law were moved to make this allowance: that the law would not "extend to the surgeon, who opened the vein of a person that fell down in the street with a fit." Blackstone, *supra*, note 14, vol. 1, Introduction, section 2, p. 60.

25. *Supra*, note 22, p. 732.

26. 475 U.S. 503.

27. Ibid., at 504–5.

28. In another essay on the Bill of Rights, Herbert Storing glimpsed—though he did not pursue—the alternative understanding I am putting forth here. "Without a

bill of rights," he wrote, "our courts would probably have developed a kind of common law of individual rights to help to test and limit governmental power." As Storing recognized, those rights would be defended against the power of the government by an appeal to natural rights; and on the other side, the government would bear the burden of showing that it is restricting rights in any case for the sake of *ends* that are *legitimate*. In that way he partially anticipated my argument: "Might the courts thus have been compelled to confront the basic questions that 'substantive due process,' 'substantive equal protection,' 'clear and present danger,' etc., have permitted them to conceal, even from themselves? Is it possible that without a bill of rights we might suffer less of that ignoble battering between absolutistic positivism and flaccid historicism that characterizes our constitutional law today?" See Storing in *supra*, note 19, pp. 25–26.

29. Marshall, Address on the Constitutionality of the Alien and Sedition Acts, in Morton Frisch and Richard Stevens, eds., *The Political Thought of American Statesmen* (Itasca: Peacock Publishers, 1973), pp. 99–116, at p. 113.

30. For an emphatic statement of this position in our own day, see Felix Frankfurter's dissent in *West Virginia v. Barnette*, 319 U.S. 624: "The right not to have one's property taken without just compensation has, so far as the scope of judicial power is concerned, the same constitutional dignity as the right to be protected against unreasonable searches and seizures, and the latter has no less claim than freedom of the press or freedom of speech or religious freedom."

31. See, for example, *Virginia State Bd. of Pharmacy v. Virginia Citizens Consumer Council*, 425 U.S. 748 (1976); cf. *Valentine v. Chrestensen*, 316 U.S. 52 (1942).

32. There could be no clearer statement on this point than Justice Field's dissenting opinion in the Slaughter-House cases, 16 Wall 36, at 83–111 (1873). See also Bernard Siegan, *Economic Liberties and the Constitution* (Chicago: University of Chicago Press, 1980), chap. 5. Field understood that it could be quite appropriate, in certain cases, to grant exclusive franchises for bridges and ferries, which provided a public service. But he regarded that kind of arrangement as "a very different thing from a grant, with exclusive privileges, of a right to pursue one of the ordinary trades or callings of life [as, in this case, the slaughtering of animals], which is a right appertaining solely to the individual." It was one thing to provide inspections for the safety of the product, but it was quite another to impose an arbitrary limit on the number of people who could work at an ordinary trade, and require, in effect, a "tribute" to the government for the permission of working at a legitimate job. See Field at 86 and 88.

33. See, on this point, Bernard Siegan, ibid., p. 76 and *passim*.

34. For a commentary on the case in Skokie, see my piece, "Marching Through Skokie," *National Review* (May 12, 1978), pp. 588–92.

35. For an extended consideration of this matter, see Arkes, *Philosopher in the City* (Princeton, N.J.: Princeton University Press, 1981), Chaps. 2 and 3.

36. *Shaare Tefila Congregation v. Cobb*, 481 U.S. 615 (1987).

37. The most notable case here has been *Cohen v. California*, 403 U.S. 15 (1971), which undercut *Chaplinsky v. New Hampshire*, 315 U.S. 568 (1942), the classic case on "fighting words" and verbal assaults. For an extended discussion of these cases, see Arkes, *The Philosopher in the City, supra*, note 35, pp. 53–74 and *passim*.

38. 410 U.S. 113 (1973).

39. See Blackmun in ibid., p. 157.

40. In fairness, Herbert Storing reminded us that the decision to attach the Bill of Rights as an appendage to the Constitution was made at the behest of Roger Sherman, who bore no enthusiasm for making these additions in the first place. The partisans of a Bill of Rights preferred to have the rights declared, as principles, in the preamble of the Constitution. There these maxims could take the position of founding principles, from which the character and powers of the government could be drawn. But Federalists such as George Clymer preferred to keep the amendments distinct from the body of the Constitution, so that "the world would discover the perfection of the original and the superfluity of the amendments." Storing apparently thought that this change was more compatible with the ends of the Anti-Federalists than their own design would have been: The Bill of Rights was converted from a grand statement of natural rights into the operative principles of a constituted government. As I have suggested, we may properly doubt that this distinction made any substantive difference for the judging of rights in the law. But Storing would help make the accounts clearer: To the extent that the confusions of the Bill of Rights have emanated from this decision, to place the protection of natural rights as an appendix to the Constitution, the responsibility for this distraction must lie with some of the Federalists themselves. See Storing, *supra*, note 19, pp. 31–34.

41. *The Federalist* #84, *supra*, note 6, pp. 560–61.

42. Chief Justice Burger was content to argue, in the Bob Jones case, that the policies of the school ran counter to a public policy confirmed over the years in statutes, executive orders, and the decisions of the courts. But when he sought to explain the principle contained in that public policy, Burger insisted on the narrowest construction. Within the space of two pages, he managed to state five times that the weight of federal policy had been set firmly against the practice of "racial discrimination in education." See *Bob Jones University v. U.S.*, 461 U.S. 574, at 592–95 (1983).

CHAPTER FIVE

1. See *NAACP v. Alabama*, 357 U.S. 449 (1958).

2. See the attempt of the Court to skirt around this issue in *Buckley v. Valeo*, 424 U.S. 1, at 69–74 (1976).

3. 314 U.S. 160.

4. 36 U.S. (11 Peters) 102.

5. Ibid., at 143.

6. *Supra*, note 3, at 174–75.

7. Ibid., at 176–77.

8. See Arkes, *First Things* (Princeton, N.J.: Princeton University Press, 1986), pp. 168–69, and see also Chap. 4, pp. 116–33.

9. *Supra*, note 3, at 177.

10. Ibid., at 182.

11. See, for example, Lincoln's First Inaugural Address in Roy P. Basler, ed., *The Collected Works of Abraham Lincoln* (New Brunswick, N.J.: Rutgers University Press, 1953), vol. 4, pp. 263–64.

12. W. W. Crosskey collected the strands of a plausible argument here in his re-

doubtable treatise, *Politics and the Constitution in the History of the United States* (Chicago: University of Chicago Press, 1953), vol. 2, pp. 1083–1118.

13. *Supra*, note 3, at 178.

14. Ibid., at 181.

15. *Truax v. Raich*, 239 U.S. 33, 39 (1915), quoted in ibid., at 184.

16. Ibid., at 184.

17. Ibid., at 184–85.

18. See, for example, *Cooley v. Port Wardens*, 53 U.S. (12 Howard) 299 (1851), and *New York v. Miln*, *supra*, note 4.

19. *Edwards v. California*, *supra*, note 3, at 172–73.

20. For an extended consideration of this question, see Arkes, *First Things*, *supra*, note 8, pp. 92–99, and *The Philosopher in the City* (Princeton, N.J.: Princeton University Press, 1981), chaps. 2, 3, and 9.

21. *Edwards v. California*, *supra*, note 3, at 181, emphasis in original.

22. See 118 U.S. 356 (1886).

23. 316 U.S. 535.

24. Ibid., at 545.

25. Ibid., at 543.

26. The estate consisted of a few items of personal property and a savings account with a value of "less than $1,000." *Reed v. Reed*, 404 U.S. 71, at 72, n. 1.

27. Ibid., at 72–73.

28. Ibid., at 76.

29. Brief for the appellee, p. 12. This argument was not reported in the opinion of the Court in the Reed case. It was cited by Justice Brennan about a year later in the related case of *Frontiero v. Richardson*, 411 U.S. 677 (1973), at 683 and note 10.

30. *Reed v. Reed*, *supra*, note 26, at 75–76.

31. *Frontiero v. Richardson*, 411 U.S. 677, at 680 (1973).

32. Ibid., at 688–89.

33. *Bolling v. Sharpe*, 347 U.S. 497, at 499 (1954).

34. For a fuller argument on this point, see *The Philosopher in the City*, *supra*, note 20, chap. 9, and *First Things*, *supra*, note 8.

35. In this respect, see Justice Jackson's separate opinion in *Beauharnais v. Illinois*, 343 U.S. 250, at 294–95 (1952).

36. *Railway Express v. New York*, 336 U.S. 106 (1949).

37. Ibid., at 109–10.

38. Ibid., at 110.

39. Ibid., at 112–13.

40. See Marcus Singer, *Generalization in Ethics* (New York: Knopf, 1960), and R. M. Hare, *Freedom and Reason* (New York: Oxford University Press, 1963), chaps. 5 and 6.

41. See Immanuel Kant, *Groundwork for the Metaphysics of Morals* [1785], trans. and ed. H. J. Paton (New York: Harper and Row, 1964), p. 88 (p. 421 of the edition of the Royal Prussian Academy).

42. See chapter 2 and Roy P. Basler, ed., *The Collected Works of Abraham Lincoln* (New Brunswick, N.J.: Rutgers University Press, 1953), vol. 2, p. 222, emphasis in the original.

43. *Railway Express v. New York, supra*, note 36, at 112.
44. Ibid.
45. See Field's opinion in the *Slaughter House Cases*, 16 Wallace 36, at 83–111 (1873).
46. See 2 Samuel 12:1–7.
47. Plato, *The Republic*, book 5, 454c–e.
48. Charles L. Black, Jr., *Structure and Relationship in Constitutional Law* (Baton Rouge: Louisiana State University Press, 1969), p. 33.

CHAPTER SIX

1. *Monroe v. Pape*, 365 U.S. 167, at 203 (1960).
2. Apart from the passage cited above, see Frankfurter's remarks in ibid., at 210.
3. 325 U.S. 91 (1945).
4. Ibid., at 92–93.
5. Ibid., at 138–39.
6. *United States v. Williams*, 341 U.S. 70, at 71 (1951).
7. See Frankfurter in ibid., at 74.
8. Thurman in the *Congressional Globe*, 42d Cong., 1st Sess., at Appendix, 218; cited by Frankfurter in *Monroe v. Pape, supra*, note 1, at 234.
9. *Congressional Globe*, 39th Cong., 1st Sess., at 1758; cited by Frankfurter in *Monroe v. Pape, supra*, note 1, at 226, and in *Screws v. United States, supra*, note 3, at 143.
10. *Supra*, note 3, at 143.
11. See Frankfurter in *United States v. Williams, supra*, note 6, at 81–82.
12. 144 U.S. 263 (1892).
13. 212 U.S. 564.
14. *In re Quarles*, 158 U.S. 532 (1895); *Motes v. United States*, 178 U.S. 458 (1900).
15. *Guinn v. United States*, 238 U.S. 347 (1915); *United States v. Moseley*, 238 U.S. 383 (1915); *United States v. Saylor*, 322 U.S. 385 (1944). This understanding was extended to the primary elections for members of Congress in *United States v. Classic*, 313 U.S. 209 (1941).
16. *United States v. Waddell*, 112 U.S. 76 (1884).
17. 203 U.S. 1 (1906).
18. *Baldwin v. Franks*, 120 U.S. 678; and see, especially, pp. 695–96 in Harlan's dissent.
19. *Monroe v. Pape, supra*, note 1, at 243.
20. *Screws v. United States, supra*, note 3, at 160.
21. *Monroe v. Pape, supra*, note 1, at 242.
22. See, on this point, Arkes, *First Things* (Princeton, N.J.: Princeton University Press, 1986), chaps. 4 and 5.
23. See, as the most notable example, Charles Black, *Structure and Relationship in Constitutional Law* (Baton Rouge: Louisiana State University Press, 1969).
24. See *Logan v. United States, supra*, note 12; and Frankfurter in *United States v. Williams, supra*, note 6, at 81–82.
25. *In re Neagle*, 135 U.S. 1 (1889).
26. *Griffin v. Breckenridge*, 403 U.S. 88 (1971).

27. See Harlan's dissent in *Plessy v. Ferguson*, 163 U.S. 537, at 555 and 562 (1897), and *Hodges v. United States, supra,* note 17, at 28 and 29.

28. On this revival of the Thirteenth Amendment, see *Jones v. Alfred Mayer Co.*, 392 U.S. 409 (1968), and Note, "The 'New' Thirteenth Amendment: A Preliminary Analysis," 82 *Harvard Law Review* 1294 (1969).

29. See Madison's notes for June 6, 1787, in Max Farrand, ed., *The Records of the Federal Convention of 1787* (New Haven: Yale University Press, 1911; rev. ed. 1937), vol. I, pp. 133–34.

30. Madison, in the *Federalist #10, The Federalist* (New York: Modern Library, n.d.), pp. 60–61.

31. See, for example, Hume, "That Politics May Be Reduced to a Science," in *David Hume's Political Essays,* ed. Charles W. Hendel (Indianapolis: Bobbs-Merrill, 1953), pp. 12–23.

32. Most notably, in the *Federalist #9.*

33.

In its larger and juster meaning, ["property"] embraces everything to which a man may attach a value and have a right; and *which leaves to everyone else the like advantage. . . .* [In that enlarged sense,] a man has a property in his opinions and the free communication of them. He has a property of peculiar value in his religious opinions, and in the profession and practice dictated by them. He has property very dear to him in the safety and liberty of his person. He has an equal property in the free use of his faculties, and free choice of the objects on which to employ them. In a word, as a man is said to have a right to his property, he may equally be said to have a property in his rights. (Madison, letter of March 27, 1792, in *The James Madison Letters* [New York: Townsend Mac Coun., 1884], vol. 4, p. 478, emphasis in original; cited by Bernard Siegan, in *Economic Liberties and the Constitution* [Chicago: University of Chicago Press, 1980], pp. 58, 342.)

34. 6 Wallace (73 U.S) 36, cited in *The Slaughter-House Cases,* 16 Wallace (83 U.S.) 36, at 79 (1873).

35. *Carter v. Carter Coal Co.*, 298 U.S. 238, at 294 (1936).

36. *Monroe v. Pape, supra,* note 1, at 242.

37. See ibid., at 220–22.

38. *Screws v. United States, supra,* note 3, at 143.

39. See *Bradwell v. Illinois,* 83 U.S. 130 (1873).

40. See *Katzenbach v. McClung,* 379 U.S. 294, at 297 (1964).

41. See Grodzins, *The American System* (Chicago: Rand-McNally, 1966), chap. 12.

42. 469 U.S. 528.

43. Ibid., at 538–40.

44. *Dartmouth College v. Woodward,* 17 U.S. (4 Wheaton) 518, at 629 (1819).

45. See *Loving v. Virginia,* 388 U.S. 1 (1967).

46. See, for example, *Fountaine v. Fountaine,* 9 Ill. App. 2d 482, 133 N.E. 2d 532 (1956). *Fountaine* involved the case of children who had been born to a white mother and a black father. The parents were divorced; the mother married a white man; and she petitioned for the custody of the children. Her former husband countered her petition by claiming that the children would "make a better adjustment to life if al-

lowed to remain identified, reared and educated with the group and basic stock of . . . their father." Ibid., at 484, 133 N.E. 2d at 534. The judge found nothing unfit in the mother or her home, but he was persuaded by the argument of the natural father. He explained quite frankly that, were it not for the difference in color, he would not have paused for "a moment in awarding custody to the mother." Ibid., at 485, 133 N.E. 2d at 534. This decision, however, was later reversed on appeal. Ibid., at 486, 133 N.E. 2d at 535. See also, Susan J. Grossman, "A Child of a Different Color: Race As a Factor in Adoption and Custody Proceedings," 17 *Buffalo Law Review* 303 (1968).

47. Quoted in 228 F.2d 446, at 447.

48. See Judge Bazelon's opinion for the Court of Appeals, in overturning the decision of Judge Holtzoff, 228 F.2d at 448.

49. See 466 U.S. 429, at 430–31 (1984).

50. The Chief Justice summed up the matter in this way: "The effects of racial prejudice, however real, cannot justify a racial classification removing an infant child from the custody of its natural mother found to be an appropriate person to have such custody." Ibid., at 434.

51. As Hamilton remarked in the *Federalist* #31, "there ought to be no limitation of a power destined to effect a purpose which is itself incapable of limitation." See *The Federalist, supra*, note 30, at 188; and see also #32 and #33.

52. See *Shaare Tefile Congregation v. Cobb*, 481 U.S. 615 (1987).

53. The passage is drawn, of course, from Justice Matthews's classic opinion in *Yick Wo v. Hopkins*, 118 U.S. 356, at 373–74 (1886).

54. *The Federalist, supra*, note 30, p. 248, emphasis in original.

55. Quoted by Madison in the *Federalist* #40, *supra*, note 30, p. 251.

56. *Federalist* #39, *supra*, note 30.

57. *Federalist* #40, *supra*, note 30, pp. 252–53.

58. *Congressional Globe*, 39th Cong., 1st Sess. (1865), at 475; cited by Gerhard Casper, "Jones v. Mayer: Clio, Bemused and Confused Muse," in *The Supreme Court Review 1968*, ed. Philip B. Kurland (Chicago: University of Chicago Press, 1968), pp. 89–132, at 106.

59. 660 F.2d 1345.

60. 419 U.S 565.

61. 452 F.2d 640.

62. 424 U.S. 693 (1976).

63. The book of photos had been seen by Davis's employer, who was apparently disturbed by the incident and placed Davis on "warning." See ibid., at 696.

64. I sought to demonstrate this point at length in *The Philosopher in the City* (Princeton, N.J.: Princeton University Press, 1981). See, most notably, chaps. 2, 3, 9, 14 and 15 (and as a short explanation, pp. 10–13).

65. See Martin Diamond, "The Federalist's View of Federalism," in *Essays in Federalism*, ed. George C. S. Benson (Claremont, Calif.: Institute for Studies in Federalism, 1961), pp. 21–64, especially pp. 46–51, 55–56. The writers of the Federalist papers had celebrated the value of the states for local administration, but Diamond pointed out that "the emphasis on 'local administration for local purposes' does not, as *The Federalist* makes the argument, call for any kind of federalism. It requires decentralization, but not necessarily *federal* decentralization. Hamilton and Madison were

perfectly aware that in England there was a division of labor but not of sovereignty, between national and local government." Ibid., p. 56.

66. Justice Brennan suggested precisely this point in his separate opinion in *Paul v. Davis*, and in making this point, he recalled this passage in Justice Douglas's opinion in *Monroe v. Pape*: "It is no answer," said Douglas, "that the State has a law which if enforced would give relief. The federal remedy is supplementary to the State remedy, and the latter need not be first sought and refused before the federal one is invoked." Quoted in *Paul v. Davis, supra*, note 62, at 715; from 365 U.S. 167, at 183.

67. There is probably no better example than reasoning employed by the government and the Court in *Katzenbach v. McClung, supra*, note 40, at 299–300. See the analysis of this case in *The Philosopher in the City, supra*, note 64, pp. 243–46, 332.

CHAPTER SEVEN

1. A notable and sufficient example may be found by considering the way Harlan was able to render a more luminous understanding of *Shelton v. Tucker*, 360 U.S. 479 (a case involving the firing of teachers) through his opinion, a year later, in *Konigsberg v. State Bar*, 366 U.S. at 53 (1961).

2. 403 U.S. 15 (1971).

3. For an extended analysis of the quality of Harlan's judicial mind in this instance, see my own book, *The Philosopher in the City* (Princeton, N.J.: Princeton University Press, 1981), pp. 63–74.

4. 354 U.S. 476 (1957).

5. Ibid., at 487; see also 488–89.

6. Ibid., at 498–99.

7. I have recalled, in this vein, the story of Cecil Partee, the redoubtable ward committeeman in Chicago. See *First Things* (Princeton, N.J.: Princeton University Press, 1986), pp. 94–97.

8. The question of pornography has fostered the most distracting confusions, precisely on this matter of confounding the wrong in principle with tenuous arguments over material injuries. For a fuller discussion of this problem, see Arkes, *The Philosopher in the City, supra*, note 3, chap. 14.

9. *Supra*, note 4, at 504, 502.

10. See *Beauharnais v. Illinois*, 343 U.S. 250. The layers of questions contained in this case are explored at length in *The Philosopher in the City, supra*, note 3, chaps. 2 and 3.

11. For Jackson's argument in *Beauharnais*, see ibid., 287–305, especially 294–95.

12. *Roth v. United States, supra*, note 4, at 505–6.

13. 32 U.S. (7 Peters) 248.

14. See Leonard Levy, *Jefferson and Civil Liberties* (Cambridge: Harvard University Press, 1963), chap. 3, pp. 42–69.

15. On this point, see Harry Jaffa, *The Crisis of the House Divided* (Garden City: Doubleday, 1959), pp. 291–92.

16. 268 U.S. 652.

17. Ibid., at 666.

18. See his dissenting opinion in *Adamson v. California*, 332 U.S. 46, at 68–123.

19. 367 U.S. 643.

20. *Duncan v. Louisiana*, 391 U.S. 145, at 179 (1968).

21. *Supra*, note 16, at 666.

22. Ibid., at 672.

23. 302 U.S. 319.

24. Ibid., at 323. For the fuller background of this case, see *State v. Palko*, 186 Atl. Reporter 657 (1936), and 191 Atl. Reporter 321 (1937).

25. *Palko v. Connecticut, supra*, note 23, at 324.

26. Ibid., at 327.

27. Ibid., at 325.

28. Ibid.

29. Ibid., at 326.

30. Ibid., at 327.

31. Ibid.

32. Ibid., at 325.

33. Ibid., at 327.

34. Ibid., at 325.

35. *Rochin v. California*, 342 U.S. 165, at 172.

36. See *Irvine v. California*, 347 U.S. 128, and Frankfurter's opinion, at 142–49 (1954).

37. *Palko v. Connecticut, supra*, note 23, at 325–26.

38. Ibid., at 328.

39. See *First Things, supra*, chaps. 5 and 8.

40. See Gary McDowell, "The Problem With Amendments," *Wall Street Journal*, January 26, 1983, p. 30.

41. 402 U.S. 424.

42. Ibid., at 442.

43. Ibid., at 456.

44. For an account of this case that carries the problem through the layers of complexity disclosed in the precedents—a complexity that Justice Black conveniently screened from his own historical account, see Bernard D. Meltzer, "Privileges Against Self-Incrimination and the Hit-and-Run Opinions," *The Supreme Court Review 1971*, ed. Philip B. Kurland (Chicago: University of Chicago Press, 1971), pp. 1–30.

45. See *Ward v. Coleman*, 598 F.2d 1187, at 1192–95 (1979).

46. *United States v. Ward*, 448 U.S. 242, at 248–51 (1980). For a discussion of the act and these cases, see D. Gary Beck, "The Federal Water Pollution Control Act's Self-Reporting Requirement and the Privilege Against Self-Incrimination: Civil or Criminal Proceedings and Penalties? *United States v. Ward*," 1981 *Brigham Young University Law Review* (1983).

47. Readers may find another, reinforcing example, if they consider the cases dealing with the requirement of a warrant in carrying out inspections for health and safety. A question may properly be raised as to whether the requirement of the Fourth Amendment would really apply with any utility or justification for inspections of this kind, especially if they are arranged with proper notice, for the convenience of the owners or residents. The same judges who have been convinced that there is really a constitutional principle engaged in these inspections have been willing to apply the same, stringent requirement to the states and cities, as well as to the federal govern-

ment. And the same plausible points of doubt would work, with the same reasoning, to empower the federal government to carry out inspections for safety and health, without a burden of securing warrants in every instance. Compare in this respect *Camara v. Muncipal Court [San Francisco]*, 387 U.S. 523 (1967) and *Marshall v. Barlow's, Inc.*, 56 L Ed 2d 305 (1978) [involving the federal Occupational Safety and Health Administration].

CHAPTER EIGHT

1. 350 U.S. 422.
2. Cited in ibid., at 423–24.
3. Ibid., at 426.
4. Ibid., at 438–39.
5. See *Brown v. Walker*, 161 U.S. 591, upholding a statute enacted in 1893, 27 *Stat.* 443.
6. 116 U.S. 616.
7. See ibid., 620–21.
8. Ibid., at 638.
9. Ibid., at 634.
10. Jeremy Bentham, *A Comment on the Commentaries* [on Blackstone's Commentaries], ed. J. H. Burns and H.L.A Hart (London: University of London, Athlone Press, 1977), II.4, pp. 189–90. (These commentaries were originally written in 1776, but they were not published until 1828.)
11. 1 *Annals of Congress* 782 (ed. J. Gales, 1834), cited in Robert Heidt, "The Conjurer's Circle: The Fifth Amendment Privilege in Civil Cases," 91 *Yale Law Journal*, 1062, at 1082–83 (1982).
12. See ibid., at 1064–65.
13. Ibid., at 1133–34.
14. Ibid., at 1084.
15. *United States v. James*, 60 F. 257, at 264 (1894), cited by Douglas in *Ullmann v. United States, supra*, note 1, at 450.
16. Ibid., emphasis added.
17. Ibid., at 442.
18. Ibid., at 455.
19. *Lefkowitz v. Turley*, 414 U.S. 70 (1973).
20. *Spevack v. Klein*, 385 U.S. 511 (1967).
21. *Uniformed Sanitation Men Association v. Commissioner of Sanitation*, 392 U.S. 280 (1968).
22. 97 L Ed 2d 315 (1987).
23. *Palko v. Connecticut*, 302 U.S. 319, at 326.
24. See Friendly, "The Fifth Amendment Tomorrow: The Case for Constitutional Change," 37 *University of Cincinnati Law Review* 671 (1968); and see also, Wallace Mendelson, "Self-Incrimination in American and French Law," 19 *Criminal Law Bulletin* 34 (1983).
25. Bentham, *supra*, note 10, p. 189.
26. See *Boyd v. United States, supra*, note 6, at 621–22.
27. Ibid., at 630.

28. Ibid., at 631–32.

29. 3 *Hind's Precedents* 181 (1907), cited by Judge MacKinnon in his dissenting opinion in *Nixon v. Sirica*, 487 F.2d 700, at 735 (1973), emphasis added.

30. *In re Subpoena to Nixon*, 360 F. Supp. 1, at 6 (1973). Sirica annexed to his argument this passage from Chief Justice Marshall's opinion in the Burr case: "The propriety of introducing any paper into a case, as testimony, must depend on the character of the paper, not on the character of the person who holds it." Cited in ibid. The Chief Justice had issued a subpoena to President Jefferson, but the balancing of protocols threw only a thin disguise over the fact that Jefferson, nevertheless, made his own decision on the papers that would be excised from the record or delivered to the courts. See ibid., at 7, n. 18.

31. See *Zurcher v. Stanford Daily*, 436 U.S. 547 (1978).

32. Compare John Stuart Mill:

> [W]e do not call anything wrong unless we mean to imply that a person ought to be punished in some way or other for doing it. . . . [The notion of deserving, or not deserving, punishment] lies at the bottom of the notions of right and wrong; that we call any conduct wrong, or employ, instead, some other term of dislike or disparagement, according as we think that the person ought, or ought not, to be punished for it; and we say it would be right to do so and so, or merely that it would be desirable or laudable, according as we would wish to see the person whom it concerns compelled, or only persuaded and exhorted, to act in that manner. (Mill, *Utilitarianism* [Indianapolis: Bobbs-Merrill, 1957 (1861)], p. 61.)

See also, on this point, Arkes, *First Things* (Princeton, N.J.: Princeton University Press, 1986), pp. 24–25 and *passim*.

33. Some recent writers have sought to rescue the case for a "right" to withhold evidence, but the efforts have proven lame precisely because the writers have been inattentive to the irreducible moral ground for this argument. Hence, they usually fail to notice the contradiction that would immanently affect any claim of a "right" to withhold evidence of "wrongdoing." They fail to notice that rudimentary problem because they seem to have forgotten the older axiom, recalled by Lincoln and Aquinas, that we cannot have "the right to do a wrong." For that reason, we cannot have a "right" to succeed in our wrongdoing, or a "right," then, to conceal our wrongdoing. When they are detached from these ancient understandings, the recent arguments over self-incrimination must be rendered vacuous. In this class are the arguments, often heard these days, that we honor the "moral autonomy" of defendants by confirming to them a "right" to remain silent and conceal their own wrongdoing. But of course we could never claim, in the name of our "moral autonomy," the "right to do a wrong." Therefore we would not violate the autonomy of moral agents when we ask them to acknowledge their own, moral responsibility and do justice to their victims. Nor do we inflict a "harm" on a person when we impose a justified penalty. And therefore it cannot rightly be said that we compel people to collaborate in their own "harm," when we oblige them to offer evidence that may lead to their own, just punishment. Even an estimable writer such as Professor Kent Greenawalt could show a surprising credulity in the face of these kinds of arguments. See R. Kent Greenawalt,

"Silence As a Moral and Constitutional Right," 23 *William and Mary Law Review* 15, at 18, 36–39 (1981). See also Robert Gerstein, "The Demise of Boyd: Self-Incrimination and Private Papers in the Burger Court," 27 *UCLA Law Review* 343 (1979), and "Privacy and Self-Incrimination," 80 *Ethics* 87 (1970).

In a more recent piece, Professor David Dolinko has surveyed, with an exhausting detail, the efforts to furnish more novel and ingenious arguments for the "right" to withhold evidence. Dolinko has reviewed the arguments in a detail that runs beyond their merits; but he has managed, I think, to show that these recent outpourings of novelty have been uniformly untenable. Dolinko, "Is There a Rationale for the Privilege Against Self-Incrimination?" 33 *UCLA Law Review* 1063 (1986).

34. See also my own book, *First Things, supra*, note 32, pp. 83–87, 169–73; and Arkes, " 'Autonomy' and the 'Quality of Life': The Dismantling of Moral Terms," 2 *Issues in Laws and Medicine* 421 (1987).

35. See Max Rheinstein, ed., *Max Weber on Law in Economy and Society*, trans. Edward Shils (Cambridge: Harvard University Press, 1954), pp. l–li, 59, 63–64.

36. *Palko v. Connecticut, supra*, note 23, at 326.

37. See the *New York Times*, July 30, 1974, pp. 1 and 13; August 8, 1974, p. 1; August 10, 1974, pp. 7 and 27; April 18, 1975, p. 1 [acquittal]; April 22, 1975, p. 12 [Department of Justice had warned the special prosecutor about plea bargaining with Jake Jacobsen as a means of securing testimony against Connally].

38. See the *New York Times*, July 17, 1987.

39. See the *New York Times*, May 11, 1988.

40. For the account of these developments in the case of St. Germain, I am relying on the account in the *Washington Post*, August 22, 1987, C1, C8.

41. See the account by Walter Pincus and Joe Pichirallo in the *Washington Post*, March 14, 1988, A1, A4.

42. See, for example, the analyses in the editorials of the *Wall Street Journal*, "The Blackmailing of McFarlane," March 15, 1988, p. 34; "No Pardon for Walsh," March 18, 1988, p. 26.

43. See Langbein, "Torture and Plea Bargaining," in 68 *The Public Interest* (Winter 1980), pp. 43–61.

44. Ibid., pp. 51–52.

45. Ibid., p. 48.

46. Ibid., pp. 48–49.

47. Abraham Goldstein and Martin Marcus have found, for example, that the courts in France, Italy, and Germany have come under the same pressures that have compelled the use of shortcuts in procedure in the United States. More and more discretion, they find, has been shifted from the supervising judges to the police and the prosecutors. And as in the United States, there has been a comparable tendency to "correctionalize," or scale down, the charges for the sake of producing an uncontested trial, which can be dispatched far more quickly. In this vein, the authors report the experience of one French prosecutor, specializing in "check fraud," who claimed to have participated in sixty cases in a sitting of three hours. On the other hand, Goldstein and Marcus would yield this one confirmation to the argument offered by Langbein: They do not find, among the Europeans, an active, ongoing conversation in "trading" confessions for the reduction of charges. See Goldstein and Marcus, "The

Myth of Judicial Supervision in Three 'Inquisitorial' Systems: France, Italy, and Germany," 87 *Yale Law Journal* 240, at 269, 267, 278, 281–82 (1977).

48. 384 U.S. 436 (1966).

49. 384 U.S. 757 (1966).

50. Ibid., 761, emphasis added.

51. Ibid., at 765, emphasis added.

52. See, for example, *Gilbert v. California*, 388 U.S. 262 (1967) [on taking samples of handwriting and compelling a suspect to appear in a lineup]; and see also the sources cited by Brennan in ibid., 764, note 8.

53. See *Blackford v. United States*, 247 F.2d 745 (1962), and for a dissenting opinion, see Judge Stephens at 754. For a case appealing even more strongly to a prurient interest, see *United States v. Holtz*, 479 F.2d 89 (1973), and the dissent of Judge Ely at 94. For other cases involving the search of bodily cavities, see *Rivas v. United States*, 368 F.2d 703 (1966) [sustaining a search]; and *Henderson v. United States*, 390 F.2d 876 (1967) [overturning a search].

54. *Schmerber v. California*, *supra*, note 49, at 767–68, emphasis added.

55. Ibid., at 770–71.

56. Ibid., at 771.

57. Ibid., at 771–72.

58. *Rochin v. California*, 342 U.S. 165, at 172.

59. See, as a recent and notable case in point, *South Dakota v. Neville*, 459 U.S. 553 (1983).

60. *Miranda v. Arizona*, *supra*, note 48, at 458.

61. Ibid., at 457.

62. Ibid., at 467.

63. Ibid., at 457.

64. Ibid., at 497–99.

65. For the review of these techniques, see ibid., at 449–58.

66. Ibid., at 444–45.

67. For Harlan's dissenting opinion, see ibid., at 504–26.

68. *Watts v. Indiana*, 338 U.S. 49, at 59, quoted by Harlan in ibid., at 516, n. 12.

69. Ibid., at 512.

70. See ibid., at 460.

71. William Tucker has made this point movingly, in an essay on the Miranda case:

Despite all their efforts to "put themselves in the criminals' place," the Warren majority never seems to have realized that, at bottom, most people who commit crimes know somewhere in their minds that they have *done something wrong*. As Dostoyevsky showed in *Crime and Punishment*, criminal acts separate people out from normal society in a way that most people eventually find too difficult to bear. At bottom, there is a great psychological relief in finally admitting guilt—even if it means opening the way to punishment. (Tucker, "True Confessions: The Long Road Back from Miranda," *National Review* [October 18, 1985], pp. 28–36.)

72. 446 U.S. 291, at 293–95 (1980).

73. 467 U.S. 638, at 651–52 (1984).

74. See ibid., at 654.

75. Ibid., at 676.

76. The Court in *Miranda* was concerned about such devious stratagems as contriving, with a phony "witness" (perhaps a member of the police) to identify the suspect. In one version of this ploy, the "witness" would identify the suspect for a more serious crime, which he did not commit. By putting suspects under this kind of pressure, many of them would confess to the real charges as a means of clearing themselves from the false charges. See the Miranda case, *supra*, note 48, at 453. Justice Stewart recalled this point in *Rhode Island v. Innis*, *supra*, note 72, 306–7.

77. *Rhode Island v. Innis*, *supra*, note 72, 311.

78. 352 U.S. 432 (1957).

79. 378 U.S. 1.

80. Cited by Brennan in *Schmerber v. California*, *supra*, note 49, at 762.

81. *Boyd v. United States*, *supra*, note 6, at 632.

CHAPTER NINE

1. See the interview with Lenzner in *Boston Globe*, September 10, 1978, p. A2.

2. See Arkes, *First Things* (Princeton, N.J.: Princeton University Press, 1986), pp. 88–90.

3. *Supra*, note 1.

4. See *United States v. Binder*, 769 F.2d 595 (1985).

5. *Kentucky v. Stincer*, 96 L Ed 2d 631 (1987), at 644.

6. Ibid., at 649, emphasis in original. The minority raised the proper question of just why there was a compelling need to make these kinds of discriminations in the stages of the trial: Why was it especially necessary or legitimate to suspend the rule on the confrontation of witnesses in the initial phase of the trial? Why in the initial phase and not in any other stage of the prosecution?

7. *Boston Globe*, *supra*, note 1.

8. At the time of this writing, the U.S. attorney in Manhattan has brought charges against two officers in the transport police in New York who have been charged with making a business of "false arrests." The officers had been working under an incentive system that provided the best jobs to the officers who made the most arrests and issued the most summonses. This team of officers produced a series of suspicious arrests, which had led to an investigation by the Transport Authority, at the urging of the district attorney in Manhattan, Robert Morgenthau. But when the evidence was collected, Mr. Morgenthau's office was not confident that the evidence was sufficient to justify a prosecution. But a few years later, in May 1988, the U.S. attorney, Rudolph Giuliani, did file the charges and procure the arrests. And yet, how did this matter become the business of the U.S. attorney's office? How did it come within the reach of the federal government? The two officers were charged with a conspiracy to violate the Civil Rights Acts. As Giuliani remarked, "It's an allegation of false arrest, and false arrest is clearly a deprivation of civil rights." See *New York Times*, May 13, 1988, pp. A1, B4.

9. Wilson, "Of the Natural Rights of Individuals," in *The Works of James Wilson* (Cambridge: Harvard University Press, 1967), vol. 2, pp. 585–610, at p. 592.

10. See the account of Andrew in Eric McKitrick, *Andrew Johnson and Reconstruction* (Chicago: University of Chicago Press, 1960), pp. 215–38, and especially 221–22:

When the call for troops went out from the War Department, Andrew was the first of the governors to respond. . . . "Despatch received. By what route shall we send?" The first United States soldiers killed in Baltimore were members of the Sixth Massachusetts. Andrew became the man of action, personally overseeing an incredible range of detail as all energies were hurled into the stupendous work. . . . Constituting himself, as one writer puts it, "unofficial secretary of war for New England," Andrew never hesitated to seize the initiative from others when he thought it necessary. . . . He told [Secretary] Cameron that the government should strengthen the defenses of Fortress Monroe and offered to send two regiments there himself. He advised protection for Harpers Ferry. He wanted an immediate increase in the arms output of the Federal arsenal at Springfield. He offered the results of experiments on a new projectile being carried on by his own staff. His impact on the administration must have been quite overpowering.

11. See Bray Hammond, *Sovereignty and an Empty Purse; Banks and Politics in the Civil War* (Princeton, N.J.: Princeton University Press, 1970), p. 13.

12. See Donovan, "Judging Teenagers: How Minors Fare When They Seek Court-Authorized Abortions," 15 *Family Planning Perspectives* 259 (1983). Cf., also, *H.B. v. Wilkinson*, 639 F. Supp. 952, 956 (1986). In this latter case, a teenager seeking an abortion was asked by a judge whether she had used contraception. She replied that she had not, since she understood that she could obtain an abortion fairly easily, without her parents learning about it. See the amicus curiae brief submitted by Dennis Horan et al., on behalf of Americans United for Life, in *Hartigan v. Zbaraz*, June 22, 1987.

13. Jonathan Elliot, ed., *The Debates in the Several Conventions on the Adoption of the Federal Constitution* (Philadelphia: J. B. Lippincott, 1836), vol. 2, pp. 355–56.

14. See, for example, the memoir left by Nadezhda Mandelstam in *Hope Against Hope*, trans. Max Hayward (London: Collins and Harvill, 1971), see p. 305, and pp. 298–99, 316–17. She recalls the evening that the secret police came, suddenly, and arrested her husband, Osip Mandelstam. The translater David Brodski was visiting that night, and he seemed to prolong his stay with maneuvers that did not become explicable until after the police had come—and spent the night ransacking the apartment. In the midst of this drama, "Brodski slumped into his chair and sat there motionless, like a huge wooden sculpture of some savage tribe." Later, Brodski raised his hand, like a schoolboy, and asked permission to go to the bathroom. "The agent directing the search looked at him with contempt. 'You can go home,' he said. 'What?' Brodski said in astonishment. 'Home,' the man repeated and turned his back. The secret police despised their civilian helpers. Brodski had no doubt been ordered to sit with us that evening in case we tried to destroy any manuscripts when we heard the knock on the door" (pp. 5–6).

15. Tocqueville, *Democracy in America* (New York: Random House, 1945), vol. 2, book 2, chap. 5 ("Of the Use that Americans Make of Public Associations in Civil Life"), p. 118.

16. For an extended consideration of this problem, see my analysis in *The Philosopher in the City* (Princeton, N.J.: Princeton University Press, 1981), pp. 243–46, 332.

17. See 42 U.S.C.A, Sec. 2000e, paragraph (a).

18. See *McClure v. Salvation Army*, 460 F.2d 553 (1972), and *Coon v. Tingle*, 277 F. Supp. 304 (1967).

19. See, of course, the ever remarkable case of *Shelley v. Kraemer*, 334 U.S. 1 (1948), and consider *Burton v. Wilmington Parking Authority*, 365 U.S. 715 (1961), *Reitman v. Mulkey*, 387 U.S. 369 (1967).

20. P.L. 92–318, 86 Statutes at Large 373, Section 901(a).

21. "The Equal Rights Amendment: A Constitutional Basis for Equal Rights for Women," 80 *Yale Law Journal* 872, at 893–96 (1971).

22. Very recently, this line of argument has been taken up by federal judge Ruth Bader Ginsburg in "Some Thoughts on Autonomy and Equality in Relation to Roe versus Wade," 63 *North Carolina Law Review* 375 (1985).

23. *Grove City College v. Bell*, 79 L Ed 2d 516 (1984).

24. Ibid., at 530–32.

25. Cited in 134 *Congressional Record*, January 28, 1988, p. S218.

26. Ibid., pp. S216–17.

27. 10 U.S.C., Section 1093.

28. 22 U.S.C., Sections 2151b (f)(1) and (2).

29. 42 U.S.C., Section 300a–6.

30. 42 U.S.C., Section 2996f (b)(8).

31. *Congressional Record, supra*, note 25, January 28, 1988, p. S219.

32. Ibid., p. S226.

33. The text is reprinted in ibid., p. S219. The amendment was adopted in the Senate by a vote of 56–39. The bill containing this amendment was passed in the House by a vote of 315–98. See ibid., March 2, 1988, pp. H597–98.

34. See "NOW Walks Away from CRRA [Civil Rights Restoration Act] Debacle," *National N.O.W. Times* (December/January 1988), p. 1.

35. *Congressional Record, supra*, note 25, p. S218.

36. Ibid., p. S227. In the face of these concerns, Senator Kennedy pleaded his own problems as the chief manager of the bill. According to the National Center for Educational Statistics, there were 3,331 institutions of higher education in the country. Of those, 794 reported a religious affiliation. "Therefore," Kennedy reasoned, "it is conceivable that as many as one-quarter of all such institutions could apply for and receive exemptions." Ibid., p. S209. Apparently, moral judgments were to be drawn with calculation. An exemption that was thought to be justified in principle somehow ceased to be justified if it became too costly, or if it shrank, too noticeably, the number of institutions that were subject to the law. But if it were justified to exempt an institution such as Catholic University from the obligations of this law, how could it make a difference whether Catholic University stood by itself, or whether it was joined by other schools bearing the same religous concerns? Moving along this path, the managers of the bill could not escape all of those moral confusions that arise when exemptions are granted in the law on the basis of religious belief. On the reasons that make such exemptions morally suspect, see Arkes, *First Things, supra*, note 2, chap. 9.

37. I have sought to offer an extended demonstration of how an argument of that kind would be framed. See *First Things, supra*, note 2, chap. 16.

38. *Congressional Record, supra*, note 25, p. S236.

39. The form read in this way:

[College X — fill in the name] is in violation of Title IX.

Specifically, the student health insurance offered by this college *does not* treat childbirth, pregnancy, false pregnancy, termination of pregnancy and recovery therefrom in the same manner and under the same policies as any other temporary disability with respect to any medical or hospital benefit, service, plan or policy which such recipient administers, operates, offers, or participates in with respect to students admitted to the recipients [sic] educational program or activity.

I am quoting here from the copy of the complaint received by Biola University, and contained in the files of the Office of Civil Rights. The original was received on October 15, 1985, by the Department of Education, Office of Civil Rights, Region IX.

40. Copies of letters in files of the Department of Education, Office for Civil Rights.

41. See the letter from Philip G. Kiko, acting director, Policy and Enforcement Service, Department of Education, to Alicia Coro, acting assistant secretary for civil rights, June 11, 1987; reprinted in *Congressional Record, supra,* note 25, p. S228.

42. See *supra*, chap. 6.

43. See, for example, *Harris v. MacRae*, 448 U.S. 297.

44. I made this point on another occasion with a discussion of the Human Life Bill of 1981. See *First Things, supra*, note 2, pp. 417–22.

45. 476 U.S. 610 (1986).

46. 87 Statutes at Large 394, 29 U.S.C., Section 794.

47. U.S. Supreme Court, Oral Arguments, Vol. 8, Cases Nos. 84-1573–84-1560; October Term, 1985, pp. 16 and 23 [Oral argument in *Bowen v. American Hospital Association*].

48. See *United States v. University Hospital, State University of New York (Stony Brook)*, 729 F.2d 144, at 146 (1984).

49. Oral argument in *Bowen v. American Hospital Association, supra*, note 47, pp. 17–18.

50. Ibid., pp. 18, 19.

51. Quoted in *Bowen, supra*, note 45, at 662.

52. Cited by Justice White in ibid., at 659–60.

53. This point was reiterated by Charles Cooper in his argument for the government. See Oral Argument, *supra*, note 47, p. 7.

54. Arkes, " 'Baby Doe': It's Not a 'Medical' Question," *Washington Post*, April 17, 1983.

55. *U.S. v. University Hospital (Stony Brook), supra*, note 48, at 162.

56. Daniel Robinson, "Whatever May Happen to Baby Jane," *Washington Post*, December 4, 1983.

57. 98 Stat. 1749 (October 9, 1984).

58. Oral argument in the Bowen case, *supra*, note 47, pp. 18–20.

59. Ibid., pp. 25–26.

60. Ibid., p. 26.

61. 2 Dallas 419, at 464 (1793).

62. The *Federalist* #31, *The Federalist Papers* (New York: Random House, n.d.), p. 188.

INDEX